FIELDS of MEMORY

FIELDS OF MEMORY
A TESTIMONY TO THE GREAT WAR

ANNE ROZE

Photography
JOHN FOLEY

Preface
Jean Rouaud

CASSELL

The author and publishers would like to thank everyone
who has helped with the research for this book.

Photographic acknowledgements

NOTE: t = top, b = bottom, r = right, l = left, m = middle

Boyer-Viollet: p.32 t. Photothèque Hachette: pp. 15; 18 t l; 23; 31 b r; 32 b; 35; 38 t m b r; 39 m l; 42 b; 50 t l; 58 t b; 60; 65; 70; 76; 77; 90 b r, l; 96; 100 b l r; 104 b; 111 t l, b r l; 118 m b r; 126 m l; 128 b r; 132; 134 b r; 135; 140 t; 146 t r; 147 t l r; 150 b r l;170; 171; 176 t l; 191; 196; 197; 200 t l, m l, b r; 215 t; 216; 220 t r; 226. Collection of Jean-Pierre Verney: pp. 13; 14; 18 t r; 24; 26 t r; 27; 31 b l; 34; 37 b; 39 t l, m b r; 46; 50 t b r; 51; 54 t; 66; 78 b; 81; 83; 84; 90 t r l; 92; 103 t; 104 t; 106 t r; 110; 111 t r; 113; 126 b l; 131; 134 b l; 139; 140 b; 141; 159 t r; 185; 200 t r; 202 b l; 209 b; 215 m; 220 t l b; 224 t. Collection of Jean-Claude Kermazyn: pp. 18 m b l; 38 t l; 103 t; 138. Journaux de l'époque: pp. 22 b r; 50 b l; 58 m; 106 t r b r l; 118 t r; 126 t l, m r; 146 t l, 159 t l; 174; 176 m l, t m b r; 200 b l; 204 b r l; 205. Journal *Le Miroir*: p. 18 b r; 19; 22 t; 26 b. Collection of the author: p. 22 b l. Bild Archiv Prussicher, Berlin: p. 64.

This edition first published in the UK 1999 by
Cassell
Wellington House, 125 Strand
London WC2R 0BB
www.cassell.co.uk

Copyright © 1998, Éditions du Chêne-Hachette Livre
English translation © Cassell 1999

Original title: *Les Champs de la Mémoire*
Illustrated by: John Foley
Written by: Anne Roze
With the collaboration of Jean-Pierre Verney
Preface: Jean Rouaud

Extracts from *A Working Party* copyright © Siegfried Sassoon
by kind permission of George Sassoon and Viking Penguin USA

Published by Les Éditions du Chêne-Hachette Livre 1998

Distributed in the United States by
Sterling Publishing Co. Inc.
387 Park Avenue South
New York NY 10016–8810

British Library Cataloguing-in-Publication Data

A catalogue record for this book is available from the British Library

ISBN 0-304-35324-8

Printed and bound in Italy by Milanostampa

CONTENTS

Preface

What is left of the Great War? A handful of centenarians at Remembrance Day ceremonies straining to hear the names of the dead, inscribed on the solemn memorials that reveal the history of contemporary sculpture, the pages of memoirs … ?

To this day, no other event has generated so many books, many of which credit France and its system of state education, which, by making it obligatory for rank and file soldiers to learn to read and write just before they were sent to slaughter, made it possible for us to consider another point of view. Before that time, military histories had given us the privileged outlook of aristocrats, who had their own deeply entrenched ideas about war and the chivalric spirit. This prevailing view was so far removed from the realities of life at the front that the high command, with an elegant disdain for the realities of fighting, had chosen the colour red for the men's trousers because it looked so smart with the blue of their tunics and caps. This uniform, which gave a slightly comic air to the soldiers, was perfect for the parade ground and for attracting girls, but those fields of corn in the early months of the summer of 1914 were not, as the heavy loss of life proved, the place for a fashion parade.

Scraps of contemporary film show French soldiers weighed down with equipment – crossed leather straps for the water canteen, a grenade carrier, a rifle, a gas mask – advancing with jerky steps, at which, in these silent films, one might laugh. But those soldiers who found themselves facing the camera lens forced themselves to smile to maintain the morale of those who were far from the front, as if it were necessary to make us believe in the pleasures of life in the trenches. Sometimes we see short clips of soldiers mounting an attack. Leaving their dug-outs, their bayonets at the ready, they faced the enemy lines across land that was pitted with shell holes. How could anyone describe the grim determination that those on the other side were going to witness? In fact, however, there was nothing at all to see, because if you pay attention to the angle of the camera, you will realize that these well-ordered assaults are an exercise and have been filmed for training purposes. This was the logic that lay behind Verdun, the Chemin des Dames and three weeks of heavy artillery shelling before an offensive began – but this was not the time to have someone behind a camera.

If one adds to that the spectacular fields of crosses, geometrically laid out, as if an artist had lent a hand, what is there left for us? What is the ephemeral evidence that will leave its mark on the history of these four years of war on every inch of the front line?

Our sister, our mother the earth, eighty years after these events, has been subjected to soundings, scans and all kinds of tests to cover every aspect – that is, the earth has offered its scar-covered shell to be studied in every possible way. And there really are scars here, the results of the most enormous open-cast quarrying operation ever carried out, even though this was not really the first time the earth has been so treated. Centuries ago the emperors of China amused themselves by moving mountains, which is not an impossible task, even for men, if there is sufficient manpower. But these huge changes were undertaken to enhance the beauty of the countryside and out of a concern for cosmic harmony, just as if the imperfect original could be recreated or even improved upon.

Here, however, along the front line, it was nothing of the kind. Destroy, they said. Destroy the body of a man lying in ambush behind the hill, and in order to do this we will demolish the hill itself and flatten the countryside and rip up the ground to reveal the man who is by then running away, like someone who hides in a river in order to shelter from the rain, or we will root out the forest where there is still a tiny corner of hope, so that there is nothing left to see at the end of this long night but a lunar landscape. People remember a land that had been ploughed up and ripped open; people remember the terrible struggles to gain control of the ruined stones of Douaumont or the mud of the Somme and the Marne. Our sister the land has disguised these wounds with grass and has tried to smooth over the harsh angles in the countryside that rise up so strangely and to cover the fortresses with vegetation, filling in the underground trenches where these people used to live. All the bodies have returned to the earth in the great recycling of nature. So what is left? A vision of a devastated playground.

Jean Rouaud

CHRONOLOGY

1914

28 JUNE
Archduke Franz Ferdinand is assassinated at Sarajevo

28 JULY
Austria-Hungary declares war on Serbia; Russia, Serbia's ally, mobilizes its troops.

1 AUGUST
Under the terms of its treaty with Austria-Hungary, Germany declares war on Russia, an ally of France.

3 AUGUST
Germany declares war on France and invades Russia.

3–4 AUGUST
Germany invades Belgium and Britain declares war on Germany.

6 AUGUST
Austria-Hungary declares war on Russia; Serbia declares war on Germany.

12 AUGUST
Britain and France declare war on Austria-Hungary; Europe is at war

14–25 AUGUST
Battle of the Frontiers, including Battles of Lorraine, Ardennes, Sambre and Mons

21–24 AUGUST
Battle of Charleroi; followed by retreat of French troops

26–27 AUGUST
Battle of Le Cateau

4–9 SEPTEMBER
First Battle of the Marne; Germans fall back to a line from the Vosges to Picardy

SEPTEMBER–OCTOBER
The 'race to the sea'; Germans reach the English Channel

OCTOBER–NOVEMBER
Battle of Flanders, including Battles of Messines, Armentières and the Yser and First Battle of Ypres

20 DECEMBER
First Battle of Champagne continues until March 1915
By the end of the year the front line is more established with complex trench systems; thousands of men on both sides were killed in numerous offensives

1915

10–13 MARCH
Battle of Neuve Chapelle

APRIL–MAY
Second Battle of Ypres; British forced back

MAY–JUNE
Second Battle of Artois (Vimy Ridge)

JUNE–JULY
Battle of the Argonne

SEPTEMBER–NOVEMBER
Second Battle of Champagne

SEPTEMBER–OCTOBER
Battle of Loos

1916

21 FEBRUARY–18 DECEMBER
Battle of Verdun

1 JULY–18 NOVEMBER
Battle of the Somme, including Battles of Albert, Delville Wood, Pozières, Thiepval and Ancre

1917

APRIL–MAY
Battle of Arras

16–20 APRIL
Nivelle offensive, including Second Battle of the Aisne and Third Battle of Champagne

JUNE
American troops land in France

JULY–NOVEMBER
Third Battle of Ypres (Passchendaele); Allied offensive leading to thousands of deaths but no strategic advantage

7 NOVEMBER
Bolsheviks seize power in Russia leading to Treaty of Brest-Litovsk and withdrawal of German troops from Eastern Front

NOVEMBER–DECEMBER
Battle of Cambrai

1918

21 MARCH–5 APRIL
'Michael' offensive, including Second Battle of the Somme

9–29 APRIL
Lys offensive, including Battle of Messines and First and Second Battles of Kemmel

27 MAY–17 JUNE
Aisne offensive, including Battles of Château-Thierry and Belleau Wood

9–13 JUNE
Montdidier–Noyon offensive

15 JULY–4 AUGUST
Second Battle of the Marne

26 AUGUST–12 OCTOBER
Assault on Hindenburg Line

12–16 SEPTEMBER
Battle of Saint Mihiel

28 SEPTEMBER–11 NOVEMBER
Flanders offensive

17 OCTOBER–11 NOVEMBER
Picardy offensive

31 OCTOBER
Austria is declared a republic

9 NOVEMBER
Wilhelm II abdicates and flees to the Netherlands

11 NOVEMBER
Armistice signed by the Germans at Rethondes near Compiègne comes into effect at 11 o'clock

Eight million men died in the First World War; as many again were wounded.

INTRODUCTION

It was the start of a wonderful summer, sunny and bright. In July 1914 the countryside of northern France held the promise of a fine harvest, and as they watched the grapes ripening on the vines, farmers told themselves that it was going to be a vintage year. Families on holiday along the Atlantic and Channel coasts relaxed in the cool of the evenings after enjoyable afternoons on the beach.

Some people talked about the likelihood of war, but no one really believed it would happen. 'We thought about it sometimes,' noted the Austrian writer Stefan Zweig, 'but in much the same way as you think about death – as something that will happen, but not for a long time.'

This period at the beginning of the century later came to be called the *belle époque*. Europe was at its height. There had been peace for fifty years, and people went about their everyday lives, enjoying the tranquillity and largely indifferent to events elsewhere. It was, in effect, the calm before the storm.

It was true that there had been rather more tensions between the countries of Europe in the previous ten or twelve years. Increasingly, German had been concerned about its 'living space' – *Lebensraum* – but pacifism had been spreading in all countries. None of the governments wanted to go to war, and every time a problem arose it had been resolved by the diplomats in the chancelleries throughout Europe. Nevertheless, the balance of power between the two blocs – the Triple Alliance and the Triple Entente – had become increasingly fragile, and after every crisis the nationalists within each country ratcheted the tension up a notch and popular sentiment was inflamed. Nevertheless, during the early months of 1914 nothing that had happened suggested that the situation had become more dangerous. Winston Churchill himself commented on the 'exceptional tranquillity' that was enjoyed during the spring and summer of 1914. There seemed to be no reason to feel anything but confident about the future, and mothers hoped that they would be free of the ancient threat that their sons would be killed in combat.

War was to break out 'on a day when the corn was golden and rich, the vines were heavy with fruit, homes were full of couples, and my son was bursting with health'. This was how Jean Giraudoux made Andromache speak in *La Guerre de Troie n'aura pas lieu* (1935; *Tiger at the Gates*, 1955) some twenty years later.

At the end of June 1914, Archduke Franz Ferdinand, the heir to the Habsburg monarchy, and his wife, Sophie von Hohenberg, were assassinated at Sarajevo in Bosnia-Herzegovina by the student Gavrilo Princip, a Serbian nationalist. The heads of the European countries sent their sympathies to the old Franz Josef, Emperor of Austria and King of Hungary, who had already suffered many family bereavements. Diplomats asked themselves if this act of terrorism was going to create any unforeseen problems in an area that was inherently unstable and always threatening. But no one suspected that one act would set the world alight.

Who in 1914 would have thought that, forty years later, there would have been no Emperor of Germany, no Emperor of Austria-Hungary and no Tsar of Russia? That France and Britain, although victorious, would be terribly weakened. That the United States would have intervened in Europe and begun to take its leading role on the world stage. That more than eight million young men would be buried in the soil of Europe. And who could ever have thought that among the survivors of a war that no one had foreseen, and that no one could have imagined would be on such a scale, were those who would be wounded and scarred for life by the terrible events they were to live through?

In mid-July diplomatic activity was stepped up. Disturbing news was coming from Central Europe. Austria found the terms for Serbia's reparations to be unacceptable, and she called for – and received – support from Germany. When the alliances came into effect, the whole of Europe ran the risk of a fatal clash. Then, on 25 July, newspapers published the news of an ultimatum from Austria-Hungary to Serbia, and many people thought that the die was cast.

In France and Germany old antagonisms awoke, and in both Paris and Berlin feelings were inflamed. Young men dreamed of fighting and of returning home as heroes. The President of France, Raymond Poincaré, who returned suddenly from an official visit to Russia, was greeted on his return to Paris by cries of 'Long live France' and 'Down with Germany', while in Berlin crowds cheered the statue of Bismarck, the 'Iron Chancellor'.

The general staffs of all countries were put on war footing and began to put the finishing touches to their plans of attack. War was a way of life for these men. Diplomats, however, continued to make feverish attempts to stop the terrible chain of events that had been set in motion.

The situation began to change quickly and to move irrevocably towards the abyss. On 28 July Austria-Hungary declared war on Serbia. Two days later Russia, an ally of Serbia, ordered general mobilization. Germany, despite a certain degree of hesitation on the part of Wilhelm II, declared solidarity with Austria-Hungary on 1 August. France, an ally of Russia's, began to prepare for war. On 31 July one of the leading figures of the French Socialist movement, Jean Jaurès, was assassinated by a fanatical nationalist. Only a few days before, in a lecture to students at Albi, he had said: 'Humanity is cursed if, just to prove it has courage, it is condemned to eternal killing.'

This time the diplomats failed to neutralize the crisis. On Saturday, 1 August, in all the towns and villages of France, at exactly 5 o'clock in the afternoon, the tocsin sounded. In the little township of Saint-Lormel in Brittany, an old woman who was waiting murmured with prescience: 'That was the death knell of our young men.' White notices were attached to the walls of town halls the length and breadth of the country: it was the order for general mobilization, which was to come into effect on the following day.

It was war.

Colette was in Saint-Malo on that day: 'How can I ever forget that hour? It was 4 o'clock on a beautiful summer's day by the sea, the sky was misted over, and the golden-yellow ramparts of the town faced the sea, which was green near the shore but blue on the horizon – children in red bathing suits were leaving the beach for their afternoon tea and making their way through the busy streets. ... And in the centre of the town, the uproar burst forth all at once: alarm bell, drum, the shouts of the crowd, the crying of children. ... Women ran from the groups, stopping short as if they had been struck, then running again, with a look on their faces that seemed to say they had gone beyond some invisible boundary and plunged into another world.'

Farm-workers left the fields. In the towns crowds filled the roads. The old, brutal times had returned. Men, who felt as if they were drunk, began to realize that they had lost control of their lives and that they would not regain that control. Millions of people had a last night together, preparing for a future that no one could imagine.

The whole of Europe was in arms. Each country was threatened and was, in turn, convinced that it was going to have to defend itself to the utmost. Maurice Paléologue, the French ambassador in Russia, thought: 'The part of the mind that governs people's powers of reasoning is so feeble that within a week universal folly will be unleashed in the world.'

'No one can escape their destiny,' wrote the Russian minister of the interior as he signed the official order for national mobilization, to which he added the sign of the cross.

In the country consternation followed surprise. Who would do the harvesting? Horses were already being requisitioned. Women would have to do the work of gathering in the grain and wine harvests if the men were not back before autumn. They got ready to do their work.

On 2 August the French learned that uhlans – a name that had filled them with terror since 1870 – had already hurried past the frontier posts in Lorraine and had arrived in the village of Nomeny. At Joncherey, near to Belfort and 10 kilometres (6 miles) inside the French frontier, a German patrol killed Corporal Peugeot, the first French soldier to die in the war. A German aircraft dropped bombs near Lunéville. The old enemy was again occupying France's territory.

Germany declared war on France on 3 August. The next day German troops invaded Belgium, despite the international treaties guaranteeing that country's neutrality – treaties that the German Chancellor, Theobald von Bethmann Hollweg, described as 'scraps of paper'. Several years later Prince Bernhard Bülow described the promises to Belgium as 'unspeakably stupid'.

Britain, which had until then remained aloof, reacted to the violation of Belgium's neutrality by declaring war in Germany.

Everything was in place for the slaughter that was to follow.

1914

ARMÉE DE TERRE ET ARMÉE DE MER

ORDRE
DE MOBILISATION GÉNÉRALE

Par décret du Président de la République, la mobilisation des armées de terre et de mer est ordonnée, ainsi que la réquisition des animaux, voitures et harnais nécessaires au complément de ces armées.

Le premier jour de la mobilisation est le *Dimanche Deux Août 1914*

Tout Français soumis aux obligations militaires doit, sous peine d'être puni avec toute la rigueur des lois, obéir aux prescriptions du **FASCICULE DE MOBILISATION** (pages coloriées placées dans son livret).

Sont visés par le présent ordre **TOUS LES HOMMES** non présents sous les Drapeaux et appartenant :

1° à l'**ARMÉE DE TERRE** y compris les **TROUPES COLONIALES** et les hommes des **SERVICES AUXILIAIRES**;

2° à l'**ARMÉE DE MER** y compris les **INSCRITS MARITIMES** et les **ARMURIERS** de la **MARINE**.

Les Autorités civiles et militaires sont responsables de l'exécution du présent décret.

Le Ministre de la Guerre,   Le Ministre de la Marine,

◀ Page 12: The German cemetery at Langemarck in Belgium.

◀ Page 13: The French order for general mobilization dated Sunday, 2 August 1914.

'*I set out as a soldier of the Republic for what seemed to me the worst of reasons – universal peace and general disarmament.*'

Charles Péguy

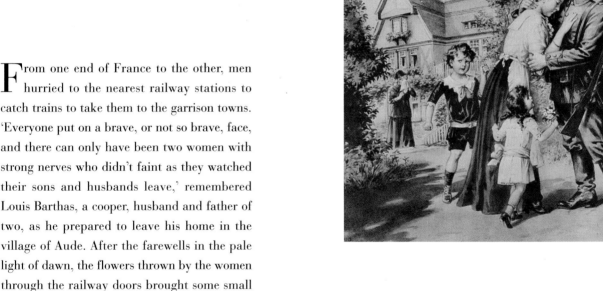

From one end of France to the other, men hurried to the nearest railway stations to catch trains to take them to the garrison towns. 'Everyone put on a brave, or not so brave, face, and there can only have been two women with strong nerves who didn't faint as they watched their sons and husbands leave,' remembered Louis Barthas, a cooper, husband and father of two, as he prepared to leave his home in the village of Aude. After the farewells in the pale light of dawn, the flowers thrown by the women through the railway doors brought some small consolation to the men setting out for the unknown.

Improvised barracks were hastily set up to accommodate 'all the men who hurried to enlist so promptly that the military authorities were taken by surprise,' continued Louis Barthas. The regiments and battalions were organized; and the soon-to-be combatants were provided with uniforms that were often too large or too small for them and were all imaginable colours: red kepi, blue-grey greatcoat, madder-red trousers

for the infantrymen, who, in addition, had to wear hobnail laced boots and carry a pack weighing 25 kilograms (55 pounds), an ammunition pouch, an 8mm Lebel rifle and a bayonet, which journalists soon came to call 'Rosalie'. The would-be soldiers were the centre of attention among the girls when they were seen walking about in their uniforms. But in just a few short weeks, these same uniforms were to offer the perfect targets amid the meadows and stubble of the first battles.

The German forces wore uniforms of field grey – *Feldgrau* – a shade the Kaiser was said to have found too dull. But the wisdom of the general staff in adopting this colour was soon evident: the German soldiers did not stand out against the background.

Farm-workers, craftsmen, office-workers, priests and financiers were crammed together into the railway wagons that jolted slowly along the crowded tracks as convoy followed convoy, one after another. All the would-be soldiers,

▲▶ Reservists mobilized in Berlin (above) and Paris (right).

drawn from every class of society, found they shared the same patriotic spirit. Day after day, hundreds of trains made their way towards the German frontier, carrying men from Brittany, Normandy, Corsica and Savoy, many of whom had never before left their home towns.

'All along the route of the trains, at level crossings, in the towns, there were crowds,' noted Lieutenant Désagneaux in his diary. The soldiers were cheered, people sang *La Marseillaise*. French women quickly took up their new role, handing out drinks, writing paper and cigarettes. The prevailing feeling was that the Germans had caused this and that it was their fault; the French would never have a better opportunity to get their revenge for 1870. The stations were decorated with bunting and echoed to the sounds of patriotic songs – *Sambre et Meuse* and *Chant du départ* – which increased the feelings of excitement. Very quickly the warlike rituals needed to generate patriotic fervour reappeared. Within a few days, once the initial shock of the mobilization had passed, the whole of France came together, from the pacifists on the left to the nationalists and revanchists on the right. It was the 'sacred union'.

'You had to live through a time like that to understand that "nation" wasn't just a word,' wrote the alpine chasseur Ferdinand Belmont, who was just twenty-four years old. 'It was good to be French then. It was especially good to see the upsurge of dedication, energy, self-sacrifice and patriotism from all corners of the country.'

For its part, Germany experienced the same overwhelming sense of unity and of nationalism, even among the powerful socialist party, which had been pacifist just a few weeks before. In Germany, as in France, everyone was convinced

> '*They are completely mad! A war between European nations is a civil war, the most monumentally stupid thing that has ever happened!*'
>
> General Louis Lyautey

of the rightness of the cause, and the feeling of unity that was generated was made up in equal parts of excitement, resignation and a sense of duty. In both countries, and in Britain, volunteers rushed to the recruiting offices. Hundreds of thousands enlisted in the German army; some were barely sixteen years old. The writer Ernst Jünger later remembered: 'We left lecture rooms, school desks and workshops and after a few weeks' training we had become a team and we had been made into a proper unit, which was full of enthusiasm. Raised in the ethos of a materialistic age, an unexpected desire and intense feeling overcame us.

'The war made us feel as if we were drunk. … It seemed to us a masculine thing to do, like a carefree contest between sharp-shooters in fields full of flowers, damp with a dew of blood. There could be no better way to die. Everything was on the move; nothing stayed still.'

Another German writer, Erich Maria Remarque, in *All Quiet on the Western Front*, recalled especially the type of indoctrination to which his hero, after the war, felt he had been subjected. 'When we met up at the recruiting depot, we were still nothing more than a class of students, made up of twenty young men, who, filled with pride, went to shave before we penetrated to the heart of the barracks. … We were filled with unsettling ideas that, as far as we could see, gave our lives and the war itself an idealized, almost romantic character.

'Our military training lasted for ten weeks, and that was sufficient time to transform us more fundamentally than ten years at school could have done. … We had seen that the classic idea of nationhood, the one that had been inculcated by our masters at school, was brought to nought here with a denial of personality that one wouldn't dare ask of the most humble domestic servant.' Remarque's book, published in 1929, was an impassioned denunciation of war.

Across the whole of France young men – and fathers and retired soldiers – went to sign up to defend their threatened nation. 'What good recruits we had at our disposal,' wrote Raymond Poincaré. 'The writers themselves and even greater people who, like Ernest Psichari or Charles Péguy, were not really old enough to go to fight in the first wave and to sacrifice themselves, claimed the honour of being useful behind the front.' These men included Edmond Rostand, Anatole France, Pierre Loti and several other intellectuals.

In Britain, from the moment the country entered the war, thousands of volunteers, horrified by the German invasion of Belgium and the violation of the treaties, responded to the calls from the Secretary of State for War, Lord Kitchener, and joined up to swell the ranks of the 100,000 soldiers of the regular army. They began to embark for Rouen and Boulogne from mid-August.

From 29 July the writer Blaise Cendrars, who had been born in Switzerland but who had, like many artists, lived in Paris since the beginning of the century, launched an appeal, which appeared in the Paris newspapers. Cendrars called on 'all the foreign friends of France' who, like him, had moved to France during the early years of the century, to defend the country of the Enlightenment and the Rights of Man against Germany, a country led by the Kaiser, the representative of another age and a man who supported the actions of another emperor in suppressing minorities. Cendrars was made a French citizen after the war.

Following his example, other groups were formed in major towns in France – Marseille, Toulouse and Lille – and so many foreigners wanted to enlist to show their support for France that some recruitment offices were unable to deal with them quickly enough. Among those who volunteered was Guillaume Apollinaire, who had been born Wilhelm Apollinaris de Kostrowitzki in Rome of an Italian father and a Polish mother. At the age of thirty-four, he found himself waiting for several months in a barracks at Nîmes before being sent to the front. In 1916 he was severely wounded in the head when a shell exploded while he was fighting on the Aisne.

Painters and poets mingled with Polish miners from the north and Spanish and Italian farm-workers from the southwest; the son of Gorki, the grandchildren of Garibaldi, who swept along with them thousands of Red Shirts, many of whom perished alongside them in 1915 in the Forest of Argonne. The Black American boxer Jack Monroe, and the champion cyclist from Luxembourg, François Faber, joined with Russians, Armenians, Czechs, Romanians, Jews from Central Europe and the countries of the eastern Mediterranean littoral, Americans, Argentinians ... By the end of 1914, 88,000 men were ready to fight for France. Cendrars fought in a unit that was linked to the Foreign Legion – which drew recruits equally from Alsace and Lorraine, as men deserted from the German army to fight for France – and he was joined by the Italian Rossi, who died on the Somme; Segouana, the furrier from the rue de Babylone, who was killed at Navarin Farm in September 1915; Goy, who was originally from Dalmatia; the Pole Przybyszewski; the American Victor Chapman, the son of a Chicago multi-millionaire; the Canadian Colon, who arrived from Winnipeg with his horses, which he wanted to give to France, and who lost a leg in Champagne.

The 80,000 men of the North African army began to arrive in Marseille – spahis, the native Algerian infantry, or zouaves. Troops arrived at Bordeaux from Senegal, Mali, Guinea and Niger, and the French got to know their colonies. At Narbonne Louis Barthas, the cooper from Aude, saw 'a magnificent Algerian division. It was impossible not to admire their appearance as they marched past, the ranks of the zouaves and the infantrymen, looking so proud, so gallant in their unusual uniforms.' The colonial and North African forces were to be sent directly to the fronts in all the major battles. 'A few days later some sensational news was heard, which made everyone extremely curious,' continued Barthas. 'It was said that a huge army of Hindus had arrived in Marseille and would be passing through.' These men from the Indian Army were sent north to join the British forces. The war was already global.

In the euphoria of the early days, a swift victory seemed assured, and this view was encouraged by the newspapers. It was reported that there had been so many advances in the technology of warfare that the initial engagements would be decisive. Only Lord Kitchener seemed to have read the omens correctly: he

▲ The chapel at the Château of Tilloloy on the Somme after the war. The front line crossed the grounds, and the Swiss writer Blaise Cendrars described the fighting here in his novel *La Main coupée* (1946).
▲ The forgotten grave of one of Cendrars's comrades at Tilloloy.

▼ The writer Blaise Cendrars was one of the many foreign volunteers who supported France. He fought on the Somme and in Champagne, where he lost an arm in 1915. After the war he became a French citizen.

'*Among us were foreigners who had committed themselves to the cause more from a love of France than a hatred of Germany. It wasn't only intellectuals and artists; there were businessmen and bankers. It wasn't just that they had left behind their shops, their businesses and their social life in Paris or the provinces so that they could become naturalized citizens or put their political or family circumstances on a regular footing. Many had come from other countries, some even from overseas. They had left their wives and children; some were no longer young. They came to France, without in any way regarding it as an adventure, and signed up for the duration of the war, after which they would be able to return to their homes.*'

Blaise Cendrars

▼ The chapel at Tilloloy was restored after the war.

Arrivée à Narbonne
de l'équipe du Cantonnement
de la 53e Cie du
1er Zouaves

▲ French mobilization was for the 'sacred union'.

◀ Native Algerian infantry and zouaves were sent to the front from French colonies in North Africa.

L'ANGLETERRE LÈVE UNE ARMÉE DE 500.000 HOMMES

▲ The first waves of volunteers rushed to the Central London Recruiting Depot, as French newspapers reported that Britain was raising an army of 500,000 men.

◀ Newly arrived British soldiers regrouped into their units.

◀ Far left: Mobilization depended on the smooth running of the railways.

predicted that the war might be a long one. As for the Kaiser, Wilhelm II promised his soldiers that the war would be 'quick and happy' and that they would be home 'before the leaves had fallen'.

The French counted on the Russian steamroller, the huge army that would advance smoothly to Berlin and bring the impudent Germans to their knees. As far as the Western Front was concerned, everyone was confident that they would make short shrift of the war and that everyone would be home for the wine harvest and the hunting season. The French made jokes about the German machine-guns, which jammed easily and would not offer any resistance to the French 75mm, the best field gun in the world. They would quickly recover Alsace and Lorraine; justice would soon be done.

THE OPENING SHOTS

It was precisely in the direction of the two 'lost' provinces that General Joffre, commander in chief of the French army, directed his forces. Some 4 million men were mustered in the east of the country, together with 600,000 horses, which had been transported there by rail.

From 4 August French troops had been attacking a ridge in the Vosges, where they pulled out the German posts marking the 1870 border. On 8 August the French entered Mulhouse in Alsace, a symbolic victory, which triggered a wave of enthusiasm through the whole country. French soldiers unfurled flags and played fanfares. 'The torrent of our army has by now flowed into Alsace,' claimed *Le Petit Parisien*. But victory was short lived. Mulhouse was retaken on the next day, then recaptured and lost again by the French, who withdrew a short distance to their rear and clung to the slopes of the Vosges. From de la Schlucht, the col of Bonhomme or the heights of Donon they couldn't help but look with longing over the plains of Alsace. The general staff set up headquarters at Thann, which they had just recaptured and which they were able to hold. The townspeople watched as the cavalrymen pitched camp in their orchards, the men's sky blue jackets harking back to the Napoleonic Wars.

► The view towards
France from Haguenau in
the Vosges.

Scarcely before the twentieth century had made its mark on the war, 'everyone had their noses in the air,' commented Lieutenant Désagneaux on 10 August. 'A German airplane flew over Épinal. It was attacked by the artillery in the fortifications there. It was the first time such a thing had been seen, and we watched the shells burst around it.'

Many of the new young soldiers in the garrisons longed impatiently for their 'baptism of fire'. Ferdinand Belmont, the young alpine chasseur based in a garrison in the Alps, was one such. On 20 August he wrote to his parents: 'We are still here, for I don't know how long, stuck in the boring valley, useless, forgotten, unwanted.' He had been in a hurry to find out what the field of battle was like, and he was sure that 'the longed-for moment would be wonderful'. Like his comrades, he was ready if necessary to sacrifice himself heroically in hand-to-hand combat. The fighting would, in fact, be nothing like he imagined.

The training they received did little to prepare the recruits for what was to come. As far as the French general staff was concerned, winning meant advancing. Despite the Russo-Japanese War of 1904–5 and the recent conflicts in the Balkans, which might have made them think seriously about developments in machine-guns and cannon, they continued to think in terms of the Battle of Austerlitz and the colonial

▲ From the 1870 frontier at Belfort the French looked into occupied territory.

wars. For most of the generals, superiority in battle depended on sheer force of numbers. The infantry were sent forward, bayonets at the ready, flags unfurled, following their officers, who dashed forward, their swords drawn. But bayonets are of little use against machine-guns. The men were cut down, falling in their battle formation without even having seen the enemy.

'The war played the cruellest trick on the soldiers by not being how they had imagined it would be,' wrote the poet and playwright Jules Romains after the war. Instead of 'real battles', for which they were ready, they were deafened by horrific detonations and showered with bullets and fire. They panicked and scattered everywhere.

'*Beneath their carefree laughter, most of my comrades hadn't given a second's thought to the horrors of war. They looked upon it as something they had seen only in patriotic colour prints.*'

Jean Galtier-Boissière

Jean Galtier-Bossière, who later founded the leading newspaper of the trenches, *Le Crapouillot*, described the bewilderment felt by French soldiers in the early days of the war. 'The officers drew their swords; we fixed our bayonets and marched forward. A thrill ran through the ranks. ... Today, God willing, would be the day for hand-to-hand fighting, when we would be able to show what we were made of. In front of us was a bare hillside. ... Bullets whistled overhead, shrapnel burst over us; huge shells exploded, making craters in the ground. ... Deafened, struck dumb, almost intoxicated with dirt and noise, I walked as if in a trance. I had but one idea, a single wish. ... Advance! Advance! I vaguely saw men collapsing on my right, on my left. The captain leapt into the smoke. A bugler stood to sound the charge as loudly as he could; then he fell. The ranks were thinner ... now we advanced by fits and starts. We struggled forward, weighed down by our packs, impeded by our cartridge pouches and water cans, swaying under our knapsacks ... then we threw them to the ground. ... Men bumped into each other as they advanced, others were struck in the head as they stood up. Bursts of gunfire swept over us, low down. ... "They are cutting us down with machine-gun fire," said the man next to me. A second later, he was dead.'

At last, after what seemed to be a never-ending hail of bullets from the enemy, Jean Galtier-Bossière heard with amazement the order to fall back. The infantrymen moved as quickly as they could across a field of potatoes to a ditch along a road bordered by trees. 'As far as the eye could see, the French line had withdrawn across the field, and I kept on saying, as if I was in a stupor, "But we had to retreat. In the name of God, we had to retreat!" Our losses, alas, were very great. The lieutenant-colonel, our major and three-quarters of our officers were dead or wounded.'

Newspapers did not get as far as battle zones in the east of the country, and news travelled slowly. During the first weeks letters from home did not reach the troops, who were continually on the move. The soldiers felt completely isolated, and, naturally, they knew nothing about the overall direction of the war. Increasingly confusing rumours began to circulate, and although they were afraid of spies, people picked up information from those who were coming back from the front line as they tried to find out exactly how far the enemy had advanced.

Just a few kilometres behind the front line, however, it was impossible not to know what was happening.'All the talk was of the great heavy artillery guns that fired from 10 kilometres and against which our 75s were useless,' noted Désagneaux. Soon the first convoys bearing the wounded were brought from the front in 'mobile hospitals, which were really nothing more than

▶ A less than successful camouflage.

◀ One of the earliest reconnaissance aircraft. Within four short years aviation became a determining factor in war.

◀ The first casualties.

trucks for livestock that had been converted', or in requisitioned buses. By now the real war had begun, and with it the reality of the hardship and suffering to come.

'Spirits are definitely not as high as they had been,' wrote Lieutenant Désagneaux on 12 August. He was in Lorraine, taken there by railway after mobilization. 'At Baccarat,' he noted on 20 August, 'it was possible to guess what was happening at the front. It seemed as if the numbers of the wounded would never end. The courtyard in front of the station was full of men waiting to be moved.' The numbers of the wounded quickly became so serious that it proved impossible to look after them locally. Convoys of casualties were sent to hospitals throughout France, and as the wounded were taken to the provinces, the sight of the mutilated bodies and the soldiers' accounts of the fighting quickly dispelled the illusions of the early days.

In addition to the wounded, scared refugees, both French and Belgian, began to flood into the towns behind the line, fleeing from territory taken by the Germans. 'At Badonviller there were terror and devastation in equal measure – townspeople stood huddled together, frightened and moaning, still terrified by the last few days.' The Germans had entered the small town on 10 August, and on the first day things had been relatively calm. But then the cellars had been ransacked, and the soldiers got drunk and lost control, venting their anger in shocking ways. Lieutenant Désagneaux recounted in his diary the horrific events that he heard from the survivors who had managed to escape. 'After they had finished drinking, they set up their field guns and machine-guns in the streets and began to fire at the houses at point-blank range. The church was shelled from a hundred metres, while the priest was standing in the main porch.'

It was possible to see houses burning in the

CROQUIS DE GUERRE 1914

129   Une Charge de Cavalerie française

1914... Chasseurs délogeant l'ennemi d'un bois   Light Infantry soldiers removing the enemy
10me Série   from a wood

distance, and news of other destroyed villages was brought by those who had succeeded in escaping. 'There were people from all over the area who had no idea where they were going – women, children, the elderly, the sick – they piled into whatever transport they could find and fled. … All these people were waiting, drawn to the station. The railway was their only hope. They crowded into livestock wagons, the children not understanding what was happening, their parents demanding to know where they would be taken. The crowds were indescribable.'

The alarming news spread throughout the region near the front line and soon began to affect the whole country. It was now obvious that no one would be singing about a victory.

THE BATTLE OF THE FRONTIERS

While violent fighting for the hillsides continued in the Vosges, General Joffre, from his head-quarters in a school in Vitry-le-François, was conducting a parallel assault in Lorraine, which became known as the Battle of the Frontiers.

At Sarrebourg the German troops, commanded by Crown Prince Rupprecht of Bavaria himself, fell back to the shelter of the concrete trenches that they had built for this very purpose and that were protected by barbed wire entanglements. The French, filled with excitement at the prospect of regaining lost territory, **took the town** of Sarrebourg and the hilly land to the north. Suddenly, they came under fire from

an enemy who had hitherto been nothing more than grey shadows. The infantry, decimated by the heavy shelling, abandoned Sarrebourg, the houses collapsing around them. The French were confronted by what General Dubail described to Joffre as 'real siege warfare'.

Around Château-Salins and Morhange the situation was pretty much the same: French troops liberated the borders of Lorraine, singing *La Marseillaise*. The cavalry took part in the operation, the cuirassiers wearing brilliant metal breastplates and the light cavalry armed with long lances and wearing plumed helmets.

◄ In the first weeks of the war the cavalry was seen as the key.

▲ Mounted troops were quickly abandoned in favour of the infantry.

► A turret survives amid the ruins of Fort Loncin.

Normally very swift, they were unmounted because their horses were exhausted through lack of food and rest and could advance no further. In the attacks, the infantry hurried behind the officers, some of whom – those who had trained at Saint-Cyr – wore helmets adorned with cassowary plumes and white gloves. Every time

▲ German troops advancing across Belgium.

CROQUIS DE GUERRE 1914

136   Fantassins allemands dans les tranchées au coin d'un Bois

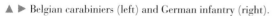

▲ ▶ Belgian carabiniers (left) and German infantry (right).

◀ Belgian cavalrymen in the streets of Liège.

▶ The Belgian royal family.

they advanced, a hail of shots held them back. Some divisions suffered losses of 80 per cent.

The infantrymen were completely demoralized by the insane advance, and increasing numbers of deserters were being captured. Soldiers who fled from the front line were maimed by being shot in the hand, and the general staff, which ignored the advice of superior officers and generals, handed out strict instructions about the treatment of deserters.

All the same, it was agreed that the famous madder-red trousers worn by the infantrymen would be covered by blue overalls. It was not to be until April 1915 that soldiers were given their famous sky blue uniforms.

The Invasion of Belgium

None of the men who fell at Montcourt, Charmes or Rozelieures knew that while they were bravely advancing under enemy fire, the future of the war was actually being decided elsewhere.

At the French headquarters General Joffre was annoyed by the warnings of General Lanrezac, the 'Lion of Guadeloupe'. Lanrezac, who was not only arrogant and quick-tempered but did not mince his words, continued to caution against a German attack from the north, and his view was borne out by reports from the air force and from aerial reconnaissance from airships. The King of the Belgians himself asked for help, but Joffre could not believe that the Kaiser would deploy his forces into Belgium, a neutral country, even though the French general staff had been aware of the Schlieffen Plan since 1911. Thus it was that while the French army was on the offensive in Lorraine, German forces were engaged in mounting a pincer movement that completely encircled Belgium.

From 4 August the farmers in the countryside around Liège, who had been busy harvesting corn, began to see German cavalrymen – uhlans – with their shakos, boots and lances. Laurent Lombard, writing in *Ceux de Liège*, described the extraordinary scene: 'At the top of a wooded headland a score of Belgian lancers crowded around a lieutenant, who was looking at a sunlit path. … There was silence as the officer kept his binoculars trained on the golden band whose furthest point disappeared into the shadows. Yes, there they were – a troop of uhlans. They advanced at a gentle pace, the sunlight glinting off their accoutrements. Their helmets bobbed up and down rhythmically, in time with their trotting horses. It was possible to make out the details of the grey uniforms. Their equipment was brand new. A cloth covered their shakos.'

The lieutenant immediately released a carrier pigeon, and at the same time the cyclists set out to warn the villagers. Suddenly, from the hilltop, the mounted scouts saw a mesmerizing sight. 'The invasion, terrible and unforgettable, had begun in front of them. It was a nightmare, a human anthill, from which arose a long-drawn-out rumble, made up of a thousand discordant sounds. The huge grey mass came to life and began to move and seethe. Here and there, camp fires glowed. … As the long hours passed, Picard and his men, completely hidden in the shadows, kept watch, spying on the sinister horde.'

After the cavalry followed the infantry, in a grey tide that spread out across the entire countryside. Cyclist troops were posted at crossroads and spooled out telegraph wires. The occupation had begun.

'I crossed Belgium as easily as I moved my hand,' said Wilhelm II, according to Cartier. But the Belgians resisted. They demolished bridges and tore up railway tracks to slow down the German advance, and King Albert I, who was known to his subjects as the Chevalier, personally took command of the tiny army of 117,000 men.

The city of Liège, which was surrounded by a series of fortresses, appeared to the German general staff as an inconvenient obstacle in its way to taking the country. It ordered the Belgian commander of the city, General Leman, to capitulate, but he refused out of hand. Then began the first aerial bombardment in history. Zeppelins flew overhead, dropping bombs on the city, while below them German troops began the attack. Nevertheless, the fortresses withstood the assault, and five days later the Germans had still failed to achieve their object.

They were then sent the latest howitzer from the Krupp factory on the Ruhr, the 420mm, a monster weighing 18 tonnes, which was dismantled before being dispatched on low-loaders and then transferred to articulated vehicles. The Belgians had blown up the tunnel at Herstal through which the convoy had to pass, but on 12 August the German artillerymen, who had taken up their position more than 300 metres (330 yards) away, launched the bombardment. The shells, each weighing almost a tonne, fell on the fort at Pontisse, which was razed to the ground; the remaining forts were then attacked, one after another. The last to fall was Loncin, to which General Leman had withdrawn. He was found unconscious among the ruins.

The Allies were in total disarray. It had been believed that the fortresses around Liège would withstand a siege lasting several months. Despite the heroic resistance of the Belgians, the superiority of the German firepower had broken through the fortifications in just a few days. Albert I decided to respond by withdrawing with the army to Antwerp and by surrendering Brussels. On 20 August 320,000 German soldiers – cavalry and infantrymen – paraded through the streets of the Belgian capital.

In order to break down Belgian resistance,

► The fortifications
around Liège were
unable to withstand the
heavy shelling from
German artillery.

◄ The crater that
resulted when a shell fell
on the magazine at Fort
Loncin.

the German general staff immediately instituted a reign of terror. At Liège on 22 August General Karl von Bülow had posters stuck up telling the inhabitants that at Andenne, where 'traitors' had attacked German soldiers, 'The general who commanded these troops has reduced the town to ashes and shot 110 people.' The general's poster continued: 'I bring these facts to the attention of the inhabitants of the city of Liège so that they might understand the fate that awaits them.' The same words were displayed in other occupied towns.

All over the territories, both French and Belgian, henceforth controlled by Germany, the Kaiser's army enforced the methods of 'total war', looting, burning, holding people to ransom, taking hostages – in short, acting in a way that horrified international opinion. In one act of

reprisal, the city of Louvain was burned – its houses, its fine public buildings, its library were destroyed. Hostages were shot as a warning, including a hundred in the town of Arlon. It was estimated that more than 3000 civilians were killed in Belgium, a number that included women, children and old people.

One German soldier noted in his logbook that the reprisals were carried out to frighten the free-shooters – the *francs-tireurs*. 'Behind Merlemont we crossed Villers-en-Fague, which was in flames. The population had warned the French that the soldiers were coming by signalling to them from the top of the church tower. The enemy artillery had fired on them, and shrapnel had wounded and killed some soldiers. At that, the hussars set the village on fire; the priest and some other people were shot.' Later

on he described the German advance, which was marked by further senseless cruelty. 'At Leffe, about 200 people were shot. It was done as a warning to others. Some innocent people may have suffered, but it was inevitable. It was also necessary to find out who was to blame.' Everywhere in France, as the German troops advanced – at Nomeny, Gerbéviller and Sarrebourg – eminent citizens were arrested and shot, civilians were attacked, the number of deportations increased, and the terrified inhabitants began to flee from their villages and from these acts of violence.

Eventually, General Joffre withdrew his forces to the frontier towards the west, and on 21 August the French attacked in the Ardennes, towards Neufchâteau in Belgium. Despite their superior numbers, thousands of infantrymen

▲ The ruins of Fort Loncin.

Germans suffered grievous losses too – the poet Georg Trakl, Ernst Wilhelm Lotz, Ernest Stadler, Alfred Lichtenstein and Hans Leybold – while among the British writers killed were the poets Rupert Brooke, Leslie Coulson, Julian Grenfell and Wilfred Owen. In addition to these, painters and sculptors, students and philosophers also fell. One can only wonder what these men would have achieved had they lived.

While the French were trying to advance into Lorraine, the Germans went on the offensive at Dinant, from where they wanted to cross the River Meuse. On the day before, the 33rd infantry regiment arrived at the stronghold under the command of a colonel who was on the point of retiring. His name was Pétain, and he had under his command a young sub-lieutenant named de Gaulle. The men had travelled on foot for more than 30 kilometres (19 miles) and were so exhausted they even slept in the street. The German bombardment began at dawn, and de Gaulle, who was in position on a railway embankment, was wounded in the knee. 'The road was covered with the dying, there was a chorus of groans and cries for help.' In his notes, de Gaulle continued: 'The officers were calm;

fell under the battery of guns hidden in the woods. Ten thousand men were cut down in just a few hours, among them the writer Ernest Psichari, the grandson of Joseph-Ernest Renan. The news of his death sent reverberations around the literary world. He was one of the first writers to perish in this war, just a few weeks before Charles Péguy, who was one of his friends, and a few months before Alain-Fournier and Louis Pergaud, who had just won the Prix Goncourt and whose body was never found. It was the start of the slaughter of an entire generation of intellectuals and artists, most of whom were non-commissioned officers and fell in the early months of the war at the head of their troops. In all, 133 French writers had been killed by the end of 1914; 430 in the whole war. This loss of talented young men was not confined to the French; the

▼ The interior of Fort Lantin, one of the dozen fortifications around Liège. The garrison surrendered without offering any resistance, which explains why it is undamaged.

they would be shot where they stood. With bayonets fixed to their rifles, just a few units stood firm; a bugler sounded the advance; isolated acts of supreme heroism. ... Nothing happened. In the wink of an eye it seemed as if all the goodness in the world could not prevail against the fire.'

General Joffre decided to concentrate the Allied troops against the Sambre and the Meuse, to the south of Charleroi, where the Belgian troops had joined up with the British Expeditionary Force (BEF). But the German forces facing them had also had time to regroup. The night before the French attack, Captain Spears of the BEF was talking to a French officer on a nearby hill when he suddenly saw a haunting sight. 'Without a moment's warning ... we saw the horizon burst into flame. To the north, the whole sky was lit by innumerable incendiaries. It was almost as if hordes of demons had suddenly been given their freedom and, swooping above the distant plain, had set fire to every town, every village.'

There, near to Charleroi, was to be the site of a major battle, in a countryside where, as Pierre Drieu la Rochelle put it, even blackbirds spat out songs of bullets.

From the start, the battle was unequal – fifty-two German divisions faced thirty-two Allied divisions. The French infantry were driven back, and on 23 August General Lanrezac recognized that his men were surrounded. He ordered a

▲ Fort Loncin was razed by the German shells.

retreat to save part, at least, of his army. General Helmuth von Moltke, who had taken 4000 prisoners, gave the order to pursue the French.

THE RETREAT

It was the retreat that etched itself with such horror in the memories of the survivors, so great were the effects on their morale and physical

condition. The army began to fall back under a blazing hot sun. The roads were already crowded with fleeing civilians, and Captain Spears remembered that: 'We began to pass long, slow-moving columns of the wounded, limping along. Sometimes they were alone; sometimes they were in pairs, trying to support each other. Their clothes were torn; their faces were smeared with dirt and dust. There were a very few officers,

▼ The tiny Belgian army, struggling to reorganize itself in the face of the German threat, went to war with enormous courage.

crammed to overflowing; in each hand his wife held a huge wicker basket, each covered with a napkin. They walked quickly, their eyes filled with distress and fear, back to their home, which they hadn't wanted to leave and which now, perhaps, had been reduced to a heap of smoking ruins.'

Everywhere there were 'groups of infantrymen, covered in dust and marching in the sparse grass along the sides of the road … carts were crammed with the wounded', farm wagons jolted along, piled high with mattresses and bundles of clothes and with women, children and old people.

The retreating soldiers, attacked from the rear by the advancing Germans, had to march non-stop for ten days. They lifted potatoes from the fields as they passed; they drank water from stagnant pools; they were numb with exhaustion and their feet were covered with blood. They abandoned along the side of the road those who could walk no further.

Roland Dorgelès later wrote about the retreat: 'The forced march from Charleroi to Montmirail was appalling; there was no rest, no food and nothing to drink; all the regiments were mixed together – zouaves with infantrymen, riflemen with engineers – and there were the wounded, frightened and stumbling; the gaunt stragglers, who had been beaten by the guards. Knapsacks and weapons were thrown into ditches. The fighting and pursuit went on day

their men straggling and looking completely exhausted; they dragged their legs from fatigue. These men were not injured; they were worn out.'

In the north of France, where people were hastening from the German army, there was panic. The huge influx of Belgian refugees and their accounts of the atrocities inflicted on them exacerbated the exodus. The mayor of Maubeuge decided to evacuate the town just two days after General Haig had established his headquarters in the town. Maubeuge was a garrison town, surrounded by six forts, but it was unable to withstand the German shelling.

Lille, which had declared itself an 'open' (unfortified) town, no longer concerned the Germans who were making swift progress south. The British had fallen back after a hard struggle to Lanrecies, then to Le Câteau, where there was hand-to-hand fighting in the streets. The Germans occupied Valenciennes, Cambrai, Saint Quentin (which became their headquarters), Bapaume, Péronne, Laon, Senlis. As the banks in the coastal areas transferred all their funds to Britain, the Kaiser was ordering medal after medal to be struck to celebrate the German victories.

Marc Bloch, who fought during the retreat, with 'a rifle that had never fired', saw 'poor evacuees in their cars, which filled the roads and squares of the villages. They were lost, stupefied, ordered about by the guards, in the way and pathetic.' Everywhere, from Flanders to

Lorraine, similar scenes were being enacted. Lieutenant Maurice Genevoix watched the villagers escaping from Montfaucon, which had been shelled. 'I watched the columns of smoke with a kind of numbed pity … the flames shot up everywhere, joining together and spreading, until there was a huge pall of smoke, black and deadly, hanging above the whole village. Vehicles carrying injured people passed me; some of the people were dying. The wounded who could still walk dragged themselves along, about half were supporting themselves on crutches or using two sticks to bear their weight. … There was an especially pathetic old couple: on his back the old man carried an enormous basket, which was

▲ ▶ In Belgium and in northern France thousands of refugees fled before the lightning advance of the German troops.

after day; there were occasional victories – Guise, where the Germans fell back. We slept whenever we stopped, on the embankments or on the road, in spite of the wagons that passed us, weighed down with looted groceries, farm animals and mouldy bread, which people argued over. There were machine-gunners without their mules, dragoons without their horses, units from Senegal without their captains. The roads were completely covered with ox-carts, filled with weeping women and children and with goats tethered behind them. Villages were in flames, bridges were blown up, comrades, bleeding and exhausted, were left behind, and still the sound from the shells continued to harass the sad procession.'

In the rest of France, accurate information was impossible to come by. It was believed that the Germans had completely conquered Belgium and it was understood that they had also taken Picardy. 'The great farms of the plains and the haystacks burned in the distance,' wrote Marc Blanpain, 'together with the fields of beetroot and the stubble in the fields. Hundreds of terrified horses roamed about, still wearing their bridles and dribbling helplessly.'

At Guise the French troops summoned up a sudden burst of energy and gave battle, and, thanks to the artillery, they managed to slow down the German advance for a while. The Germans crossed back over the bridges of the River Oise and briefly were in retreat. This was the first time since the war began that the German advance was delayed. Whether or not the morale of the Kaiser's commander-in-chief was affected by this, the German advance towards Paris was at least halted.

But, dressed in their dark uniforms and carrying their long lances, the uhlans – the Prussian lancers – who had been in the first wave of the invasion, were able to see in the distance, through the heat haze of the early days of September, the top of the Eiffel Tower.

THE BATTLE OF THE MARNE

On 31 August General Joffre, who had just learned of the Russian defeat at the Battle of Tannenberg, recommended that the French government should withdraw to Bordeaux. While 500,000 Parisians were attempting to get to the south, General Gallieni set about organizing the defence of the capital after entrusting the command of his newly formed army to General Maunoury. Meanwhile, the German First Army under General von Kluck had reached the Marne and was continuing to advance towards the Seine, despite the orders of the German high command. By his actions, von Kluck had exposed his right flank, and when they realized this, Joffre and

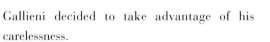

Among the French forces at the First Battle of the Marne were 5000 native Moroccans.

Gallieni decided to take advantage of his carelessness.

Joffre got the agreement of the British to attack. On 4 September Maunoury was ordered to march his army to the east and to launch a surprise attack on von Kluck's army on the River Ourcq. The first bullets were fired at about noon; by 5 o'clock in the afternoon Charles Péguy had fallen, hit in the head by a bullet. He had been on an embankment running along a little road near Villeroy, not far from Meaux. 'I set out as a soldier of the Republic for what seemed to me the worst of reasons – universal peace and general disarmament,' he had written just a few days before.

On the night of 5 September the exhausted soldiers had to sleep where they stood. In the Île-de-France, after the very warm days earlier in the month, the cool nights caused a cold mist to accumulate in the bottom of the valleys. In the morning the soldiers listened to the details of the order of attack, read out by their general. The French army was to execute an about-turn and engage the enemy 'according to the lie of the land. … Troops that could advance no further were to defend the territory they held, no matter what the cost, and to die rather than give way.'

Exhausted after the ten days' march, the soldiers turned towards the enemy and, summoning up their last reserves of energy, began to fight.

The future of France, of Europe itself, depended on the outcome of this great battle, in which 2 million men faced each other along a front 200 kilometres (125 miles) long, running from Verdun to Paris along the River Marne. For five days the battlefield rang with rifle fire and the sound of field guns, mingling with bugle calls, while as far as the eye could see the sky was lit by flames. The infantry from Provence and Brittany fought side by side with zouaves and colonial troops against soldiers from Bavaria, Prussia and Württemberg. Tens of thousands of men fell among the ricks of late-summer hay.

The first engagements took place near the River Ourcq, to where the French had initially fallen back. Gallieni, all too aware of the time it would take reinforcements to reach him from the capital, commandeered all the taxis in Paris. That night, under cover of dark and unobserved by enemy aircraft, they ferried to Nanteuil-le-Haudouin, to the north of Meaux, all the soldiers who had arrived in Paris by train from the east of France.

The main fighting shifted to the centre of the front, to the area between Sézanne and Fère-Champenoise, on the borders of the Île-de-France and Champagne, in the very place where, several centuries earlier, Attila the Hun had halted the Roman legions and hastened the collapse of the Empire. Somewhere in the fields around here the golden headdress of the barbarian leader still lay buried. The Germans attacked around the marshes of Saint Gond, where they came up against the troops under the command of General

◀ The First Battle of the Marne, fought in September 1914, quickly became the subject of paintings.

Foch, who was determined not to give way, despite the exhaustion of his men. For Foch, winning was, above all, a question of morale. 'Victory is a matter of will.'

The Germans attacked with the famous Prussian guard, who were supported by an impressive artillery battery. The blazing hot days were followed by thunder storms, and the rain soaked the uniforms of the North African troops, who were unused to such cold weather. The Germans managed to take Château Mondement, which had been held by the Moroccan divisions. It was a beautiful house, with a tower at one side that was known as the 'donjon' and that looked out over the low-lying marshes round about. This marked the furthest forward that the Germans were able to advance.

On the order to regroup, the French infantry began to fight furiously. Reinforcements were brought by General Grossetti, who was renowned for his great speed and who arrived riding on horseback amid his troops. The attack was launched against the German rear, from the garden of the great house, and it was led by Captain Beaufort, who had first spent some time in meditation with a priest. Then he pulled on his white gloves and threw himself forward, through a breach made in the wall by the 75mm field guns, urging forward his men: 'Onward, men! For France! Charge!' He was brought down a few moments later, shot through the chest. A few minutes after that, Captain Montesquieu fell, his sword in the air, just as he was leaping through the same breach. The fighting continued until 9 o'clock at night, when the Germans began to retreat.

Along the entire length of the front the Germans were being forced to fall back. The First Battle of the Marne had been won, and the German advance into France had been halted. The Schlieffen Plan was in ruins. Prince Bernhard von Bülow was aware that the invasion of Belgium had turned out to be a terrible error. 'Some of the things that were done could not be justified by the results.' And he quoted Machiavelli: 'Cosa fatta capo na.'

After the battle the dead had to be buried. So many bodies were beginning to decompose

that the water supplies to Paris were being polluted and there was no drinkable water in the capital. Everywhere – under hedges, in fields – the swollen bodies of horses lay next to the shattered wagons and carts. The unburied bodies of countless mutilated men were becoming bloated. 'The mild breezes carried the vile stench; it was all-pervading and unbearable,' wrote Maurice Genevoix. 'All day long I smoked, one cigarette after another, trying to disguise the frightful smell, the stench of those poor dead men who had fallen in the fighting, abandoned where they fell because no one had time to throw a little earth over them so that their putrefying bodies wouldn't be seen.'

Émile Henriot, a young journalist, travelled the length of the field of battle. 'The village of Varreddes, lying in a valley, was in chaos. Exhausted men went to and fro, as if they were in a daze. I crossed the village in the direction of the plain. … Beyond was a huge, empty space; the stubble-covered fields lay beneath the wide sky. There were black hayricks in the distance; something was burning there and further away, and the smoke was billowing out. The sun shone, the sky was blue. I did not know what the nauseating smell could be; it made my gorge rise and my heart pound. Was it the smoke? I walked on. Close by, on my right was a field of red poppies, glowing in the sun. It looked strange. I moved nearer. They were not poppies; they were rows of red trousers, covering the whole field. … One of the units that had been in the attack had been cut down like corn. … The plain was covered with bodies. Trousers of flowing white material, the little blue jackets, edged with braid; Moroccans and zouaves with their fezzes. They lay in battle order, line on line. These men had launched the attack, their bayonets fixed to their rifles. They lay where they had fallen. … The heavy stench hung everywhere. It clung to me like glue. The fine September day drew to a peaceful end on this stinking scene.'

The villagers were ordered to bury the corpses. 'Some of the people living here,' recalled

▲ ◄ The battle was waged amid abandoned sheaves of corn in the first autumn of the war.

▲ Château Mondement today.

◀ The marshes of Saint Gond.

▶ The fierce fighting that took place at Château Mondement according to a contemporary print.

10. Bataille de la Marne
6 au 12 Septembre 1914
Maurupt (Marne)
Champ de bataille à l'est du chemin
de Pargny-sur-Saulx

◄ ▼ After the First Battle of the Marne.

'Along the side of the trenches, in ever-longer lines, stood the makeshift crosses, made from two pieces of wood or even from sticks. Sometimes there were dozens of unnamed dead, a single cross marking all their graves. "Soldiers of France, killed on the field of honour," we wrote. From their little mounds, green once again, they watched us pass by, and someone said that their crosses were bending towards us, to choose those of our number who would be joining them tomorrow.'

Roland Dorgelès

La Tombe du Fils.

'*It was only when night fell that Joseph became too tired to hold any longer in his arms the stiff, cold, dead body. He had watched Jules's life ebb away. "Ah, yes!" he said. … Then he took his medal. He checked to make sure that he had both the medals in his pocket, and then he set out along the road. There was nothing but the sound of his footsetps in the terrible silence.*'

Jean Giono

▲ The First Battle of the Marne halted the German advance and saved Paris.

'*Poor old village! The church was left standing ignominiously around its profaned nave. The beautiful houses that were still standing were little more than two triangles of stone, which looked sadly at each other.*'

André Maurois

BATAILLE DE LA MARNE (6-13 Sept. 1914). — Prise de Clermont-en-Argonne incendié par les Wurtembergeois (Extrait de '' En Plein Feu '').
Visé Paris n° 36

◀ The armies came face to face on a line that, according to William Faulkner, cut across France, from the Alps in the east to the ocean in the west, in a single line of mud-stained men.

▲ The ruined village of Montfaucon in Lorraine, which lay on the top of a knoll taken by the Germans in September 1914. It was recaptured by American forces in September 1918.

a sub-lieutenant in the African corps of riflemen, 'excavated a huge ditch. … A cart arrived, driven by an old farmer. It was a haycart. It was full, to the top of the rails, with bodies that had been picked up. … It was possible to see the awful swollen faces – some looked so young with their close-cropped hair – which looked ghastly as they began to decompose. I hurried away. In spite of the respect I felt for these men who had fallen on the field of honour, I could not bring myself to watch these carts with their macabre loads.'

THE GERMAN WITHDRAWAL

On 10 September the order was given for the Germans to fall back, but the French had neither the ammunition nor the troops to pursue them with any vigour. The Germans withdrew for about 40 kilometres (25 miles) to beyond the River Aisne and then began to establish a line on high ground running from the east through the Argonne and along the heights of the Meuse. Although the men were exhausted, fierce fighting occurred here and there over small pockets of land. Despite this, the Germans continued to stabilize their position along the higher ground, in a line they were to maintain for the next four years.

An irony of the war was that, during their withdrawal, the Germans occupied some of the huge fortifications that the French had built after 1870 to protect themselves from invasion. These fortifications had been marked on the maps of the French general staff and offered, in theory, protection for the main towns in the north and east of the country. They created barracks from solid concrete, surrounding them with ditches that could only be crossed by bridge. Around Reims only the fortress at Pompelle remained under French control. The German forces installed themselves in the forts at Berru, Brimont and Nogent-l'Abbesse, from where they attacked the city, which was within firing range. For months Reims suffered an almost daily bombardment, during which houses, hospitals and churches alike were damaged.

fought relentlessly to contain the German threat. In Lorraine, the town of Lunéville was retaken, but it was little more than a shell, with German notices still attached to the ruins. At Grand-Couronné the French defence of Nancy was especially difficult. Within a few hours 8000 shells fell on a single hill. General de Castelnau, whose headquarters were at Maizières, witnessed the tragic events. Just as he was about to receive his orders, he was given a personal message: one of his sons, Xavier, had just been killed. The general turned away to one side for a few moments, then he composed himself and, his face pale, spoke to his officers: 'Let us continue, men.' A few days later he learned of the death of his son-in-law, and in the course of war he lost three more children.

In the Vosges the fighting to occupy the mountain ridges was desperate and bloody. The Germans had had time to fortify what had, since 1870, been their own border. To the north of the mountain range soldiers from Bavaria held Spitzenberg, where they installed themselves in the ruins of an ancient château that had belonged to the Counts of Lorraine. They had riddled the steep slope of the mountain with bunkers and emplacements for machine-guns, ready for the French to begin the attack from the bottom of the valley. Around Saint-Dié, a small town on the

On 14 September, Captain Edward Spears, who later became a major-general, watched the assault on the city. 'Whistling like a dozen express trains and appearing to dance a saraband above our heads, the 210mm shells went on crashing into houses with the force of planets hurling themselves at each other. ... The air became thick and yellow, just like a London fog, and began to stink of explosives.' He saw people falling in the streets and then 'the enemy began to bombard the cathedral', an act that horrified the entire population of France and seemed to the Allies to be a manifestation of utter barbarity. For Rudyard Kipling, who visited the city in 1916, the ruins of the 'blind and mutilated' cathedral became a potent symbol of the city's courage.

Towns near the front line suffered throughout the war from the same kind of bombardments as Reims. At Soissons, for example, some of the townspeople were determined to stay, no matter what happened. The novelist Pierre Loti later remembered: 'Here and there it was possible to see little notes, written on white paper and attached to whatever wall remained standing. They bore the message: "This house is still lived in." ... An hotel greeted the intrepid traveller who

risked the journey there. In some places, people were thinking about the front line: ditches had been dug along the streets and in the garden of the town hall. Barricades, trenches, barbed wire entanglements and fences, holes in the road and other building works were used to isolate remote suburbs.'

Although the decisive action had taken place on the Marne, towards the east French troops had

▲ The Fort of Pompelle, one of the fortifications around Reims.

◄ German prisoners were led through the streets by French cavalrymen.

▶ Fort Brimont near Reims was held by the Germans throughout the war.

west flank, the enemies alternately advanced and retreated, conducting hand-to-hand fighting among the pine trees and shooting each other at point-blank range. The town was taken and retaken several times in the course of a fortnight, until, eventually, it was in French hands.

The young sub-lieutenant, Ferdinand Belmont, arrived at Saint-Dié with his unit of alpine chasseurs at the end of August. He had left his home in the Alps for the battle zone while the Battle of Charleroi was taking place, but he knew absolutely nothing about it. He waited impatiently until he could go to the front line and was anxious to confront the enemy and show his courage, but when he arrived in the little town in the Vosges he found out what war was really like. The troops that a few days earlier had been

fighting at Sainte-Marie-aux-Mines fell back in disorder, 'harassed by the German artillery. … The men were afraid, unshaven and visibly exhausted. They had been fighting for three weeks, and they had slept as often under the stars as in haystacks.'

The young man received a baptism of fire three days after he had arrived. He was in the pine woods when some 'men began to fall, heavily but silently onto the moss'. They had been shot at close range by the Germans, 'whom we hadn't seen, thanks to their grey uniforms, which merged with the thickets of bramble and bracken'. It was a 'terrible and sad' introduction to the screams of pain and to death.

A few days later Belmont was pleased to be leaving for the battle front, and he wrote to his

parents. 'I think I shall see France tomorrow, cleansed by the sacrifice and strengthened by the test. … Who knows if this terrifying rush into whatever confronts the power of the world is the desolation allowed by God to remove the spots that stain the Church?' But on the evening of one of his first days in battle, Belmont wrote: 'War is absolutely terrible, and there are times, like this evening, when we are, despite ourselves, overcome by a black horror.' A few days later he added: 'Say that the men who march past, and whom I see move, are men like us, like me, and they are the enemy. We spy on each other from afar. We want to kill each other one day or another.' Nevertheless, Belmont added, 'We are at war; we have to fight. It is a large and serious undertaking to accept and to

► The plains of Berry-au-Bac on the north bank of the Aisne to the west of Reims.

◄ The ruins of Reims. By 1918 there were only about a score of habitable dwellings in the entire town.

'Across the fields only little red mounds indicated the positions of the graves that were dug, with rough crosses put at their heads. Personal belongings, broken weapons, equipment lay by the side of the roads and all along the trenches. The stench from an enormous number of dead horses, abandoned in the fields, polluted the air.' Henri Désagneaux, who was near Harancourt in Lorraine, made the same observation. 'There are nothing but graves. Everywhere you turn there is a cross, marking the position of a body, then there are the holes made by shells. The vast fields are desolated. Ruins cover the country.'

'I do not know how many men have been killed or are injured,' wrote Ferdinand Belmont on 30 August. 'There are no captains left, and half the lieutenants and sub-lieutenants have been killed or wounded. There are men who are lost whose bodies we have not found.' On 3 September he noted: 'So, the last two captains of the 11th company have been killed. This is a state of affairs common to all the companies – the loss of officers is proportionately greater than the loss of men. We are noticeably short of officers, and the result is that those who survive are assured of preferment to important postings. My God! How far will I, with my limited experience, be promoted!' Three days later he wrote: 'Another lieutenant of the battalion was killed yesterday. If this continues there won't be any officers left to take command of 1600 or 1700 men!' On 7 September the losses had become so great that Belmont was made a lieutenant.

An entire section of French society was on the point of disappearing altogether. The elite of the nation was being killed: 833 specialist engineers, 146 graduate teachers and almost half the primary school-teachers had been killed in the war, and the children of those families who had traditionally entered the armed forces from loyalty to the idea of serving the nation were being killed, one after another.

It was rumoured that the Germans regarded killing officers as a priority. But was this supposition necessary to explain the disproportionate number of deaths among those who had been brought up to believe in the value of self-sacrifice

fulfil. But pray for me; I need you to, I need you to very much.'

He was not granted an overall view of the battle; he knew only that he and his men had to hold a little valley. If they lost ground, 'every day they would be leaving behind a little of the world as they moved on, and losing their supplies,' with a battalion of which 'all that remained was fragments'. Faced with the fortified entrenchments of the Germans, they excavated ditches to protect themselves. 'We went to earth in our holes, keeping perfectly still and hidden in the red earth, in the middle of the clover and the potatoes [while] an enormous German airship hovered overhead, large and yellow, like a huge caterpillar, above the valley.' They were attacked by the enemy artillery before they were able to bury the bodies that lay on the damp ground in the fields and by the sides of the roads.

The countryside was devastated by the artillery battles, but it was still beautiful, especially in the pale evening light – until the calm was shattered by the sound of gunfire. 'From time to time German reconnaissance aircraft appeared in the clear sky. The evenings were peaceful as the sun set, lengthening the shadows cast by the pine trees. It was enough to make one weep, to feel so alone and to have to do what we were doing in such surroundings.'

The contrast was even more poignant when 'the desolate countryside was ravaged by shells which left bodies, like dark stains, scattered across the fields'.

On the evening that he went to the front, Belmont met a soldier who questioned him. It was his brother Jean, who did not immediately recognize him in his soldier's uniform. 'We had two minutes alone together by the side of the road. He had just arrived behind the lines and didn't know where he was being sent.' Jean was killed the next day, in his first battle, but it was several weeks before Ferdinand heard the news. He had searched in vain for his brother at the time of the battle in which his brother had taken part, but he left the Vosges two weeks later without having heard any news of him. It wasn't until he was in Toussaint in Picardy, to where he had been transferred, that he learned of his brother's death in a letter from his parents who had themselves just received the terrible news.

Like his comrades, he knew nothing of the overall direction of events. When he was in the Vosges, he had no idea what was happening on the Marne. All he knew was that he didn't know where he would be the next day. He saw only the events that took place around him – and he saw men die.

and in the concept that honour was a virtue? The young officers were the first to rush to lead the men under them, and they were the first to die. With them was dying a concept of duty and morality that until then had helped to bind society together.

In fact, the Germans were suffering in the same way. The two armies experienced the same problems with the loss of officer-class men and the example that such men provided to the young, inexperienced recruits who often panicked as soon as they came under fire.

The officers were not, of course, the only ones to die. The number of dead reached such levels during the early weeks of the war that it proved necessary to regroup those who survived into new battalions and to appeal for new recruits to take the place of those who had fallen. In September it became necessary to mobilize the 1914 intake of recruits, who were hastily trained. These were, noted the journal *L'Illustration*, 'only just men, of whom their mothers could be proud', and Roland Dorgelès saw them arriving on the Aisne from November, 'with their kitbags and worn out' but wanting to know where the enemy was. 'They said nothing about going to the front when they saw, on the other side of the barbed wire, the furtive movements of the Germans, who vanished as quickly as they were seen, and in no man's land, beneath the thickets that glittered with snow, the bodies of their older comrades in their red trousers.' The young men were seen passing through Sommedieue in Lorraine in December.

On 2 August Maurice Genevoix had written of 'the feeling of euphoria, the surge of delight that swept through Europe, the cheering as trains passed by, the waving handkerchiefs', but now 'after us, come others, like us, who are lost'. Thrown into the attack during that first winter, about 80 per cent of these young men were killed or wounded.

They fought on the Oise, on the Aisne, in Champagne, in Argonne and in Lorraine for the sake of taking a single hill or knoll to gain a slight advantage over the enemy. There were machine-guns and explosions everywhere and bursts of artillery fire; and the bodies piled up. The

▼ The remains of a small fortification in the Vosges, near to Saint-Dié.

▲ A monument near to Ban-de-Sapt marks the early months of the war.

number of empty places around dinner tables increased. In villages everywhere people dreaded the sight of the mayor or police bringing the awful news. When they saw them in the distance, people would stop working in the fields and ask which farm they were going to this time.

The philosopher Alain (Émile-Auguste Chartier), who was forty-six years old, left his teaching post and enrolled as a private. On 14 December 1914 he wrote to E. and F. Halévy: 'When I see the infantrymen, I am unable to do anything but long for the end of the war because, if it continues, they will all die.'

The Race to the Sea

It was not long before Ferdinand Belmont, like many of those who had been fighting in the east of France, was transferred to the Western Front, where most of the important events of the war were to take place. Belmont was sent to Dompierre in Picardy, an area of extensive plains and flat horizons, where it was possible to deploy the artillery. 'There were major engagements lasting several days and on very long fronts in the enormous plains that exist round here, where the artillery has vast fields in which to fire countless rounds.' Soon, 'in the intervals between rounds, it was possible to hear the calls of partridges that had been disturbed by the war'. The frightened birds flew 'between the abandoned sheaves of corn that had begun to rot'.

'Despite the optimism of the general staff,' noted Belmont at the beginning of October, 'it seemed that the hostilities were going to continue for much longer than anyone had initially believed. For even if the formidable German attack had been worn out … there still remained a lot of work to do to force the savages back and to make them retrace their steps through the lands they had taken.'

◄ The French cemetery at Fontenelle in the Vosges.

▲ In the west the armies faced each other across the vast plains of Picardy.

AVIS
à la Population

A partir du 16 AVRIL, les horloges des monuments publics ainsi que celles des lieux affectés au public **DEVRONT ÊTRE AVANCÉES D'UNE HEURE.**

La circulation sur la voie publique est autorisée de cinq heures du matin à neuf heures du soir (nouvelle heure allemande).

Marcq-en-Barœul, le 12 Avril 1917.

Le Commandant de Place.

Marcq, Imp. P. Cornille, 23, rue Saint-Patrick

▲ Towns were forced to accept German standard time.

▼ Occupied towns were either terrorized or charmed.

▲ The town of Arras was bombarded by German shells.

For the time being at least, from the Vosges to Picardy, the front was impassable, and there was only one direction in which the troops could move forwards: the west. Each army tried to pass the other at the far end of its front lines in the only territory where movement was possible, each time moving the front a little further northwest, across the Somme and Artois, to Flanders. This period of the war came to be known as 'the race to the sea'.

The fighting spread across Picardy, around Roye, Rosières and Péronne. In October Arras, the capital of Artois, was threatened, surrounded and shelled. The belfry collapsed, and buildings dating from the seventeenth century were destroyed. But, despite the bombardments, which the Kaiser himself came to watch, the town held out, thanks to the reinforcements provided by troops from Senegal and by zouaves. The German cavalry attacked the mining area, where they were opposed by British troops, who gave battle at Neuve Chapelle, Armentières and La Bassée in the mountains of the north, which separated sections of the front.

Lille, which had been abandoned by the Germans in August, was occupied in September. Maxence Van der Meersch recalled that the first Germans who wanted to take the city arrived by way of the area around the Porte des Postes. 'At the beginning of October 1914 they began to attack a group of firemen, who were armed with rifles and who fired back. A few shots were also fired from windows in that part of the city. The Germans retreated, leaving half a dozen dead on the street. But the next day, thousands of men overran the neighbourhood. The siege of Lille had begun, and in reprisal for the earlier deaths Prince Rupprecht of Bavaria ordered that that part of the city should be sacked. The assault was savage, and people looking out from their doors and windows were shot at. Men and women didn't understand what was happening, and when they heard the bullets shattering the windows and roofs they thought it was a shower of pebbles. When they went outside to see what was happening, they were killed. It is impossible to imagine how the townspeople so misread the war. Hordes of drunken soldiers forced their way into their houses, looting and pillaging, sprinkling petrol over the furniture and floors, and releasing cats, soaked with petrol and set alight, into the houses. A large part of the neighbourhood burned down almost instantly. The terrified people rushed outdoors, into the streets where they were in danger of being hit by bullets fired by Lille's defenders. Amid this indescribable confusion, the German soldiers, who had already taken the town, swept through the area like a tide.'

From then on, throughout the occupied territory, there was no more news from the rest of France. 'A barrier of iron fell around the occupied north of France, cutting it off from the rest of the world. What happened to our forces? … No one had any idea of what had happened at the Battle of the Marne or about the race to the sea. People thought that the occupation of Lille, Roubaix and Tourcoing was nothing more than a stage in the retreat of the German army and that very soon the French soldiers would be on their heels.'

Those who had been either unwilling or unable to escape soon found themselves under the terrible rule of the invaders. The occupied areas were unable to support the war effort of the French

KOMMANDANTUR DE MARCQ-EN-BARŒUL

AVIS

Comme suite aux Ordonnances du 7 et 30 juillet écoulé, tous les propriétaires ou locataires d'arbres fruitiers :

Poires, Pommes, Prunes, etc.

doivent faire à la Kommandantur, une déclaration écrite indiquant le nombre, la nature des arbres fruitiers, l'époque à laquelle les fruits seront cueillis et la quantité approximative.

Ces déclarations devront être remises à la Kommandantur (Rue Nationale, 43, près du Pont) le

2 AOUT, jusqu'à 2 heures du soir.

Les fruits actuellement mûrs doivent être immédiatement cueillis et apportés ensachés à la Kommandantur, tous les jours, de 3 à 6 heures du soir. Les sacs devront être munis d'une étiquette indiquant : la catégorie, le poids et le nom du fournisseur.

Tout commerce ou exportation des fruits dans le territoire de la Kommandantur est sévèrement interdit; les infractions seront punies outre la confiscation des fruits, d'une peine de prison et d'une amende équivalente au moins au double des fruits vendus ou exportés.

Marcq-en-Barœul, le 31 Juillet 1917.

Le Commandant de Place.

Marcq. Imp. P. Cornille, 23, rue Saint-Patrick

▲ Fruit farmers had to account to the Germans for all their produce.

► Even today this land near Dompierre in Picardy bears the scars of the trenches.

but had to supply goods to the Germans. The enemy controlled everything, even displacing people and bringing in forced labour. They imposed a curfew and people were shot if they went out at night, even into their gardens or for the most innocent of reasons. They requisitioned everything, from crops in the fields to mattresses, from door handles to copper pipes and church bells, which were melted down to make weapons. The population was forced to live by the decrees and pronouncements of the Commandants. Gradually, people got used to living under the occupation, with its mixture of hostages, collaborators and supporters of the resistance movement. For many of the men in the trenches it was for this part of France, for this part of their country, and for these families, who had been cruelly separated from their loved ones, that they continued to fight.

THE WAR IN FLANDERS

From this time on, from the end of 1914, it was in Flanders that the most savage fighting of the whole war took place. The Allies wanted, at all

▼ The Menin Gate in Ypres was built as a memorial to the British soldiers who perished there.

▲ In October and November 1914 the town of Ypres suffered dreadfully from the German bombardment.

costs, to prevent the Germans from reaching the Channel ports, through which British soldiers arrived in France.

In Belgium on 6 October shells from the 420mm guns fell on the besieged city of Antwerp and destroyed the chain of forts around it. The city, to which King Albert and his army had withdrawn, was the last bastion of Belgian resistance. On 3 October Winston Churchill had arrived there, and 2000 Royal Marines were despatched in an attempt to save the port, with its vital access to the southern coast of England, but this time the situation was desperate. The army prepared to evacuate the city with all speed while the bridges over the Scheldt held, and on 7 October, at 3 o'clock in the afternoon, the king left Antwerp, but only after the last of his army had withdrawn. Soldiers mingled with civilians as they rushed to escape to neutral Holland. The German bombardment of the city continued: 25,000 buildings were eventually destroyed.

Antwerp fell on 9 October; it was followed by Gand on the 11th, Bruges on the 14th and Ostend on the 15th. King Albert fell back with 50,000 soldiers across the River Scheldt towards Dunkirk. The British and French managed to hold the road against the Germans who were pursuing the Belgian soldiers, who were easily

recognizable among the Allies in their black greatcoats and flat hats. It was essential that their retreat was protected at all costs. Foch, who had been in command of the armies on the northwest front since the beginning of October, had just established his headquarters in the old town hall at Cassel, from where he dominated the plain of Flanders. It was from Cassel that he decreed that the natural line of defence represented by the River Yser must be held at all costs. It is accurate to call the line 'natural', but in fact, it was a very slight line, marked by the narrow river that meandered gently across the flat land as far as the eye could see. In this landscape the only high land was the network of embankments that had been built up along the river banks, and the land was dominated by a few lines of trees and windmills. While the British were repulsing a German attack on Ypres, a chain of communication, which proved vital to the Allies, was organized by the French between Nieuport (Nieuwpoort) and Dixmude (Diksmuide).

The young recruits from Brittany, the marines of Admiral Ronarc'h, had been sent there. 'There is water everywhere, in the air, on the ground, under the ground. ... It rains for three days out of four in this part of the world.... And when the rain stops, the mist rises from the

▲ The River Yser and, in the distance, the town of Dixmude.

soil, a white mist, almost solid, in which both men and things look like spectres.' As part of the resistance, French and Belgian soldiers excavated trenches in soil that was already sodden along the line of the railway between Nieuport and Dixmude. Their feet in the oozing mud, they continued to work to contain the German threat, even though they were being shelled.

The Germans kept on sending reinforcements to the area and were easily able to take control of the ports. A large number of their forces were enrolled as students in the universities, young men who were barely fully grown. The young volunteers, who had responded *en masse* to the Kaiser's call and who were scarcely old enough to shave, sang while they advanced towards the front line.

On 25 October the town of Dixmude, which had been bombarded by the Germans, became an inferno. On the next day the Belgians, in an attempt to halt the German advance, decided to open the sluices at Nieuport, an action they had previously taken in 1793 when they were fighting the Spanish, in order to flood the land between the sea and Dixmude. The seawater flooded into the canals, slowly at first so as not to alert the Germans, then more quickly to cover the fields, as the water arose around the low-lying farms and windmills, transforming the countryside into a huge, calm lake beneath a cloudy sky. From the surface of the water, which was 2–3 metres (7–10 feet) deep, emerged the bare outlines of the trees that bordered the roads. Here and there, the carcasses of cows and dead bodies floated by.

Despite everything, the Germans continued their advance across the flooded polders. Around Dixmude, the most exposed point, Admiral Ronarc'h, who shared the hard, daily grind in the trenches with the men, said to his marines: 'In order to save our left wing until reinforcements can get here, sacrifice yourselves. Try to hold out for ten days.' They actually held out for four weeks with some Belgian detachments in the most appalling conditions, against odds of twenty to one. There were only 6000 marines and 5000 Belgians against a total of 250,000 German soldiers. Falling back to the west of the Yser, into trenches through which water was pouring, they survived a bombardment by the heaviest German guns that went on all night and day, and also repelled fifteen night attacks. They replied by

► The Belgian line at
Boyau de la Mort – the
Trench of Death – was only
a few dozen metres from
the German front line.

◀ Allied artillery arriving on the North Sea beaches of Belgium.

◀ A wounded Belgian solider is stretchered away from the front.

◀ Allied soldiers looking at the flooded polders.

◀ Belgian soldiers on the road to Ypres.

firing at point-blank range with their machine-guns, which jammed because they were overloaded or because the barrels were clogged with mud. One Belgian brigade fought for seventy-two hours without respite. Colonel Jacques, their commander, was wounded three times and was created Baron Jacques of Dixmude by the king. There were only a few survivors among the French fusiliers when reinforcements arrived in the shape of an elite unit, the Senegalese riflemen and African chasseurs.

On 7 November a fusilier, G. d'Audierne, wrote to his mother: 'As I write a few lines to you to give you my news, I am, as ever, ready to be shot in a hail of fire from German guns. I am well, and I hope you are too, mother, and all the family, and that we meet again, but I am not counting on it because none of us will return. In the end, I have given my life to do my duty as a solider and as a marine.'

The Germans attacked Dixmude again on 10 November and succeeded in taking the town, which was by then little more than a 'pile of stones', according to the contemporary account in *L'Illustration*. The town remained on the front line for a further four years. In the months that followed the Belgians went on to reinforce the position that they had managed to establish behind a slightly raised line on the Yser. It was known as the Boyau de la Mort (Trench of Death), because of the huge number of people who died in these trenches, which were only about 30 kilometres (19 miles) from the German lines and were under constant fire.

While the French and Belgians were fighting on the Yser, the British were defending Ypres, which the Germans had attacked from the north and east. They fought from Bikschote and Poelkapelle to Zonnebecke and Geluveld, all around the town, which had been for so long associated with the cloth trade. Ypres was sited on a crossroads of important routes and was at the point where the French and English forces met. Each army continued to send reinforcements, but on 1 November the Kaiser himself arrived at Château Coquinage so that he could enter Ypres in triumph. Despite the overwhelming superiority of his army, the professional soldiers of the British

◀ The statue of Baron Jacques was erected in Dixmude's town square after the war. The town itself had to be completely rebuilt.

◀ Spahis – members of the Algerian cavalry in French service – near Nieuport in Belgium.

▼ A French marine.

▶ Traces of the trenches can still be seen in summer meadows.

army managed to hold out against the German troops, which were largely composed of inexperienced young men, recently arrived at the front.

On 11 November the Kaiser decided to throw the famous Prussian guard into the battle, and it was then too that he decided to order the systematic bombing of the town. The cathedral itself was blown up on 22 November. The fighting continued in December around the Messines Ridge, and it was near the village of Wijtschate (Wytschaete) that a young soldier in an infantry regiment from Bavaria was wounded – Adolf Hitler. He was sent to the church of Messines, which had been turned into a military hospital, where he soon recovered.

Throughout the war the Ypres Salient became an obsession with both sides, and hundreds of thousands of men died there.

After the war the question of what to do with the ruins of Dixmude arose. The townspeople wanted to return to their home and rebuild their houses. Eighty years later, under the white winter sky, seagulls fly above the brick buildings while sparrows nest in the façades. Dixmude has the calm appearance typical of a small town in Flanders, and only the bronze statue of Baron Jacques in the centre of the square serves as a reminder of the town's terrible experiences at the end of 1914: life can overcome anything that takes place on the field of destruction and death. Ypres, too, was rebuilt after four years' continuous bombardment, despite Churchill's suggestion that the site should be bought and the ruins left as a reminder of the barbarity of which men are capable.

Meanwhile, a little way away in the countryside, death still makes its presence felt. There is the Belgian mausoleum at Ramskapelle, and countless British cemeteries line the roads here or lie between the buildings in the outskirts of Ypres, for in this one area alone tens of thousands of men died between 1915 and 1917.

At Langemarck in Belgium more than 44,000 German soldiers are buried. In a corner of the cemetery the traces of the bunkers that formed part of the Hindenburg Line are still visible. Separated from the vineyards by a low wall, the soldiers rest under the tall trees, in groups of six or eight beneath marble slabs that lie flat against the ground among the grass. Some of them are known only by a number: 10724 to 10729. In the centre, a communal grave, planted over with low-growing shrubs, is the last resting place of some 25,000 men. On the black wooden panels that have been erected there are inscribed the names of 3000 students who volunteered to join the army and who died in this region during the last months of 1914. At the far end of the cemetery, facing the entrance, can be seen the silhouettes of four sculpted soldiers, plain and unadorned, seen standing in profile against the light streaming across the empty polders.

At Vladslo cemetery, also in Belgium, there is the same arrangement of tombstones, with the name and date of death inscribed on the flags. From time to time a German-registered car pulls up. A couple get out and search for the name of a grandfather they never knew. At the end of the central path are two statues, of a man and a woman, their bodies bowed in grief. They were sculpted by Käthe Kollwitz-Schmidt, who worked as an expressionist artist after her son

was killed at the end of 1914. At first, she wanted to sculpt her son's face, but in the end she could not bring herself to do that and decided instead to create a lasting memorial to the grief of all parents who had lost children during the war.

STALEMATE

From now on, from the dunes around Nieuport in the west to the dug-outs of Belfort in the east, the front line was established. The armies were immobile, staring at each other almost face to face, and the soldiers dug themselves in into two lines of trenches, some 800 kilometres (500 miles) long, which, as the months dragged by, became filled with men. Thousands of cubic metres of earth were dug out as the trenches were constantly dug and re-dug to keep them repaired.

Rudyard Kipling described them as a 'terrible wound' passing right across France.

For four years the long line of trenches followed the contours of the land, passing over hills, across rivers and through villages. Millions of men were to die in unspeakable conditions, both physical and spiritual, in what became a regular cycle of attacks that were little more than macabre, bloodstained rituals. During these years the battle front along this line scarcely moved – one side might gain a few metres or even a few kilometres, while the other would gain a village or a farm, each slight loss or gain costing thousands of lives. The soldiers fought for months for a hill or a small ridge crowned with a few trees, and the names of these small gains became well known – Bois-le-Prêtre, Bois Bourru, Bois Bolante, Bois de la Gruerie, Bois de la Folie …

▲ The German cemetery at Langemarck in Belgium.

▶ At the German cemetery at Vladslo, Belgium, the statues of parents weeping for their sons were sculpted by Käthe Kollwitz-Schmidt.

'From here you could get to Switzerland along this trench,' an officer said to Rudyard Kipling in 1916. 'And from here to the other end, you will find the same mess. This isn't war. It's worse. It's an entire people who are being engulfed, swallowed up: They arrive here, fill up the trenches and then die here, they die and they die. And they watch others, who die just as they will die.'

In this narrow track of land, which soon became isolated from the rest of the world and which was, in effect, a world consecrated to

violence and death, the men 'were nothing more than a bluish stain, scarcely more than nothing'.

At first, the soldiers excavated holes in which they could shelter from machine-gun fire, but later they began to join the individual dug-outs together with ditches, which became the trenches, a word that has come to epitomize the First World War. To start with 'they were long, narrow ditches, about as deep as a man, with straw in the bottom to stand on'. Later, infantrymen and ordinary soldiers worked like labourers, digging with spades and picks. 'There was no shelter,' wrote Ferdinand Belmont, 'and we believed that if we made the trenches deeper we would be able to shelter in them like foxes, so that we would not be as easily shelled or at the mercy of hails of German bullets.'

They added parapets to the side of the trenches facing the enemy, just as the Romans had done. At intervals they left gaps through which they could observe the enemy lines, and these were protected with metal shields. They stretched wires along the trenches on which they could hang empty food tins and bottles, which would warn them if the enemy tried to approach, and they built ledges from which they fired on the enemy. 'Along the entire edge of the front facing us, the Bavarian troops had made trenches like ours, and they spied on us from behind their parapets, firing on us every time an observer risked his beret or helmet over the top of our parapets.'

To discourage the enemy and to stop them advancing, the soldiers in the trenches erected barriers of barbed wire entanglements and coils of wire, like pigs' tails, which were attached to posts. These entanglements came to haunt all the soldiers during the assaults. How many of them would find themselves caught on the wire and be shot by those they were supposed to be attacking, and then left hanging there, unable to break free?

Between the two series of trenches was an empty space, belonging to neither side and called no man's land. This was where, after an attack, those who could not be rescued were left to die.

The distance between the two armies varied along the length of the front. Usually it was several hundred metres, but sometimes, as in Alsace and Flanders, it was scarcely 30 metres (100 feet). Here, at night, as the sound of the firing died away, it was possible to hear fragments of conversation from the enemy line. At the Trench of Death in Belgium men bound strips of

▲ A German soldier caught for ever in barbed wire.

'We looked at their nervous faces and at their helmets – they were French. ... I watched one of them fall on the barbed wire entanglement, his head was held high but his body was sagging under him, like a sack. His hands were crossed as if he wanted to pray. Then suddenly the body was completely detached, and only the hands were left, shot from the body, together with the stumps of his arms, which were still there, caught on the wire.'

Erich Maria Remarque

they exchanged cigarettes and food and information. On the Somme, at the Bois de la Vache – named because the rotting carcass of a cow, killed by a shell, was caught by its horns on the barbed wire – Blaise Cendrars remembered how they had been warned by the Saxons, who had left them 'relatively alone', that reinforcements were coming from Bavaria, and these 'led them to the devil himself – grenades, mines, explosions, endless shelling, which shook the poor little wood as if it had been a pocket handkerchief'. Cendrars arrived at the front just as men were beginning to visit no man's land and to fraternize with the enemy, which happened only in the first year of the war. After that the general staff of both sides took measures against all attempts at subversion and punished the guilty.

The trenches could not be anything more than a temporary shelter given the way of life. On both sides, men tried to hide in the ground, their protector, but for many the trenches became their grave. 'The earth mattered only to the soldiers, to no one else,' wrote Erich Maria Remarque. 'When one has pressed one's body against it so closely for so long, it comes to be part of one's face and limbs. Although it is part of one's death throes, it is also a friend, a brother, a mother. ... The earth welcomes soldiers, then it lets them go for ten seconds in the course of their lives before taking them to itself again.'

When they arrived behind the lines the soldiers were allowed to rest for four days, during which they stayed in uncomfortable billets, barns or abandoned houses. They had often had to march for many hours through difficult terrain in order to relieve their comrades in the trenches at the front line. After the four days they found themselves sitting on the clayey ground, huddled together, on the alert for bombardments and sudden attacks. They slept there, sometimes dozing off where they stood, in the holes dug out of the sides of the trenches, unable to undress or to wash, dirty, covered in mud, unshaven and flea- and louse-ridden. The French soldier of the trenches became known as the *poilu* (hairy or shaggy one), an affectionate nickname given by the soldiers behind the lines to each other and a name that quickly spread. 'I saw three soldiers

cloth around their boots to muffle the sound of their steps. The trenches were sometimes so near to each other that during the night some soldiers, returning from the latrines or fetching food from the mess, made the mistake of going into the wrong trench. The fate befalling such men was tragic, of course, but was as nothing in the overall progress of the war.

In some sectors soldiers hurled abuse and rubbish at each other over the parapets; in others,

from the trenches coming towards me,' wrote Louis Barthas. 'They were covered with mud, from their shoes to the tops of the helmets, as if they had just swum through a lake of slime. Their hands, their faces, their moustaches, their eyelids, their hair … everything was covered with sludge.' It was only when one of the men called to him by name that he recognized three old friends.

The French had only one concern: to liberate the occupied territory. Everyone thought of the trenches as a temporary stage, a view that was reinforced by communiqués from the general staff and by the propaganda published in the newspapers. But would it have been possible to attack and return to a 'war of movement' to free France of the enemy? Unfortunately the evidence suggests otherwise: the situation had reached deadlock, and the war was going to last in conditions that had never before obtained and for which no one could have been prepared. Nevertheless, some people realized what was happening at a very early stage. Lieutenant Désagneaux had, for example, noted in his journal as early as 26 September that Colonel Marchand, a veteran of Fashoda, who now found himself fighting side by side with the British, had said that in his opinion the war would be a long one. 'He spoke of three years, and all those who heard him laughed to themselves at this madness.' In any case, at the front it didn't do to be pessimistic, and those who were seen as

defeatist were pilloried in the newspapers. At the bottom of their trenches the soldiers knew only too well that it wasn't going to be easy to get away, and they just wanted to know if they were going to have to spend the winter there.

Meanwhile, everyone was well and truly stuck in something quite unforeseeable: an immobile war, which consisted of nothing but the heroism of the combatants; a war of siege tactics, which was fought at a medieval pace but with new technology that was becoming more and more sophisticated. But it was not siege warfare in which one of the sides was trying to conquer a fabulous city or a palace with pennants fluttering from its turrets. The Greeks surrounding Troy

coveted the city's wealth, just as the Romans envied the riches of Carthage. The unfortunate soldiers in the trenches, lost in the middle of an increasingly desolate countryside, were not part of a quest for a fabulous city. They were fighting against rain, mud, rats, lice, shells and horrific sights of wounded men; against physical and mental hardship; and against an increasing feeling that the situation was absurd.

'The sense of disenchantment is widespread,' wrote Jean Dumont, a primary school-teacher, to his family. 'The world has shrunk, and the war has become nothing more than infantry battles and tunnels. We are no longer men; we have turned into moles. We cannot see the sky; we see the ground and the mud.'

▲ ◄ As 1914 drew to a close, men settled down to a period of stalemate.

Ferdinand Belmont, who tried hard to reassure his family and to describe the situation with humour, wrote: 'We live underground all the time, a cross between moles and foxes. ... Yesterday evening, when I was in my little den, I watched with fascination as small lumps of soil kept falling from the ceiling of my lair onto the straw next to me. I was getting a bit worried and was wondering if my little refuge was about to collapse and I was going to be buried alive. Today, the same thing was happening, and so I went to find out what was causing it: it was moles, who were digging their own tunnels and, coming across my hole, decided to make a window.'

Autumn brought bad weather and rain. Water got into the food, down necks and coated helmets with mud. 'I doubt if there will be any advantage to either side in this dreadful autumn rain, which is turning our trenches into mud baths, slippery and unhealthy,' wrote Ferdinand Belmont to his parents. In Champagne it was the white, sticky clay that made the soldiers' boots heavy; in Picardy and Artois there was particularly runny mud, and infantrymen in the trenches were sometimes up to their knees in it. French soldiers were less well prepared for it than the troops of other countries. They did not have waterproof clothing and wrapped themselves in canvas – the same material in which the dead were wrapped.

In November Louis Barthas, who was in Artois, wrote: 'The rain keeps on falling; it rains all night. The walls of the trenches are giving way, and in spite of the steep slopes, the water forms pools, held back by landslips. In the foot of the trenches there are streams of water, which keep getting wider, moving towards us like a huge pool. The sentries could not stay in position, giving way before this water and mud. Some left the trenches, others began to dig new holes, which very quickly filled with water.'

In December, after a 'victory' that enabled them to retake Vermelles, a little town that looked as if it had been hit by a tornado, they occupied a new line in what had previously been German-held territory. As night fell, so did the rain. 'I found myself crouching in a little shelter made with the handles of three spades and a piece of canvas, through which water rushed as if it were being poured through a ladle. Others sheltered as well as they could under a short plank, under cloaks and under pieces of sacking. Two teachers were so demoralized and discouraged that they didn't have the energy even to try to protect themselves against the weather. They told me that they had stood in the trench, putting up with the cold rain, as if they had been beasts of burden.'

The Germans had quickly prepared themselves for a long war, but even they suffered from the same miseries as their enemy. 'Night duty,' recalled Ernst Jünger, 'interminable and exhausting though it was, was just about bearable in good weather and even when it was cold. It became torture when it was raining. ... When the rain began to get under the canvas of the tents, then on to people's heads, then under the hoods, people fell into a kind of stupor, which was broken only when the relief came splashing towards them. Dawn broke over exhausted men, white with dried mud, who threw themselves, white faced, on the piles of rotting straw in the dripping shelters.'

In November in the Vosges it was already snowing. As winter approached, men along the whole front began to suffer dreadfully from the cold, which stopped them from sleeping, their feet were so chilled. Their boots were frozen so hard that they could not take them off. 'People with freezing, rotting and lifeless feet were being evacuated every day, by the dozen,' noted Jean Benier, writing about the unfortunate infantrymen, who were nicknamed *biffins* (rag-and-bone men), a name that they had given themselves. They muffled themselves up in whatever they could find – woollen clothes sent by their families, bits of cloth or blankets found here and there in the abandoned villages, layers of newspaper, the skins of rabbits they were

Mon appartement à "Aquatique City" (Carnoy Xbre 1914)

◀ 'Hell – it's mud.' Soldiers in the trenches somehow managed to retain their sense of humour despite the appalling conditions.

▶ The countryside still bears the marks of the gashes of the trenches, as here in the undergrowth of the Vosges.

▲ ▶ The remains of the trenches at Hill 62, near Zilebeke Wood, Belgium.

'As night fell, it was still possible to make out the network of ditches. These were the trenches. The bottom was covered with a layer of slimy mud, and each time a soldier lifted his foot to take a step it made a noise. ... I saw shadows emerging from the dug-outs along the sides, advancing, huge and formless, like a bear, squelching and groaning. It was us.'

Henri Barbusse

sometimes able to poach and rags, which they wrapped round their feet. When they could, they wore German shoes, which were of better quality than their own, even though there were prohibitions about taking things from dead Germans.

'Our hoods and our damp clothes,' wrote Louis Barthas, 'became stiff as they froze. We couldn't feel our feet they were so cold. Despite strict prohibitions, I had to take off my boots and rub my feet as hard as I could with a little brandy, which I kept in reserve, then wrap them in the driest corner of my blanket. At the start of the day, the supply truck would bring some coffee, which we would be looking forward to, but it would be frozen in the can.'

Cendrars, who was near the village of Frise, wrote that in the trenches 'people spent the night with water up to their stomachs in temperatures of 0–2°C [32–36°F].' According to Louis Barthas, it was impossible even to attempt to describe how they suffered. 'I never thought that the human body could withstand such hardship. Almost every morning snow and ice had caused icicles to form on our beards and moustaches, our feet were like blocks of ice. Then during the day or during the night the temperature would rise a little and the rain would begin to fall, like a waterfall, filling our trenches with mud and then transforming them into rivers.'

Faced with an enemy who was better prepared for this type of warfare, it was crucial that the French held on. The Germans had fought hard in September 1914 to keep their positions on the high land, and they had organized their lines of communication so that their forces at the front received regular supplies of arms and food. They made every effort to provide for the troops and to ensure their safety through the construction of strong fortifications, which were reinforced with concrete, and underground shelters, for which they burrowed deep below the surface.

The French had been forced to provide some form of protection in this war of stalemate. The trenches that were excavated in October were improvised and dug in a hurry. Louis Barthas thought that they were dug before the soldiers really knew what they were doing, and although these gradually improved, the French never attached the same importance to their construction as the Germans, so they were not built to the same high standards or by special teams of builders. The Germans admired the French soldiers, who, despite the conditions in which they fought, did manage to gain possession of sections of the enemy line from time to time.

Over time, the double line of trenches across the land was transformed into an increasingly elaborate network, in some sections made of triple lines and communication trenches, creating a complicated spider's web below the surface of the soil. The first lines, the parallel trenches, were the point from which the attacks were launched, and they were topped by lines of sandbags, which provided some protection from enemy bullets. The trenches were dug at angles to avoid raking fire, as were the ditches that led to the second line. Behind these were narrow passages between banks of earth, through which supplies were carried, through which reinforcements arrived at the front and through which the wounded, and if possible the dead, were carried away.

The soldiers covered the floor of the trenches with duckboards to make it easier to walk around and tried to turn the warrens into shelters. Very soon the sides had to be reinforced to provide additional protection against bad weather and pounding artillery attacks from the enemy, who were so close to the forward positions. The walls

▲ The entry to one of the German tunnels at Hartmannweilerkopf in the Vosges. The area is still riddled with dugouts and excavations.

were supported with pieces of timber and any other materials that came to hand – in forested areas tree trunks were used; pit props were found in the abandoned mines in the north; and sometimes sections of houses whose owners had fled were used.

The soldiers did their best to make the dug-outs and shelters away from the immediate front line as habitable and secure as they could, but even these were never anything more than hovels in the ground, simple shelters dug out of the ground and scarcely protected, providing the rudest shelter for eating and sleeping, littered with rubbish, and dark and airless. 'This hole is wet, very wet, and there are lice everywhere.'

The Germans were, on the whole, fortunate in having better conditions, but in places the front line was scarcely any better than that of the enemy to whom they were so close. Ernst Jünger

recalled the dug-outs in Champagne in which he found himself in 1915. 'They were just holes cut out of the chalk, opening on to the trenches and with a roof made out of a couple of planks with some shovelfuls of earth on top. Whenever it rained the water dripped down for days on end. Someone with a black sense of humour put up signs reading "Cave with stalactites", "Men's showers" and the like. If anyone wanted to rest for a while, they had to stretch out their legs along the trench, which made walking along the trenches like an obstacle course. In the circumstances, there was really no question of lying down during the day. Everyone had to be on guard duty for two hours, then clean out the trenches, go to get supplies or something to drink, and do other chores.'

Ferdinand Belmont tried hard to reassure his parents about the conditions in which he was

living. 'We occupy ourselves by working hard every day to make our shelters better. Our little mole cities have corridors between the various passages so that we can communicate with the other trenches. They lead to the mess and to the officers' dug-outs. It's possible to get there after about half an hour going round in circles in this maze of trenches and traverses, all about the height of a man.' But in the maze there was no Ariadne's thread to aid the soldiers, and there was not just a single Minotaur to slay. The monster they faced was in this never-ending quagmire, between two narrow walls that stretched as far as the eye could see.

▶ A French shelter, cut into the hillside at Hartmannweilerkopf.

▼ Everyday life for French soldiers, including (below left) making coffee.

Au Cantonnement : Préparation du Café.

Behind the front line were the artillery and the horses. About eighty animals were needed to pull the four pieces of a battery of 75mm field guns. The army had requisitioned thousands of horses from farmers, but they had to be fed with tonnes of oats. Since the end of 1914 the losses had been considerable, and the French had had to buy from overseas, especially from Argentina. The field guns had to be dug in and camouflaged. Both the calibre and weight of gun increased exponentially as the months passed, and the sound of the artillery shells could be heard from further and further away. The French 75mm field gun was able to fire twenty rounds a minute.

The Germans had the 77mm field guns (known to the British as 'whizz-bangs') and light guns designed for use in a war of movement, but artillery with a greater range quickly followed – 120mm, 150mm and 210mm – that could fire shells with 60–100 kilograms (130–220 pounds) of explosive, which soldiers quickly learned to recognize from the noise they made. There were also shells crammed with shrapnel that exploded, showering hundreds of balls of lead everywhere, and percussion fuse shells, which released masses of coloured smoke. There was the German trench mortar, the *Minenwerfer* (known to the British as 'moaning Minnies'), and the French equivalent, which had wings so that they would travel further. Above all, there were the machine-guns, which the Germans built pillboxes and concrete fortifications to protect. Throughout the war on both sides the weaponry continued to become more and more effective, and both armies used vast quantities of munitions.

The front, that 'different and strange country' barely 80 kilometres (50 miles) from Paris, became part of everyone's consciousness, but discovering the reality of life there was not easy. New recruits went to the front for the first time with a mixture of curiosity and anxiety. They went part of the way by train and then had to march for several hours. The first time that the philosopher Alain rejoined his regiment at Toul, he tried hard to imagine what happened beyond the 'threatening horizon' and to understand what it was that the non-commissioned officers called

'serious hospitality'. He arrived at the woods near Remières during a bombardment. 'I had time to see the lines of fear etched on the faces of those who were waiting for the terrible moment when the wood would be blown up around them. Then later, when I was on leave, I could see the same fine lines around my own eyes. The soldiers who live through this are as different from other soldiers as dogs are different from cats.' The front was 'a line of fire', which devoured men indiscriminately along its entire length.

Louis Barthas, who arrived near to the front line in Artois in the early hours of the morning, could see nothing but 'mounds and heaps of earth and ditches, which seemed unplanned and confusing'. He remembered that he had to make

saw what seemed to be an amazing display of fireworks, as the intermittent light from rockets illuminated the network of trenches zigzagging across the fields. It was a sight that reminded him of the music-hall and conjurors, albeit amid the whistle of bullets and crashes of shells, which fell around him in the mud.

In the morning, by the pale light of dawn, he at last saw the front. 'From the top of the mound of mud where I was crouched, I could see nothing but desolation from one trench to another. Someone was taking pot shots at my feet. And now that the darkness of night no longer disguised the shower of shells bursting around us and the depth of the holes, echoing to the sound of the shells, everything I could see seemed small,

'*For the whole length of these trenches, which resembled nothing so much as intestines, men stood in the mire, their legs and feet huge from being encased in mud, their faces greenish-grey and marked with lines caused by the unremitting tension, fear and boredom, scarred just as the hillside around them had been disfigured by the trenches and the shelling.*'

John Dos Passos

a real effort to remind himself that he was next to a 'volcano', from which thousands of men were watching them, ready to kill them. He felt that he was at the very edge of a different world: 'I was at the limit of civilization, just two kilometres from men who had been overcome by a barbarity that seemed to belong to twenty centuries ago.'

Cendrars and his squad arrived near the front at Dompierre in Picardy 'after an exhausting march lasting several days'. They went up to the front at night, through a maze of sodden ditches, in a world in which there were no signposts and in which men could lose themselves again and again. Soon he noticed 'a loud noise, which sounded like the roar of the sea, coming from the north – it was the sound of cannons, firing in the distance. An indefinable smell was borne on the wind – a mixture of chemicals and decay.' As they got nearer to the front, Cendrars

shabby and grey – everything was covered with mud. Despite the kilometre after kilometre of trenches and barbed wire entanglements, there was nothing grand about it – it was almost as if the barrier had been created between two neighbours who were arguing about a line of dirty laundry, not about the conquest of nations. ... And it was so that they could end up in this miserable corner that all the finest young men in the world had been asked to leave the most beautiful cities on earth.'

The immediate impression given by this world within a world was of death – visible everywhere and always present. 'When I arrived at the front I was nineteen years old,' an old soldier recalled eighty years later. 'The first thing I saw was a dead man on the parapet. The body was left there, and people walked by without paying any attention to it. Dying itself, of course,

▲ The French soldier at the Museum of the Great War at Péronne on the Somme.

is an everyday event, but the death of a single man is different.'

During the first night that he was at the front Louis Barthas was awakened by a strange noise. 'It was being made by pickaxes and shovels. I got up trembling, keeping my head below the parapet, and asked the men what kind of work they were doing at night. "Can't you see that we're burying the men who were killed in the last attack?" one of them told me rudely.' In the early morning, when it was just light, they looked out across no man's land. 'Here and there they could see little mounds, sad, grey shapes, above which the crows circled. They were the dead French and Germans, waiting to be buried.'

Going up to the front for the first time took courage, which could suddenly evaporate in a group of men, the majority of whom were scarcely out of their adolescence. This world of madness and horror united all those who lived in the trenches in a world that they could not share with people who had not experienced it. It was a world in which the values that most people held dear were as nought; it was a world in which the dead were abandoned; it was a world in which even Antigone would not have sacrificed herself to provide a resting place for her brother.

'God absents himself from the field of battle,' wrote Cendrars. In one of the wide, flat fields near Frise 'those who had died at the start of the war, those poor young men in their madder-red trousers, lie forgotten in the grass, making innumerable little hillocks that are no more important than piles of cow dung in a field. … Seeing the dead left, abandoned, everywhere is appalling. They rot away in the open air,

surrounded by green, and they are washed and washed again by the autumn rains and shrivel up a little more every day. Their only shrouds are their bright red trousers, from which the red dye seeps into the puddles, dandelions and autumn crocuses that surround them.'

Disobeying orders, Cendrars and his friend Sawo tried to recover the bodies lying, in 'desperate solitude', on the rain-swept land between the two worlds, but they were unable to get as far as the field. On the way back, they discovered a shack, which was out of sight of the lines. 'There were three dead Germans in the hut or, rather, there were three skeletons, collapsing under their uniforms, around a machine-gun.' They were the men who had cut down the young French soldiers, who were even then rotting away in the field outside, abandoned just as the Germans had been. 'I forgot to say,' added Cendrars, 'that there were slugs in the dead men's eye sockets.' He and Sawo returned from 'the ends of the earth' but only after they had taken the three men's wallets, in which they found letters and photographs of their wives and children. 'It was foul,' commented Cendrars, and Sawo, a gypsy, added: 'What a sight it was. We thought we had seen everything there was to see.'

But not quite everything. Sometimes it was necessary to leave wounded men in no man's land, where they died in agony. They were just a dozen or so metres from the trenches, and it was possible to hear them calling for help. 'They were so close,' wrote Roland Dorgelès. 'They fell on their own side of the wire, the Germans spread out along the other side. The body would curl up, and we would say a prayer for the dying. … In the heavy shadow, the little blue shape kept on groaning. It was awful to see these brave young men who didn't want to die.'

Sometimes, soldiers couldn't bear to watch their comrades die like this, and they broke from the trenches, in spite of the bursts of machine-gun fire, to try to rescue their wounded comrades. Louis Pergaud, who had won the Prix Goncourt in 1910 for his novel *De Goupil à Margot* and who was to die in Lorraine on 8 April 1915, wrote about one such occasion in a letter to his wife. At the end of an attack, 'dedicated to an

unsuccessful advance', which left several wounded men lying between the lines, 'a brave little doctor yesterday volunteered, in broad daylight, to go to get them. Then followed an agonizing minute for those of us who were watching. Would they fire at him and at the stretcher-bearers? He didn't seem to care. He raised a flag with the Red Cross on it and, wearing his doctor's armband, he climbed over the top of the trench. … The Germans were very correct. They raised themselves up onto the parapet, and each side looked at the other.' The doctor 'arrived near the wounded, who were about six metres from the Germans, to whom he saluted, just as if it were happening in the reign of Louis XIV. Then he turned to the wounded. As the stretcher-bearers carried them away, he saluted again, as he had done before, and this time the Germans saluted back.'

'Just as if it were happening in the reign of Louis XIV' … but there was less and less room for a code of honour between men who were face to face like this, even when they respected each other. In general, 'people saw nothing from the other side of the coils of barbed wire. It was a war without enemies, death without fighting. … The dead, nothing but the dead.'

The French general staff had not resigned themselves to a static war, and they were looking for a way to break out of the trenches and return to a war of movement. Joffre also wanted the

British to understand that he could not properly equip his army, so that they would not relax their own war effort. He was still convinced that the war would be won with 'legs of the infantrymen', and he wanted to retake, inch by inch, all the land that was occupied. In November 1914 he gave the order for the distance between the front lines to be reduced to 150 metres (500 feet) wherever possible. Along the whole length of the front small-scale assaults were launched with a grim determination; they proved both costly and ineffective. The men were forced to attack wearing neither breastplates nor helmets. It was not until April 1915 that metal skull-caps were distributed to the troops to protect their heads under their kepis, but these proved to be useless and were mostly used for carrying food from the mess. Proper metal helmets that protected the back of the neck were only later made available to all the troops.

Perched on their firing positions, the men waited for the signal. When the officers blew the whistles, the men jumped over the parapets, bayonets fixed in their rifles, and ran across the barbed wire, which had been cut with clippers in various places during the previous night so that they could get through. Then they had to run across no man's land, straight towards the machine-guns and the trenches facing them. Those who managed to survive that far had to get across the enemy's barbed wire entanglements, then over their parapets before they could

take on the Germans in hand-to-hand combat. The French suffered terrible losses in these attacks. The Germans had the advantage of their high defensive positions, from which they could shoot down on their desperate attackers, who fell one after another, the pitiful bodies jerking like puppets in no man's land long after the attacks. 'It was possible to count the dead, lying on the yellowing grass. They fell as they advanced, head first: unquestioning, fighting on their knees, always looking ready to leap forward, into the attack.'

In spite of the repetition of the action and the numbers, each one of these infantrymen was still gripped by fear before he had to jump over the parapet. He would think in those terrible moments of his family and how they would be waiting for him and if he would be able to look after them. Each one of them had a mother, who prayed, day after day, that her son would be safe. They were men who had hopes for the future but who now had to cross a deadly space, under a bombardment of howling shells, which exploded, mingling the bodies with the blood and iron underfoot.

'Forward! Follow me! Advance! Follow me!' Maurice Genevoix recalled one such attack with the men under his command. 'I believed that my men were behind me. I saw a human figure leap forward, over the ditch. He was wearing a muddy greatcoat, and his head was bare. On his skin, on his colourless skin, was some blood, very fresh and very red. It glowed and grew deeper in colour.'

Alain remembered the aftermath of one of these attacks, which he felt were carried out by condemned men. 'They arrived through the trench at a kind of uncovered area, at the edge of the wood, from where it was possible to see for about 300 metres [980 feet] in all directions, towards a field between Remières, French, and Le Sonnard, German: sinister woods. Two lines of trenches crossed the field, and between them was a line of infantrymen, crouching down, then falling as they moved forwards. … How can we encourage our young men to cross the field? They already have enough honour.'

Jean Giraudoux, who was wounded in the thigh during an attack on Vingré on the Aisne, later remembered the confused feelings experienced by the soldiers at such times. 'In an hour we would be gone, marching towards an enemy who were already waiting for us. The greatest words rose inside me this morning. Words about the infinite and words about the material world; words about life and about death. … The lieutenant's whistle sounded harshly. It was time to go. The word "cowardice" vied with the word "country".'

Ferdinand Belmont let himself go, 'the better to be able to do the will of God,' he said. 'In fact, and it went on happening until the end of the war, we lived from day to day. We followed the path that led to Providence and no one thought about examining his own soul. People had to be reminded to say their prayers every day.' And he went on to add at the end of his letter: 'Pray God have pity on us. Let him accept the sacrifices that we have committed for the sake of poor, dear France.'

In the French trenches not everyone accepted the inevitable with the same fortitude or used the same justification of the intolerable. Louis Pergaud wrote about the useless attacks that were launched and, in particular, of one in which he took part in Lorraine. 'There is no doubt that it was a three-star general commanding the division of the line. Without saying anything, the regiment obeyed him to the letter, and they were shot to

pieces by the machine-guns and heavy shells. I will never forget the tragic scene – the dead, the wounded, the pools of blood, the bits of brain, the groans, the dark night lit by shells from our 75mm field gun finishing off our wounded. There were bodies everywhere one stepped.'

Louis Barthas was amazed by the ploys sometimes used by the leaders to minimize the risks to their men of future attacks. And he was equally surprised that none of his comrades thought of disobeying orders. 'People made so much about honour that we were incapable of making even the slightest gesture of protest when they were about to lead us to the abattoir. We were citizens still, but in reality nothing more than a cheap group of beasts of burden.'

To bolster the nation's morale official communiqués made it seem as if the taking of a group of ruins and an advance of a few dozen metres at the cost of hundreds of lives were important victories, even though they had no effect at all on the course of the war. Ferdinand Belmont admired the courage the troops continued to show as they threw themselves into the attack on the German trenches at Mont-Saint-Éloi near Arras, but Louis Barthas, who was fighting in the same sector, railed against an attack that went

ahead 'in spite of common sense and the certain prospect of defeat' and in spite of the protests of the captain of one of the companies, who 'obeyed against his better judgement, launched himself into the attack and fell after just a few steps'. He saw an adjutant, a revolver in his hand, drive his men forward, and he was astonished at the triumphalist tone of the communiqués. 'Nothing was added, in order not to tarnish our honour, about our having failed to take a centimetre of land from the Germans. Nothing was said about our having simply and stupidly got within range of mortars, bombs, mines and grenades, and that's as it should be, after all – to ignore the sacrifice of those who are fertilizing the land in this corner of Flanders with their bodies.'

Not all soldiers refused to admit to the number of fatalities, and some officers even refused to send their men into the attack. Sometimes it was infantrymen who disobeyed orders, either giving themselves up to the enemy or even deserting. The general staff were alarmed by these events and issued draconian orders in an attempt to restore discipline. Courts martial were held at which a number of soldiers were sentenced to death for self-mutilation, for desertion in the face of enemy fire or for refusing to obey orders. The condemned men were executed by

The region of Soissonais saw almost uninterrupted fighting during the last months of 1914. During their withdrawal to the north of the Marne, the Germans tried to keep to the high land dominating the valley of the River Aisne, and the French suffered terrible losses as they crossed the river and began to climb the mountain slopes. The men were thrashed with bayonets when they tried

In the months that followed heroic battles continued to take place for the possession of ruins – at Confrécourt, at Quennevières and at Rouvent. Eighty years later in these fields that have been brought back into cultivation farmworkers are still finding skeletons, whose nationality can be determined by the equipment or even buttons that are found with them. Tractors

▲ The monument to those who were executed by the French at Vingré in December 1914.

'Twenty-four of us were court martialled. Six of us were condemned to death. I was among those six, and I was no more guilty than my comrades, but my life was sacrificed for theirs. This is my last letter; I am to die for a reason I do not understand.'

The last letter of Private Quinault to his wife

their comrades, some of whom, it was believed, had a blank charge in their rifles. 'The man to be shot was tied to a stake by his wrists. A handkerchief was bound around his head like a crown. Ghastly pale, the chaplain said a prayer, his eyes closed so that he could see nothing more.'

At Crouy in Champagne and at Souain lance corporals fired their rifles as an example. In Soissonais Private Leymarie, who had been injured in the hand by an enemy bullet, was accused of shooting himself and was executed on 13 November. Private Bresot, who, just a few days before he had been granted leave to go to see his wife and baby daughter, had refused to wear the red trousers stained with the blood of a dead comrade that had been given to him as part of his uniform. He was hastily found guilty and executed as an example to others moments before the arrival of his pardon, which had been signed by the President of France himself.

At Vingré, after an abortive attack, six men out of a company of twenty-four were found guilty and executed on 4 December 1914, following the instructions handed down to the court martial by General de Villaret to encourage soldiers to regain a taste for obedience.

to occupy the deep caves that covered the surface of the chalk cliffs and that could have been used as shelters and dug-outs for billeting men and equipment behind the front lines. In the end, both sides dug trenches across the plains, where hectares of corn and beetroot had been ploughed up by shells, and around the huge farms that gradually fell into ruin until they were no more than heaps of stones.

are still disturbing the rest of men who were lost in the war and whose families had waited, day after day, for a letter, even when it seemed that all chance of their survival was long gone, keeping alive a faint hope that their loved one had been taken as a prisoner of war – anything rather than admit that he had been lost in action.

The bitter fighting that took place along the entire front throughout the last months of 1914

▼ A field hospital in a cave near Soissons.

▲ Ruins on the plains around Soissons.

to gain possession of the higher ground and thereby take a more defensible position meant that this period saw the greatest number of casualties of the entire war. The French alone lost 340,000 men in five months.

In Lorraine Maurice Genevoix learned the news of the death of one of their comrades from a friend. 'Have you never thought about the deaths of other men, those whom we do not know, all those in the other regiments who have died? We know about our own comrades, hundreds of whom lie scattered behind us. Everywhere we have passed through, the little crosses have been raised behind us, the two sticks with a red kepi fastened to them. ... But at the same time other regiments have been advancing; hundred of regiments, each of which left behind it hundreds upon hundreds of dead men. Do you think about that? Do you think about this multitude? It scarcely bears thinking about. ...

And then there are all those old carts we have seen rattling along the road, with their bloodstained heaps of hay and all the Red Cross wagons that trundle to the towns in France – there are the dead in the ambulances and in the hospitals. Still more crosses; the ranks of crosses are filling the military cemeteries. ... But I have thought about something worse than these massacres. ... Perhaps the dead will be forgotten very quickly. ... Stop and think for a minute.

There have been deaths since the very beginning of the war. There are going to be many, many more.'

The soldiers watched the time of the corn harvest pass; then that of the wine harvest. They understood that they would spend Christmas at the front. Ferdinand Belmont wrote to his parents: 'To you all, together in the family home so far away. I wish I was safe with you and far away from these two walls of earth.'

In Artois, at Tracy-le-Val near to Soissons, in Champagne and in the Vosges the soldiers were to attack on Christmas Day. At Frise, Cendrars and some of his companions mounted a commando operation against the enemy line without the knowledge of the general staff. They wanted to rig up a gramophone in the German-held village so that at midnight they could play *La Marseillaise* in response to the sound of *Tannenbaum*. Even in sectors that were not fighting, Christmas was a sombre affair. The men tried in vain to buy oysters or to find wine hidden in the nearby villages, or they shared the parcels sent by their families, as feelings of hopelessness and melancholy pervaded all parts of the front line. Everyone was thinking about their homes and wondering if they would ever see them again.

In some places Christmas was a time for fraternization with the enemy. A tacit agreement was reached in a very few places by which the soldiers did not open fire on each other across their respective trenches, and, for that one day, men could show their heads above the parapets without fearing that they would be blown off. The soldiers even sang hymns together. In the British sector in particular soldiers went into no man's land and exchanged cigarettes and buried their dead. Then they said goodbye and returned to their trenches. The war began again the next day as if nothing had happened.

No one dared wonder what would be happening on Christmas Day the following year. Maurice Genevoix wrote to one of his friends: 'Because war has covered the world like a canker, who can say if there won't come a time when everyone is so used to fighting that they go on living with this infection within them? Things just happen, you know, and the war is tolerated, accepted. And it could become the normal course of events for young men to be condemned to death.'

The long months of the war were now effectively turning into years.

▼ This house in the village of Bernanval near Tracy-le-Val, which was behind the lines, served as a hospital.

▼ The command post of Colonel Reboul was hidden in the woods near Chapeaumont, just 3 kilometres (less then 2 miles) from the German lines.

▲ Christmas for the French …

'*Everyone is looking forward to peace, and even the officers talk openly about the useless loss of life and senseless destruction of both countries.*'

Alain

▼ … and for the Germans.

'*It's far away, the enthusiasm of heroes. We have ended up by understanding. The shells, day after day, have finally managed to teach us.*'

Ernst Johannsen

1915

LE RÊVE D'UN CHOUCROUTMANN.

▲▼ Zeppelins brought terror to civilians behind the front lines.

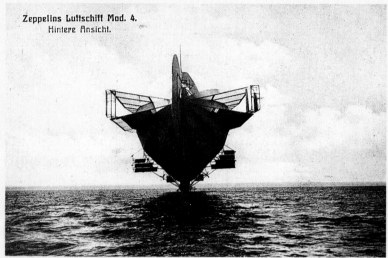

Zeppelins Luftschiff Mod. 4.
Hintere Ansicht.

▼ On Christmas Day 1914 the German Zeppelin sheds at Cuxhaven on the North Sea were attacked by British seaplanes.

1914-15... L'attaque de CUXHAVEN «Port allemand, mer du Nord, par les hydravions et contre-torpilleurs Anglais
1914-15... The CUXHAVEN action « German port in the north sea » by the English

Guerre 1914-15-16... GUERRE AÉRIENNE. | War 1914-15-16... AERIAL WAR — The Fall
Chute du Zeppelin L. 19 dans la Mer du Nord | of the Zeppelin L. 19 in the North sea
55me Série | Visé, Paris N° 1355

Visé Paris N° 873
CAMPAGNE 1914-1917
Manœuvre du ballon captif « La Saucisse ». — Manœuvre of the captive balloon « The Sausage »

▲ A blockhouse near Aubers Ridge in Flanders.

Neither the horror of the fighting nor the number of deaths brought a halt to events. On the contrary, both sides settled down for the long haul. Factories worked flat out to make guns, and women were employed to make shells while their menfolk stood in freezing mud, preparing to throw themselves at the barbed wire.

It was a war of attrition, but it was also total war in that civilians behind the front line were involved. In 1915 the Germans stepped up their aerial raids over towns. As early as October 1914 three people had been killed in the streets of Paris, and the Michelin company offered a reward to every French airman who brought down a German plane. Air attacks were renewed over the capital in March 1915 and over Brussels and Maubeuge, and also over Britain. More dangerous

than airplanes, however, were the Zeppelins, the long airships, shaped rather like cigars, which cruised silently through the night above sleeping villages, dropping bombs on the houses and vanishing before they could be spotted.

Those behind the front waited impatiently for the soldiers to achieve the victory that would liberate their country and bring to an end the danger that now threatened everyone.

Since December 1914 the French general staff had sought to 'boot the enemy out of France' by trying to breach the German front line and bring the fighting back into the open country. It had identified two sectors in which to concentrate its efforts: Artois and Champagne. It hoped to effect a pincer movement in both areas to surround the German troops and then advance

across Belgium, driving back the occupiers before them. Both attacks were to be launched at the same time, the first in the sector at Carency near to Arras and the other in Champagne, where the attack was cut short because of a lack of shells.

In January, still basing their strategy on the same analysis, the French renewed the attack in Champagne, this time in the hilly area to the east of Reims. This higher ground could hardly be called mountainous, but the numerous ridges, among which the Germans had excavated an extensive network of carefully defended trenches, were to account for thousands of lives. Supported this time by 600 field guns, the French infantry, largely made up of colonial troops, advanced for several hundred metres to Perthes-les-Hurlus; to Beauséjour, where the fort was taken and then

▲ An English cemetery at Neuve Chapelle.

a violence that was remarkable even in this period. Despite the heavy losses suffered by the British on their wings, notably by the Indian regiments whose officers were all killed, at the centre the German line was pushed back. But a lack of reinforcements meant that the British could not continue to push forwards. An Irish battalion entered Neuve Chapelle two hours after the start of the attack and saw, spread out in front of it, the vast plain of Flanders. But rather than follow up the advantage, General Haig preferred to erect a barrier of barbed wire, giving the Germans a day in which to regroup. The next day, when Haig gave the order for a new attack, the British infantry were unable to advance under the German machine-gun fire. It was this incident that is said to have led Colonel Max Hoffmann, Ludendorff's adjutant, to have replied to the general's remark that the British fought like lions, with the comment that they may have fought like lions but they were led by donkeys.

retaken by the marines; and to the region of Main de Massiges, a ridge that, on the map, looked like the five fingers of a hand. But the soldiers could not make progress over land that was beginning to thaw. Men and entire convoys slipped in the mud.

Further assaults against the same ridges were made in February. They fought for a month around the little Bois Sabot, at Beauséjour and at Souain. The number of casualties continued to rise. The dead were buried quickly, their resting places marked by a makeshift wooden cross, on which the name of the dead soldier was carved with a knife; sometimes the dead man's kepi was fixed to the cross. In three months 10 square kilometres (less than 4 square miles) were gained at a cost of 90,000 French lives.

FLANDERS

At the northwest end of the front the British launched an offensive at Neuve Chapelle, southwest of Armentières, in March. In December 1914, in the same part of the Flemish plain, they had already lost several divisions of the Indian army in a costly and useless attack on the enemy's barbed wire entanglements. Writing in his diary,

Major Leeds described the action as 'a dreadful waste of fine men'. He added: 'Let us hope that the generals, who are so far away, will understand that local attacks like this are pure folly.'

This time 40,000 men were massed along a front two kilometres (just over a mile) long. The bombardment that preceded the assault was of

In May the British carried out a similar assault on Aubers Ridge, but their guns were insufficient to break down the German fortifications. An Irish battalion, which managed to get as far as the enemy trenches, found itself isolated and was not able to withdraw until the evening, although three

▲ The ruins of a pillbox in Flanders.

◀ A memorial to the Indian troops who fought at Neuve Chapelle.

men were taken prisoner. During the day more than 10,000 soldiers were killed or wounded.

In Belgium in April the British undertook a much greater offensive with the intention of taking the Ypres Salient. British engineers dug tunnels to make mine holes beneath the German lines. The mines exploded on 17 April, and the greatest explosion created an artificial hill 60 metres (about 200 feet) high, which was near a railway line. It quickly became known as Hill 60.

One of the war's paradoxes was that while science brought enormous advances to the technology of weaponry, the methods used were those that had had their moment of glory in the preceding century. In the early months of 1914, when faced with furious enemy fire, the French turned to old-fashioned breastplates and wore them to protect them against the German infantry. Men surrounded wheelbarrows with metal shields behind which the attackers sheltered as they advanced. These were quickly abandoned, but wheelbarrows and similarly protected vehicles were the forerunners of the tanks that later appeared in the ravaged countryside, changing completely the face of warfare in the twentieth century.

In the trenches men used whatever they could find to improvise items of equipment that depended more on day-to-day need than on science – for example, periscopes were made from cartons and pieces of tin so that soldiers could look into no man's land without having to raise their heads above the parapets, and small bombs were made by packing explosive into empty food tins or bottles. Grenades and underground mines, which had been used in the siege warfare of the sixteenth and seventeenth centuries, came back into use at the front. Sappers dug out narrow tunnels in which they edged cautiously forward so that they could excavate mine holes under the enemy's front line. Sometimes they needed to steal a march on the other side, which was doing exactly the same thing. Men on both sides heard with horror the dull thuds under their feet and wondered where and when the explosion would happen and whether they would be engulfed in the enormous crater that

▶ Adolf Hitler stayed in this blockhouse near Fromelles before the Battle of Aubers Ridge in May 1915.

▶ The remains of a concrete fortification on Hill 60 at Zillebeke, near Ypres.

▲ A gas attack.

'Gas! Gas! Quick, boys! – An ecstasy of fumbling,

Fitting the clumsy helmets just in time;

But someone still was yelling out and stumbling,

And flound'ring like a man in fire or lime ...

Dim, through the misty panes and thick green light,

As under a green sea, I saw him drowning.'

Wilfred Owen, *Dulce Et Decorum Est*

would result. The British, among whose forces were a large number of sappers, used this strategy before important assaults on a scale not seen elsewhere. In April 1915 they had a major success on the Flanders front, but the Germans responded with another weapon – gas.

On 22 April at 5 o'clock in the afternoon, between Poelcappelle (Poelkapelle) and Bikschote, a part of the front held by the Belgians, British and French, the Germans released thousands of canisters of chlorine gas, placed at intervals of about a metre (3 feet). A yellowish-green cloud, blown by a light breeze from the north, moved towards the Allied lines. In the château where he had established his headquarters, Colonel Mordacq had a strange telephone conversation with one of the commanders of the North African regiments, who breathlessly explained that enormous plumes of yellow smoke were drifting around them and that his men were leaving the trenches and falling down, choking. The first soldiers to have been affected were the Algerian riflemen and the zouaves, regiments from Brittany and Normandy, and a Canadian division. Those who managed to get away were 'running as if they were mad, rushing headlong, crying out for water and coughing up blood, and some were rolling about on the ground, trying to breathe'.

The men had been subjected to a brutal attack of chlorine gas, which caused them to choke and suffocate. At the same time they were subjected to a horrific bombardment from the German field guns. Ranks of German troops, who had been concentrated in an area near the wood at Houthulst, advanced with fixed bayonets. The soldiers' faces were covered with crude masks, and they advanced towards the abandoned trenches in front of them.

This first gas attack left about 5000 men lying dead on the ground, their faces blue from asphyxiation. The attack opened up a breach about 6 kilometres (almost 4 miles) long in the Allied front line, but the Germans failed to exploit the advantage because they had insufficient men in reserve. The ground they took was retaken by the British in the following month and, in July, the most appalling fighting continued around Ypres. The Germans approached to within 4 kilometres (2½ miles) of the city, which was subjected to such a heavy bombardment that the last townspeople were forced to abandon their homes.

During this period the cemeteries in the countryside around the front lines continued to increase in size, and little enclosures appeared in which the unidentified bodies of those who fell fighting were interred. Around the field hospitals organized by the British behind the front lines, meadows were filled with rows of crosses.

The German use of chemical warfare – which was in contravention of the Hague Convention of 1899 – introduced a new dimension to the war,

'*We are the Dead. Short days ago*
We lived, felt dawn, saw sunset glow,
Loved and were loved, and now we lie
In Flanders fields.

Take up our quarrel with the foe:
To you from failing hands we throw
The torch; be yours to hold it high.'

John McCrae, *In Flanders Fields*

and, sadly, to all those that have followed. The commander of the German forces attacking Ypres, who seems to have had a conscience, noted in his memoirs that: 'I must acknowledge that the plan of poisoning the enemy with gas just as if they were rats affected me as it would any decent soldier: it disgusted me.'

Nevertheless, on the Belgium front in late April 1915 the bells of the cathedral of Gand announced that a deadly cloud of gas had been released over the trenches of Ypres. The Germans continued to work to perfect their new weapon. After releasing the toxic gas in Argonne, they replaced the chlorine that had been in the first canisters with something even more deadly: for an attack at Ypres in July 1917 they had an invisible substance that burned the eyes and skin – mustard gas.

At first, because insufficient gas masks were being made, all that soldiers could do was cover their mouths and noses with damp cloths, which they soaked with their own urine when nothing else was available, in order to protect their throats and lungs. No matter what doubts were expressed, both sides eventually started to use this awful and feared weapon. Chemists went on experimenting with new formulations, which had progressively worse effects. Although gas actually killed proportionately fewer men than other types of weapon, it was probably more feared by all combatants in the war, who had no real protection from it and who were powerless to act against the cloud that 'blocked out the sun and got into every hole, like a vast, fluid Medusa'. In the course of

▶ A wayside cross erected near Boesinghe, Belgium, in memory of the territorials from Brittany, who were killed in a gas attack on 22 April 1915.

PATIENCE....
JE LES.. GRIGNOTE

▲ A postcard with a caricature of Joffre, the French
commander-in-chief. The caption reads: 'Be patient. I
am wearing them down.'

the war gas caused the agonizing deaths of
thousands of men, but its effects lasted, and
thousands more, blinded and with damaged lungs,
lingered on after 1918, before dying in misery.

The French general staff was more than ever
concerned with the need to achieve a breach in the
enemy's front line, but it also understood the
importance of artillery fire to open the way for the
infantry. It had to play for time until French
factories could produce more field guns and shells,
although this did not mean that localized attacks
did not continue to harass the Germans or to win
back a tiny parcel of land. Joffre wanted to wear
down the enemy, as he himself said. He had a
theory, and to this end 1915 became the year of
useless and bloody tit-for-tat encounters.

THE VOSGES

At the other end of the front line, in the Vosges,
the confrontations were especially primitive,
partly because of the geographical conditions and
partly because of the weather. The fighting always
took place along a line of ridges about 1000
metres (two-thirds of a mile) long. In winter
wounded men died from cold before there was
time to rescue them and take them to the valleys
where the ambulances were stationed.

Hartmannweilerkopf (Hartmannswiller-
kopf), which the French soldiers came to call *le
vieil Armand*, is an outcrop overlooking the south
of the plain of Alsace. The observation post was
bitterly fought over by élite forces from both the
German and French armies for several months.
The Germans held the side of the mountain and

▶ ▼ The slopes of Hartmannweilerkopf in the
Vosges, which the French called *le vieil
Armand*. It was the scene of bitter fighting in
April 1915.

had had time to fortify their position, excavating underground shelters and dug-outs for the officers and creating a network of tunnels, which provided far better means of communication and defence than the trenches of the front line further west. A telegraph cable led to the plain of Alsace, which the Germans had held since 1870, and they had had time to build up stocks of men and materiel. The defences they had excavated in the granite were reinforced with concrete.

The French infantry, on the other hand, had to make do with the most basic of shelters and dug-outs on the steep mountainsides, protecting their positions with logs and trunks cut from the trees they found around them. Supplies had to be carried up from the valley by sled, on the backs of mules or by the men themselves.

In 1915 Hartmannweilerkopf was taken and retaken several times, often in hand-to-hand fighting, as men battled amid the remains of trees and shattered rocks. On each side the soldiers performed great acts of heroism, which, while widely celebrated, were largely pointless. On 21 December, for example, a French attack on a machine-gun emplacement cost 2000 lives in two days.

Another peak that saw an equally tragic loss of lives throughout 1915 was the Linge, a small, rocky spur with steep, tree-covered slopes in the centre of the Vosges. The site offered no important observation point; it did not control a major supply route; it did not represent in any way a strategically significant position. Nevertheless, it was the location of some of the most terrible fighting – terrible because it was pointless. The French general staff was anxious to overrun the enemy on the higher ground, and the Linge was one of the summits it selected to surprise the enemy and enable it to take Colmar. The alpine chasseurs were among the brave soldiers sent to the area. The preparations for the attack during the early months of the year alerted the Germans, who were already established on the summit, to the French presence. The sound of picks, the noise made as trees were felled and exploding mines, which were noticed by some French battalions in the valley, suggested that the Germans were in the process of preparing to withstand a new attack. In fact, they were reinforcing their

▲ A German trench on the Linge in the Vosges. In the distance is a pillbox from where machine-gun fire rained down on the attacking French.

▶ The German front line at the Collet du Linge. A cross has been erected to a French soldier, whose body was recently discovered.

trenches, which had been dug out of the rocks, and constructing new concrete emplacements for their machine-gunners, which they hid among the trees. The French general staff brought forward the assault to July, but it was carried out in such a way that all element of surprise was lost.

In January Ferdinand Belmont found himself in the mountains, where he had been at the start of the war and where his brother had been shot in the very first days. At the end of December he had taken part in the attack on Artois, and he also learned that his younger brother, Joseph, who had been attending a seminary, had joined up. When he arrived in the Vosges, he was given leave to go to Gérardmer to return to 'civilization': to sleep in a bed, to have his hair cut, to have a drink in a café. Then he was sent to the valley of the Fecht, where he fought to take the wooded peak of Reicherkopf and was astonished to find himself still alive while those around him were killed.

On 8 July Belmont was awarded the Croix de Guerre for his courage in the fighting in the valley of the Fecht. Three days later he learned that Joseph had been killed in Argonne. In a letter to his parents he searched desperately to find the words to comfort them, and he ended his letter: 'Now, you must not worry about me. Try to live your lives, accepting, without fear, that we will meet again in another life.' He was allowed to visit his parents again and visited Gérardmer for

'In the past there were battles; between the battles people marched and then rested. Now, there are no battles and no truces. There is nothing but war without a minute's rest, without a morsel of unoccupied land. It's progress that does this. There is no more strategy, no more planning, no more skill and no more intelligence. There are only endurance, tenacity, patience and obstinacy. I no longer know which of the strategies is the more difficult. War today, despite this, or perhaps because of the negation of the individual, is probably better than the old-fashioned kind.'

Ferdinand Belmont

another three days. Then he returned to the front line, for the attack on the Linge. There, he wrote to his parents, were 'the Germans [who] had brought their finest troops to stop us'.

The assault began on 20 July on the little peak, on a front 4 kilometres (2½ miles) long, after some initial rounds of artillery fire, which were intended to create an opaque cloud that would obscure the slopes and summit. In order to conquer the Collet du Linge, the alpine chasseurs set off for a position on a lower level, but were immediately peppered by shells from above. One entire rank of the chasseurs was wiped out on the first day, and the survivors who had reached as far as the level of the enemy were forced to retreat. Some managed to bring back notices that had been attached to the barbed wire and that bore the legend: 'Notice: The Linge will be the graveyard of the chasseurs.' This quickly became the mountain's nickname.

After this check, many other attacks followed, but they were uncoordinated, and each time hundreds of soldiers were left on the increasingly deforested slopes. Nevertheless, on 26 July the alpine chasseurs returned, despite the machine-gun fire, which cut down numerous men at point-blank range, and they tried to reach the ridge of the Linge and the blockhouse there. They were also under fire from the batteries hidden on the mountain at the Ravin des Chênes and the German counterattack was unexpected. The chasseurs were driven back, although they managed to hold on just below the first line of Germans, in trenches they had quickly dug out, in one place only about 30 metres (less than 100 feet) from the enemy. Attacks and counterattacks continued throughout the summer in an attempt to take the summit. At the beginning of August, between the valley of Combe and the summit of the Linge, there were 2000 French bodies lying on the ground, covered with flies and beginning to decompose.

On 18 August, before a new attack, Ferdinand Belmont wrote to his parents: 'Our guns will be loosed on the German trench that dominates our position from the ravaged ridge of the Linge from where we can see, despite the crenellations, the greenish sandbags. At 6 o'clock the artillery will be silent; it will be our turn. We have to climb upwards to cross the area where the trees have been cut down, the twisted lines of barbed wire and the scattered boulders, then we will seize the enemy blockhouse and stay there. We are ready. The men have filled their cartridge pouches, hooked their tools to their belts and filled their knapsacks with grenades. They know where they are going. While

◀ Alpine chasseurs.

▶ The site of the fighting for the Linge in the Vosges.

► Hartmannweilerkopf, with the plain of Alsace on the right. The memorial was built over the last resting place of 12,000 unknown soldiers.

▲ A French trench.

we are waiting for the signal to advance, men chat about this and that with a calm and a confidence that it is impossible not to admire.'

When they reached the ridge, mines exploded under the trench and under the blockhouse, 'filling the air with flying baskets, bags, weapons, bits of blue material and arms and legs. Ten minutes later the survivors of the two companies went back down the mountain to where we set off. A crowd of crested helmets once again swarmed along the ridge. A barrage of artillery, a deafening din and irritated telephone calls. I was given the order to start the attack again. So that the same thing didn't happen again and in order to avoid senseless slaughter, I took it upon myself not to try again. I have about seventy men

left under me. This mountain is truly called the graveyard of the chasseurs.'

At the end of the summer the Germans used gas, then flame-throwers, to clear out the trenches nearest to their own. Autumn arrived, the beautifully clear skies looking down upon this military disaster. On 4 November Ferdinand Belmont was awarded the Legion of Honour. But this honour, he wrote, 'had been earned by others, who had paid for it. And how many of them rest in the shadows, unrecognized, sacrificed and ignored?' He thought about all those who had died in the pine forests of Alsace or on the plains of Flanders. 'What does this red ribbon, which is stained with your blood, matter to you and what does it matter to all those who weep? Where are the heroes? They have neither ribbons or medals; they are invisible and uncountable.'

The French continued to cling to the slopes. 'Through the fog it was possible to see the torn stumps of the pines, looking a bit like tombstones in a graveyard. This terrible mountain is, indeed, a graveyard, and no one will ever know all those who sleep their last sleep under these stones, this rubbish, these heaps of earth and the shattered dug-outs, and no one will ever dig them up.'

On 24 December Ferdinand Belmont set out for *le vieil Armand*, where he began a new attack. On the 27th he wrote to his youngest brother, Maxime, who had, in his turn, just left home. On

'*We have got entirely used to staggering along or being bent double in our dug-outs and in trenches under beams and telephone wires. … As a result of staying awake all night and living in our dark and damp shelters we are completely exhausted.*'

Ludwig Renn

the 28th, fighting among the chasseurs, Ferdinand was wounded; he died that evening.

Soon the front line on the Vosges was static. Attention was directed elsewhere, and by the end of 1915 both the Linge and Hartmannweilerkopf were regarded as 'closed'.

◄ Hartmannweilerkopf in the Vosges.

► The entrance to a German tunnel excavated in the mountainside.

► A German trench.

'The enemy lines,' Ferdinand Belmont wrote one evening, 'face each other, a short distance apart, creating a watershed. Between these two lines, the land has become a charnel house. The bodies of dead chassseurs, fallen in a succession of attacks; the bodies of Germans, killed by our guns in the counterattacks, lie stretched out in all positions in the middle of strands of barbed wire and smashed pine trees.'

Fifty years later people voluntarily started to move blocks of red sandstone and to clear away the soil from around the heather and pines, which had regrown along the summit of the Collet du Linge. Metal shields, coils of barbed wire from which some could not be disentangled, barbed wire fences … all the weapons from the trenches are still there. There are also little pieces of belt under the bracken, cartridge cases and rusty cans, bringing back, albeit fleetingly, the reality of these soldiers who already seemed to belong to a different age, and the death of these forgotten men. The resting places of many 'lost' men were found beneath the earth. Crosses – black for the Germans, white for the French – are mixed together over the ground, testifying over and over again to the dreadful events in the Vosges that were ultimately meaningless.

The Heights of the Meuse

Among the names associated with Joffre's policy of 'wearing down' or 'nibbling away at' the enemy, some have assumed a terrible resonance – in Lorraine, for example, the names Bois-le-Prêtre, Bois d'Ailly and Bois Brûlé. Jacques Vaché, who was about to leave for Bois-le-Prêtre, wrote to a friend: 'This evening I am going to the most stupid place in the whole war – a place from which few return.' Vaché, whose letters to his parents described everyday events in the war in an allusive, intentionally humorous way, suddenly became serious. 'I am going to the trench that is known as "the trench of bodies", a nickname that was given long ago to a place that defies belief. This evening we have to go to the front line for, I imagine, a major assault. And we shall have to witness this inferno so that we can understand, calmly and objectively, what will be an important

▲ The writer Alain-Fournier is buried in the cemetery of Saint-Rémy-la-Calonne in the Meuse.

The battlefield at Bois-le-Prêtre.

A glass pyramid has been erected in the wood at the site of a mass grave in which the bodies of Alain-Fournier and twenty of his comrades were found.

attack in this area. It will be necessary to count the 70 per cent losses in this dismal trench – that's the percentage of those already lost in the doubtful honour of defending this spot. Don't worry, though, my friend, I hope to be among the survivors and one of the survivors who are sound in mind, because it is especially heart-rending to see those who come back with their spirit broken. In any case, immediately after the skirmish I will write to you – or someone else will write to you. If I have to stay here, you will sort out the things I have told you about. … I send you the warmest greetings. But why? Why?'

Vaché, although wounded in other offensives, survived the war. However, two other writers of his generation lost their lives in the woods on the heights of the Meuse. Louis Pergaud died there, as did Alain-Fournier, author of *Le Grand Meaulnes* (*The Lost Domain*, 1913), who 'disappeared', like the protagonist of his novel, until his body was found in 1991 and identified from a fragment of one of his boots, which had been covered with dead leaves in the undergrowth. He was lying in a hastily dug pit alongside the others who had accompanied him on the reconnaissance mission in which their lives ended. A small glass pyramid has been erected where their bodies were found, and their remains have been reinterred not far away in the little cemetery of Saint-Rémy-la-Calonne.

THE ÉPARGES

The fighting was particularly intense in the countryside around Verdun, a town the Germans were determined to occupy, and both sides struggled to control the uplands, especially the ridges, which provided valuable observation points.

To the east of Verdun the Germans had managed to advance in the region of Saint Mihiel and create a 'bulge' in the French front line. As part of his overall plan, Joffre tried to dislodge the enemy by carrying out a series of what proved to be costly assaults on the heights of the Meuse, particularly on the ridge of Éparges. This seemed to him to be an ideal point from which to oversee the artillery battles on the plain of Woevre, some 350 metres (380 yards) away. But there, as

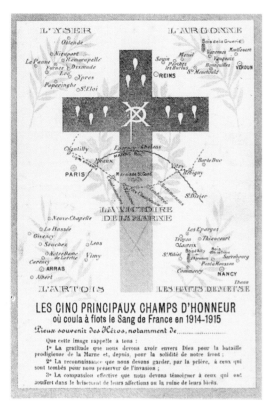

▲ A token of remembrance for French soldiers who fell in the five main battles of 1914–15, when the land 'ran with the blood of France'.

elsewhere, the Germans had consolidated their position. They had created a series of tunnels and dug-outs, which were properly supported with timber posts, and they had even managed to excavate under the railway line. On the sides of the hill they had, in places, established up to five interconnected lines of trenches.

The French tried to make their way through the forest, which covered the west side, leaving behind them the valley of the River Longeau and the little village of Éparges, which found itself about 600 metres (656 yards) from the German line. The clay ground underfoot was particularly difficult to cross, and in the cold rain that fell that winter the mountain was transformed into a 'pile of mud'. The young teacher Maurice Genevoix was a lieutenant near Éparges in the early months of 1915, when the preparations for the French attack were being made. The forest was both damp and cold, and, when the men had to climb the side of mountain to relieve their comrades who were waiting in the crannies dug out of the clay near the summit, 'the soles of their shoes stuck to the ground, squelching with every step. People slipped about all over the place, holding their hands out in front of them, sticking in the mire, up to their wrists in muck. We made progress by crawling along on our elbows and knees in the mud.' The French dug out tunnels on the slope, which enabled them to put mines beneath the German position on the summit. Before long the little peak was riddled with trenches and tunnels, which zigzagged all over the place around the ridge.

The attack took place on 17 February. Crowded together in their dug-outs, the men had to keep perfectly still and quiet while sappers crawled along the tunnels on their stomachs to light the fuses. Maurice Genevoix looked at his men, among whom were only fifteen survivors of the fighting of the previous autumn, and he wondered how to position them for the moment after the explosion, when they would throw themselves over the crater just created to take the land around the enemy. It was hard, waiting for five hours, isolated from the world. Then came the explosion. 'At first there was a shudder in the earth, which we felt as we crouched against the ground.' Four blasts went off simultaneously under the German positions at the summit. 'We were on our feet when the hideous white fumes, filled with flying black shapes, flowed down over the plain, behind a line near to the horizon. … There was a cracking noise in the sky, which seemed to split and crumble. The ground groaned and trembled. We could not see anything more because of a reddish powder, which was like flames or blood, and then, across the smoking, stinking cloud, came a glimpse of the wonderful sun, a flash of faint light.' Then guns began to fire all at once.

With the terrible noise of the shells going on all around them, the men kept crouched down close the ground, but then the order was given to advance to occupy the huge holes that had been made in the hill. As they moved onto the land that had been turned upside down, they began to distinguish 'pieces of shredded wood and splinters, fragments of light-coloured wood lying in shards all over the dark earth, bits of barbed wire, a rag of a charred cloth caught on some wire'.

On the evening of 17 February the French had taken what remained of the German front line, and began to discover the dead and wounded lying among the wooden beams that had been dislodged from the tunnels. They also took prisoners, among whom Maurice Genevoix noticed someone who stayed at the back, 'a child

▲ A mine exploding.

in tears, a huge lump on his forehead, which he kept covered with his hand all the time, in an unconscious gesture'. He kept saying 'Dreadful!' over and over again to the captain who was interrogating him. He said he was seventeen and a half years old and that he was a volunteer in the army. The officer, who was forty-eight years old, 'looked at this weeping child with a wound on his head and gave him a piece of chocolate' before sending him to join the other prisoners.

On the following day the Germans began a counterattack, during which the French suffered terrible bombardments. The infantry, who were standing at the edges of the areas they had just taken, could not understand why their artillery was unable to provide protection against the enemy shells raining down on them and they felt abandoned, 'sacrificed'. Maurice Genevoix later learned that the distribution of ammunition had been arranged when the positions they had taken had not posed a threat to the lives of the men, and the bulk was now with the officer who was commanding the attack taking place further away. The soldiers put up with this with 'dignified resignation'. The fighting on the ridge lasted for five days. Attacks, shelling and explosions followed one after another, crushing the men in the trenches and covering them with earth in which were mixed 'bits of people, who could not be recognized from a leg, an arm or a head'. In the awful fighting and bombardments and in the horror of what was happening around them, the men lost all sense of time and did not even know if they were hungry or thirsty, 'we could have been sleep walking'. Nothing was more important to the men who remained and who were trying to hold on to the ridge, at no matter what cost, than the telephone message from headquarters. 'The German infantry kept on firing at us, at those who were left up there, covered with mud, sitting among the dead, and on land that had so recently been green and fertile but was now made irrevocably vile by our suffering.'

The peak of the hill was held by the French, but at the most dreadful cost on both sides. The fighting continued unabated, and every week of the winter of 1915 saw the dead and wounded being evacuated on the backs of their comrades down the slippery, muddy slopes.

In April another major assault began. It lasted four days, under continuous rain. The

▼ The crater made by a mine on the ridge of the Éparges has been reclaimed by vegetation.

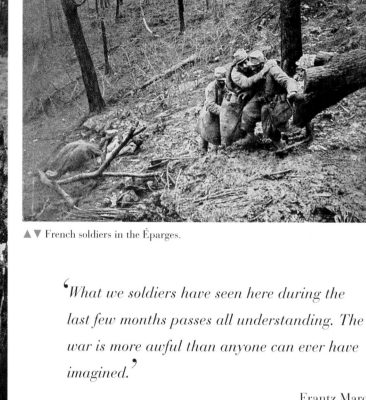

▲▼ French soldiers in the Éparges.

'What we soldiers have seen here during the last few months passes all understanding. The war is more awful than anyone can ever have imagined.'

Frantz Marc

▲ The monument to the Revenants (Ghosts) created by Maxine Real del Sarte.

'And still they keep on coming, their eyes wide, walking in the same fast, unsteady way, breathless, half-mad and fantasizing about the ridge, from which they long to escape, to get away from this ravine in which death whistles through the leaves destroying the calm, to reach the valley below, where their wounds can be dressed, and where they can be looked after and, perhaps, be safe.

Maurice Genevoix

▲ The trench of Calonne, the old name given to a straight route across the Éparges.

trenches were piled high with bodies, and as the holes created by the mines filled with water, the men slid about, fighting and drowning.

The ridge continued to be divided between the two sides until the end of the war, with each side holding onto one of the slopes. The advantage gained by this 'wearing down' of the Germans was negligible. The view over the plain of Woevre, which the April attack was intended to achieve, was not of great strategic importance, and the attack itself ended in slaughter.

Lieutenant Genevoix was wounded fighting in the Woevre sector at the end of April. 'My war is over,' he wrote. 'I have left behind me all those who died next to me, all those who died on the forest tracks.' He continued to be haunted by the suffering of those who had disappeared and those who were still fighting, but life, almost despite himself, began to reassert itself. 'Oh my friends, is it my fault that I have changed so much? … I believed that I was going to die, but because I am alive, I am filled with a sense of good fortune that I cannot shake off. My eyes fill with tears as I look through an open door.'

The Argonne

Lying between Champagne and Lorraine on the other side of Verdun, the Argonne is a huge forest where the Germans halted during their withdrawal in 1914. The line they held ran from east to west, dividing the forest almost exactly in two.

The land was covered with stands of tall oak and pine trees, separated by ravines shrouded in dense undergrowth, and the forest was crossed from north to south by a straight road, the Haute-Chevauchée, which recalled the hunts that used to take place around there. The whole countryside was littered with places whose names were redolent of a more peaceful time: the Grange-aux-Bois, Bagatelle, Saint-Hubert and Les Islettes. Streams gurgled and splashed everywhere, giving rise to the names of villages such as Fontaine-Madame and Fontaine-aux-Charmes. But the very characteristics that made the forest so beautiful proved to be a nightmare for the soldiers, who had to fight in coppices where the clay in the soil made it impossible for water to drain away. The men had to live in a constantly damp environment, squelching about in a glue-like mire and always having to empty the water out of their mud-coated

◀ ▲ Dug-outs in the forest of Argonne near Verdun.

▲ A fortified shelter near the route to the Haute-Chevauchée.

▲ Crown Prince Wilhelm's dug-out.

trenches and dug-outs and to use the maze of rough tracks that criss-crossed the forest to get about and to bring supplies up to the front line.

The layout of the trenches that had been so hastily excavated quickly became haphazard in the uneven terrain and changed hands almost overnight. The two sides were often only a few dozen metres apart, glimpsing each other hiding behind trees or firing at machine-gunners who sprayed the forest with bullets to protect them from a surprise attack. The men harassed each other day and night, and skirmishes with grenades and knives were not uncommon in the threatening surroundings. The little Bois de la Gruerie was quickly given the nickname Bois de la Tuerie. Losses on both sides were very heavy, especially when one camp strayed onto a part of a ravine held by the other. It was in one such, the ravine of the Meurissons, that Bruno Garibaldi, grandson of the famous revolutionary leader, was killed with other Italians who had volunteered for the Foreign Legion. His brother, Constante, was killed a few days later, when he returned to see the spot where his brother fell.

The Germans quickly concentrated resources in this sector from which they wanted to interrupt

▼ In the forest of Argonne.

'*Oh, those shelters. The sun scarcely lit them. Even when the sun was at its brightest, a pale candle would have provided more light in a dark night. But when the rain drowns the forest, when, as now, the cold causes branches to break, our little hovels have a familiar calm, the quiet of an ancient house. … I hope that some of them will be saved after the war so that we can come back together to see them.*'

Maurice Genevoix

the channels of communication that enabled supplies to get to Verdun. The Crown Prince himself sheltered in a dug-out nestling in the undergrowth so that it would not be visible from the air. His retreat was to the east of the forest, not far from Varennes, a little town whose name is remembered by the French because Louis XVI was arrested there on the night he tried to get to Austria to escape from the Revolution.

For successful combat in this difficult terrain the Germans used *Minenwerfer*, whose shells created holes 8–10 metres (26–32 feet) deep; gas, which collected in deadly pockets in the bottom of the ravines; and, after 1915, a new weapon, flame-throwers. Even so, actually getting to the French trenches was difficult in the terrain, and since it was almost impossible to wage war successfully on the surface, the enemy went

underground. The Germans sent General von Mudra to the area. A sapper of some repute, he was put in charge of mine warfare. The French soon began to use the same tactic, and each side excavated numerous tunnels so that they could place explosives under the other's trenches. The ground under the forest floor is honeycombed with tunnels and galleries, built so that one side could destroy the enemy's own constructions before he had laid his charges. Each side tried to blow up the other before it was itself blown up.

The sappers made slow progress, simply because it was so difficult to remove the soil from a tunnel as it was excavated. In addition, it took several days to move the boxes of explosive through the narrow tunnels, which might easily collapse around them if an enemy mine went off nearby. Then, before they could actually finish laying the

charge, they had to pack in sacks of earth in order to minimize the shock of the counterblast that would occur when the fuse was lit. The men on the surface waited in terror, on the lookout while they listened to the monotonous sound of the pickaxes underground, counting the moments until the end of the shift and knowing that the safety of them all depended on the actions of just one man.

'The war in the Argonne was a very special kind of war, waged in unique ways,' wrote General Apremont in the journal *L'Illustration*. 'There were terrible deaths and … the proportion dying later from wounds received is noticeably greater than elsewhere.' Praising the endurance and self-denial of the 'brave little soldier of France', he added: 'The worst is over; the darkest days have passed. Winter has already come to an end. The

days are beginning to lengthen, and spring will bring victory in its train!' How wrong he was.

After 1915 enemy encounters became less violent, until the great battle took place at Verdun, which no one could yet imagine.

Today, in the forest of Argonne it is possible to follow the lines of the craters that cut through the network of trenches around the old front line. On all sides the undergrowth still cannot conceal the scars that reveal the positions of the trenches or the humpbacks of the dug-outs and shelters that rise among the trees. In the short grass all along the track that runs from Vienna to La Harazée, at the foot of the steep, tree-covered slopes, are holes and hidden openings, that used to swallow up men, just as Jonah was swallowed by the whale, only to spit them out further up the mountain, as they climbed towards the

ridges, where they would be killed in new fighting. A strange brick staircase, now covered with moss and ending half-way up, climbs towards the peaks amid the pine trees. In the thick layer of damp leaves that covers the ground lie pieces of corrugated iron, now brown with rust, which were used to cover the dug-outs. Metal posts still support a winch on which it was possible to raise supplies to those at the front line and to lower the wounded to the valley below. A little further away there are holes in the side

▶ The monument to the soldiers of the Great War at Vauquois.

▼ The remains of an ancient building in the woods on the slopes of the ravine of Meurissons, where Bruno Garibaldi and his brother, Constante, came under fire over a period of several days.

of the hill. Here, during the terrible year of 1915, the soldiers watched the buttercups bloom while, like General Apremont, they waited for the war to end. They watched the trees in the fields across the valleys turning to the emerald green so typical of the area and saw the white blossom appearing on the hawthorn bushes in the distance – the same blossom that was appearing in the little military cemetery at La Harazée where their comrades lay.

Vauquois

The ridge at Vauquois, to the east of the forest of Argonne, was a veritable laboratory of mine warfare. The soldiers eventually blew up the end of the village that is perched half-way up the side of the hill. From a strategic point of view, the peak represented an important observation point over the area around Verdun. Since September 1914 the Germans had held the summit and had fortified the village there. After a fruitless attack in October, the French soldiers would raise their eyes from their trenches, precariously established in the orchards at the foot of the hill, towards the ridge whose conquest began to assume a national significance for them. In February they began a new offensive against the bullets that rained down on them when they got near to the village. Almost all the men were killed on the first day. More men were sent into the attack on the next day. They had been given cartridges and supplies for two days and full water cans, so they rolled up their cloaks and tents and attached them to their shoulder belts, then hung their shovels and pickaxes from the belts. Some of them got to the summit, and it was possible to see, from several kilometres all around, the silhouette of a French soldier, brandishing the national flag before he was shot.

Soon, under the bombardment of shells, the remains of the village 'disappeared like a head of oats shaken in a turbulent wind'. Sadly, the German counterattack soon took the form of the inevitable hand-to-hand fighting behind the remains of walls and in caves, and scenes of sublime and banal heroism were enacted in the ruins of a village that had been cut in two.

'Move him into the sun –
Gently its touch awoke him once,
At home, whispering of fields unsown.
Always it woke him, even in France,
Until this morning and this snow.'

Wilfred Owen, *Futility*

Then the mine warfare began. Each side tried to excavate a tunnel, about 60 centimetres (2 feet) wide, under the enemy line, each time trying to get below the other side's mine hole. The men rested during the day, but at night, in the damp and cold, they took off their shoes so that they would make no noise on the frozen ground, and excavated mine holes to a depth of 40 metres (130 feet) in attempts to dig while making less noise than the enemy. As they worked they risked revealing the communal ditches, when the light of candles lit the night, and the soldiers lay, unmoving, alone in the crushing silence and the darkness, feeling the weight of the earth above them.

The first mine – a German one – went off on 3 March; 4 tonnes of explosive blew a giant hole in part of the village. On 25 March the French exploded 12 tonnes of dynamite, which blew the church to pieces. Following that, each side tried to outdo each other in the laying of mines until, on 14 May the Germans laid and exploded a mine of 15 tonnes, which engulfed 108 men in a crater 100 metres (330 feet) across. Nothing was left of the village, nor of the summit of the hill, and the soldiers on both sides, despite their desire to explode the ridge, which had become an anthill, stopped because they had no more explosives.

On the ridge of Vauquois wild grasses have sprouted in the huge wounds that were open to the sky. Today, an information board stands next to the sites that were the church and the town hall. In 1918, when the Americans arrived in the Argonne with their tanks, they just skirted round the ridge as they pushed to the north.

▲ ▶ At Vauquois the
exploding mines caused
both the village and the
top of the hill to disappear.

▶ A trench.

▶ The entrance to an
underground tunnel dug
by sappers.

Artois

The repeated assaults resulted in massacres on all sides. General Joffre, who wanted nothing more than to break through the German front line, planned a large-scale attack in Artois in May 1915. It was to be known as 'the spring offensive'.

While the British attacked towards Loos, French soldiers were sent into the attack at Vimy Ridge and Notre-Dame-de-Lorette, where the Germans threatened Arras. They poured across the coal-mining area, towards the towns of Lens and Douai. The combined force that set out was divided at Mont-Saint-Éloi, which the French had used in the past as an observation point. The hill was surmounted by an abbey, whose twin towers had been reduced to ruins by German shelling.

From there, the plan was that the French would descend into the valley of the River Souchez, take the line of villages occupied by the Germans and advance into the hills facing them.

This time they would make the greatest possible use of an artillery bombardment to prepare the way for the infantry. The Eighth and Tenth Armies were assembled for the attack. New trenches were dug and carefully camouflaged, engineers built dug-outs and first-aid posts, the artillery was brought into position, reconnaissance aircraft criss-crossed the sky, and the soldiers wanted nothing more than to believe in the success of an attack the scale of which had never before been contemplated. They were ready to throw themselves wholeheartedly into an assault on the mountains to bring an end to life

in the trenches, where they had just spent the long winter months. Several generals were sceptical about the reasons for the attack, however. General Fayolle, for example, wrote in his journal: 'This is, definitely, the attack. After the lessons of the Yser, Champagne, Neuve Chapelle, the Éparges, they want to begin again. ... There will be 1000 men lying underground for every kilometre of land.'

The Germans, for their part, had not been slow to strengthen their position. All the villages in the valley – Carency, Neuville-Saint-Vaast and Ablain-Saint-Nazaire – had been turned into fortresses. The caves, now reinforced with concrete, were linked with access tunnels along which supplies could be carried. The walls around gardens were topped by barbed wire. In

▲ The basilica of Notre-Dame-de-Lorette. The national cemetery contains 20,000 named graves, while the eight ossuaries, including the lantern tower, house the remains of 20,000 unknown soldiers.

◄ The ruins of the Abbey of Mont-Saint-Éloi, which served as an observation post for the French.

the plain, the 'Labyrinth' was a network of strongly fortified trenches, extending over about a kilometre (two-thirds of a mile) and supported by extensive underground passages. The French soldiers were impressed by the formidable defences they could see in the distance, which they nicknamed 'white works', because of the white material (taken from the sheets found in houses) that was used to cover the sandbags piled up beneath the parapets.

At dawn on 9 May a bombardment by 1200 guns began. The ground shook beneath the feet of the ranks of men ready to attack. In the distance, through the clouds of smoke, the French soldiers could see debris of all kinds flying through the air. The weather was exceptionally good, and at 10 o'clock in the morning the attack began. A human tide advanced from the French base. In the spring sunshine the infantry moved forward confidently towards the plain, astonished to hear birds singing now that the guns were silent. After they had advanced a few metres, German machine-guns suddenly opened fire, and men fell everywhere. The French guns had not reached as far as the German defences. The trenches in the front line had been destroyed, but no Germans were in them.

At the centre of the offensive line, meanwhile, soldiers of the 33rd division took Carency and its defences, La Targette and the Bois de la Folie, and began to mount the long cliff-face at Givenchy and Vimy Ridge. The men of the Moroccan division took the ridge, from where they could see the Germans who had infiltrated the plain of Lens. They had broken through the German line! In just a few hours they had advanced 4 kilometres (2½ miles). Exhausted and dying of thirst, they waited for reinforcements. But the reserve forces were about 12 kilometres (more than 7 miles) away; those who did manage to reach the front line – territorials who were too old to join up – did not arrive until the following day, by which time the Germans had managed to regroup.

▲ Muslim graves at the mausoleum of Notre-Dame-de-Lorette.

'We haven't left the plain, the vast, scarred plain, but meanwhile we are in Souchez! The village has vanished. I have never seen anything disappear as this village has disappeared. ... The bombardment has so changed everything that it has diverted the course of the river running by the mill and the river is now creating a marsh over the remains of the little place where a cross used to stand.'

Henri Barbusse

▶ The ruins of the village of Souchez after the war.

Cendrars and his companions in the Foreign Legion joined up with part of the Moroccan division that was waiting in vain for reinforcements, but then, unbelievably, they found themselves being fired on by the French artillery. 'People would have done better to have a square of white material stitched to their backs or to wave pennants and flags to attract attention and ask people to stop firing. The noise and confusion were indescribable. The intensity of the firing got louder and nearer every minute, and soon the Germans in the rear line, the fortieth, whom we had just got past, were taking aim and picking us off one by one.'

The same evening the Germans retook the ridge and bombarded the French who had to fire back from the side of the road running between Béthune and Souchez. The trees along the side of the road fell, one after another. The dressing station collapsed. 'The survivors of the attack,' remembered Colonel Humbert, 'had no time to dig themselves in deeply. They crouched down in the grass or behind little piles of earth – there was no protection against the bullets. The number of wounded increased at an alarming rate.' In the following days Carency and Neuville were retaken, street by street, cellar by cellar, but the Germans could advance no further.

Of this famous 'breakthrough', the one fact that is recalled today is that the 33rd division was commanded by General Pétain.

The offensive continued, and the battle raged bitterly over the hill of Notre-Dame-de-Lorette. Since the end of 1914 the two sides had shared the hill that gave its name to the chapel built on

▶ Indian troops in Artois.

▶ British infantrymen.

the summit. The chapel was in ruins, but these had in turn been fortified. The ridge was held by the Germans who, in March, had launched an attack designed to make them the masters of the whole hill, and had taken the 'Ridge of Arabs'. To retake it, the French fought for many days, 'in terrain that was confused and slippery, where groups of men, bayonets facing guns, assembled chaotically, chilled to the bone and standing in holes filled with mud,' recalled Captain Joubert. After losing 3200 men, the French had managed to retake 600 metres (660 yards) on the ridge.

In May the French undertook a new attack, this time on the northwest side, fortified with five rows of trenches protected by barbed wire and parapets, behind which stood the machine-gunners. French and German soldiers alike lived through what they thought was their last day. Amid the explosions, with bullets hailing down on them, they saw 'those who had been killed in the earlier fighting and buried in the ground being blown out of their graves by shells'. The men fought for thirteen days in the heat and surrounded by an unbearable stench. The French soldiers, crawling up the slope from one shell hole to the other, managed to reach the small fort from where the Germans fired on them and took the ridge and the whole plain. Louis Barthas took part in the fighting in the Lorette sector, 'those places of horror and hopelessness'. 'Here comes the dawn,' he wrote. 'The disinterested sun rises over the field of horror; everywhere there are bodies and misshapen human limbs, left on the ground for the rats, braver than the crows, that fear keeps at a distance.'

The struggle continued in the valley, at Ablain-Saint-Nazaire, the 'Labyrinth' and Souchez, where the sugar refinery, one of the

'*Such, such is Death: no triumph: no defeat:*
Only an empty pail, a slate rubbed clean,
A merciful putting away of what has been.'

Charles Hamilton Sorley, *Sonnet*, 12 June 1915

▲ The ruins of the church of Ablain-Saint-Nazaire.

▲ On 5 May 1915 from the top of Vimy Ridge the zouaves and Legionnaires managed to break through the German lines to the plain of Douai. But the reinforcements did not follow them.

'*The blackbird sings to him, 'Brother, brother,*
If this be the last song you shall sing,
Sing well, for you may not sing another;
Brother, sing.'

Julian Grenfell, *Into Battle*

centres of fighting, fell in June. 'Souchez was almost another Verdun,' said Pierre Mac Orlan. Around Neuville-Saint-Vaast 300,000 shells were fired in twenty-four hours.

Not one of the original houses in the villages remained. A fragment of the portal of the ancient church of Ablain was left standing and has been preserved in the middle of the new brick houses as a reminder of the hundreds of thousands of soldiers who died in the little valley. At Souchez a notice board by the side of the main road identifies some stones on a nearby hill: the remains of the sugar refinery, which cost so many lives.

In mid-June General Foch, who was in command of all the armies of the north, ordered an end to the offensive. The French had lost 140,000 men, and 300,000 wounded had been sent away from the front line.

During the summer a British officer accompanied a French colleague to an observation point from where they could see the trenches and the land ravaged by the May fighting. 'It would have been impossible to liberate this devastated area without some kind of land boat that could have been raised and lowered to provide a mobile gantry.' Captain Keller, who reported the conversation, said that the major 'matched his words with actions, using his arms and chest to suggest how such a vehicle would move. The major was Winston Churchill … who had foreseen the development of tanks.'

Despite the setback experienced by the French forces in May, Joffre's enthusiasm was unabated, as was his faith in large-scale offensives; after the catastrophic naval operation at Gallipoli he was more than ever convinced that victory would be won only on the Western Front. Joffre and Sir John French, the commander-in-chief of the BEF, met that summer to prepare a major joint offensive. This was to take place in September, in Artois and in Champagne, partly over the same terrain but also on new fronts, and the artillery was to have a far more important role. The chief theatre of attack was to be Champagne, with Pétain commanding the armies in that sector. The attack on Artois would be launched the day before as a diversion.

▶ The statue of General Maistre on the hill at Notre-Dame-de-Lorette.

Ammunition and materiel were stockpiled around Arras, and men were assembled there, including a hundred French divisions, giving a total of 300,000 men. Thanks to Lord Kitchener's campaign for volunteers, the British had thirty divisions in the north of France, among whom were troops from India, Australia and New Zealand.

This time, the initial artillery attack lasted for four days. The British, who attacked at Loos, used gas for the first time. The Irish, throwing a football in front of them, and the Scots, playing the bagpipes, led the attack on the German front line. Among them were the young volunteers who had arrived at the front the previous summer and who were now fighting for the first time. Losses were terrible. At Lens the 15th Scottish division lost 5400 men in a single day.

As in May, the French attempted to mount an attack at Vimy and Notre-Dame-de-Lorette, where one of the ridges was still in German hands. At Vimy, the units ranged along the slopes of the hills, taking three rows of trenches and managing to get as far as the borders of the Bois de la Folie and onto the plain of the ridge. The swift arrival of German reinforcements from Lille, Douai and Valenciennes compelled them to defend themselves on the plain, where machine-gun fire was forcing them back when a sudden thunderstorm transformed the trenches into swamps. Weighed down by the clay clinging to their shoes and clothes, the men staggered about and fell into the bomb craters. 'The shells were bursting everywhere, and no one could tell what was happening or make anything out,' recalled Colonel Humbert. 'As night fell it went on raining, and the ditches and trenches were filled with the wounded and dead. The battalions that had led the attack were scattered over the ground, hiding in shell holes. There was blood and mud everywhere.'

Terrible fighting was also taking place at Souchez. Roland Dorgelès described the battle, which raged in the cemetery itself. 'The blinding light [of the rockets] suddenly illuminated the scene. The men stood perfectly still, not even moving their heads as they watched. In a single instance, they saw the crosses, the tombstones and the cypress trees; we were in a cemetery. There was a huge area littered with broken stones, shattered trees and, dominating the ruins, the solemn figure of a saint, holding in its arms a marble book in which, each evening, the flying splinters engraved the details of the events.' In

◀ The cenotaph to the war dead of Souchez and the statue of General Barbot, who was killed during the fighting at Artois.

the terror of the bombardment the living sheltered in the holes dug to house the dead. 'We were more dead than they were, trembling under the stones.' A German soldier was found there, 'abandoned by his regiment. He did not speak. He was terribly thin, with huge eyes, his sunken cheeks dirty and unshaven, his hands emaciated. He did not seem to be able to feel the terrible wounds in his broken legs, but a terrible thirst made him whimper.'

They waited for three long days, sheltering behind the gravestones, until the enemy attacked again. 'The cemetery rang to the sound of grenades, and fires crackled. It was like an inferno, and the noise suddenly burst into the night. ... The mines, the shells and even the tombstones shattered around them, things

exploded into the air – it was like an erupting volcano. The explosions in the night crushed everything. ... Help! Men are being killed!'

The ruins of Souchez were eventually taken. 'Ah, our reports could sing of victory,' wrote Louis Barthas, 'but perhaps they should have been edged in black.' Although 25 September was regarded as a French 'victory', there was widespread horror. On the slopes of Vimy Ridge, remembered Colonel Humbert, 'were scattered bits of bodies and men, convulsed in agony, writhing and racked with pain. ... So many dead. ... They were lying in the shell holes, sinking into the mud. Every evening the carts before the dressing station were filled up. ... But the most memorable sight was, perhaps, that seen on Hill 119, on the ramp in front of the trench

▲ A lonely tomb by the side of a hole made by a shell near the German emplacement at Navarin Farm.

▶ In the undulating countryside of Champagne the ordinary French soldiers launched themselves into what they believed would be the 'ultimate' battle.

at Brême, where hundreds of men were spread out, and as one looked at them lying on the cropped grass, they looked like a sky blue carpet.' Meanwhile, the Germans did not stall. During October Prince Rupprecht of Bavaria, trying to retake Loos, left 20,000 dead soldiers in front of the Allied lines.

Then trench warfare was resumed, with its daily bombardments and the daily suffering in the mud.

CHAMPAGNE

While the attack on Artois was under way, the principal offensive was about to take place in Champagne, to the east of Reims, between Aubérive and Massiges. Enormous resources were put in place: roads were constructed so that heavy field guns could be transported, enormous spaces were cleared on which the soldiers could be stationed – one of these, nicknamed the 'Place de l'Opéra' by the men, was protected by 20,000 sandbags – and new trenches were dug so that troops could attack from positions nearer the German line. The French were counting on the element of surprise, but the Germans could hardly have failed to hear the sound of the convoys of vehicles, and their reconnaissance

aircraft had reported on the existence of the white marks made by the new trenches in the chalky ground of Champagne. They were, therefore, able to reinforce their positions and bring up reserves, especially to the opposing side of the mountains, where the French could not see them.

Four days before the assault, a continuous bombardment began, with the purpose of clearing the way for the infantry. It was a real hail of steel, and in the German trenches, under the deafening sound of the explosions, some men went mad. The underground shelters collapsed, crushing their occupants. It has been estimated that 3000 shells were launched every hour at each 100 metres (330 feet) of the German front line and to a depth of a kilometre (two-thirds of a mile). The French soldiers were reassured by the exhaustive

artillery rounds. This time, they thought, would be *the* great offensive.

'There had never been firing like it. ... It never stopped,' said one of the characters in Roland Dorgelès's *Croix de bois*. 'I knew we could advance.'

'Me too. ... I agree.'

'For the first time, there is a sense that preparations have been made for a proper battle and not for one of these tragic scuffles or one of those farcical advances that preceded other attacks.' If they were to die, they would at least know that it wasn't for nothing. 'I tell you that after this assault, the war will be over. It is the men's last attack.' The ordinary soldiers were certainly reassured. 'You can be sure that you won't be winning a wooden cross.'

'These are the last minutes of life for many of us. We dread it, and we look around to try to understand the sacrifices.'

Gabriel Chevallier

▲ On the morning of 25 September 1915 Colonel Desgrées du Lou took the head of his troops. A few minutes later he was dead.

▼ This area in Champagne was given the nickname 'Place de l'Opéra'.

On the evening of 24 September, the day before the attack, Joffre read out a proclamation to his soldiers. 'Behind the blizzard of iron and fire that has been unleashed, thanks to the hard work in the factories of France, where your brothers have worked day and night for you, you will go into the attack together. Your attack will be irresistible.'

On the morning of 25 September, despite the rain that had begun to fall, the men were confident. For four days they had watched the artillery attack on the enemy. Facing them, everything had been smashed. 'All the ditches, all the trenches were full, and all these men, side by side in their hundreds and thousands, felt a fierce assurance. Whether they were confident or resigned, each one was nothing more than a grain of sand in that vast mass of humanity. That morning, as one, the whole army scented victory.'

The soldiers had to attack by crossing the undulating, chalky plains of Champagne that are barren apart from occasional thickets of pine trees. At 9 o'clock in the morning 130,000 men got ready to launch themselves over the parapets, tightening their belts with one hand, clutching their rifles in the other. '"You're sure you know where I live," said Sulphart to Gilbert [characters in *Croix de bois*] … They looked at the wide, empty plain. … Advance! It's time to go. Quickly now.' The men threw themselves over the parapets to the sound of *La Marseillaise* and began to move swiftly towards no man's land. But they could already hear the sound of machine-guns. Not all had been destroyed. Maimed bodies began to fall.

The first day was a success for the French troops, who managed to get beyond the German front line and take part of the Main de Massiges, the ridge at Tahure and Navarin Farm, where Cendrars, who was still fighting with the Foreign Legion in the Moroccan division, lost an arm. General Marchand, the hero of Fashoda, was wounded in the stomach by a burst of machine-gun fire. The Moroccan division advanced as far as the ridge at Souain, but the salient at Mesnil could not be taken, despite the courage of the cavalry, who charged towards the machine-gun emplacements, their swords in the air, and who did take a small section of the German trenches.

By the evening of the first day the soldiers were exhausted. Reinforcements came up behind the front line, but they were in such confusion that they stopped each other from being able to exploit the breach in the German line. The next day they made some further progress, to the side of Souain and Perthes, but when they reached the second line of German defences, which had not been destroyed, there was carnage. The waves of infantry who threw themselves into the attack on the slopes were cut down by machine-gun fire and paralysed by a gas attack. The dead and wounded mounted up in the despoiled fields. Some units lost their officers, and although the fighting continued for another two days, the men on both sides were exhausted. 'The dead were everywhere: caught in the crossfire, lying on the grass, piled up in the shell holes. Blue greatcoats here, grey ones over there.'

In *Paroles d'un revenant* Jacques d'Arnoux remembered the days following the September offensive. 'Dawn broke above the smouldering ruins of Perthes-les-Hurlus: trenches famous for walls made of humans, where the dead sheltered the living. … Rotting limbs, empty sleeves lying around everywhere … there was not a foot of ground that had not become a tomb.' On 6 October the French renewed the attack and took Tahure – a village erased from maps by the war – and the Moroccan division reached Sommepy, where the men were bombarded by French artillery because no one realized who they were. On 1 November the general staff halted the offensive. The greatest gain had been 4 kilometres (2½ miles) although the advance at Main de Massiges was only 800 metres (½ mile) at a cost of 138,000 dead, not counting wounded and missing. All in a month.

In the years after the war the land on which it had been fought could not be brought back into cultivation because of the large number of unexploded shells that remained. At first, the land was returned to the farmers, but there were so many accidents that the land was declared too dangerous to work, and in 1922 it was taken over by the military. In some areas only dwarf trees

▲ The ruins of a dug-out in the second line of the German defences on the opposite side of the mountains of Champagne.

▲ The Russian cemetery at Saint-Hilaire-le-Grand, where lie the bodies of the members of the Russian brigade who fought in the area in 1916.

and lichens would grow. Several villages had completely disappeared, and their names were added to those that were to be rebuilt so that they would not be forgotten. Thus Souain became known as Souain-Perthes-les-Hurlus, in memory of one of these villages of which all that

remains are the foundations of a few houses, the flagstones of the church and some shattered tombstones. All that remains of those who died are the immense cemeteries, both German and French, with their ranks of gravestones behind the huge rectangles of the communal graves.

▲ The French cemetery at Souain-Perthes-les-Hurlus.

▼ The remains of the ancient church of Mesnil-les-Hurlus.

▼ The church of Souain seen from the presbytery.

▲ The monument at Navarin Farm, east of Reims.

▼ The German cemetery at Souain-Perthes-les-Hurlus.

▲ All that remains of Perthes-les-Hurlus, one of five villages in Champagne to be totally destroyed.

▲ The gravestones of North African troops in the French cemetery at Suippes.

LIFE AT THE FRONT

The great offensives of 1915 brought death to Europe on a scale that had never before been witnessed. The Allies had lost 600,000 men for derisory territorial gains, and the French army alone had lost 29,000 men for each month of the conflict.

Since the war of movement ended, more than a million men had fallen along the length of the front. It was as if a strip of land, 800 kilometres (500 miles) long, had simply become a graveyard for the dead. In places men had been buried so hastily that their bodies rose to the surface, and those that had been interred in cemeteries behind the front line before a retreat were occasionally blown out of their graves by shells exploding

around them in subsequent battles whenever the position of the front line changed by a couple of hundred metres. At the front lines the men lived in what was, in effect, a charnel house. Whenever soldiers had to excavate new trenches their spades would cut into human bodies in various stages of decomposition. Memoirs from this period abound with references to the presence of bodies. Louis Barthas, who was stationed near to Notre-Dame-de-Lorette, noted: 'The rain caused landslips, which revealed several French corpses along the side of the trench, which we had taken on 25 September. They had been insufficiently covered with earth. It was not uncommon to fall over a skeletal hand or a rotting foot … we became so used to seeing such things that we hardly paid any more attention when we were tripped up by them than if they had been the roots of a tree.'

'*The evening silence gently weaves its mist, forming a huge grey shroud for all those who do not have their own.*'

Roland Dorgelès

On the German side the novelist Ludwig Renn wrote: 'One would notice a leg sticking out from a wall that had collapsed. Who is it? But that's Emile, as you know very well. He used to make us laugh. Now he weeps.'

As if that were not enough, the decomposing flesh attracted both flies and rats. 'Those flies in the open graves at Lorette,' recalled Louis Barthas, 'spread from the front line; they filled us with the most tremendous disgust. They got everywhere –

'*The dead wait there, in long rows. We cannot go out to look for them; we do not know what we can do for them.*'

Erich Maria Remarque

◀ Wounded French soldiers watching an entertainment.

▼ Soldiers who had lost limbs continued to play their part in the national effort.

If death was appalling, the manner of dying was even worse. Soldiers in the trenches could see comrades with whom they had just been talking blown to pieces in front of their eyes or disappearing into holes suddenly created by an exploding shell. Stretcher-bearers often needed to use shovels to dig out wounded men. Infantry-men, many of whom were scarcely more than teenagers, were splattered with their comrades' blood or had to watch the head or arms or legs of a friend being blown off before their eyes. Everywhere they looked, the living saw scarred and wounded faces, which often they could not recognize as belonging to their comrades, whom fear and suffering had changed beyond all recognition. What could they say to those lying in agony before their very eyes that would offer the slightest comfort?

in the mugs, the mess tins, the cooking pans – buzzing about us all the time, flying from the dead to us and from us to the dead, like bees carrying pollen from flower to flower.'

Those who had lived through the terrible days of the major offensives could not but be affected by the violence, which exceeded every-thing any human could be expected to bear. Writing of Artois, where he was a stretcher-bearer, Henri Barbusse likened it to being in the most awful of storms when the thunder and lightning continued, with no let-up, day after day. It wasn't only on the days of the offensives that people would die – guns went off at any time. The strain was intolerable. People could be wounded when they were doing the most ordinary of things, such as going to get soup from the mess or just looking over the top of the parapet to see the sunlight glinting on the countryside, to remind themselves that there was another world somewhere. They could be killed by a shell landing near someone who was just lighting up a cigarette to enjoy a few moments' solitude in the overcrowded trench or who wanted to block out the all-pervading stench of rotting flesh. 'It's only by accident that people did not die,' commented Erich Maria Remarque.

In Ancient Rome gladiators had to fight each other to the death in one-to-one combat. On average they survived for two years. How many

months did men have in the Great War? The men crouched on their firing ledges, watching along the entire 800 kilometres (500 miles) of the front line for an enemy who was invisible, but who would wound even if he did not kill. They waited in what felt like a permanent state at the doorway separating them from life and death. They knew that they might have to die alone, staring at the huge, empty sky, 'facing the last agony and closing their eyes without a mother's kiss', alone with their thoughts and despair, without even being able to share their last words with another.

Supplies of morphine ran out, and doctors and orderlies in the dressing stations and field hospitals worked in wholly unhygienic con-ditions, made worse in some places by the overcrowding. The number of wounded was enormous and outstripped the total number of those killed. In the first aid posts, said Jean Giono, 'we had to move the meat from the stretcher'. Most of those who survived being wounded were scarred for life. Amputations were carried out as if on an assembly line in the hospitals and in the towns behind the front line, and townspeople saw increasing numbers of

young men in wheelchairs, pushed around either by orderlies or by one of the women who corresponded with soldiers at the front line. The techniques of medicine and surgery made huge advances, but the maimed, the blind and those with severe facial injuries became an important part of everyday life behind the front.

Some soldiers dreamed about being wounded so that they would be sent away from the front. Roland Dorgelès and Henri Barbusse included in their novels conversations between men waiting for the next assault in which they discussed the 'best' type of wound to have, to ensure that they would not have to return to the front – whether it was better to lose a leg, an arm or even an eye. Maurice Genevoix recounted the words of an officer to a young soldier whose hand had just been blown off and who was worrying about the kind of life he would lead. 'At least you are safe,' the officer said.

The men withdrew into themselves after the shock of the first deaths, simply because of the numbers involved. 'Ten agonizing deaths cannot all affect us in the same way,' remarked Pierre Chaine. In the Éparges Maurice Genevoix experienced a kind of desensitization after the death of one of his close comrades, 'a hard coldness, a dry indifference, accompanied by a shrinking of my soul'. But it was difficult to forget the distressing images. Some men became psychologically disturbed; some were suicidal. Many things were not spoken of at all.

Some men were amazed to find themselves experiencing a state akin to euphoria after an

'The dead for whom they are mourning did not watch them die.'

Jean Bernier

attack, even an assault in which they had seen their comrades disappear in terrible circumstances, simply because they had come through the ordeal unscathed. They later suffered profound reactions. Many soldiers felt that they had become little better than animals, and believed that they were living in a world that was becoming less, rather than more, civilized in its indifference to death. There was no doubt that

'God had absented himself from the field of battle'.

To add to this tragic backdrop were the appalling conditions in which the soldiers lived. In addition to continual fear, there were dirt, discomfort, exhaustion and illness. Nerves were constantly frayed by the sounds of explosions and by bullets whistling around their heads. Even in the billets behind the front lines, where the men might have looked forward to a brief respite, 'suddenly the violent roar of a field gun would rend the air, close to the barracks we had built, and bring us back to reality'. The soldiers were malnourished, slept little and badly, and were

'Lice, rats, barbed wire, fleas, shells, bombs, dug-outs, bodies, blood, alcohol, mice, cats, artillery, filth, bullets, deaths, fire, metal. That's war. It's the Devil's work.'

Otto Dix

infested with fleas and lice. 'The fleas attacked everyone, from the leathery skinned farm-worker to the effeminate Parisian; they did not discriminate between social class. To get rid of them people would rub themselves every night with petrol or paraffin. Some people carried sachets containing camphor or powdered insecticides, but nothing worked. You could kill ten, but another hundred would appear,' wrote Louis Barthas. There was little that they could do to improve the living conditions of an environment in which they felt they were kept like animals. The rats brought diseases with them, just as they had carried the plague in the Middle Ages. They were attracted by the dead, which they quickly came to confuse with the living, and they would run over the bodies of sleeping soldiers. Rewards were offered to the soldiers who killed the largest number of them.

It was impossible, too, for the men to ignore the weather when they had to live under the sky and on the bare earth. It rains a lot in the north of France, and even when they had managed to repair part of their trenches, the rain continued to flood the dug-outs. 'Torrential rain fell,' remembered Henri Barbusse. 'People would eat standing up, one behind the other, with no shelter, and the heavens would open. The men had to go to extraordinary lengths to keep their bully beef and bread away from the torrents of water that gushed from all sides.'

'We were turned into statues of clay,' wrote Champion, 'with mud up to our mouths.' In comparison, the German dug-outs were much more comfortable, but life for the infantrymen in their trenches was, nevertheless, just as unbearable as for the French because they could not see how it would end.

'Hell is mud,' wrote Henri Barbusse. Blaise Cendrars, writing in a trench known as Clara in Picardy, noted: 'Heroism consists of nothing more than being able to withstand for four days being sucked down into the mud, which grips you by your socks.' Even so, mud killed. 'Those who deserved the most sympathy,' according to Louis Barthas, 'were the telephone operators, the men who drove the supply trucks and the liaison officers. In normal conditions they would be envied because they were exempt from the everyday chores. But at that time they were expected to set out alone, and they could sink into the mud with no one to help pull them out. They would then have to wait for hours before someone set out to help them. In the end, we would get to the place where the one who had set out before us was in such difficulties. The unfortunate man would be stuck, without any way of getting himself out. We would try in vain to pull him out, almost pulling his arms and legs out of their sockets. If he thought that we were going to leave him, he would ask one of us to shoot him to put an end to his suffering. We would promise to return the next morning and we would leave a shovel so that he could try to save himself.' The nightmare was the same everywhere – in Artois, the Éparges and in Champagne – and the same stories were told from one end of the front to the other.

'This war,' wrote Henri Barbusse, 'means unremitting and unbelievable exhaustion; it means being soaked to the skin; it means mud, excrement and filth.' Every day the men were obliged to build or repair the trenches, which wore them out; at night they had to keep guard on the ramparts; they had to take part in long marches to reach the billets behind the front line, where they slept in ruined barns or in the open air, scarcely protected against the bad weather. The inhabitants of the villages who had not deserted their homes had become accustomed to their misery and showed less and less sympathy for their lot. They had come to treat the war as a

'If, despite everything, these men are happy at the exit from hell, it is precisely because they have a way out. They return, they are safe. Once more death, who was there, had mercy on them. Each company's tour of duty lasts for six weeks. Six weeks! The soldiers of the war have, for both the large and small things, a childish philosophy: they never look at anything around them or anything in front of them.'

Henri Barbusse

business like any other, and many soldiers complained about the price they were forced to pay to be allowed to sleep in damp straw. After a few days' 'rest' or just a breathing space, they were back on duty, with long hours of night marches, having to cover several dozen kilometres with their heavy packs on their backs in order to take their turn in the trenches. Again, they waited in trenches for whole days behind the same ramparts, facing the same desolate landscape, with death as far as the eye could see.

In the early assaults the fighting took place amid forests, where the trees looked like trees, and in fields covered with sheaves of corn. As the months

passed, however, the countryside became increasingly devastated. As they stood on guard duty, soldiers could see around them where shells had burned the ground or made craters that filled with muddy water whenever it rained. They could see the stumps of burned trees, ruined houses and a countryside that was becoming progressively depopulated and colourless, a countryside that looked much as it must have done before the Creation. Under the sound of shells the front had become a terrible ribbon of land, suffering as much as the men suffered.

'The land!' wrote Henri Barbusse. 'The pools, the craters … the tracks made by the troops and convoys that move by night in this sterile land; the ridges created by the carts gleam like railway tracks in the half light; the piles of mud that appear hear and there, propping up broken posts; the rolls of barbed wire, twisted into heaps.'

'We're alive! Forgive us, you comrades who have died. We're alive! We're going to enjoy this moment and make the most of our good fortune.'

Louis Botti

Even behind the front line, in the countryside across which they marched to relieve their comrades, the men saw all around them the inexorable progress of the devastation, like a developing cancer. In the areas immediately behind the front line where Jean Giono fought 'there were no trees and no grass, no long furrows in the fields, and the bare meadows revealed nothing but holes in the chalky land'. The farms and the big houses were increasingly being damaged by artillery, and the forests were despoiled. The surface of the roads was broken up, and along the way lay the rotting bodies of horses and broken wagons. The infantry marched through deserted villages, like those in Lorraine, which Maurice Genevoix described: 'Along the sides of the roads the ghosts of houses receded into the fog. The doors and windows were closed and blank, apparently waiting for us to reveal the mystery of their empty rooms. But suddenly, an ugly breach opened up where one of the white stone walls had collapsed; it was possible to see directly into one of the rooms, with its broken wooden floor, a bed lying under a heap of rubble, splinters of broken furniture and, amid all the devastation, a red curtain fluttering in the wind. The fog smelled of cold ashes, and, for a few moments, on the air was carried the stench of dead flesh.'

The ordinary soldiers, who were mostly countrymen, suffered terribly from the despoil-ation of the countryside, and the transformation of fields into heaps of soil and scrap metal by an all-pervading purpose that represented to them the systematic destruction of nature. In spite of the desolation of the landscape, the soldiers in the trenches watched the changing seasons as a kind of talisman, looking out for the young shoots of oats as they began to sprout in the fields or waiting for the light wind that heralds the arrival of spring and the song of a lark. In the observable manifestations of nature they looked for proof that life went on.

In the horror of the front, strange periods of peace occurred, including those enjoyed by Cendrars on the Somme with a few of his com-rades in the brigade. They formed themselves into a little troop to help other people out, and every

'*These days there is a sea of mud. Those who have been slightly wounded drown in it as they try to get to the first-aid post. The mud clings to my legs. … It's almost impossible to get rid of it. At the bottom of the hole, which is filled with water, my foot struck a tangle of wires, among which I recognized telephone wires, which are usually attached along the length of the trench but which have been swept away as they fell. … There are mud and bodies everywhere. Oh, the bodies. The dead who fell in the autumn, and who were buried quickly, reappear bit by bit as the trenches collapse.*'

Paul Truffaut, *Carnets d'un combattant*

night they managed to get away from Frise to make contact with other groups of French soldiers posted on the other side of the marsh of Cappy. Instead of walking right round the water's edge, they used a barge covered with reeds. Each night, without anyone's knowledge, they managed to glide over the surface of the marsh, isolated for a few hours from the two sides that continued to fight, in the middle of aquatic plants and in a hidden, almost calm world, where nature, bizarrely, continued to assert itself. In the centre of all the devastation, life, despite everything, went on.

But apart from thinking about an improb-able truce, it was not possible to escape from the gloom of the trenches. 'People rested behind the lines for four days,' continued Cendrars. 'Then

they went up to the front for four days and into the attack for four days, and so on, right on to the end if it were possible to have an end to this sad history. … All that was missing was a siren at the entrance to the trenches – a siren and a clock and a system of controlling a stamp, so that it would be possible to issue a ticket and have an automatic gate. The siren would summon the poor devils to their work, not to mention the wounded, who thought they were safe but who have to come back, to the factory of death, one, two, three, four days at the front line, then four days' rest.'

'I have stopped complaining,' said Barque, one of the characters in Henri Barbusse's novel. 'At first I complained about everything, about those

► The marsh of Cappy on the Somme. During the battle here Blaise Cendrars and Georges Braque fought on one side, Otto Dix on the other.

▲ The caves in the Soissonais were used as shelters by the French.

had abandoned their ploughs for rifles in order to save their country. They had the courage of ordinary men. They wanted to accomplish their job without getting engulfed in it, but hoping to do what they had to do as well as they could, which often led them to do more than was expected of them.

For the millions of men who were trapped in the 20,000-kilometre (12,400-mile) network of trenches it was a question of surviving instead of having a proper life and of organizing themselves as best they could. They tried to establish a familiar routine, and when the sector they were in was relatively calm, they decorated their dug-outs, even going so far as to give them the names of houses or hotels, using humour to help make the intolerable tolerable.

at the front, about civilians, about the locals, about the shirkers. Yes, I complained, but that was at the beginning of the war, when I was young. Now I accept things more.'

'You have to take things as they come.'

'Of course. Otherwise you go mad. We're already half mad anyway, aren't we, Firmin?'

The men in the trenches were living in the lowest ground, continued Barbusse, stuck in the closed world of the trenches while they waited to learn their fate. 'Men are buried beneath the battlefield; but like the tick-tock of clocks in our homes – in another time, in an almost mythical past – they were heard without being listened to.'

The soldiers existed, but, despite everything, they didn't give up. They did what they regarded as their job, doing their modest, unglamorous work. Most of the infantry were countrymen, who

Some of the soldiers stood a better chance than others. A garrison was based in the caves of the Soissonais and the hills of the Chemin des Dames. They lived in the honeycomb of caves quarried in the rock by the ancient rock-cutters, where they cut new underground corridors and ventilation shafts and found a relative degree of comfort in the troglodytic life, although they were aware of the contrast with the more dangerous lot of their comrades who enjoyed no such protection. Their understanding of the harshness of life in the trenches made them appreciate more that in the caves they were protected from shells and from the rain or heat by several metres of rock above their heads. From the confusion and noise of

▼ The quarries at Confrécourt in the Soissonais were turned into garrisons.

▲ ▼ Evocative traces of the soldiers' presence are still visible.

machine-guns, they entered the shady silence and calm of the caverns, where they were able to rest safely. In the quiet solitude they carved their hopes and dreams on the cave walls, which are today an archive of this period. They drew portraits of their wives and pictures of bunches of grapes ripening in the sun in a countryside from which they were so distant; in a cave at Confrécourt is a bust of Marianne (the personification of France) not far from an altar – on one side the image of the Republic, and on the other the Catholic Church, fighting shoulder to shoulder.

Before returning to the daylight and the front line, they would pray in the chapels they had carved out. They would ask St Therese of Lisieux, who had died at the age of twenty-four, the same age as many of the soldiers, to intercede on their behalf to save them. At Chemin des Dames the frescos, sometimes by an anonymous hand and sometimes identified by a first name only, sometimes in a naïve style and sometimes in a more elaborate style, remind us of the drawings in the Catacombs and of the parallel between the lives of the soldiers and those of early Christians in the brutal world of the Roman Empire.

Even now the caves that mark the flanks of the outcrop of this area in the east of Picardy speak of the misery endured by these men who had been brought face to face with death.

When they were not fighting the soldiers had to find a way to fill the emptiness and come to terms

'And I saw white bones in the cinder-shard,
 Bones without number;
For many hearts with coal are charred,
 And few remember.

I thought of some who worked dark pits
 Of war, and died
Digging the rock where Death reputes
 Peace lies indeed.'

Wilfred Owen, *Miners*

with the restricted life that was left to them. 'Here we are, still buried in our holes,' wrote Ferdinand Belmont to his parents. 'We sleep or watch what is happening around us. Some people rest, dozing on the straw; others smoke and think about this and that; still others stitch on a button or repair a tear in their uniform; some of us write; others talk interminably to each other, returning always to the same subject. It's a life that is slower, both physically and intellectually.'

The men talked about the past all the time. Indeed, how could they talk about the future when it was so uncertain? The periods of inactivity were broken by card games or just by pottering about, as some of the more skilful used cartridge and shell cases to make small pieces of jewellery, cigarette lighters, writing cases and other items that quickly became 'souvenirs' of the

war. Soldiers had to battle constantly against boredom and depression. 'A kind of intellectual torpor takes over. Everything becomes black. One is even tired of living. External events cease to be of interest.' Thus wrote the author of one of the little diaries from the front that first saw the light of day early in 1915. The soldiers used this method to communicate what they had experienced, which they could otherwise talk about only with each other. They started to use their own language 'created from a mixture of the slang used in factories and barracks with dialect words, heightened by some neologisms, which bound us together, like a sauce, crowded together as we were, whatever the season, emptying France and gathering in the northeast of the country,' wrote Henri Barbusse. The diaries and journals described the everyday life of the soldiers and

▼ ▶ The gulf between the lives of those at and those behind the front line was wider than ever.

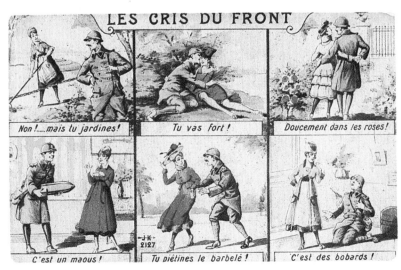

standing in the pouring rain, the ground turning to mud beneath him, his face turned to the greyness of no man's land where a shell might burst at any moment, would be sent some fond advice about looking after himself – so removed from the reality of his experience – accompanied by some redcurrants or strawberries from the family garden.

The difference between life on the front and life behind the lines increased. Soldiers became more aware of this gulf not only from the letters they received but also with the advent at the front of inexperienced new recruits and the granting of leave from mid–1915. Roland Dorgelès remembered the arrival in the trenches of 'three astonished soldiers', around whom the men formed a curious circle. 'They looked at us and we looked at them without saying anything. They came from behind the lines, they came from towns. Just yesterday they had walked in the streets, they had looked at women, they had seen tramlines and shops. Tomorrow they would live like men. And we looked at them, amazed and envious, as if they were travellers setting out on a journey to a fantastic country.'

showed how they went about their miserable lives from one end of the front to the other, using humour, a safeguard against the despair that took hold in the squalid trenches.

They wrote to their loved ones, often sending a letter every day and hoping that those of whom they dreamed loved them in return; they also wrote to their parents, asking for news of events on the farm and of the crops that had been sown. They knew that letters were read and censored in case they gave away important information, but on the whole they did not relate in their letters the horrors they faced. They did not wish to reveal everything, perhaps from delicacy or from a desire to protect their families or from a feeling that their families could not truly understand the suffering they were enduring.

them, could take comical or tragic turns according to circumstances. 'My uncle wrote to me to sympathize with my suffering,' wrote Gabriel Chevallier. 'He congratulated me on being able to relax, and, as I was reading, some cooking pots fell on my head.'

Sometimes a letter would arrive from the parents of a soldier who was already dead. Sometimes the replies from a fiancée or wife were delayed or increasingly rare. Overdue leave would only confirm the doubts that the soldiers had not dared put into words: for more than one soldier, leave showed that nothing would ever be as it had been. When he came back to the trenches and turned his face to the wall, his comrades tried not to ask the wrong questions. Long-awaited parcels, containing woollen clothes and shoes or some

'I've been given leave to return home for ten days. … My mother came out of the house and ran to meet me and embrace me. If she had known the state of my soul and that I was thinking of nothing at all, she wouldn't have kissed me.'

Ludwig Renn

They waited for the letters back, which were like bridges between them and their families and which they read in the dug-outs by the light of a candle. The difference between their circumstances and the news in the letters, made more intense by the time it took for the letters to reach

extra food, were welcome improvements on everyday conditions. Food assumed a great importance as a means of breaking up the awful hours spent in the trenches.

Sometimes an echo from the other world would take on an unreal aspect. A soldier,

increasingly estranged from their old lives. 'I seemed to be isolated in a completely different, faraway world,' wrote Jacques Vaché. 'We're barely 100 kilometres [60 miles] from Paris … but how can we explain the inexplicable, especially when the propaganda describes the soldiers' heroism in the language of a different era?'

The soldiers in the trenches chose to say nothing of their experiences. They withdrew from the world that meant nothing to them and returned bravely to the front line, where they risked their lives for their comrades and relied on their companions' support in their misery. 'The most important thing,' wrote Erich Maria Remarque, 'was the strong, practical bond of solidarity that sprang up among us. The war eventually created something that was worthwhile – camaraderie.'

Among the soldiers of the trenches a relationship developed between men who would not, in other circumstances, have ever met. They became like brothers, and, as Maurice Genevoix described, the bonds that had been forged in the war proved indissoluble and old comrades continued to meet for years after the war was over.

The chance of a few days' leave would mean that men, covered in mud, would arrive behind the lines from a world that was completely incomprehensible to civilians. 'I passed beyond the intermediate billet, where soldiers could stay before going away from the front,' an old soldier later recalled. 'I wanted to get home as quickly as I could and did not stop on the way. My mother did not recognize me.' In the towns life went on as before, cheerfully and pointlessly. One soldier arrived in Paris after a ten-hour train journey and found there was not a spare seat in any of the cafés. 'They did, after all, have money, so the wars are not altogether bad for those who do the fighting,' he said, disillusioned, adding that for those who were away from the front line, this was an exciting time.

The men at the front gradually became

1916

◀ Page 142: A blockhouse near to Tavannes railway tunnel.

◀ ▼ The ruins of Fort Bois Bourru and Fort Marre near Verdun.

In December 1915 Joffre, in agreement with the other Allied commanders, decided to launch a major joint offensive in the Franco-British sector on the Somme. It was to be under the overall command of General Foch, who did not want to launch another assault of the kind that had characterized the previous year. Meticulous preparations were put in hand.

VERDUN

Meanwhile, General Falkenhayn, who was now commander in chief of the German armies on the Western Front, advanced. He wanted to launch a crushing attack on a limited but symbolic objective, whose capture would destabilize all France. Unable to break through the front, he decided to maintain maximum pressure on a single point that the French would feel obliged to defend to the last man. His plan was to bleed France white and exhaust it utterly. The place on which he had decided to concentrate his forces and to which his soldiers had been brought for months was Verdun.

After the war of 1870 Verdun had been heavily fortified and was capable of withstanding a

German attack. The town itself was well defended and was surrounded by a score of fortresses, built, according to the plans of General Séré de Rivières, so that each could protect the next. Surrounded by huge ditches, the immense fortifications were deeply entrenched and had been equipped with pivoting fortress guns, which were able to fire over the whole region. The most important of the fortresses and the one that dominated the area was the fort at Douaumont.

Some of these concrete monsters to the south of Verdun were scarcely affected by the war until 1916. They remained virtually intact, standing hidden amid forests, which have since been replanted. Nowadays young conscripts come to the fort at Bois Bourru to practise firing, and their graffiti mingles with that of the soldiers of an earlier generation who confided their dreams and desires to its walls. The other fortresses have been abandoned to silence and to the elements. At Marre and Rozelier long passages, hidden in the undergrowth, open out into rooms. There are several storeys, with immense staircases rising to stone-clad rooms, lit by a diffuse light that enters through arrow-slit windows from which it was possible to keep watch over the surrounding countryside. Sometimes, where a wall has collapsed, the rotting vault of the roof is exposed. In the courtyards moss and creepers have smothered the ancient walls, which are stained with rust and saltpetre, but the might of these enormous ruins can still overawe us.

In September 1914 the German advance had been halted north of Verdun, but they dug in for about 15 kilometres (more than 9 miles) to the east, west and north of the town, establishing a line of observations posts, and they fought fiercely throughout 1915 to maintain their position. If they attacked, they were in a position to threaten the city, which formed a significant bulge in the German front line, and the French would be prepared to protect this point at any cost. Such was Falkenhayn's reasoning, and he was right in thinking that the French general staff, despite the alarming signs, would not count the cost.

The French had thought that a German attack on Verdun was so unlikely that the guns

▲ Top: The Germans built a 'village' behind their front line at Verdun, camouflaging the buildings in the forest. The remains are today known as the 'black village'.

▲ Above: The interior of Fort Rozelier.

▲ The French prepare for a counterattack.

▲ Preparing to fire a trench mortar.

had been largely dismounted from the fortresses and taken elsewhere on the front – the collapse of the fortresses around Liège had made the French doubt their value. With the Germans just a few kilometres away, the town began to make frantic preparations, cancelling all leave and transforming a small provincial sub-prefecture, which was usually very quiet, into one that saw some of the worst fighting of the war. Journalists came to the town to gather impressions of the front, and they found that local businessmen had not suffered too much from the war and the soldiers who had been stationed in the barracks in the town contributed to their prosperity. People believed themselves to be safe in the town and paid scant attention to the continual arrival of convoys of vehicles that could be heard all night behind the German lines nor to the reports of deserters from Alsace and Lorraine.

'The situation is disastrous,' noted General Chrétien, who had assumed command in September 1915, when he saw that the French defences had been virtually abandoned. As early as August 1915 Lieutenant Colonel Driant, the sixty-year-old local deputy, who had, on the declaration of war, requested that he be re-appointed to his command and who held a sector in front of the Bois des Caures to the north of Verdun, had written to the president of the Chamber of Deputies to warn against the ramshackle state of French defences and to explain the dangers inherent in this situation. At the end

of January General de Castelnau visited Verdun to inspect the area, and he gave orders that the defences be strengthened. Unfortunately, he was too late.

For several weeks trains ran regularly from the north and east, across the German-occupied countryside of Lorraine, through villages whose inhabitants had fled and from which they took building materials to construct garrisons and hospitals. On the way, the men who were being transported so hastily to the front, could see enormous stocks of munitions, hundreds of guns

of all calibres, millions of shells laid out in rows and huge piles of wooden stakes and rolls of barbed wire. They saw other trains pulling low-loaders, on which were carried the bases of heavy howitzers, under their camouflage tarpaulins, and other wagons full of horses. Night after night the equipment necessary for a great battle was accumulated. Entire villages and marshalling yards were built under the cover of the forest, in which most of the trees were cut down, leaving only the great oak trees, whose wide canopies provided cover from aerial reconnaissance. 'One

▼ ► Lieutenant Colonel Émile Driant's headquarters in the Bois des Caures.

▲ A first-aid post.

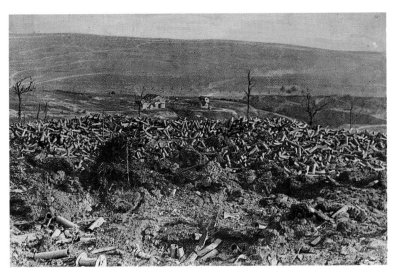

▲ Piles of shell cases.

hundred hours' preparation went into organizing that!' was the rumour that spread among the German troops. The soldiers understood what they were aiming at and that it was going to be a massive assault. Perhaps it would, after all, be preferable to the insane immobile war in which they had been bogged down, face to face with the enemy, for seventeen months.

The offensive that Falkenhayn had planned for the beginning of February had to be put back because of bad weather. It started to snow, and for two weeks the soldiers had to wait, crammed

into the underground tunnels hidden in the woods close to the front. On the night of 20 February the sky cleared, and it froze. The attack was to take place the next day, led on the right bank of the River Meuse by Crown Prince Wilhelm in person.

At dawn on 21 February the French soldiers, who were in the woods to the northeast of Verdun, rose with the sun, which made the hoar frost glint on the branches. Reconnaissance aircraft circled in the blue sky. At quarter past seven in the morning a mysterious tremor ran through the

air – thousands of shells had been fired simultaneously from the German guns. Then a mind-numbing attack was launched. Clods of earth shot up in all directions; trees were flattened; dug-outs were ripped open. It was the beginning of an unbelievable assault, of a hitherto unimagined violence, that was to last for ten hours. More than a thousand field guns, concentrated in a front 10 kilometres (about 6 miles) long, battered the French position to the north of Verdun. A shell landed on the French every three seconds, and in all a million shots fell, slaughtering men and destroying the fortifications.

The men who survived this shattering offensive thought that the hail of bullets signalled the end of the world. They saw their comrades fall, one by one, crushed by the terrible onslaught as they tried to get their bearings amid a landscape that had, within a few hours, become unrecognizable. From the citadel in Verdun it had been possible to witness the destruction of the heights of the Meuse but without fully realizing what effect such a scorched earth action had on the men. The wood at Spincourt seemed to be in flames from morning to night. At 4 o'clock in the afternoon the firing intensified, and German soldiers began to advance slowly, flame-throwers in their hands. Then, standing in the churned-up ground amid heaps of bodies, those French soldiers who survived rose and fought with whatever weapons were left to them – grenades, the butts of their rifles and even spades.

► The remains of Fort
Souville, the limit of the
German advance during
the Battle of Verdun.

'The great forts of Verdun,
Douaumont and Vaux, which
dominate the plain and which
are often shrouded in mist,
today resemble abandoned
quarries. … In winter, though,
they are imbued with the aura
of death.'

Pierre Mac Orlan

On the preceding day Joffre had made General Pétain responsible for reversing the situation and given him command of the forces at Verdun, which were now engaged in one of the greatest battles of the century. Joffre's chief of staff set out to find Pétain, who was with a woman in a hotel in Paris, but on receiving Joffre's orders he set out for the east, reaching the little village of Souilly to the south of Verdun, on the road running from Verdun to Bar-le-Duc. Pétain was sixty years old, and before 1914 his career was not especially remarkable. Since the beginning of the war, however, he had become convinced of the uselessness of large-scale

Lieutenant Colonel Driant, who was with battalions of infantry in the Bois des Caures, withstood the German attack all night and all the following day. A first-class marksman, he made his way to the front after having taken off his wedding ring so that it could be sent to his wife. At the end of the afternoon on 22 February he was shot.

Because of the frenzied resistance of a few handfuls of men, the Germans were unable to advance as quickly as they had expected. In three days they had, nevertheless, taken the ridge of the Herlebois, the Bois de Wavrille, the Bois des Fosses, the Bois des Caurières and the villages of Ornes and Haumont. The area to the north of Verdun itself was in danger of being overrun, and on 25 February the Germans arrived at Fort Douaumont, the best fortified section of the French line.

'The Voie Sacrée made it possible to make an unparalleled
offertory at the most formidable altar man has ever raised.'

Paul Valéry

infantry attacks and had kept on repeating 'rifles kill' and 'artillery conquers, infantry occupies'. His concern for the conditions in which the men under his command operated had already earned him great respect among the soldiers, who felt that too often insufficient attention was paid to their circumstances, and Pétain's appointment restored confidence among the troops.

When he arrived in the village hall at Souilly, which he made into his headquarters, Pétain learned that Douaumont had just fallen to the Germans. On 25 February a patrol of the Brandenburg regiment entered the fort through a breach in the moat and took it without having to fire a shot. The fort had been disarmed the previous year and was guarded only by about sixty territorials, who were so surprised to see German soldiers arriving at the fort that they surrendered without offering any resistance. French attempts to retake the fort on the following day proved futile. While German communiqués were telling the whole world about their conquests and explaining how their success at Verdun was the prelude to a final victory, French soldiers were preparing to retreat.

Pétain, who was confined to bed because he was suffering from pneumonia, began to give orders for the rationalization of the defences of the salient and to hold the line in the face of the appalling situation that was confronting the French. He established a defensive line to the east of the River Meuse, began to rearm the fortresses and looked for the best ways to use the existing supplies of weapons to defend the most threatened points while he awaited the arrival of new armaments from the factories behind the lines. He recognized the value of support from aircraft, both for reconnaissance and photography, and it was at this time that 'aces' began to have dogfights in the skies.

He reinforced the defensive positions on the right bank of the river because he was convinced that the Germans would broaden their attack on that side, and he took control of the only road by

◀ The *Voie sacrée* (Sacred Way), the road to Verdun.

▶ During the weeks of the fighting the forests around Verdun disappeared.

'*Each of these forests had cost a sea of blood, in the strict sense of the word.*'

Arnold Zweig

which supplies could be carried to Verdun and the front line, the road from Bar-le-Duc to Verdun, which the writer Maurice Barrès called *la Voie sacrée*. Each week 90,000 men and 15,000 tonnes of supplies were transported along this road, which was only 7 metres (23 feet) wide. It was constantly repaired by teams of territorials, who threw stones under the wheels of 11,000 trucks, which travelled in two uninterrupted lines, one towards Verdun, the other away, one truck every five seconds, under orders never to halt. This conveyor belt of supplies was the life blood of the French. It allowed the transportation not only of equipment but also of men, to relieve – and replace – those at the front line. Because of it, almost all the units saw action at the front and almost every French soldier fought at Verdun, which came to represent the battle for France itself.

At the end of February the situation on the eastern sector of the Meuse settled down, but then the Germans tried again to take the village of Douaumont, at which Pétain gave the order that the position, which he thought untenable, should be abandoned. Among the thousands of prisoners was Captain de Gaulle, who had been wounded for the third time.

In March Falkenhayn threw new battalions into the attack, some of which were moved from the eastern sectors of the front, and he broadened the offensive to the west of the river, which he believed was tactically important if the Germans were going to make progress on the east of the river. The Germans launched an attack on the ridge of Mort-Homme, and took the slopes, despite the French bombardment from Hill 304. At the end of March the German artillery unleashed against this new salient an onslaught just as fierce as on the first day of the attack. Communications between French soldiers and the commanding officers at the rear of the front line were broken, and it was thanks only to a captured air balloon that the general staff learned that the infantry who had survived the hail of shells were now threatened by flame-throwers.

The German forces could not manage to break through the French defensive line, and the Crown Prince's troops failed to take the summit of the ridge, which the French soldiers held in a remarkable display of courage and tenacity. The men were subjected to a barrage of shells from the twin peaks, which had originally been wooded but from which, in just a few weeks, all the vegetation had disappeared. In some places, too, the slopes had become precipitous as shells had blasted into the ground. The woods of Avocourt, Corbeaux and Cumières were reduced to blackened stumps and bare trunks, standing amid unidentifiable remains.

Fighting continued on one or other banks of the Meuse with a violence never before seen, and attacks and counterattacks followed each other without interruption, both sides showing equal ferocity and each side suffering terrible losses. For both French and German soldiers the battle became known as the 'hell of Verdun'. A storm of metal fell on the men every day, in what Henri Désagneaux called 'a race to destruction: man against gun'. In no other part of the front did the concentration of artillery fire reach such intensity, nor did it last for so long in an area that was no more than a few kilometres long. Later it was calculated that more than one shell had fallen at Verdun for every square centimetre of ground. Whatever moved in the countryside, where the men were now completely without shelter, was immediately shelled. The movement of troops, the changing of guards and even performing fatigues could be done only at night. In some places the trenches were nothing more than holes in the ground where the soil was piled higher than elsewhere, and the men huddled together and sheltered as best they could, next to the bodies of those who had already fallen.

In some sectors the telephone wires were severed and it was impossible to send messages, cutting off the men from all contact with the rear of the front line. A new kind of combatant

> '*A magnificent stretch of uninhabited land, with Douaumont in the centre, was turned completely upside down, like the smashed shell of a giant tortoise.*'
>
> Arnold Zweig

◀ An observation post built over a fort.

appeared at Verdun; someone who was known as the runner, a volunteer, tried to reach headquarters by running from one shell hole to the next under a hail of machine-gun fire.

The stretcher-bearers showed an equal degree of heroism, every night carrying their miserable burdens to the dressing stations, which were often 'holes covered with planks and branches' on the other side of the hills. The stations were not large enough to accommodate all the wounded, and some men were evacuated from the area after a few days. Charles Delvert described the arrival of a stretcher-bearer, 'his eyes round and blue and almost starting out of his head. "Captain, I can't go on. There are only three bearers left; the others are dead or wounded. I haven't eaten for three days, and I haven't swallowed more than a drop of water." This was a brave man,' added Captain Delvert. 'He did his work without thought to the bullets and shells that were bursting around him.'

The wounded who could get to the area behind the front were taken care of by the ambulance drivers, a corps that included Frenchmen among its numbers as well as many British and American volunteers. As for the dead, those that could be rescued were carried on carts to the cemeteries, which were becoming ever larger, and buried there, side by side.

'Our men suffered and endured hardship in ways we cannot begin to imagine. They did what was asked of them straightforwardly, without bragging about it. They were almost beyond reproach,' said Pétain. From the steps of his headquarters at Souilly he saw the troops passing on their way to the burning horizon. 'My heart sank when I saw our young men, only twenty years old, going towards the fire of Verdun. I loved their confident look as they saluted me. But how dismayed I felt when they came back, one by one, limping and wounded, or in groups with their companions, sadly diminished in numbers. My blood ran cold when I saw how what they had seen had changed them. They were bowed under the weight of hideous memories; they could scarcely reply when I asked them about their experiences.'

On 9 April the Germans launched a general offensive on both banks of the river at the same

▲ The ruins of the church in Ornes, one of the dozen villages around Verdun that were completely destroyed.

time, and yet again the attacks were repulsed. The French resisted with a ferocity that impressed the enemy, and even the youngest recruits, who had joined up in 1916, charged, their bayonets fixed, singing *La Marseillaise*. It was on that day that Pétain issued his famous decree: 'Infantrymen, artillerymen, sappers and airmen of the Second Army have vied with each other in displaying heroism. Honour is due to all. The Germans will attack again. Everyone must labour day and night to equal our earlier success. Courage! We shall have them yet.'

On the day of the offensives a German officer who would die several hours later at Mort-Homme wrote a letter that was found on him. 'The circle around Verdun closes up again little by little. … We will not take Verdun. So many men have fallen there. It would take months of fighting for us to take it.'

Falkenhayn had wanted to bleed the French army, but German losses had started to mount. Despite this, the fighting continued for several months, after which the French and Germans found themselves in more or less the same positions as in February 1916. When Crown Prince Wilhelm realized how seriously depleted

his forces had become he wanted to withdraw from a conflict that he had begun to regard as a dangerous drain on German resources, but Falkenhayn did not want to change his policy. Nor did Joffre, who wrote: 'It is certain that we will wear ourselves out at this game; but the

'*When may we, like other people, have our place in the sun?*'

Lieutenant Gandy

enemy will wear themselves out, too, and my aim must be to organize ourselves wisely so that we can last longer than they can.' So each side continued to fall into the other's trap.

'The entire French army has passed through here,' wrote Lieutenant Gandy. 'If the politicians could see it, they would make peace immediately.'

The fighting continued. Pétain's demands for additional men and equipment so that he could hold out were beginning to get on Joffre's nerves, and Pétain himself was regarded as too timid. He

► The monument on the ridge at Mort-Homme takes the form of a skeleton; the sculpture was created by Froment-Meurice.

was, therefore, promoted to the command of the Central Army Group, while the command at Verdun was entrusted to General Nivelle.

In May hostilities broke out again on the right bank of the Meuse between Douaumont and Vaux, where the Germans were able to take several dozen metres of land, although at great cost. On 22 May Joffre gave orders for an attack to retake Douaumont, and responsibility for the assault was given to General Mangin, a man of legendary courage but controversial because of his excessive fondness for attack, a trait that had been seen in the colonial wars in which he had fought, and because of his hopes for revenge. His forces got as far as the exterior fortifications of the fort and even managed to get inside the blockhouses, but the Germans got the better of the French efforts. Some 2000 French soldiers were taken prisoner, and Mangin was relieved of his command. In this period 10,000 Frenchmen died defending Hill 304.

The soldiers who marched the 20 kilometres (more than 12 miles) of the Sacred Way to the front line felt the ground beneath their feet tremble from the shock waves of the shells, and the noise could be heard in the Ardennes, in Reims and even, on some days, outside Paris. Before their eyes was a horizon from which arose the flames of an unceasing fire in which at least a quarter of them would die. As they advanced, the terrain became increasingly difficult. The German shells reached them before they had got as far as the front line, and in order to relieve the men they had been sent to replace, they had to move from one shell hole to another. They found it difficult to get their bearings in land that was covered in craters and mounds of earth, often mixed with human bodies, while they were deafened by explosions and blinded by bursts of fire.

Every soldier found that getting to the front line was a journey through hell, and each knew only too well the sacrifice that he was likely to have to make. Too many men had already given their lives there. They were bound by a kind of solidarity, strengthened by the suffering endured by all, yet every day scores of soldiers performed miracles

of courage, which remain unknown except among those who shared the honour and misery.

The snow of the first weeks gave way to a thaw and then rain, which turned the ground into an 'ocean of mud, without a shore and without a base', wrote Arnold Zweig. 'In the funnel-shaped craters bodies floated, like flies in a basin,' noted one of the soldiers. Then the warm weather arrived, turning the ground into a desert of rubble and dust. The men suffered terribly from thirst and from the stench of the bodies, which piled up because no one could bury them in a land that was continually bombarded by shells.

'My dear wife,' Private Eugène Bouin wrote in May. 'You cannot imagine the countryside in which we live. There are no plants and scarcely any ruins. ... Between us and the Germans, apart from the barbed wire entanglements, everything has been reduced to dust by the shelling. ... You may have heard people talk of Mort-Homme, of Hill 304, of the Bois de la Caillette, of the village of Fleury or of the Ravin de la Mort. Well, imagine that in each hole is a man like me, alone, with no means of communication, often separated from his unit. Do not ask me to talk about it and do not ask me to explain. I would not be able to answer you.'

The Germans knew that an Allied attack on the Somme was imminent, and they wanted to bring an end to the offensive at Verdun. In June, therefore, they decided to mount an attack on the fortress at Vaux, which they had been bombarding for four months. As many as 8000 shells had already fallen on the fortress, which was said to be impregnable as the walls were reinforced with 2.5 metres (more than 8 feet) of concrete, but the domed roof had been penetrated in several places. At the end of May the fort shook under a terrible onslaught of shells.

On 1 June the German artillery began a systematic bombardment on the fort itself and its approaches, which was followed by an infantry attack designed to surround the fort. All the defenders in the Bois de la Caillette were killed or taken prisoner, and the village of Damloup fell to the Germans, who then succeeded in getting to the top of the huge concrete structure, where they installed machine-guns, thus preventing the arrival of reinforcements. The men inside the fort, who were under the command of Major Raynal, were completely cut off and had no hope of outside help. On 3 June Raynal learned that the Germans were digging a tunnel to lay mines under one of the walls of the fort and that they intended to launch grenades containing burning oil and gas canisters through the holes in the roof on to the remaining garrison. He and his men took refuge in the basement corridors where there was no fresh air while the exterior of the fort blazed. The only thing that could save the garrison was an immediate artillery attack, and on the morning of 5 June they sent a distress

> 'We can have only a vague idea of the grandeur of the dead. They have given their all.'
>
> Henri Barbusse

signal: 'Attack immediately or we are lost. We can last no longer.' The men crouching in the cellars were short of food but suffered especially from a lack of water, since the cistern had dried up. Some of the men even licked the walls in the hope of finding some moisture. On 4 June Raynal sent his last carrier pigeon, which died on its arrival from the effects of gas.

On 5 June Fort Souville intercepted a message: 'We have reached the limit of our endurance, but the entire troop, men and officers, have, in all circumstance, done their duty to the very end.' Then there was nothing but fragments, to which the listening post at Souville could only respond: 'Have courage.' Raynal attempted to send out 500 men that night, but the Germans, alerted by a fall of rock, fired on them and took them prisoner. The next day a hundred soldiers managed to escape. Inside the fortress more and more men were delirious or in the throes of death. Major Raynal noted in his diary: 'My men hold out only through a tremendous act of will.' On the morning of 7 June, before those who remained died from exhaustion, Raynal chose to surrender. His men had held out for seven days.

The Germans watched as the ghost-like men withdrew from the ruins of the fortress. They were so impressed by the men's feat that they gave them water and presented Major Raynal with a sword as a mark of honour.

In June the fighting on the right bank of the Meuse reached new heights around Douaumont and the village of Fleury. 'It's a hell of fire,' wrote Lieutenant Désagneaux, who, after a change of duty, found himself one evening with his men in a 'ditch that had almost completely collapsed, without shelter, without anything'. When it was light the next day he found a platoon of machine-gunners buried in the ground, their arms and legs thrusting upwards. 'No sleep, no water, impossible to stand up in the hole or even to show one's head above the top of the ditch. ... The ground shakes, the air is filled with smoke and dust. ... [At night] the fatigue parties have to come and go in this whirlwind of madness, and getting soup involves going to outskirts of Verdun, 6 kilometres [3½ miles] away, and then coming back. The men go and say nothing.'

In the sector in which Jean Giono was fighting 'soup rations did not arrive for eight days. The fatigue parties left in the evening, into the dark night, and that was it. They melted away, like sugar in coffee. Not a single man returned. They were all killed, every one, each time, every day, without exception.'

The Germans attacked Thiaumont and Froideterre, which stood on a ridge overlooking Douaumont. The ridge was the last natural defence before the town of Verdun, and the two structures, originally built on a small scale, had, through force of circumstance, become the main focus of the French defence at the time when Falkenhayn launched what he hoped would be the final attack. Excavated in the rock lower down, on the other side of the ridge, were the

▲ The site of Thiaumont; the observation tower was smashed by a shell.

ammunition magazine at Fleury and the dug-out of the Quatre Cheminées, which served as a shelter for the wounded while they waited until the stretcher-bearers and volunteer ambulance-drivers could evacuate them at night through the Ravin des Vignes to which it was linked.

sensation we have; people are feverish but there is no water. Instances of insanity were reported in several units.' At the same time an official communiqué noted: 'The events before Verdun are of such a uniformity that all those who try to explain them begin to repeat themselves. The

'*The pretty villages were reduced to ruins, then to heaps of stones and, finally, to rubbish. The forests were cleared, then flattened and then turned into graveyards, where the bits of shattered wood were made into rifle stocks – then they became bare land.*'

Arnold Zweig

From 20 June the bombardment on the whole sector was stepped up. From the valley in which he found himself, Lieutenant Désagneaux waited for the order to relieve the front lines. On 21 June he noted: 'The night was spent under a barrage of fire. Bursts of gunfire were followed by shrapnel; the 210mm guns showered fire on us for twenty-four hours without a second's halt. Then it all began again. It's madness. Everything trembles, our nerves as well as the ground. Everyone is exhausted, with no thought of life. ... No one can eat, and thirst is the only

Germans bombard, attack, are driven back, then bombard again. And nothing happens there that has not already happened; there is nothing about which anyone could split hairs.' No fewer than 100,000 shells containing poison gas were sent to this sector. As the roof of the Quatre Cheminées dug-out shook continually above them, the wounded who had inhaled gas because of faulty masks suffered terrible convulsions that could be relieved by none of the doctors, who were themselves close to exhaustion and despair.

People could read in *Le Petit Parisien*: 'The battle of Verdun took its course without perceptible change. The decision was a long time in coming, and that was all the better, because the length of time worked in our favour.'

During the day the men crouched on the ground in the shell holes, in the heat and stench, waiting desperately until night when they could stand up in the light of the shells on a ground covered with bodies. 'It was dark. It was possible to feel something soft under the feet – it was someone's stomach. People lay down to sleep on top of corpses.' It was difficult to make out where the enemy were in this frightful world. In the last days of June the number of attacks and counterattacks around Thiaumont and the ruins of Fleury increased, and the village was taken and retaken sixteen times. The wounded could not be evacuated, and, by the sides of the first-aid posts, where people were left to die, the doctors piled up the limbs they had amputated.

'Night after awful day,' wrote Henri Désagneaux about Sunday, 25 June, 'we lived in blood and in madness.' The French managed to block the German advance, but only at a cost that the journal *Le Matin* described as 'very appreciable',

▲ An aerial view of the fort at Vaux, riddled with shell holes.

'*No one could believe that it was possible for people still to be living in this flattened landscape.*'

Erich Maria Remarque

and on 30 June they attacked with artillery and managed to retake the fort. For Henri Désagneaux and his men, who were in their trench nearby, this day was one of the worst they had lived through. 'My head was spinning, I was no longer afraid. … We sank into our trench,

▼ The national mausoleum and the ossuary at Douaumont contain the remains of 130,000 unidentified soldiers.

huddling together. … It was madness. The wounded crowded around us; the poor devils, not knowing what to do with themselves, kept coming to us, believing that we would help them. What could they do? There were clouds of smoke everywhere, and the air was unbreathable. There was death everywhere. At our feet, the wounded kept whimpering through their blood; two of them, who had been hurt more seriously, were groaning. One – a machine-gunner – was blinded, one eye was missing from the socket, the other was crushed; he had also lost a leg. The other man's face had been blown off, he had lost an arm, and he had a terrible wound in his stomach. They were crying and suffering, and they begged us: "Lieutenant, don't let me die. I'm in pain, lieutenant, please help." … The other, more seriously hurt and possibly close to death, asked me to kill him, to finish him off, with the words: "Lieutenant, if you won't help me, give me your revolver." Awful, terrible moments, while the canon fire tormented us and the shells splattered us with mud and earth and surrounded us with clouds. The death rattles, cries and wailing continued for hours – eighteen hours – and they died there, under our eyes, before anyone could help them.'

'I do not know what kind of monument the country will later erect in memory of the battle,' wrote Teilhard de Chardin, who was a stretcher-bearer in the area of Froideterre and Thiaumont. 'A single one should be put up: a great figure of Christ.'

After the war it was at the point on the front where the greatest number of deaths occurred that the ossuary of Douaumont was built, where the remains of 130,000 unidentified soldiers, both French and German, found in the soil in all sectors of Verdun, were interred. A tower surmounted by a lantern house dominates a huge cemetery containing 15,000 graves. Not far away, near the ancient Ravin de la Dame, a monument has been built above the Tranchée des Baïonnettes (Trench of Bayonets). The trench has been filled in, but in it still lie the bodies of the soldiers who were buried during the attack, their positions identified by their bayonets, still in their rifles, which protruded from the earth. Perhaps the reality will slowly be transformed into a archetype, which will subsume the legend. But what is important, after all, are the men who died at Verdun and those who were, like many others, simply buried by a shell. The events were no less tragic for those men than they were for those who lived through the nightmare. In a sense, the dead do not matter more than the living. 'It's absurd, isn't it?' remarked the German writer Ernst Johannsen, who fought in the war. 'We are dead, but we are still alive.'

Only 200 infantrymen out of 3000 survived the last attack on Thiaumont. When they managed to get away from the artillery barrage into the secure zone and into the villages behind the front line it was as if they were the survivors from a different world, their appearance altered by an unutterable horror. Lieutenant Georges Gaudy saw the men who had lived, the survivors from two regiments, pass by: 'They marched or, rather, shuffled forwards, their knees bent, propping each other up. … They said nothing, they didn't even complain. They hadn't got the strength to grumble. When these men, whom we might call prisoners of the war, raised their eyes to the roofs in the village it was possible to see in their faces an extraordinary degree of melancholy. In this moment their features seemed to be frozen in dust and etched by suffering. … Some territorials, who were standing next to me, were thoughtful. Two of them were weeping silently, like women.'

On 1 July the attack on the Somme, the great Allied offensive that had been planned since the beginning of the year, began. Falkenhayn was immediately forced to withdraw men and artillery to send to the western sectors of the front, and the situation at Verdun became more difficult for the Germans, despite some setbacks for the French. On 11 July the Germans made a final attempt to break through the line. After a tremendous bombardment, including the use of gas and heavy shells, which reached as far as the fort at Moulainville, the Germans managed to advance to the Bois de Vaux-Chapitre, the Ravin de la Dame and Fleury and were approaching Souville when they were forced back. About sixty soldiers and a lieutenant in the ruined fort held the Germans at bay with grenades and machine-guns. Already exhausted, the Germans eventually fell back. Once more, in the fighting around Verdun, a handful of men, cut off from their front line, performed almost superhuman feats of courage and desperation and managed to beat off the enemy. The Germans did not advance beyond the fort.

'*What candles may be held to speed them all?*
Not in the hands of boys, but in their eyes
Shall shine the holy glimmers of goodbyes.
The pallor of girls' brows shall be their pall;
Their flowers the tenderness of patient minds,
And each slow dusk a drawing-down of blinds.'

Wilfred Owen, *Anthem for Doomed Youth*

▲ The remains of Fort Douaumont.

Thus it was that the huge wave that had been launched against Verdun on 21 February ebbed away at the feet of Souville. From then on the attention of the chiefs of staff was concentrated on the Somme, and the front at Verdun became of secondary importance, even though the battle there continued for six months. In August the Germans mounted a surprise attack near the quarries at Haudromont, but Mangin and a regiment of colonial troops counter-attacked. They retook the ridge between Fleury and Thiaumont and took 1000 prisoners. Already, however, German public opinion, for so long enthusiastic about the offensive, had begun to question its value, and its initiator, Falken-hayn, was replaced by Hindenburg and Ludendorff. In September they decided to concentrate instead on a completely new offensive, and Crown Prince Wilhelm in person thanked them when they met at Charleville.

In August, with a loss of 1500 men, including thirteen officers, the French retook the village of Fleury, of which nothing remained. A series of actions enabled the French to achieve a symbolic success by retaking Fort Douaumont, whose recapture had become a national obsession. The Germans had carefully organized it into a logistic centre, and despite heavy shelling by the French, similar to that experienced by the French themselves in February, the interior of the fort was still relatively unscathed, even after the accidental explosion of a stock of grenades, which caused the death of 700 Germans – whose bodies are still interred there. In October the French launched a wide-ranging operation to retake it, and on 24 October the Germans who were lying low in the fortress felt the impact of the tremendous artillery barrage that preceded the assault. That night a 400mm shell set alight a munitions depot, and on the next morning, taking advantage of a thick fog, Mangin led his colonial troops in a surprise attack. The Germans shelter-ing amid the ruins were thrown into confusion by the zouaves, and the fort was retaken.

On 3 November Nivelle, who was in com-mand locally, took Vaux and ordered the retaking of the other fortified positions that had been lost. The front at Verdun was restored almost to its February position. It had taken the Germans four months to occupy the 4 kilometres (2½ miles) between Fort Douaumont and Fleury, but they were retaken in a matter of hours. The extra-ordinary energy shown by the French soldiers in defending this tiny scrap of French territory and the degree of self-sacrifice of which they showed themselves capable have remained for France potent symbols of the Great War.

The hill of Mort-Homme, which the Germans had transformed into an underground garrison, was retaken in August 1917, at the same time as the hills of Talour and Oie. By this stage the front was almost exactly as it had been in February 1916, although the town of Verdun was not decisively liberated until the American offensive in 1918, two months before the Armistice.

The battle of 1916 had lasted for ten months and had cost the lives of 700,000 men, French and German, including 320,000 who had died on a front some 10 kilometres (6 miles) long. The guns had not stopped for 300 days and nights, and the horizon had been like an unquenchable furnace that had instilled fear in the men who walked towards it. The land that had witnessed this fearful fighting and had been the site of the sacrifice of two nations became a sterile desert, littered with wreckage, scraps of metal and human remains, clothed in rags of blue and field grey.

Yet several months earlier, not far away, fields of corn could be seen and cottage gardens surrounded the houses in the little villages in Lorraine that had been built at the edge of the woods. But a dozen of the tranquil villages that had existed before the war had been completely wiped from the map and were never rebuilt. According to Pierre Mac Orlan, when he returned some years after the Armistice, the ground had been poisoned through and through. 'Death is everywhere in the countryside, in the merciless sky, in the woods, imbrued with bones and rusty weapons and absolutely infertile.'

After the war nothing could be grown in the ravaged land. The field of battle, where the watercourses had been polluted and where, for several decades, shells continued to explode, was declared a 'red zone'. In some places nothing would grow except for the occasional conifer. Today, in the woods where the fighting took place, a strange kind of vegetation has taken over: the trees are dying back but from their branches hang shrouds of creepers, which intertwine over the barren land with brambles and wild roses. In the undergrowth still lie tens of thousands of men whose bodies have never been recovered.

THE SOMME

On 1 July 1916, after several days of rain, a bright dawn broke over the Somme. It was the day chosen by the Allies for their great offensive.

Since the end of 1915 General Joffre, who was convinced that the failures in Artois and Champagne were the result of insufficient supplies of men and materiel, had been trying to persuade the British that it was essential to mount a large-scale campaign in the west. Forestalled by the German offensive at Verdun, the Allies put off the attack until the summer, when the assault would be concentrated on a front 35 kilometres (21½ miles) long. The larger part of the French army was still in Verdun, despite the niggardly way in which Joffre had responded to the pleas of Pétain and others for support. Because of this the Somme offensive, which was under the command of General Foch, was carried out by mostly British forces. They attacked on a front 25 kilometres (15½ miles) long to the north of the Somme, between Beaumont-Hamel and Maricourt, in the direction of Bapaume. The French were along a line to the south of the river, facing towards Péronne.

This time, British and French soldiers fought side by side in a real collaboration between the armies, even though there were clashes between the chiefs of staff. In a letter to Field Marshal Haig, Sir William Robertson, Chief of the Imperial General Staff, summarized his impressions of the French in terms that did not hide his feelings: 'Often they display excellent qualities but sometimes they are very primitive and insubordinate. In dealing with them it's necessary to remember that they are French and not English. ... No doubt,' he conceded, 'they find us odd, I imagine. Waiting and working with allies is not easy; it is necessary to exercise permanent control over ourselves and to show a great deal of tolerance.'

▼ Beside a field on the Somme.

► Lochnagar Crater at La Boisselle, which is 100 metres (330 feet) deep, was created by the explosion of a British mine under German lines on 1 July 1916, the first day of the attack. It has become a place of symbolic importance: on the anniversary each year, pilgrims throw poppies into the crater in remembrance of the Great War.

The French divisions were under the command of General Fayolle, an officer who had always shown his concern to spare the infantry while advancing the artillery and whose prudence since 1914 contrasted with the confidence of most of his colleagues. 'Do they hope to break through,' he had noted in March, apropos the earlier offensive.'I do not think so. Anyway, what does this battle mean?' In April, becoming sceptical more about the means than the purpose of the offensive, he wrote: 'Foch has shown us his plan. … The battle of which he dreams has no goal.' He increasingly argued that the French should relieve the pressure on Verdun and exhaust the Germans on another front.

> '*I have a rendezvous with Death*
> *At some disputed barricade,*
> *When Spring comes back with rustling shade*
> *And apple-blossoms fill the air –*
> *I have a rendezvous with Death*
> *When Spring brings back blue days and fair.*'
>
> Alan Seeger, *Rendezvous*

The British forces were commanded by Field Marshal Sir Douglas Haig, a graduate of Oxford and Sandhurst. He had total confidence in the courage of his men and in the outcome of the next offensives. The number of British soldiers who took part in this battle was greater than in any other assault. To the BEF and the volunteer recruits were now added conscripts, for in 1916 Britain found it necessary to introduce conscription to fill the ranks. Nevertheless, the essence of the British army and its great strength were still the volunteers of Kitchener's army, the 2 million men who had responded in the twelve months of the appeal launched with a series of posters showing the face of the Secretary of State for War, with his finger pointing forward and his eyes staring out above the legend 'Your country needs you'. These posters and others – 'Your King

◄ ▲ The British cemetery at Pozières. Australian and New Zealand soldiers are also buried here.

and country need you' and 'Join your country's army' – appeared all over the country.

This 'new army' was formed from groups of local volunteers, who joined up together and formed regiments that were often known by the name of their county or town. They left their country to defend 'good and civilization', and many of them were under the requisite age when the presented themselves at the recruiting office. One boy, only sixteen years old, who was trying to pretend he was older, was sent away by the officer with a knowing wink: 'Come back in two days when you will be two years older.' This 'army of amateurs', as Haig himself called it, was formed of men who had joined up through conviction but who quickly showed they could fight with a courage and a determination that were the admiration of their allies and enemies alike.

From the port of Boulogne, where about half the population was descended from the British, they were sent to Étaples, then Albert and onwards to the villages near the front line on the Somme. Popular songs soon combined the concept of chivalric ideals with the countryside, as in the song 'Roses of Picardy', which was sung long after the war.

Volunteers did not come only from Great Britain – they were recruited from throughout the Empire. Canadians, New Zealanders, Australians and Indians crossed the seas to fight in the trenches on the Somme. One such was the Canadian veteran Gordon Alec Boyd, who left New Brunswick, where he was born, to set sail for Europe when he was seventeen years old. He returned every year until 1998 to participate in

'*Where war has left its wake of whitened bone*
Soft stems of summer grass shall wave again.
And all the blood that war has ever strewn
Is but a passing stain.'

Leslie Coulson, *War*

'In no country of the world has so much blood been spilled as between Bapaume, Arras and Cambrai.'

Ernst Jünger

the commemorations at Vimy and in Flanders, determined never to forget the sacrifice of all those who had fallen.

After the war memorials were erected in the countryside of Picardy to honour the dead of different countries. These were often built on land that had been lost in the campaigns. The women of Newfoundland persuaded their government to buy several hectares of devastated land at Beaumont-Hamel, and a giant bronze caribou was erected on the summit of a wind-swept rock, facing towards what had been no man's land. Not far away, a few hundred metres from a tree that was petrified by gas, is a huge Scottish kilt, carved from stone, which commemorates a Highland regiment; it faces towards the remains of the German front line.

Near to Thiepval, on the summit of a hill and rising up from among the trees, is a replica of the Tower of Ulster. It was paid for by public subscription to honour the 5000 Irish soldiers who fell there within a few hours when they were holding this little mount. Near to Longueval, at Delville Wood, is a memorial commemorating 1000 young South Africans who, in July 1916, were sent to 'clean up' the wood and hold the position. South Africa bought the site and built a memorial that is surrounded with oak trees. A short distance away are New Zealand and Canadian memorials. In cemeteries of the Somme rest the bodies of not only British, French and German soldiers, but also those from Portugal, Poland and the United States. At Maurepas are Russian tombs, and at Courcelette are more Canadian graves. The great British cemetery at Pozières is surrounded by columns. Many Australians are also buried there, and the name of the little French village that stood there at the beginning of the century has since been given to a town in Queensland on the other side of the world.

▼ ▶ The British memorial at Thiepval overlooking the Ancre valley. The names of more than 73,000 missing British soldiers are inscribed on the stone pillars.

▲ The Chinese and Indian cemetery at Ayette.

'They left the equator and travelled halfway around the world, coming here to die in the cold and rain – Senegalese, Moroccans, Kurds, Chinese, Malays, Indians, Polynesians, Melanesians, Mongols and Negroes, who did not understand the password.'

William Faulkner

Near to Ayette a sunken road, barely passable in a car, leads between grassy slopes to several white pillars surrounded by low stone walls. On the pillars are inscribed, in Indian or Chinese characters, the names and sometimes the numbers of the men who were in the Chinese Labour Corps. Because the war was dragging on, both the French and British brought men from their colonies to work as labourers and do menial tasks; these men were treated as little better than slaves. The shells, however, did not distinguish between soldiers and labourers, and many of those who had spent months crossing the Indian Ocean, the Red Sea and the Mediterranean to reach the battlefields of Europe lost their lives there. In this little corner of Picardy the architecture vaguely recalls the line of a pagoda's roof, like a faint echo of their country of origin, dominating the surrounding wall, beyond which may be seen the backs of cows, grazing peacefully in the neighbouring fields.

The French army also included colonial forces from Africa, especially French-speaking North Africa, and from Indo-China. In fact, the whole world seems to have sent men to die in this corner of Picardy, where the remains of half a million soldiers rest.

Today it is almost impossible to imagine the tragedy that was played out in these lush pastures. Hundreds of little cemeteries, with lines of white gravestones surrounded by low walls, cover the countryside, and tractors drive around them. They are a reminder to us all of the events that soaked the earth here with blood. Beneath the grass mounds, decorated with roses and daffodils, lie the bodies of British soldiers, buried where they fell, next to rebuilt roads or in the middle of fields of oats or corn, which spring up here, despite the hail of bullets and shells that ravaged every centimetre of this countryside for six months.

Since the end of the 'race to the sea', the sector of the Somme had remained relatively peaceful. At the beginning of 1916, the countryside of Picardy behind the front line seemed as prosperous as it had been in peace time, even though the sound of gunfire, like the rumbling of thunder, could be heard in the distance, a reminder that the war was entering its third year.

At the end of spring the countryside was especially beautiful, with huge fields of corn as far as the eye could see. The pale green of the young crops was beginning to turn to gold, and the bright stalks rippled smoothly in the light winds. On the sides of the hills that bordered the roads bloomed bright red poppies. From the first moments of the offensive, these flowers, the colour of blood, came to have a special significance for the British soldiers, and from the terrible days of 1916 the poppy became the emblem of the Great War. Since then, the children and grandchildren of those who fell come each year to leave tributes of paper poppies

'Foreheads of men have bled where no wounds were.
I am the enemy you killed, my friend. …
Let us sleep now …'

Wilfred Owen, *Strange Meeting*

next to the white headstones or at the base of the memorials. Some throw petals into the craters left by the shells to commemorate the first day of an assault; others leave wreathes to mark the site of their pilgrimage; all come to pay homage to the hundreds of thousands of men who died in this terrible place.

From spring 1916 the area immediately behind the front line saw feverish activity. Since the end of 1914 the main British base had been the town of Albert, deserted by its original inhabitants. From their encampments, set up amid the ruins of the bombed town, now overgrown with weeds, the soldiers looked up at the gilded statue of the Virgin and Child that had once surmounted the tower of the basilica of Notre Dame de Brébières. The statue had been dislodged when the basilica was struck by a German shell in January 1915, and it now hung at an angle over the square below. Many soldiers sent home postcards of the 'Leaning Virgin', and a widely held superstition arose that the war would end when the statue fell to the ground.

In the west of Picardy roads and bridges were being built and airfields constructed. At this stage

▶ Lying in the middle of fields, one of the 410 British cemeteries on the Somme.

of the war, the Allies had mastery of the air, and gunners began to accompany reconnaissance aircraft on their expeditions, carrying out low-altitude raids on enemy trenches and firing on the German kite balloons. They also protected the planes, which had to fly slowly and in straight lines to allow the photographers to do their work. French air 'aces' had already formed elite units such as the *Cigognes* (Storks), and hangars were built to shelter the new SPADs and Nieuports that were being produced.

When observation posts were being built, the leading painters of the day were asked to help with camouflage, and the principal studio was in Amiens. Founded in 1915 by Guirand de Scévola, the number of those employed there increased steadily, and in 1916 artists such as Pinchon and Forain, sculptors such as Landowski and painters such as Braque, Dunoyer de Segonzac and André Mare added to the achievements of the workshops, which were soon producing field guns painted in a variety of colours according to the seasons of the year, imitation trees and even artificial haystacks, which were moved by night and placed near the German front line to provide shelter for observers to hide in during the day.

Hundreds of kilometres of railway track were laid to speed up the transportation of guns and ammunition to the front, and these were hidden under camouflaged tarpaulins. Factories worked flat out to deliver even more 75mm guns, the

heavy artillery needed to launch shells that would fall behind the enemy front line, and trench mortars capable of firing missiles at distances of over 10 kilometres (6 miles). The soldiers were impressed by the deployment of the powerful weapons that were found in munitions depots. Low-loaders were now bringing the first tanks, which, it was hoped, would force the Germans from the field of battle just as Hannibal's elephants had done so long before.

At the same time thousands of horses, which were needed to haul the heavy artillery, were being brought up to the front line. But it was not just the draught horses or the lancers of the Indian army that were the object of admiration in the villages through which they passed. The cavalry still played an important part in the assaults. It was always hoped that once artillery shelling had created a breach in the enemy line, a cavalry regiment would throw themselves through the gap and rid the country of the invaders. The dream always depended, of course, on their being a return to a war of movement.

While they waited, massive stocks of hay were collected for the horses and stored in the brick houses in the villages. Hay was also stored in the barns, where it was used to make palliasses

for the soldiers to sleep on. Telephone cables multiplied, and the network of trenches was extended and strengthened. The deserted schools and village halls were turned into offices and hospitals.

> *'On our return, will they believe it? Will they listen to us alone? Will they keep, at the least, the memory of death, of the countless dead?'*
>
> Ernst Johannsen

Georges Duhamel, a surgeon's assistant in Fouilloy in the south of Picardy, who had spent several months in Verdun, noticed that the countryside was being taken over by this huge army in waiting. 'Under the poplars that line the valley, an immense army is spread out like a carpet, with its battalions, its horses, its trucks, its scrap metal, its camouflaged tarpaulins, its stinking leather, its piles of rubbish. Our villages are crammed full. Soldiers are everywhere, like an illness, like a flood. … They have chased the beasts from their byres and installed themselves in the stables, in the cowsheds, in the pigsties. The countryside all around evokes a kind of sinister village fete, a fair for the war. … When I got near Chipilly I saw something strange. An immense plain seemed to undulate, covered with so many men, so much equipment and so many animals that the land was no longer visible. Around the ruined tower that dominates Étinehem a reddish-brown mass extends, like a moorland that has been scorched by fire. Much later I found that this colour was due to the masses of horses that were kept there. Every day 22,000 of them were led to drink in the muddy waters of the Somme.'

Preparations were also under way in the British camp. As in the preceding year in Flanders, coal-miners, including those from Wales, excavated galleries for 15 to 20 metres (50–65 feet) to just under the enemy lines so that they could place mines, which would explode under the German positions at the beginning of the assault. The men toiled for weeks, bent double in their narrow tunnels under no man's land, digging their way forwards metre by metre and putting the soil they had excavated into bags so that it could be taken out behind them. The

◀ A British trench.

miners relied on those above ground to keep the air pumps working, and they feared above all that a shell falling on the ground over them would cause them to be buried alive.

The Germans were installed in the high land that marked the edge of the plain of Picardy, from where the plateau rolled westwards to the sea. They held Beaumont-Hamel, Thiepval, Pozières, where there was a windmill, Fricourt, Montauban, Combles, Maricourt and the hills, which rose to scarcely more than 100 metres (330 feet); from those slopes, however, the German artillery was able to inflict terrible losses on the enemy below. The Allies believed that, with the large amount of fire-power they had amassed, they would be able to take the German defensive positions and that all the infantry would have to do would be to advance into the abandoned territory.

That view, however, failed to take account of the skill shown by the Germans. They had had eighteen months in which to dig, drill, reinforce and strengthen their trenches with concrete. Like industrious ants they had transformed every house into a stronghold and had reinforced their dug-outs, linking them to each other with underground tunnels, as they had done in Artois, but on a much greater scale. Under the hills they had created shelters that were so deep that the men in them had every reason to feel safe. 'Our great pride lies in our builders,' wrote Ernst Jünger in *In Stahlgewittern* (1920, *The Storm of Steel*). Jünger found himself in the front line at Monchy in the weeks before the offensive was launched. If the airmen who surveyed the German front line on their reconnaissance flights thought that the village looked like a heap of abandoned ruins, beneath ground life was relatively comfortable. 'Every night I rested in my dug-out with my little desk, either reading or, if some colleagues visited, gossiping. There were four officers. Every day we would take coffee or sometimes eat our dinner in one or other of our quarters, washing the food down with a bottle or two. Then we'd smoke or play cards.'

This life was very different from that endured in the muddy British trenches, which

◀ One of the little woods on the north slopes of Hangar-en-Santerre where the defenders withstood the enemy attack.

were only about 2 metres (6 feet) deep. Here, the dug-outs were on the same level as the trench walls and were badly protected from shells. When, after several months of fighting, the British had taken a few dozen square kilometres of land from the enemy, they found much to admire in the organization of the German fortifications. 'Travelling around the conquered territory,' wrote John Buchan, 'one feels respect for the work of the beavers of the German army. ... The shelter at Fricourt had nine rooms and five escape routes. It was furnished with wooden doors and anti-gas screens, the soil was covered with linoleum and the walls with wallpaper. There were even pictures on the walls, a fine bathroom and electric lights and bells.'

Thiepval was one of the sites where the Germans had concentrated their defences, and it was surveyed from several observation posts, including from the spire of the church at Pozières. As far as the summit of the hill – still wooded – which rose from the sides of the little River Ancre, every house in the village had been transformed into a dug-out and the château and its cellars were now a fortress. But below the surface of the ground – and the British had no suspicion of this – three levels had been excavated. The deep underground shelters could accommodate 5000 men, and they were linked to each other by twenty-five separate roads leading to redoubts, which had been named Leipzig, Schwaben and Stuff, names that continued to be remembered with sadness and

terror by the survivors of the Allied assault that was launched against this stronghold. It was here that the results of the disaster of the first days of the attack were the most tragic, and Thiepval became symbolic of the rout. The emplacement in the ancient château is today the site of the great British memorial, consecrated to the memory of all those who disappeared on the Somme. The imposing red brick arch, which is visible from afar, has sixteen pillars on which are inscribed the names of 73,412 soldiers whose bodies were lost in this area and who have no other tombstone.

The Germans were expecting a huge offensive on this section of the front, and they had strengthened their forces with elite troops. 'On 16 June,' wrote Ernst Jünger, 'the general sent us to our unit after making a short speech, from which we concluded that preparations were being made for a major operation on the Western Front. ... It was the Battle of the Somme that was casting its first shadows. It marked the end of the first period of the war and the hardest. We were about to embark on a completely new sort of war. What we had known until then, without having been aware of it, was the attempt to win the war by pitched battles in the old style and the development of this attempt into a static war. Now it's the battle of materiel that we're waiting for, with the deployment of fantastic amounts of equipment.'

The British artillery began a bombardment on 24 June; this bombardment was heavier than

▲ Lochnagar Crater at La Boisselle on 1 July.

decided to prolong the bombardment by two days, until 30 June. On that day a young German volunteer, Freiwiliger Eversmann, wrote in his journal: 'Haven't we suffered enough under this horrific shelling? Our heads are like those of madmen; our tongues cleave to our palates. There is virtually nothing to eat or drink. No sleep. We are cut off from all contact with the outside world. We have no news from our families, and we can't send the least word of how we are living to those we love. How worried they must be about us! How long is this going to last?'

The commanders, both British and French, were satisfied with the results of the artillery bombardment. On 30 June Douglas Haig wrote: 'The men's morale is splendid. ... Trenches have never before been so thoroughly demolished.' At the north of the front was the 'new army', which would attack the fortified sector. The French and other British soldiers would follow them two hours later on the southern flank of the front. The officers had to stay up that night so that they could properly supervise the young recruits who had no experience of combat. The British general staff was so certain that events would happen as they had planned that they gave instructions that the men should advance at walking pace across no man's land.

On 1 July the brilliant dawn promised that the day would be hot. At half past six in the morning a huge artillery barrage fell on the German positions. In the Allied trenches the soldiers got their equipment and drank some tea or coffee while they were perched on their firing ledges. They were confident, despite the distress the bombardment had caused, by preventing them from talking to each other, because it was going to make their advance easier. At twenty past seven

any that had gone before. Sadly, it is a fact that in this war, each new offensive was greater than any that had gone before. Each time, in effect, the soldiers went further in their terrible fury, showing a rage for destruction that used more and more weapons and an increasingly complex technology. There were guns every 18 metres (60 feet), and 1.5 million shells were fired in five days along a front 35 kilometres (21½ miles) long. Where the shells fell, the vegetation was killed and the ground was so contaminated that eighty years later pieces of metal are still being dug up.

'The horizon was filled with so many canons that people could hear a continual rumble, just as if a huge kettle was boiling furiously on a brazier,' recalled Georges Duhamel. The bombardment lasted for five days and nights in June, and towards the rear of the front line it was possible to hear the continuous roar of the canons. The soldiers in the trenches of the front line found the noise unbearable. When he was at Monchy Ernst Jünger discovered that he was quite close to the northern edge of what was to be the future offensive and he experienced the intensity of the shelling to which his sector was being subjected. 'Spherical mines, both light and

heavy, bottle mines, shrapnel, mortars, shells of all kinds – I could no longer distinguish among them in the noise, buzzing and bursting all over the place. I was completely deafened by the hellish sounds, which were accompanied by flames.' He saw a line of soldiers who had been overcome by gas standing before a first-aid post. 'They were holding their sides, moaning and vomiting, while the tears streamed down their faces. Everywhere, in the mess of ruins, stood those who had survived, and you could hear them repeating, over and over again, "The gas. The gas." Under the light of the shells a dazzling river ran across the black craters left by the ruined walls.'

Because bad weather had made it difficult to observe the results of the shelling, the Allies

'There is no way out. By the light of a shell I risk a glance over the meadows. It looks like a raging tide: the flames of missiles gushing like jets of water. It would be impossible for anyone to cross it.'

Erich Maria Remarque

◄ The British attack on 1 July.

► The site of the fighting at Beaumont-Hamel, in which some 700 Newfoundland soldiers died, has been transformed into a memorial park.

everything stopped for an instant. For one minute silence reigned over the ravaged countryside. Then came the explosion of 18 tonnes of dynamite in a mine under Beaumont-Hamel. At half past seven several other explosions of an incredible violence tore into the blue sky, tearing up the ground under the German trenches and hurling sandbags and pieces of wood into the air, along with the men who were there. The attack on the Somme had begun.

The British sappers exploded a dozen mines under the German lines, and the enormous holes created strange patterns in the countryside that are visible eighty years later. At La Boisselle the column of earth, mixed with human remains, rose 120 metres (400 feet) in the air, leaving a crater about 100 metres (330 feet) deep. The explosions that were set off that summer morning were heard on the other side of the Channel, even in London.

At half past seven, to the sound of the officers' whistles, 66,000 British soldiers got over the parapet and advanced confidently towards the German lines. At La Boiselle the bagpipers of the Tyneside Scottish Brigade accompanied their infantry as they advanced towards the barbed wire in front of the Germans, who were, they believed, all dead. At Fricourt an officer kicked a football, which the men passed to and fro as they advanced. At Thiepval the soldiers crossed the green valley of the River Ancre and began to ascend the slopes of the hill so that they could occupy the enemy trenches, which they believed would be empty.

Then, suddenly, there was slaughter. Secure in their underground shelters, the Germans had hardly suffered at all from the shelling, and they emerged from the dug-outs armed with their Maxim machine-guns, which could fire more than 450 bullets a minute. They calmly aimed their guns at the ranks of men who were walking up the hill towards them and had only to open fire on the pitiable sacrifice.

Wave after wave of British soldiers crossed no man's land. Corporal W.H. Shaw (quoted by Lyn Macdonald) wrote: 'Our lads were mown down. They were just simply slaughtered.' Another survivor, F.P. Crozier, later recalled the first morning of the battle: 'We set off at walking pace. I could see rank after rank of English soldiers lying dead, dying or wounded in no man's land. Here and there I could see an officer urging on the men who were following him. Sometimes I could see hands going up and a body falling on the ground. The shells and smoke made it difficult to see. We advanced. I looked again towards the south and saw clusters of British bodies hanging on the German barbed wire. The living advanced in regular formation to smash the spider's web through sheer weight of numbers. We advanced. I lost sight of the Rifle Brigade who were cut down like ears of corn before a scythe.'

A German soldier, Karl Blenk, remembered what he had seen: 'When the English started to advance … we were very surprised to see them marching – we hadn't seen anything like it before. They were everywhere; hundreds of them. The officers marched in front. I noticed that one of them was walking calmly forwards, a cane in his hand. After we had begun to fire we had to reload again and again. They fell by the hundred. It wasn't difficult to see them; we only needed to fire into the crowd.' A German officer at Ovillers wrote: 'The lines of English infantry kept on coming towards our line, like the sea against a cliff.'

The British suffered the greatest losses at the north of the front line. In just a few minutes entire regiments disappeared. Of the 800 men of the Newfoundland Regiment, 700 fell in forty minutes at Beaumont-Hamel. At Thiepval the scale of losses was unbelievable, and the soldiers who made it to the German line were cut to pieces on the barbed wire, which was virtually undamaged. The Ulster Division somehow managed to get as far as the enemy trenches and advance for 3 kilometres (almost 2 miles) against the German line, but they were soon being attacked from the sides and rear and were trapped between the German machine-guns and the British barrage. In just a few hours more than 5000 men had been cut down on the sides of the hill, where today stands the tower that was erected in their honour.

By half past eight, an hour after the beginning of the offensive, more than 30,000 were dead or wounded. Nevertheless, more than 100,000 more were sent into the attack in the hours that followed. On the next day the extent of the losses began to sink in: 60,000 in a single day, of whom half were dead.

In Britain the effect of that first day of July, the bloodiest in the country's history, was traumatic. The shock was perhaps even greater because it was felt on a local level, where the battalions had been raised. In towns across the country groups of friends, many of whom had grown up together, had joined up on the same day and had disappeared in a single day in no man's land. The young men in some villages had

▲ ▼ 1 July 1916.

▼ Everyday life in the British trenches.

been decimated. London itself lost 5000 men on that one day.

The memory of that morning haunted the survivors, and even two or three generations later the name of the Somme continues to have a resonance for the British of an incomprehensible human disaster. From that day the war began to be regarded by those who, despite everything, continued to fight as mass destruction of an unacceptable kind.

Meanwhile, the offensive continued, day after day, week after week, for six months. The 'big push' anticipated by the generals developed, like other offensives in this war, into a war of attrition, but one that lasted longer than the others and cost more lives.

In the first days the British retook a few villages, but the gains were insignificant. Fricourt, a salient in the German line, was taken by troops under Major Rappert but at such cost that six cemeteries had to be built near the village. The major himself was killed in the assault, and after the war the villagers used tractors to outline the position of his grave because they regarded him as a hero. From the field where he was first buried, his body was transferred to a small cemetery, where he now lies surrounded by his men. A street in the village is named after him, and a plaque commemorating him has been placed on one of the walls in the rebuilt church, just below a statue of Joan of Arc.

The village of Montauban was taken during the first hours of the attack, and this was followed by Mametz. It was another ten days before the nearby wood was taken by a Welsh division, which lost a quarter of its men in the process. 'There wasn't a tree that hadn't been damaged by shells,' wrote Robert Graves, who stayed in the area several months later. Today, the slope is covered with tall trees, which have regrown in the peaceful countryside, and in the fields of newly mown hay, which seem from a distance to resemble an English lawn, stands a statue of a red dragon, the emblem of Wales. But what could the mythological Celtic dragon achieve against the fire belching from the mouths of modern guns? Its feet caught in strands of

barbed wire, the dragon now faithfully keeps guard over the wooded slope where so many sons of Wales were lost.

To the south of the front the French and the rest of the British forces sustained less severe losses than their comrades in the valley of the Ancre. On the first day they were able to take the German front line, taking a number of prisoners and advancing about 10 kilometres (more than 6 miles) towards Péronne, although they could not cross the Somme, which lay between them and the town. Several villages were taken quite quickly; one of the most important was Dompierre – or, at least, what was left of it. A survivor described what he saw: 'People spoke of a sea, whose enormous waves suddenly congealed, and the most extraordinary collection of debris would rise to the surface: pieces of stone, buckled metal, crushed beams, bricks, bits of wall, clothes … wheels, smashed vehicles, everything mixed up together, higgledy-piggledy. Some black stumps would rise up: the church, perhaps, with the cemetery turned upside down like everything else.'

Then Curlu, Frise and Herbécourt were retaken. On 4 July the Foreign Legion seized Belloy-en-Santerre after terrible fighting in which more than 700 men were killed and 750 taken prisoner, a greater number than were left to continue fighting. The streets of Catalonia and Barcelona, strangely named in this village of northern France, recall the part played by Spanish volunteers in the Legion during the village's liberation in 1916. A young American volunteer also fell at Belloy. Alan Seeger had written his poem 'Rendezvous' just a few weeks before: 'I have a rendezvous with Death … I shall not fail that rendezvous.' His body was never found, but his poem lives on.

The advances made in the south in the first few days of July created the illusion that it would be possible to break through the German line. For three years the dream of 'piercing' the enemy line had held the French general staff in thrall. Joffre travelled to Méricourt, and Fayolle, always more sceptical than the other generals, noted in his journal: 'He has already seen victory and wants to bring up the cavalry. … We have taken 12,000 prisoners and seventy guns; the English

have 7500 [prisoners] and 24 [guns]. But the English already have 70,000 men under the ground, and they will not reach as far as the second German line.'

The attack on the Somme had a significant influence on the overall direction of the war. To withstand the ferocious Allied attack, the Germans were forced to transfer troops from Verdun, thereby slackening their grip on the exhausted French soldiers, who had opposed them for five months. Just as General Fayolle was writing in his journal, the Germans were attacking the fort at Souville, which marked the further point of their advance. It was now the turn of the Germans at Verdun to be on the defensive.

On 14 July, while British troops were cheering the French national day on the Champs-Élysées, their soldiers at the front were taking Longueval and Trônes Wood and coming up against the German second line. At Delville Wood (Bois Delville) the South Africans attacked for the first time in Europe. Of the 4000 men sent to capture the little wood, only 143 soldiers survived unharmed. They called it Devil's Wood.

On 20 July a new joint offensive was launched by the British and French. There was fighting at Pozières, Guillemont, Cléry and Hem Monacu, where the farm had been turned into a fortress, surrounded by machine-guns hidden in the reeds of the nearby marsh. The painter Otto Dix, who was in the German trenches, fought opposite (although he did not know it) Pierre Mac Orlan, who was based a few kilometres away in the Bois des Berlingots, where he was wounded at the end of August. 'This tragic plain unfolds before my eyes, this dirty little wood on my right, and this beautifully laid-out road, which leads to hell in all directions.' From where he was he could see the road to Bapaume; he wrote a song about it after the war.

The offensive developed into a series of isolated assaults, which did not fool the men involved about the overall situation. Each day the number of casualties increased. Jean Cocteau, who was a stretcher-bearer, helping to carry the wounded to temporary hospitals until they could be taken away from the front line by train, saw the never-ending line of blood-stained men. 'In this cataclysm,' he wrote to his mother, 'it is abnormal to be either well or safe.'

Georges Duhamel was by now a surgeon in one of the hospitals at the front, which was next to a cemetery. 'All those who fall between Combles and Bouchavesnes end up here,' he wrote in

> 'What passing-bells for these who die as cattle?
> – Only the monstrous anger of the guns.
> Only the stuttering fires' rapid rattle.
> Can patter out their hasty orisons.'
>
> Wilfred Owen, *Anthem for Doomed Youth*

Civilisation. 'You could see more wounded men here than you have hairs on your head, and more blood runs through here than there is water in the canal … The evening I took up my duties here, something had been happening in the region of Maurepas and Le Forest; it was between two days of intense fighting, one of those episodes that barely merits a mention when the communiqué is being prepared. The wounded didn't stop arriving all night.'

For wounded soldiers, hospital represented the ultimate hope – if only they could get that far. In his novel *Bob bataillonnaire*, Pierre Mac Orlan includes a probably autobiographical passage: 'Bob saw Cappy-sur-Somme again and its multicoloured barracks. Someone had given him an injection in the ambulance on the way to Feuillères. … Every turn of the wheels towards the clearing hospital at Marcelcave was balm on his wounds and brought him a joy that could be known only by soldiers who had also been wounded or by those who were condemned to death and were reprieved when they were at the foot of the scaffold.' Managing to reach the first-aid post and, from there, eventually arriving at hospital did not in itself guarantee safety, however. Surgery, like the transportation of the wounded, continued, month after month, to make remarkable progress. Nevertheless, the new weaponry caused many wounds that could not be healed.

Georges Duhamel had been at Verdun, and

his experiences there had made him believe that he was inured to what he saw, but he now found that he could never get used to the horror and torment around him. Every day he saw dying men who believed they could be saved, and he made superhuman efforts for the suffering men whose lives were slipping away. Contrary to what

he wanted to believe, it was not always individual strength that mattered. Too often he was impotent in the face of the agony of men who were no longer able to control themselves. 'In the beds that have been provided through public support, injured men wait for decisions about their future. The beds are white, the dressings are neat; many faces are smiling, waiting for the moment when fever will make them turn red or when that same fever will make all the wounded people throughout the continent begin to shake.'

> 'Cursed be the day my mother brought me into the world.'
>
> Otto Dix

Duhamel came across men who seemed ageless and those who had been spared in their first brush with death. Men who had been gassed coughed up their lungs day after day, their burns so bad that it was impossible to touch them; some had gangrene that made even the kindest orderlies go outside to vomit because the smell was so vile. Some continued to hope, despite everything, while others understood immediately what would happen. There were men who were sent home safe but blind; and there were those who had to sacrifice a limb if they were to be saved. Some of these smiled nervously when the doctor explained to them that they would have an artificial leg and would be able to walk again. Some men did not speak, nor did they smile; some

of them could only stare at the ceiling, cut off from their comrades in their suffering and tense with the effort of holding themselves back from that indescribable point from which they would ultimately set out alone on the ocean of misery.

Many wounded men accepted their lot in silence, struggling in the shadows of their solitude against a death that they believed they could delay, and they held on for weeks and even months. There were men who no longer had hands to feed themselves; some no longer had jaws, but they did not give up the struggle because help was available.

In *La Vie des martyrs* Georges Duhamel wrote about one of the wounded men. 'He carried on his own war with the sublime patience of a man who has followed the great world war and who knows that victory will not come immediately.' He described the end of some men and the recovery of others, bearing witness to the infinite misery and the extraordinary nobility of all those unknown soldiers.

Throughout the summer the offensive continued to be played out in muddled attacks, and the official communiqués became monotonous. They all omitted to mention for the benefit of the population behind the lines the numbers of dead and wounded.

The only events widely covered in the newspapers were the exploits of the airmen. Aerial combat was increasing, and René Fonck, who had the greatest number of successes in the whole war, brought down a hundred aircraft over the Somme. Even more popular was Georges Guynemer, who had not been able to fight at Verdun but who performed numerous heroic actions and would then bring down his plane on the flat ground bordering the woods at Cachy.

The Allies had more aircraft than the Germans, and they carried out regular bombing raids, 'hedge hopping' over the enemy trenches. For the first time in the autumn of 1916, in response to the bombardment of British towns by Zeppelins and the new Gothas, the British undertook strategic raids on the industrial complex on the River Sarre.

During reconnaissance flights, airmen photographed the sectors around the front, a part of the countryside that had become unrecognizable, almost unreal, but that, since the increased use of artillery at Verdun and, later, on the Somme, has become indissolubly associated with this war.

'The countryside is unforgettable, even for someone who has seen it only once,' wrote Ernst Jünger. Just a short time before, this had been a land of fields, woods, plains and villages; now it was, quite literally, impossible to find a small shrub; there was nothing but bits of straw. Each handful of earth had been turned over and over again; the trees had been uprooted, cut into pieces and ground to dust; the houses had been blown up and smashed to pieces; the hills had been flattened; and once-fertile farmland had been turned into deserts.

The fauna and flora had been affected badly. 'Moles were rare because the soil through which they dug had become so hard and filled with roots, and troops of smelly rats colonized the trenches and cellars in villages. When the night guard went on duty down the overgrown streets, they could sense the presence of the swiftly rushing silent horde.'

It was still necessary to live, even though both camps were increasingly discouraged. The British produced more and more instances of gallantry, but they were becoming ever more critical of the war in general and of the military high command in particular. The Somme brought an end to whatever illusions they may have had. Apropos British losses in the summer, Fayolle noted: 'There are 120,000 men to conquer three or four villages, and there are many more villages as far as the Rhine! ... My men are worn out; they can barely stay awake. They are fed up with having to keep on killing without achieving any decisive result.'

The Germans had had to recruit some very young troops, and adolescents were being plunged into the brutality and madness of the 'war of steel'. The soldiers began to resent the shortages that the Allied blockade was causing at home, and even the army itself was suffering from shortages of food, because reserves were kept for use by civilians. The number of prisoners was growing too, and the number of soldiers who were surrendering was worrying the chiefs of staff, who could not always launch counterattacks. Within Germany itself the situation was becoming increasingly difficult, and on 3 August marines mutinied at Wilhelmshaven on the North Sea, presaging the revolution that ended the Austro-Hungarian Empire in 1918.

On 31 August the Allies launched a new large-scale attack. The assault began after an artillery bombardment that lasted for three days. 'The artillery fire that rumbled and thundered around us was of an intensity that we had never imagined to be possible,' wrote Ernst Jünger. 'Thousands of flashes of light transformed the horizon into a burning sea of flames. An endless stream of wounded men was taken behind the line, their faces pale and drawn. Many of them had been tossed into the trenches by gunfire or by the explosions of shells, which went off all at once and with a terrific noise.' The intensity of the sound was ear-splitting. Around Combles, one of the mostly heavily defended points on the German line, 'hundreds of loud explosion were detonated, with countless shells, screaming and whining, passing in front of us. Everything was enveloped in a thick, dark fog, which was lit by flashes of various colours. Our heads ached and we had terrible pains in our ears. ... There was a sense that what was happening was inevitable and necessary, as if we were in the presence of uncontrollable elements. In the third line one of the officers went mad.'

When the men had to be brought up to the front line under enemy fire, there was no question of their stopping for those who had been wounded. 'The men fell as they ran,' continued Ernst Jünger. 'We threatened them at gun point to make a last effort with their poor, tired bodies. To left and right the wounded were falling into the craters, crying out in distress, but no one took any notice of them. The men marched forward, looking only at the man in front. We advanced along a trench that had been created by a series of enormous shell holes; the dead were waiting there, lying from wall to wall. It is the most awful sensation to feel their bodies give way under your feet. Anyone who was wounded and fell as we advanced was likely to be trampled on by those who hurried on behind.'

In many places it was impossible to distinguish between the Allied and the German dead. 'The sunken road and the land behind it were covered with German bodies; the land in front was covered with English bodies. Arms, legs and heads rolled down the slope. In front of our dug-outs were limbs and dead men, over whom we threw coats or pieces of canvas so that we weren't constantly aware of being watched by these grim faces. Despite the heat, no one even considered stopping to cover the bodies with earth.'

'*"I hope," said Ancelle, who was looking at the innumerable little crosses, some grouped in cemeteries, some standing alone. "I hope that the land that the dead reconquered will be consecrated to them and that the countryside will remain as a huge cemetery, which children will visit to learn to worship heroes."*

"What an idea," said the doctor. "There can be no doubt that the graves will be respected, but around them a fine harvest should be gathered in two years' time. This earth is too rich to remain barren. Look at the wonderful display of cornflowers growing on the craters, the scars of which can hardly be seen."'

André Maurois, *The Silence of Colonel Bramble*

► The countryside of the Somme today.

'The brutal subjugation of individual life to a single will, without any chance of appealing against it, could be seen here in all its a stark cruelty. The fighting took place on a grand scale, against which the fate of the individual was as nought.'

Ernst Jünger

The Allies achieved some success, taking fortified positions that had previously been in German hands. Guillemont was taken, a village that 'was indistinguishable from the surrounding countryside because the shell holes there were a whitish colour, like the shattered remains of the stone-built houses.' Bouchavesnes fell next, and then Combles and Thiepval after three months' fighting.

For the first time, on 15 September, the British used tanks in the battle. These tracked vehicles (to which the French gave the code name *réservoir* in order to confuse enemy espionage) had been developed in the hope that they would be able to advance over terrain in which there were deep shell holes and over barbed wire entanglements to get to the trenches. Perhaps, it was thought, they would be the means of getting away from a static war. On that first day in September forty-eight tanks were used on a front 10 kilometres (about 6 miles) long near to Courcelette. Eighteen of them got bogged down in the clay soil, but their armour plating changed the nature of the war. In September the rain began to fall, turning the field of battle into a quagmire. Rain fell for twenty days in October. The poor soldiers had to fight under a grey sky in a cesspool that swallowed up men, horses and machines. These were the last spasms of this offensive, but thousands of men were nevertheless still being forced to fight each other, even though they didn't hate each other.

In November, before his forces were entirely exhausted, Haig decided to call a halt to the offensive. The cost was monstrous: 1,200,000 men were dead or were wounded. The Allies had suffered the most severe losses, for territorial gains of just 200 square kilometres (77 square miles) and the remains of twenty-five villages in five months.

Little by little, the countries that were involved in the fighting were losing all their young men. The problem of finding people to fill the ranks of the military was common to all the countries involved. Ludendorff regarded the Somme as the worst test of the German army, but it was the British who paid the heaviest price in terms of the numbers of men lost.

The Somme changed people's attitude to war. 'The excitement and attraction of war were no more,' wrote Ernst Jünger. Not only was war now a question of equipment and machinery, but it also involved entire countries. 'The chivalric spirit has completely disappeared today.' It really was the end of one world and the beginning of the modern era. It was here that 'the new Europe' appeared and here that the machine became the master. 'The immensity and the awful solitude of the battlefield, the distance over which the metal weapons struck and the concentration in the night of all the troop movements have given the events a kind of giant, impenetrable mask. Men face death without being able to see where it is; they fall without knowing from where the blow comes. For a long time war has been conducted according to precise rules and with the straightforward firing of cannons, just like a duel, but this has given way to the massive fire-power of the machine-gun and concentrations of artillery. ... Combat was nothing more than a brutal collision of two masses, in which the production of materiel leads to blood-stained battles.'

Men from all sides felt morally outraged. 'We can do no more,' wrote Ludwig Renn. 'We will never return to Germany! In a few days we will be prisoners in France or lying dead at the bottom of some trench, and our comrades will step over our bodies.'

The men felt utterly exhausted by this crushing of the individual, which happened to all, from the lowliest soldier to the men in the elite corps. On the banks of the Somme many descendants of the great generals of the Empire fell in fighting that did not decide anything more significant than the battles in which their famous ancestors had fought. The young Prince Murat, who had joined up as a volunteer, was killed in August 1916 at Lihons, where his solitary tomb stands at the edge of a little wood. Laurent de Gouvion-Saint-Cyr was killed from a wound to the head in November at the age of twenty. In August he had written to his sister: 'I have made the greatest sacrifice.'

By the end of the offensive the countryside was laid waste in all directions. André Maurois, who served as an interpreter in the British army, travelled through the scenes of the fighting. 'The three friends travelled slowly across the silent plains, which a few months before had been the site of the terrible fighting on the Somme. As far as the eye could see, the softly rolling hills were covered with abundant wild flowers, clumps of mutilated tree trunks, which marked the position of famous woods, and millions of poppies, which gave to these dead plains a warm, coppery sheen. A few beautiful roses continued to bloom in this desert, beneath which lay an entire nation of the dead. Here and there were stakes bearing painted

'Dear Mother,
No man's land is like a body pockmarked by a foul infection. The smell is like the stench of a cancer. Under the snow it looks like the face of the moon, confusing, riddled with craters, uninhabitable, a monstrous abode of madness.'

Wilfred Owen

▲ The monument to the Welsh in Mametz Wood.

notices like those that can be seen on station platforms, recalling the names of villages that were unknown yesterday but that today are counted with Marathon and Rivoli: Contalmaison, Martinpuich and Thiepval.'

At the end of the war the inhabitants returned to an area where more than ten shells had fallen on each square metre (10 square feet). Many of those that had not exploded remained in the soil, coming to the surface week after week. While they waited for the reconstruction to begin, which was often done with the aid of the Allies who had fought there, the villagers lived in tin shacks, disinterring dead British soldiers at the rate of three francs a body. The British government, from a concern for equality, decided that

no bodies would be repatriated. The dead were regrouped according to where they fell and reburied in one of the 410 British cemeteries on the Somme.

The Battle of the Somme had sapped the morale of all the combatants. In this technological madness there was more than ever before a sense of the absurdity that had crushed everyone. In December 1916 Henri Barbusse received the Prix Goncourt for his novel *Le Feu* (*Under Fire*, 1917), a diatribe against war. In Britain the Somme was a revelation of a reality that never again brought forth the intrepid enthusiasm that had driven so many young men to volunteer. Disillusion or disgust was expressed in the verse

that stands among the masterworks of the twentieth century. Both Robert Graves and Siegfried Sassoon fought on the Somme. Their writings, like those of Wilfred Owen, whom Sassoon met in 1917 when they were both in hospital in Scotland, had a profound effect on public consciousness.

While they were fighting and confronted with the madness of the war, many British soldiers were anxious to record their experiences for future generations and to warn them. They wanted to record their memories so that they would be preserved. Only if the events of the war were written down would the suffering endured by all those who had taken part in the war never be allowed to fade from memory.

1917

Verdun had been a setback for the Germans; the Somme had been a setback for the Allies. Both armies were exhausted. The scale of losses worried the general staff and governments, which were also concerned by the misgivings that were being expressed at home. In addition to the other evils besetting families had to be added poverty, because the war consumed all the nations' resources. Queues waiting outside bakers' shops got longer, and coal was scarce. In Germany conditions were even more difficult than in France because of the maritime blockade imposed by the Allies. Strikes broke out in all countries. As for the soldiers, the newspapers tried to make them all into heroes, but after thirty months of fighting in monstrous conditions it was not possible to ask them to continue indefinitely to make a sacrifice whose purpose they did not understand.

'On marching men, on
To the gates of death with song.
Sow your gladness for earth's reaping,
So you may be glad though sleeping.
Strew your gladness on earth's bed,
So be merry, so be dead.'

Charles Hamilton Sorley,
'All the hills and vales along'

Everyone wanted the war to end, and there was much talk of peace, but it was difficult to give up a war that had already cost so many lives. No one was ready to give way; the slaughter would continue. The new leader of the Allied forces was General Nivelle, the victor at Verdun, and he had a wonderful plan to end the war: a new offensive.

Nivelle, who had replaced Joffre at the head of the French army at the end of December 1916, represented a new approach: he was determined to end the war of attrition. He had always believed that victory would be achieved by fire-power – as he had shown at Verdun – and now, with his second in command, General Mangin, he was determined to force back the Germans. Nivelle's key words were 'violence, brutality and speed', and his plan was to mount an assault in Picardy using a large artillery battery. Last-minute alterations to the plan, caused by a German withdrawal to new positions, meant that the centre of the attack was between Soissons and Reims, at Chemin des Dames.

◀ The plateau of Chemin des Dames.

▶ A French cemetery at the foot of the plateau.

◄ ► The fortress at Condé.

'*A flare went up; the shining whiteness spread*
And flickered upward, showing nimble rats
And mounds of glimmering sand-bags, bleached with rain;
Then the slow silver moment died in dark.'

Siegfried Sassoon, *A Working Party*

CHEMIN DES DAMES

At Deauville the weather in June in the third year of the war was fine. Young girls with flowers in their hair walked along the esplanade, laughing and flirting with the young men who accompanied them: this was the start of the summer. The girls had no doubt that the elegant young soldiers who were on a few days' leave were heroes. For a short time these men could enjoy

being there, breathing the clean sea air and not having to maintain a stiff military bearing or keep their eyes fixed on the distant horizon. In a couple of days they would have to return to their other life, where they were fighting for these girls and others like them in conditions that the girls could not understand, in the horror of a war that would not end until it had cut down all these young men, one after another, while they were in their prime.

The caricaturist Sem stayed for a few days on the coast of Normandy. In his notebooks he noted the extraordinary differences between a soldier's life and the idyllic days he spent at the seaside resorts some 200 kilometres (about 125 miles) from the front line. Sitting at the Tennis Club, sipping a cup of tea, he listened to the conversations at the neighbouring tables. In the middle of a 'light and witty discussion', a young lieutenant, 'whose mobile features had hardened' despite his youthful appearance, turned down the invitation of a young woman to play tennis the next day. He would, he explained to her, be on a different court, where 'the net was of barbed wire and the balls were much heavier'. He went on: 'Tomorrow I will be in an ugly place, … but one with a pretty name, Chemin des Dames.'

The charming name, which means Ladies' Way, was derived from the route used by the daughters of Louis XV when they were visiting their friend the Duchess of Narbonne at the Château de la Bove, a few kilometres to the south of Laon. The route had given its name not only to the ridge along which it ran but also to the wooded slopes of the massif itself, which dominated the valley of the Aisne on one side and the valley of the Ailette on the other. Around the large farms, which were surrounded by trees, the earth was deep and rich and produced bountiful harvests under the wide skies.

In June 1917, however, the fertile fields were fallow and suffering under constant bombardment of shells. Shattered tree trunks lay amid the machine-gun emplacements. The men were buried in the trenches, and those who had seen service at Verdun felt that they were living through a nightmare of equal proportions. Nivelle had launched his 'decisive' offensive three months earlier.

At the beginning of 1917, despite their reservations, the British had agreed to the French proposal to carry out a joint offensive at the salient of Noyon in Picardy. Nivelle had managed to persuade the British, who were more concerned with what was happening in Flanders, to participate in a large-scale offensive in Picardy on the conditions that they would not attack the strongest point of the line and that the offensive would be a surprise. In March the Russian Revolution happened, which risked upsetting the balance of power, since it was now going to be more difficult for Russia to maintain pressure on the Eastern Front. The United States, faced with increased German torpedo activity against its merchant shipping, voted to enter the war in April, but US forces would not be ready for operational service for several months. Nivelle wanted to act quickly to take advantage of the Allies' numerical superiority in the west.

Nivelle speeded up preparations for the offensive. The large quantity of canonry necessary was being produced, and factories were turning out 200,000 shells every day. At the end of February, however, an unexpected event occurred on the Western Front: the Germans withdrew between Arras and Soissons. They left the salient at Noyon and began to prepare a stronger position on the Siegfried Stellung – the Hindenburg Line – which allowed them to concentrate their resources on a line 70 kilometres (about 45 miles) long. As they withdrew, the Germans laid waste everything they had formerly held. 'The German troops reduced every village to just a heap of ruins as they fell back,' remembered Ernst Jünger. 'Every tree was cut down; every road was mined; every well was poisoned; every water course was damned; every cellar was blown up and then booby trapped; all railway tracks were torn up; all telephone wires were rolled up and removed; everything that would burn was set alight: in short, we turned the countryside into a desert before the enemy could advance into it.' At the same time the Germans blew up the medieval keep of the château of Coucy, one of whose lords had been killed when Joan of Arc besieged the château. Until the Germans destroyed it, the keep had served as an observation point in the war. The Allies were able to recover 200 villages, which had been utterly destroyed, and to advance for 20 or 30 kilometres (12–18 miles) into territory that had been thoroughly mined.

The British wanted to abandon the offensive because the salient at Noyon no longer existed and there was now no question of making a rapid advance against the new German line. Nivelle, however, was adamant: the only change in his plan was that the attack would be limited to 70 kilometres (about 45 miles) between Soissons and Reims, and the principal force of the assault would be concentrated on the central point of this line, at Chemin des Dames. This was despite the fact that this was probably the most heavily defended sector of the German line and a section that Joffre himself believed to be impregnable.

Nivelle was convinced that his plan would succeed. The artillery would bombard the German line, and with one bound the French soldiers

◄ The plateau of Chemin des Dames today.

◄ ▼ Munitions workers.

▲ The Canadian cemetery at Vimy; in the distance is the ossuary on the hill of Notre-Dame-de-Lorette.

would clear the slopes of the ridge and by the next day would be eating their breakfasts in Laon. He gave his word that this would happen, and in this period of uncertainty, his assurance told for much. Nevertheless, Nivelle was distrusted by both politicians and military men, including Pétain, who were not convinced that it would be an easy matter to get beyond the German line. Even General Micheler, to whom Nivelle had entrusted the command of the offensive, did not believe him.

In March General Lyautey, the French Minister of War, learned the details of Nivelle's plans from Colonel Renouard, the chief of the general staff. Alarmed, Lyautey said that he thought the plan was ludicrous. Then, as Renouard continued to outline Nivelle's scheme, Lyautey (according to André Maurois's later biography) had the following conversation. 'Renouard, you must answer me. Pretend I am no longer Minster of War and you are no longer a colonel. We are just two Frenchmen who have happened to meet and are concerned about the welfare of our country. What do you really think about this plan you have just described? ... Tell me the truth. What is your real opinion?' After a moment's hesitation, Renouard replied: 'Sir, I agree with you. It's madness.' A little while later Lyautey tendered his resignation, but he did not make public his views about the offensive, the preparations for which were already well under way. Hundreds of thousands of men had been sent to the Aisne, and the offensive was scheduled to begin on 16 April. It would be preceded by a diversionary operation from the British, who would launch an attack around Arras in Artois on 9 April.

On 6 April a council of war met at Compiègne. The British were not invited, but President Poincaré met Nivelle and his generals. In response to the alarmed questions that were put to him, Nivelle emphasized the importance of pressing ahead with the offensive given the Allied superiority of men and materiel. He had ordered the movement of 850,000 men, 5000 field guns, 200 tanks and 500,000 horses. He would seize the plain in twenty-four hours, forty-eight at most; if not, he would give up. Aware that he was opposed by some of the most senior members of the general staff, he offered to resign, but Poincaré himself asked him to stay. The British began their bombardment of Artois, and the plan was in train. The lunatic offensive was about to begin.

Hundreds of thousands of French infantrymen got ready for this great assault, which would, they hoped, bring the longed-for end to the war. The third winter in the trenches had been as uncomfortable as the preceding ones. In the north of France the temperature fell to -20°C (-4°F). Rivers froze, and soldiers in the trenches sometimes had to cut their bread with axes. From force of habit and from a belief that they would have to look out for themselves, they had done their best to make the shelters and dug-outs as habitable as possible, but, as Lieutenant Désagneaux noted in his journal: 'The men are worn out and every day they find the same thing: their billets are not ready and there is no straw. The villagers refuse to let them stay in their houses because they cannot pay them. And what awful quarters the men have to put up with! Here, they are in cob-built shelters, half demolished and open to the elements.' Letters written by civilians at this period complain of the poverty they were enduring, but, as one soldier wrote to his wife: 'We risk not understanding each other if you talk about "behind the lines" and I talk about the "front". We are making sacrifices in every aspect of our lives, in everything we do, and we soldiers would like to share our lives on this side of the front with life on the other side. ... Sugar ration? "How long is it since we had sugar?" asks the soldier. Taxes on cinema tickets? "How long is it since these boys went to the cinema?" No coal? Expensive wood? "How long has it been since we have been able to warm our feet?"'

The soldiers had been waiting on the plain since the beginning of April, looking at the slopes they would have to climb and standing in the freezing rain, which made it difficult for aircraft to carry out reconnaissance flights so that the artillery fire could be aimed accurately. Unfortunately, this had been one of the preconditions for the success of Nivelle's plan.

In their lightning advance towards Paris in August 1914 the Germans had quickly taken the land over a few hundred metres high. After the Battle of the Marne in September 1914, when they were forced to withdraw, they had established a front along the high ground, which formed a natural barrier, and neither the French nor the British had been able to dislodge them. Over the

◀ At the same time as the attack at Chemin des Dames was under way, the British began an action in Artois. At Vimy the Canadians commemorate their victorious attack on the ridge on 9 April every year.

◄ One of the statues at
the Canadian monument
at Vimy; they symbolize
the grief felt by women
during the war. This
statue faces towards the
summit of the hill on the
plain of Douai.

◄ The nocturnal
firework display of star
shells.

'The noise was so great that even the rats were rooted to the spot.'

On 9 April – it was Easter Sunday – at half past five in the morning mines were set off under the German lines. 'A great light came from countless tongues of flame, which sprang from the emptiness and spread as far as the eye could see, lighting the shadowy places. There was silence for a second. Then a huge explosion numbed all my senses. In front of us, where shells had exploded, a hill burst into flames.' In the fog and freezing drizzle 20,000 Canadians advanced from the village of Neuville-Saint-Vaast towards the slopes of the north ridge. After fighting all night, they took and held Vimy Ridge. This breakthrough, like so many others before it, was not exploited.

At the site where the Canadian troops had managed to take the ridge, which the Allies had been unable to retake in three years, a great memorial in white stone has been erected to the memory of all Canadians who fought in the war and those who died – more than 66,000 men. On it are engraved the names of the soldiers whose bodies were never found. At the base of two tall pillars, which are decorated with fleur-de-lis and maple leaves, on a massive raised area, is a stone statue of a veiled woman who weeps for those who sacrificed their lives in the war. The hill itself has been given to the Canadian people, and on it in 1922 were planted, amid the craters made by shells and mines, 11,285 fir trees and maples, one tree for every soldier who has no individual grave.

At Bullecourt the Australians led the assault. In the snow-covered ground of no man's land, however, they were the perfect targets for German artillery, which had not been destroyed by the British bombardment; there was another massacre. The fighting continued until the beginning of May, each wave of attackers dying on the barbed wire, where the bodies of their comrades from the preceding wave already lay. The Australians lost 10,000 men in this assault.

On 10 April the artillery bombardment at Chemin des Dames began. General Nivelle had gathered together 18 million shells, and he had positioned one heavy field gun every 21 metres (70 feet) along his front line. For six days and nights 5350 guns were fired non-stop at the

months the Germans had methodically transformed the line into a strongly fortified entrenchment. The terrain proved suitable for their purposes: the wooded hills were riddled with quarries, from which, in former times, stone had been removed to build the cathedrals at Laon, Reims and Soissons and all the great houses in the area. The Germans turned the quarries into proper garrisons for their men, and at Montparnasse they had even managed to get a railway track laid right into the interior of the caverns to bring supplies and munitions up to the battalions who were sheltering there.

The Germans had extended the galleries leading from the Caverne du Dragon (Dragon's Cave), from which there were seven exit routes, each bristling with machine-gun emplacements, and they had built a system of tunnels that enabled them to pass in complete safety along the entire length of the plain. They had also dug out wells, which provided drinkable water for the 6000 men who were garrisoned there, and brought in bunk beds so that the men could sleep comfortably in the dormitories. There were even a chapel, a field hospital and a small cemetery next to the munitions and provisions depots. On the surface of the plain each farm had been turned into a fortress, and every thicket hid a nest of machine-guns. In the blockhouses of the front line the Germans waited for the enemy bombardment, ready to

open fire on anyone who tried to scale the slopes. The French soldiers were, although they did not know it, confronted by an almost unassailable line. In just a few days, this crest would become, according to Louis Aragon, who took part in the offensive, 'the ridge that lived on death'.

The British attacked first. The soldiers left their labyrinthine underground quarters, which had been excavated to the depth of several levels beneath Arras. Australians and New Zealanders attacked towards Douai, while the Canadians launched a new assault on Vimy Ridge. They were able to advance safely towards the German lines, getting to within 50 metres (165 feet) of the German barbed wire thanks to the tunnels, which had been excavated in the valley many centuries before by the Huguenots and which they had extended and reinforced. The forces were concentrated in a single subterranean city, four storeys deep, with barracks, a hospital, a depot for munitions and a system for evacuating the wounded that ran through separate corridors so that the morale of the troops would not be affected by seeing their wounded comrades.

Before the attack began artillery bombarded the German positions for four days and aircraft dropped bombs on munition depots and railway stations. The attack was so violent that the Germans called up reserve troops to support them. In the Allied trenches an observer noted:

German defences. During this period the French soldiers advanced in their ditches towards their starting point, in the valley, opposite the plain. At the western end of the front were General Mangin and his colonial troops; at the east, near Berry-au-Bac, was General Mazel, who in addition to his army had 128 tanks, which had just been built by the factories of Schneider-Creusot and Saint Chamond and which were the first to be used by the French in combat conditions. The troops led by General Duchêne, who were in the centre, would follow the other two armies into the attack.

Snow was falling, and in the squally winds thousands of men set out, marching with difficulty in the crowded ditches as their feet slid about in the frozen mud. They huddled together in the sap holes and makeshift dug-outs, which they had only just managed to excavate. They did not know how many days they would have to wait there, lined up, one against another, without being able to sleep in the terrible noise of the shells, which were whistling over their heads. Nevertheless, they were reassured by the ferocity of the bombardment: this time, surely, it was impossible that the German lines could be unharmed. On 15 April they were given their orders to prepare to depart, and the men had the impression that the offensive was being carefully controlled. After the soldiers were given three days' worth of food rations – enough to last as they advanced through conquered territory – they wrote their last letters home and tried to rest a little.

General Ludendorff awaited the French attack without too much concern. The Germans enjoyed numerical superiority in the skies, and French reconnaissance flights had failed to provide sufficient information about the German line. Only about a quarter of German machine-gun emplacements had been damaged in the French bombardment, and Ludendorff had been able to bring up fresh troops from the east. Above all, he knew all the details of the French plan. Everybody in France had been talking about the 'offensive for victory' – it had even been reported in the newspapers – and General Nivelle had imprudently given copies of his plan to officers and junior officers. In a raid on 4 April the Germans had taken several prisoners, one of whom was carrying a copy of the plan. The French soldiers knew nothing of this, of course. They were cold, and they had been standing with their feet in mud – but they were hopeful. They believed that this offensive would end the war, and they had faith in Nivelle and in his second in command, Mangin, who had retaken the forts at Verdun and driven back the enemy. They set out for the attack full of confidence.

On 16 April at 5 o'clock in the morning grenades were handed out to the men, together with a double ration of alcohol. The countryside before them looked ghostlike in the early morning, with fog drifting across the ground. As usual before an attack, they joked with each to lift their spirits and to keep away bad luck, then they checked their rifles and tightened the straps of their helmets under their chins. At 6 o'clock, from Soupir to Craonne, the officers blew their whistles. The men leapt over the parapets and began to run towards the ridge. The silence from the German lines seemed to bode well, especially after the days of the bombardment when they had been unable to rest. In theory, they had three minutes to get across a hundred metres while the artillery behind them provided covering fire. However, once the artillery storm had ended, they could hear the sudden sound of machine-gun fire. Those 'invisible machine-guns', as one of the survivors called them, took the troops on both flanks. The Germans brought their guns to the surface and used them to sweep the slopes. The French soldiers lay down, trying desperately to shelter in shell holes. Those who continued to advance step by step towards the front on the steep hillsides found themselves caught in the barbed wire that had been placed among the trees. They fell, hundreds at a time, about 300 metres (330 yards) from where they had set off.

At the western end of the front, between Moulin and Laffaux, where the troops had gone into the attack at 9 o'clock, the same thing happened. To the east, the infantry struck against the mountains of Champagne, but they could not, as planned, seize the fort of Brimont and get on to the slopes of Moronvilliers. As for the tanks, that was a catastrophe: half of them got stuck in the mud and most of the others were destroyed by shells.

Some soldiers did, nevertheless, manage to reach the ridge in a few places, but then night fell, freezing and deadly. The men crouched on the slopes, trying to stay near the enemy lines, under the snow and the bullets. The losses were terrible: 40,000 men were dead or wounded in a single day. In one division of Senegalese riflemen, a large number of whom had been involved in the offensive, 6300 men out of 10,000 were killed or wounded in the first few hours.

For the wounded the situation was appalling. It had been thought that there would be 15,000 needing attention, but by the end of the first day there were 150,000 casualties, and the first-aid

► The château of Soupir, at the foot of the Chemin des Dames. It was General Pétain's headquarters.

◀ The remains of the
château of Soupir.

L'Aisne dévastée – PINON – Place de l'Eglise
The Church Place

◀ ▲ The ruined villages of Craonne (above left) and Pinon (above).

◀ The soldiers in the trenches were continually exhausted.

'*I have no more spirit; I have no more heart; there is no more blue sky; I have no more ideals left. I am nothing but bone, flesh and weapons. And the rain keeps on falling steadily on my metal helmet.*'

Jean Giono, 21 September 1917

'*We ended up marching as if we were dead, unconscious, out of order, without seeing and without thinking – like animals.*'

La Musette

posts were absolutely choked. Men were lying on the ground in the rain, while doctors tried to help them. In the hospitals behind the lines things changed dramatically – in one of them, for instance, there were 200 beds for 20,000 men. No one had foreseen such a bloody victory.

Nivelle, who had promised an uninterrupted offensive so that the French would be in Laon within twenty-four hours, was unmoved. 'Victory is more certain than ever,' he wrote, and on 17 April he renewed the attack on an even greater scale. In the next few days he achieved some isolated successes, particularly to the west of the ridge. Despite the cold, which affected them especially badly, the Senegalese troops managed to take the village of Chavonne and the slopes of the Grinons and the ruins of Vailly; the lancers took Sapin Hill, where they swept through the dug-outs with grenades, and the Bois des Gouttes d'Or, from where they were able to get up to the plain of Ostel. But these dearly bought 'victories' did not advance the French line by more than a few hundred metres, and the Germans, their artillery ready on the facing hillsides, were able to control the ridges and fire on any soldiers who tried to advance towards them.

Members of the French parliament, who had been invited by Nivelle to participate in the 'victory' of 16 April, denounced the folly of the plan and the arrogance of its proponent. Nivelle launched other attacks in the first weeks of May, and these enabled him to advance from Moulin to Laffaux and then to Craonne – where Bonaparte had fought in 1814 – to the sugar refinery at Cerny and the plain of Californie, at the edge of the Chemin des Dames, looking over the plain of Champagne. The French had managed to get up to the plateau and held a line of observation posts, but the losses for these gains had been huge. Nivelle was not superseded until 15 May, when he was replaced by Pétain, who took control of the whole catastrophic operation, about which he had always expressed reservations.

Between 16 and 30 April 147,000 men fell, of whom 40,000 were dead. The soldiers' initial enthusiasm for the offensive was followed by disaffection and feelings of horror at the scandalous loss of life. They felt that they had been sacrificed to the ambition of a vainglorious general, who had sent them to a pointless death. Some soldiers felt so bitter that they were driven to mutiny. On the walls of the Caverne du Dragon, which was eventually taken by the French on 25 June, an inscription bears witness to the feelings that swept through the French soldiers. An anonymous hand carved the words: 'No more 16 April.' Many soldiers began to refuse to obey orders, and men showed their disinclination to be involved in new attacks. Instances of indiscipline reached even as far as the front line,

front were affected, but even so, men did not abandon their posts – they just refused to attack. 'We have made our feelings clear,' said one soldier. 'We want them to understand that we are men, not animals that can be led to slaughter.'

Some of the general staff and some politicians put the blame for the mutinies on the Russian Revolution, on the pacifist ideals of civilian strikers or on defeatist feelings. For most of the men, however, it was less a matter of subversion than a protest about the way in which the war was being handled and the way in which they were simply being treated as cannon fodder.

▲ The ruins of the abbey of Vauclair, which was destroyed during the Nivelle offensive.

and officers heard cries of 'Down with war' and 'Long live peace'. The mutinous feelings spread into a general movement. In June 2000 mutineers gathered at Ville-en-Tardenois and at Villers-Cotterêts 4000 soldiers withdrew into the forest, although they eventually gave themselves up. The crisis grew more intense as increasing numbers of ordinary soldiers began to express the view that their generals had absolutely no understanding of what it was like to live in the trenches and then to have to go over the top towards the enemy lines. It was estimated that two-thirds of all French divisions serving at the

Pétain took the army in hand. Those who were believed to have instigated acts of mutiny were identified – almost 3500 courts martial were held and 544 soldiers were condemned to death, although, in the end, fewer than fifty executions seem to have been carried out. Repressive measures were exemplary but limited.

At the same time Pétain took great pains to do something about the conditions of the men at the front, especially improving the quality of their food and the standards of hygiene and their quarters. He also increased the amount and frequency of leave and rest periods for all soldiers. Above all, he suspended all offensive actions and decided to wait for the guns, tanks and Americans. The US Congress, angered by the naval war in which its own ships had been sunk, voted to enter the war on 6 April. Although the army was not yet fully mobilized, in June General Pershing arrived in Paris and the first troops of the American Expeditionary Force (AEF), who had disembarked at Saint-Nazaire, were sent for training.

Instances of insubordination continued to be seen in various parts of France, however. Lieutenant Désagneaux, for example, was at the Chemin des Dames in July, in the sector between Filain and Braye-en-Laonnois, and found himself in a billet with a battalion under a staff officer. 'When the men were ordered to get ready to advance, no one moved. The candles went out – it was a dark night – and no one fell in. Men responded to the orders they were given by sniggering or hurling abuse. ... It was impossible to see into the corners; it was a dark night. The officers, tired of being ignored, took out their revolvers and threatened their men. Rifles were immediately loaded; there was the sound of bolts being driven home on all sides. The officers began to negotiate with their men and look for

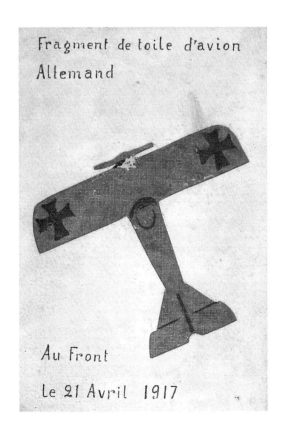

▲ The farm at Hurtebise, rebuilt on the site of the original structure, which was completely destroyed in 1917.

well-disposed soldiers who would act as an example to the others and set off as ordered. No luck. The officers got their soldiers ready themselves and made them line up one by one.'

It was not just isolated instances such as this – the wave of dissent continued to be felt throughout the summer. Pétain, who understand the dissatisfaction that lay at its root, listened to the soldiers and to their just complaints. He increased the frequency of tours of duty at the front, reported their indignation at the rubbish that was heard away from the front line and made efforts to improve the harsh reality of everyday life at the front. At long last the men began to feel that someone was listening to them, and their confidence was gradually restored.

Meanwhile, the Germans were attempting to retake the terrain that had been lost at Chemin des Dames through a counterattack. At Berry-au-Bac their sappers exploded a mine that completely destroyed Hill 108 and at the same time blew up two companies. Throughout the summer fighting continued on the eastern edge of the plain, around Craonne, in a countryside so desolate that it, like the terrain around Verdun, had come to resemble a lunar landscape. In August the French succeeded in taking the farm at Hurtebise, where, in 1814, Bonaparte had rested under the shade of a tree before defeating Blucher in 'his' battle at Craonne. In 1917 the farm was nothing but a heap of stones, and men went on dying in attacks and counterattacks.

While the British were continuing to fight in Flanders, where Haig was determined to make his own breakthrough into the German line, in October Pétain determined to return to the attack at the western end of the Chemin des Dames, an area mostly held by the Germans, and to dislodge them in a single attack. He also wanted to prove to the Allies that the French army had not completely lost its ability to fight, despite the problems experienced earlier in the year, and to restore the French infantrymen's faith in themselves. His objective was to take control of the entire line of observation points along the valley of the Ailette while also taking the plain at Laffaux and the sector around the fort at Malmaison. This fort, one of the most strongly

fortified of the German positions on the Chemin des Dames, was the site of a former stone quarry.

Pétain prepared for the limited attack with great care. Between 16 and 22 October a 12-kilometre (7½-mile) section of the German line was subjected to a bombardment by 2 million shells. Then, on the morning of 23 October, the infantry, which included a large proportion of North African troops, advanced. The Germans, who had been taken by surprise, were driven back and, an hour after the offensive began, the French had taken the fort. They then took the German positions at Moulin and Laffaux. On 25 October the Germans fell back to beyond the River Ailette, abandoning the Chemin des Dames and losing 15,000 men taken as prisoners, 200 field guns and 720 machine-guns. In this attack the Germans lost 35,000 men; 2241 French soldiers were killed. The psychological effect was as great on the Germans as on the French. 'Today we have been victorious,' wrote Lieutenant Désagneaux. 'The Germans are withdrawing, and our troops are deploying to pursue them. What a state the terrain is in. It's awful. Everything has been blown up. There are bodies everywhere – wounded

Germans and those affected by gas are dying. It is both horrific and wonderful. At the moment we are gaining on them.' The following day he wrote: 'It's a frenzy; we're taking no more prisoners; everyone has forgotten how tired he is.'

The sector remained relatively calm until the great German offensive of 1918, but the ground was terribly scarred by the months of fighting. Some trees were fossilized, and many farmers were reluctant to go back to their farms. Birds did not sing above the plains until the 1930s, when the trees began to grow new branches. Many villages were completely obliterated, and some of them – such as Craonne and Cerny – were not rebuilt on their original sites.

The Cistercian abbey at Vauclair, which had been built in the twelfth century, had been used as a munitions depot by the Germans. It was comprehensively bombarded during the Nivelle offensive, and only the ruins now remain. Visitors to the churches in the area are sometimes surprised by the Art Deco motifs they find in them; they should remember that nearly all the churches here were built between the wars.

▲ The ruins of the fort at Malmaison.

YPRES

While the fighting for the Chemin des Dames was continuing throughout most of 1917, in the far west of the Western Front General Haig, who had not been entirely discouraged by the failure of the Nivelle plan, was preparing a grand offensive of his own in Flanders around the salient at Ypres, which he believed would open the way for a cavalry attack on Berlin. He had been making his plans in this area since January. For several months miners from the north of England, who had been incorporated into Tunnelling Companies of the Royal Engineers, had been digging twenty-four tunnels between Wijtschate (Wytschaete) and Messines. They were 30–40 metres (98–130 feet) below the ground and 500 metres (550 yards) long and were built under the German line. All the mines were going to explode at the same time on 7 June. The day before, Major-General Hartington said: 'Gentlemen, I don't know whether we are going to make history tomorrow, but at any rate we shall change geography.' In fact, the course of the war was hardly changed, but the holes caused by the mining remain to this day in the countryside of Flanders. They have simply been 'recovered' to meet the needs of everyday life: they have been made into artificial ponds – albeit with a rather too regular design – to which smallholders come in the evening to fill their water trucks so that they can water their crops or to which they come during the day to water their livestock.

At exactly ten minutes past three in the morning of 7 June 1917 the mines were exploded. Only nineteen were actually set off, but they represented a total of 480 tonnes of explosive. Never before had such explosions been seen or heard – the sound even reached London and Paris. At Lille, which is about 50 kilometres (just over 30 miles) away, people said they could feel the ground tremble under their feet. On the spot, the force of the explosions completely buried German soldiers inside the dug-outs that were near to the mines, and the Allied infantry felt themselves lifted into the air. All the German defences were turned upside down, and three hours later, Allied forces, led by New Zealanders, took prisoner those Germans who were still at Messines. By the evening they had advanced by about 4 kilometres (2½ miles).

Bizarrely, Haig did not take advantage of the success. When King George V came to congratulate the troops a few weeks later, he found them still in the position they had achieved by the end of the first day. The Germans had time to regroup and were able to launch counter-attacks from their new positions.

It was six weeks later, on 31 July, that Haig went on the offensive again, this time between Dixmude and Lys. However, just when the attack was due to begin, it started to rain. People who live in Flanders say that the rain that fell in the summer of 1917 was the heaviest ever known – so heavy, in fact, that aircraft could barely carry out their reconnaissance missions and bombardments might as well have been carried out in the dark. The terrain over which the British troops were going to pass was progressively turning into a swamp. The bombardment that was supposed to prepare the way for the attack succeeded in

'*I died in hell –*

(They called it Passchendaele); my wound was slight
And I was hobbling back, and then a shell
Burst slick upon the duck-boards; so I fell
Into the bottomless mud, and lost the light.'

Siegfried Sassoon

▼ ▶ The mud of Flanders increased the suffering of the British soldiers.

▲ Australian soldiers advance beside a hole made by a mine that has filled with water.

destroying the drainage system, and muddy water began to fill the craters that were left after three years' shelling. The soldiers were sent to fight in the middle of flooded ponds, in an appalling ocean of mud in which both men and horses became hopelessly stuck up to their stomachs and were sometimes unable to get free.

Like Nivelle before him, Haig would not give up his plan. He believed that he would wear down the German army and force it to surrender. The Germans withstood the frantic bombardment, however. It was during this Third Battle of Ypres that they first used their new gas – mustard gas – which was another awful surprise for the Allied troops.

The weather improved in September. The bombardment was so intense in the sector that survivors said that it was as bright at night as it was during the day and that they could feel the ground quaking under their feet as the guns continue to sound. 'There was no way out,' wrote Erich Maria Remarque, who fought at the Bois de Houthulst. 'By the light of the shells, I risked looking over the meadows. People talked about a raging sea: the flames of the missiles spurted like jets of water.' The soldiers on both sides complained as much as those who were directing the war about the way the bad weather was prolonging the attack. The Allies eventually took the Bois de Houthulst, Poelkapelle and the Bois du Polygone.

The rain began again and a thick fog descended over the whole area, where it mixed with the smoke from the guns. The fighting had moved towards the ridge near the little village of Passchendaele, which had no significance, either strategic or tactical, but for which thousands of soldiers fought in a ghastly sea of mud in the latest battlefield. The British lost 26,000 men in a single day on 4 October. To get to the lines the men and horses had to make their way along slippery roads, pushing through the almost liquid ground and frequently disappearing before anyone could get to their help. Men sometimes had to step on bodies to prevent themselves from sinking into the mire. The night echoed in the dim half-light to moans of agony and the cries of the wounded, who could not drag themselves out of the mud and called desperately for help. An Englishman, C.A. Bill, remembered the awful nightmare from which he wanted to wake: men walked by a soldier who was choking on mud that reached up to his knees. The men could not get him out of the mud and left him there. He spent

▲ An old tank points towards the plain of Berry-au-Bac.

◀ Pages 206–7: The Lone Tree Crater was one of the huge craters left by the mine attacks of June 1917. Today it is a peaceful pool.

two more days in the same place. 'The poor man was still there; but we could only see his head and he had gone mad.' For all the men it was hell, a landscape of mud at the end of the world.

On 6 November Canadian forces managed to take Passchendaele, in which only a single wall was still standing. The Allies had advanced 8 kilometres (5 miles), but thousands of men had been lost. The British casualties totalled 300,000, of whom a third were dead, although this did not prevent Haig from being promoted to Field Marshal shortly afterwards. The Germans had lost 260,000 men.

The cemetery of Tyne Cot can be found at Passchendaele. It is the largest British cemetery in the world, and its name evokes the cottages on the River Tyne in the northeast of England, from where a large number of those who fought here originally came. The Cross of Sacrifice in the centre rises from among 11,856 tombstones and looks over the five German bunkers taken by a division of Australian soldiers in September. In addition, there are seventeen British cemeteries near the little town of Zillebeke. As you leave Ypres by the main road to the northeast, following the route of the men on their way to the battlefield, you will pass an imposing monument, reminiscent of a Roman triumphal arch: the Menin Gate. On the walls inside the arch are engraved the names of 54,896 Allied soldiers

who fell before 16 August 1917 in the Ypres salient. There was insufficient room to include the names of all those who died but were never found after that date, and their names were inscribed on commemorative plaques on the wall which surrounds the cemetery of Tyne Cot: there are 33,782 names. A further 11,451 names are recorded at the Ploegsteert Memorial to the Missing. The soldiers from New Zealand who died here are commemorated in separate memorials. In total, there are more than 600 war graves cemeteries in Belgium.

During the Third Battle of Ypres aerial combat became an ever-more significant factor in the war. The French fighter unit, the Cigognes, was still based at Saint-Pol-sur-Mer, and all the aces saw

▲ The beginnings of tank warfare.

action in the skies above Flanders. On the evening of 11 September 1917 Georges Guynemer, one of France's great heroes, was shot down over Poelkapelle; his body was never found.

The British were unable to use tanks as much as they had hoped in the fighting around Ypres because of the mud, but in November it was decided to mount a new offensive with armoured support at Cambrai in northern France, which proved how important tanks could be in the right conditions. The tanks made it possible to mount a surprise attack, without a preliminary artillery bombardment, and more than 300 were used on a front about 10 kilometres (6 miles) long. The tanks made spectacular progress, advancing 8 kilometres (5 miles) in a few hours. The Allies advanced to within 4 kilometres (2½ miles) of

Cambrai, having forced a breach in the German line and making the Germans fall back in panic. In Britain church bells were rung to celebrate the victory, but the tanks ran out of fuel and got

stuck and no reserves were available to follow up the success. Ten days later the Germans were able to mount a counterattack with their elite forces, and they retook almost all the land they had lost. The status quo was restored.

Nevertheless, the use of tanks presaged the way the war would develop in the months that followed: they made it possible to return to a war of movement.

◄ One of the earliest French tanks made in the Schneider-Creusot works.

► Pages 210–11: On Hill 62, near to Ypres, the remains of a charred tree and a number of German tombstones dating from 1914 were disturbed in the fighting in 1917.

1918

All along the front the soldiers were utterly exhausted, and this was matched by the despair that was felt by the civilian populations. Economic problems were worsening in France, where rationing was strictly enforced, and in Germany even greater hardship was being endured. The shortage of manpower was beginning to affect all the armies – the French alone had suffered a million deaths and three million wounded since 1914, and many men had also been taken prisoner. All attempts to make peace through political means in the last few months had failed, however, and it seemed that only the armies could decide the outcome of the war.

◀ Page 213: The memorial at Dormans to the victories at the Marne.

The gradual withdrawal of German soldiers from the Russian front enabled Ludendorff to increase his forces in the west. Like everyone else, he was aware of the need to end the war as quickly as possible, and he was especially anxious to bring France and Britain to their knees before American troops could become troublesome. Ludendorff decided to organize what he hoped would be the decisive offensive in March 1918. He did not use new troops but he did change his tactics: he mounted a surprise attack. A brief, but exceptionally brutal, artillery bombardment would be followed by waves of elite troops, who would open the way for the remainder of the army. In fact, throughout 1918 the offensives launched by Ludendorff were largely resisted by Allied counterattacks.

A series of particularly bloody battles was fought almost without respite from March to

November in the area lying between the Scheldt and the Meuse. On 21 March the Germans attacked in Picardy, between Arras and La Fère, on a line running through Saint Quentin, with the intention of separating the French and British forces there. The Germans advanced for 30 kilometres (18½ miles), laying waste the ground they covered. Differences of opinion began to emerge between Haig, who wanted to protect Amiens and the Channel ports, and Pétain, who wanted to protect Paris, no matter what the cost. It was clear that the Allies needed a single commander, and after a conference at Compiègne, followed by a further meeting at Doullens on 26 March, the governments and general staffs of both countries agreed that the armies would be under the overall command of Foch. When Clemenceau congratulated him on

▼ In the forest of Saint Gobain can still be found the concrete base from which 'big Bertha' could fire shells from a range of 120 kilometres (75 miles).

his appointment, Foch replied: 'A fine gift; you give me a lost battle and tell me to win it.'

On the ground the situation remained critical. The Germans entered Montdidier, retaking territory from which they had voluntarily withdrawn in 1917, and they crossed the Somme, taking the land that had been so dearly defended by the Allies in 1916. Antoine Grillet, a French solider, who was with a unit that was trying to withstand the onward rush of the Germans but was continuing to fall back, wrote: 'We cross woods and fields. ... I am so tired I feel like a rag that has been wrung out. I haven't taken off my boots for six days. It's as if a black pit will open up and swallow everything around me. This is what we've got after four years of fighting! Everything seemed to be strong, but an army of our allies has vanished without trace.' In the end, the Allies managed to prevent the Germans from advancing further but at a cost of 250,000 men.

The war of the trenches was gradually coming to an end, but the new ways of fighting were, if possible, even more costly in terms of lives and required ever-more powerful artillery.

On 24 March a German shell landed in Paris. It was fired from the forest of Saint Gobain in the Aisne valley, some 120 kilometres (75 miles) away, and it hit the church of Saint Gervais during a service; ninety-one people were killed and sixty-eight wounded. The German threat now menaced civilians. More heavy guns, the 420mm howitzers known as 'big Berthas', specially manufactured by Krupp, bombarded Paris, killing 256 people. The Gothas, heavy German bombers, carried out night-time raids over Paris, causing widespread damage and killing many civilians.

On 9 April the Germans began a second attack intended to breach the Allies' line in Flanders. On the first day the Portuguese, who were holding the line in the region of Armentières, gave way almost immediately, and the ridge at Messines was also taken. 'Burning barns covered everything with a thick red fog,' wrote Jean Giono. 'Everywhere, the ground was laid bare. ... The Germans were advancing

▲ Children in the streets of Paris.

▼ An anti-aircraft battery.

without fighting. There was no more noise, except for the loud rumbling of masses of men marching across the grass and stones and through the woods.'

The Allies fell back for 15 kilometres (more than 9 miles), and exceptionally fierce fighting took place at Mount Kemmel. 'There was a tumult of weapons. The English artillery and our own fired at full strength and the Germans replied; the sky was like a inferno. What a night! We were covered with earth and blinded by fire. Then, towards midnight, just as we were about to get some food, gas was used. In the supply trenches everyone put on a mask, but the glass got steamed up and we couldn't see anything. ... The shells kept on bursting all around us. At last our food arrived, but we could still smell the gas in the air and couldn't take off our masks. The food had to wait – and in the end it was just inedible.' Lieutenant Désagneaux, who wrote these lines, had been fighting in this sector since May: 'It was one of the sectors that wasn't relieved until the losses reached 50 or 60 per cent.'

Everyone began to hope for the same thing: a wound that would save them from death. 'Civilians don't have to think about dying all the time. But we are hoping and waiting for a way to be snatched from the jaws of death; we're not expecting to be unharmed – that would be unrealistic – we're just hoping that it will be the smallest possible injury.' Lieutenant Désagneaux's journal is full of descriptions of chaotic campaigns, shortages of supplies and the continual artillery bombardments. 'Fire everywhere and mass gas attacks. It gets in your throat, your eyes fill with blood. You live with your mask, but even so, people cough and spit. Everyone's affected to some extent. ... Every time there's an explosion it seems to be closer. We live among blood and groans.'

On 1 May Désagneaux noted: 'Whit Sunday: The weather is perfect, not a cloud in the sky and the sun is shining – and this evening we will have to march to our death. It would be better not to think about it any more and just to wake up afterwards. … And while we are here, waiting to die, for four years people behind the lines have been lounging about. All the notes, all the fine circulars didn't manage to move any of them. It's always the same people who march, and when reinforcements are sent, it's the wounded who come back after a few days, while there are others who have never even seen a trench.'

The fighting at Mount Kemmel continued throughout May. 'Night falls. Soon we will be in a hell of fire. Everything is on fire on the Clytte and in the fields, the old English camps and huts and the ruins of the farms are burning. The whole plain is blazing; it's war in all its horror.' During the attack on Mount Kemmel 230,000 British soldiers were lost; the French lost 22,000. The Germans were, however, prevented from advancing into Flanders.

On 27 May Ludendorff launched a new offensive in the valley of the Aisne. The Chemin des Dames was retaken by German troops who

advanced 20 kilometres (nearly 12½ miles) in a single day. Soissons fell, then Château-Thierry. The Germans took one of the forts defending Reims, Fort Pompelle, although a French counterattack managed to retake it. They

reached the Marne and, as in 1914, Paris was threatened. The Allies were in desperate straits.

On 11 June, however, General Mangin succeeded in holding off the Germans from Compiègne. Now, too, the first US divisions were ready to fight, and General Pershing put his troops at the disposition of Foch, although he insisted on retaining direct command of his men. The Americans were sent to the Aisne, where the marines distinguished themselves at Belleau Wood, near to Château-Thierry and the furthest point of the German advance towards Paris. It was in the fighting at Belleau Wood that George Patton and George Marshall, both later generals, first came under fire. The site of the fighting has been given to the American people, and there is now a chapel there, rising from the lines of white crosses that mark the resting places of those Americans who fell between the Aisne and the Marne.

In July Ludendorff mounted another offensive, this time in Champagne, against the defences around Reims, which had been transformed into

▲ The monument to General Mangin in the forest of Villers-Cotterêts.

◀ A listening post.

▶ An underground listening station.

► The American chapel
and cemetery at Belleau
Wood, to the north-west
of Château-Thierry.

▲ The monument of the Fantômes (Ghosts), the work of the sculptor Paul Landowski, which was raised on the ridge at Chalmont.

'*The fighting man shall from the sun*
  Take warmth, and life from the glowing earth;
Speed with the light-foot winds to run,
  And with the trees to newer birth;
And find, when fighting shall be done,
  Great rest, and fullness after dearth.'

Julian Grenfell, *Into Battle*

a fortified town, bristling with barricades. He threw as many men and as much equipment into the assault as possible, believing that this was the 'offensive for peace'. The Kaiser himself travelled to Mesnil Lépinois, 24 kilometres (about 15 miles) northeast of Reims, to witness the bombardment that would presage the final victory, and he prepared to enter Reims in triumph with his son. Leaflets were distributed to the German troops, promising that they would soon enjoy the millions of bottles of champagne stored in the cellars of the city.

However, the attack was not a surprise for the French. Reconnaissance flights had reported the movement of the troops, and information obtained from German prisoners captured in a

▲ The American cemetery at Château-Thierry near to Hill 304.

raid confirmed the intelligence that deserters from Alsace had already provided. Pétain laid his plans to foil the assault. He withdrew French troops from the front line, but packed the outposts, which had been carefully fortified for the last four years, with explosive and mustard gas. On the night of 14 July the French soldiers got ready their gas masks as they waited for the German assault. On the following day, Ludendorff's offensive failed. Although some German forces advanced around the west of Reims and managed to get beyond the Marne, crossing the river on pontoon bridges, reinforcements sent by Foch were able to force them back.

On 17 July Ludendorff stood down the assault and prepared for a final onslaught, concentrating his forces, now diminished by the fighting of the last few months, along a greatly shortened front. During the night of 17 July, however, the Allies were preparing a large-scale counterattack near to Château-Thierry. It was to be led by General Mangin, and American soldiers, who were by now arriving at the rate of 300,000 men a month, provided massive support. The troops were concentrated under the cover of the large forest of Villers-Cotterêts, from where Mangin, who had an observatory in a pylon raised above the tree tops, watched the operation unfold on the following day.

At dawn on 18 July, as the mist rose from the ground in the warmth of the sun, thousands of men emerged from the undergrowth under the eyes of the astonished German army. They were preceded by hundreds of tanks, which advanced steadily across the emerging spikes of corn in the fields. In the sky above, the sound of 800 aircraft could be heard.

In 1914 aviation had been taking its first hesitant steps – Roland Garros had crossed the Mediterranean only in 1912 – but in four years the number of French aircraft increased from 148 to several thousand. The fragile structures that had been seen at the start of the war had metamorphosed into powerful armed fighting machines, capable of flying at heights of 3000 metres (9800 feet).

The Allies ended the day by taking 10,000 prisoners. The Germans fell back to the banks of

the Aisne, completely demoralized by the result of the Second Battle of the Marne. 'You have made France feel as if it can win,' said Mangin to his men. 'You are worthy of your country.'

In spite of this the Allies wanted to know when they would be able to finish off the German army. They were afraid that the war was in danger of lasting for another year.

Ludendorff now wanted to launch an offensive in Picardy that would strike the final blow against Germany's enemies. Instead, however, it was the Allies who mounted an attack, which took place on 8 August, between Albert and Montdidier. Foch had prepared the operation in the greatest secrecy. His plan relied on aircraft and on a large number of tanks, both

British and French, which would be able to cross the trenches and would have a range of about 100 kilometres (more than 60 miles). At 5 o'clock in the morning, without any preparatory artillery rounds, which would have alerted the Germans, 450 tanks emerged from the mist, firing as they went and preparing the way for the infantry, which advanced for 10–20 kilometres (6–12 miles). Thousands of Germans fell. From the air waves of soldiers could be seen fleeing back across the Somme. It was, wrote Ludendorff, 'a black day for the German army'. His army was exhausted and demoralized.

The situation had been completely reversed, and the Allies now enjoyed superiority in both

weaponry and manpower. 'Our artillery is just about worn out,' wrote Erich Maria Remarque. 'We have too little ammunition and the barrels of the guns are so worn out that it's impossible to aim properly and they even fire on our own men. We have too few soldiers; our fresh troops are nothing more than weak children, who have to be told what to do and who can barely carry a bag, but they know how to die, by the thousand. They know nothing about war; they only know about advancing and being fired at.' The German army was, by this time, conscripting boys aged seventeen and men in their forties.

The fighting continued throughout the summer. It was more ferocious than ever, and the Allies maintained their onslaught. 'The summer

▲ The huge American army began to arrive.

◀ Long-range guns were mounted on railway track.

▲ The monument to US Marines in Belleau Wood.

of 1918 was the most awful and the most bloody of all. The days have become gold and silver angels, rising impassive above the site of so much destruction. Each one of us knows that we have lost the war. We don't talk much. We fall back; after this offensive we can't attack again. We haven't the soldiers or the equipment.' The feeling that the end had come took the edge off everything. 'Never did life, even in this miserable incarnation, seem to us as desirable as now,' wrote Erich Maria Remarque. 'The false sounds – so exciting – of the armistice and peace began to be heard. They trouble our hearts and make the withdrawal more difficult than before. … Why won't it end?'

Foch decided to launch a general offensive along the entire front. In the east an assault on the salient at Saint Mihiel was led by General Pershing, in direct command of his own forces. A total of 600,000 American and 100,000 French soldiers were supported by 1400 aircraft. The salient was taken in a day, and the Germans who fell back were taken in a pincer movement; 16,000 were captured. Pershing then moved north, towards Sedan and Charleville-Mézières, to sever German communications. He assumed command of a million American soldiers in Argonne, and on 26 September they took the hill of Montfaucon, which had been a German observation point for four years. After the tanks he had been commanding were destroyed, the young George Patton made his way to the summit of hill on foot, his boots polished, his men behind him and with a revolver in each hand.

The American success brought them face to face with the strongly fortified German line, with its machine-gun emplacements and its network of wires suspended from the trunks of trees in which tanks were caught and immobilized. The Americans were fresh and full of energy, but they were inexperienced. In addition, their provisioning system was not functioning properly, and three divisions had to go for three days without eating. The roads were filled with men and trucks, making the evacuation of the wounded more difficult. Sanitary arrangements in this sector, as in the rest of the front line, had 'all the peace of a charnel house', remembered John Dos Passos, who had worked as an ambulance driver in 1917. He was filled with the disillusion of one who had already seen a year of this war and had

► The American
cemetery at Saint Mihiel.

L'Argonne - **MONTFAUCON** - L'Eglise - The Church

◄ The ruins of the church of Montfaucon.

watched with increasing despair as 'the holocaust slowly and steadily gathered pace'.

Pershing's advance was checked, but American reinforcements arrived in ever greater number, and broke through the Hindenburg Line.

The Germans fell back on all sides before the inexorable advance of the Allies, and Ludendorff ordered a general withdrawal towards the Belgian frontier. He realized that the situation was desperate and wanted to ask for a cease-fire, but hoped to negotiate with President Wilson. The French and British refused. Ludendorff therefore sought an unconditional armistice from Foch.

The defeat of the Central Powers was complete on all fronts. Ludendorff resigned on 27 October. In Germany on 3 November German sailors at Kiel mutinied and refused to fight the British fleet, and there were riots and strikes throughout Germany. Support for revolutionary ideals became widespread, and the red flag even flew in Berlin. On 9 November the Chancellor of Germany, Prince Maximilian of Baden, announced the abdication of Wilhelm II.

▲ The American column, surmounted by the figure of Liberty, arises amid the ruins of the church at Montfaucon.

▲ The French monument to the dead at Bray-sur-Somme.

The Armistice

On 7 November Matthias Erzberger, who was head of the German armistice commission, sought a meeting with Foch, and later that day he drove to Haudroy near La Capelle on the Aisne. The French soldiers watched in silence as the cars, which flew white flags, drove past them. On 8 November the German negotiators arrived by train at Rethondes, near to Compiègne, and entered Foch's railway carriage, where Foch told them the terms of the armistice, to which Berlin was to respond within seventy-two hours. On 10 November the new Social Democratic government in Germany agreed that the armistice should be signed. There was, in the meantime, no suspension of hostilities, and men continued to be killed until the very last moment. At half past five in the morning of 11 November the agreement was signed; it was to come into effect at 11 o'clock that morning.

At ten minutes to eleven the last French solider to die in the war, Auguste Trébuchon, was killed at Vrigne-Meuse; he was carrying an order to his unit about where they should assemble at 11

'Those who come back here, even those who come back despite themselves, will, I believe, never forget this horrific time. Is it possible to kill so many people without knowing why?'

Private Jean Dumont

o'clock. In Britain on 11 November the parents of Wilfred Owen learned that the poet had been killed while crossing the River Sambre on 4 November.

At 11 o'clock along the front the sound of guns ceased as the bloodiest war then known to man came to an end. Church bells in towns and villages throughout France pealed, and civilians were jubilant. The relief felt by soldiers on both sides was immense, but mixed with their joy was sadness as they thought about the comrades they had lost. Scarcely a family was untouched by mourning. 'My grandmother,' said one woman, 'lost a son in the war and had another at the front. When she heard the bells pealing for the armistice she realized that he was safe. She

took to her bed and never got up again.' In Paris, which had been struck by 1200 shells, Clemenceau paid homage to the dead.

Some French soldiers, including Louis Barthas, could not believe the war was over. 'Tomorrow we will set off. … We ask ourselves if it's true that the war is really over. … We go on marching towards the green plain on which we see the little villages, which look so tranquil. We understand now that the war is ended and that we are still alive.'

'Yes, we won the war,' said Clemenceau, addressing the Chamber of Deputies. 'But not without great hardship. Now we must win the peace, and that will be more difficult.'

CONCLUSION

While the German Empire was collapsing, celebrations in Paris continued for several days. The fact that the heads of state of the belligerent nations visited the capital helped foster the illusion that Paris was still the centre of the world, but when the cheers faded and the bunting was put away, the great explosion of elation that had followed liberation gave way to a terrible sense of grief as people began to count the cost. It was beyond measure. Never before had so many people died in a single war.

Exact figures for the loss of life will never be established to closer than a million. It is probable that 9 million soldiers were killed and that about 20 million were injured, of whom as many as 6 million were permanently affected by their wounds. This total does not include those who were psychologically damaged by their experiences. There were also at least 3 million widows and 6 million fatherless children. In France alone one soldier in four had been killed.

The victorious nations emerged from the war either greatly weakened or in total ruin. The economies of all were shattered. Yesterday's world had definitely returned.

In the north and east of France towns and roads had been completely destroyed, fields had been churned up, and mines and industries had been devastated. In the Pas-de-Calais region alone 186 towns and villages had to be rebuilt. In Champagne and in Lorraine huge areas were declared to be too dangerous to live in, and villages that had been destroyed were abandoned and their inhabitants rehoused elsewhere. Entire tracts of land could not be cultivated.

The peace had been signed but Europe was wholly exhausted. It appeared to dominate the world, to be rich and carefree, but it was broken by the destruction and its finest young men had been lost. It was a 'sad peace', this peace of cemeteries, thought Romain Rolland, who regarded this period as an 'intermission between two massacres', as if the signal had already been given for the absolute madness that would follow and for what Georges Bernanos called 'tomorrow's terrible slaughter'.

The war was over and life began again, but under a terrible pall of mourning. The old line of the Western Front, running from the North Sea in the west to Alsace in the east, had become an enormous sepulchre for the army of the dead who lay mingled with the ground that had been churned up by the passage of men and the continual hail of shells. Along the 800 kilometres (500 miles) of the front were buried the broken bodies of millions of young men, some scarcely more than children, too soon returned to oblivion. Now it was time to begin the ghastly task of recovering their bodies: 1,400,000 French, 1,200,000 German, 770,000 British, 115,000 American, 50,000 Belgian, 50,000 Portuguese and all those men who came from distant countries in Asia and Africa and who were now mixed with the chalk of Champagne or the clay of Picardy.

Memories of the dead affected everyone, from the humblest of families to the most important in the land. At Clermont-Ferrand a

'*He pushed another bag along the top,*
Craning his body outward; then a flare
Gave one white glimpse of No Man's Land and wire;
And as he dropped his head the instant split
His startled life with lead, and all went out.'

Siegfried Sassoon, *A Working Party*

'*They shall grow not old, as we that are left grow old:*
Age shall not weary them, nor the years condemn.
At the going down of the sun and in the morning
We will remember them.'

Laurence Binyon, *Poems for the Fallen*

mother had lost six of her seven sons; the seventh was left blind and mad by his experiences. In Ariège a mother wept for eight of her eleven sons. In Paris a businessman and his wife committed suicide when they learned of the deaths of their four sons.

As the survivors began to return home, they brought with them accounts of their suffering. Some men could speak of their experiences only with difficulty, but little by little the horrors they had witnessed and the suffering endured by their comrades before they died became more widely understood, and families began to appreciate the hardships their sons had undergone and how abandoned they had felt. From all areas, parents, widows, sisters and young brothers, all clothed in black, travelled to the desolate war zone to search for the bodies of their loved ones, whether they lay beside a road or under a heap of stones, asking for the help of survivors who might have seen their sons fall. The first burial places had, however, often been disturbed in subsequent fighting, and many men now lay in communal graves. Even when bodies were recovered, they were often unrecognizable and unidentifiable.

The work of retrieving the dead began, and battlefields were dug up so that soldiers could be reburied with their comrades in military cemeteries. Each country had its own cemeteries: the lines of simple gravemarkers for the Germans; the stark white crosses for the Americans; the quasi-military graves of the French; the rectangular gravestones of the British, set around a tall white Cross of Sacrifice or, in larger cemeteries, around a Stone of Remembrance, bearing the

inscribed quotation from the Book of Ecclesiastes: 'Their Name Liveth for Ever More.'

In the years following the war national monuments began to be erected. An unidentified British soldier, the Unknown Warrior, was brought to London in November 1920 and buried in Westminster Abbey, and the Cenotaph was erected in Whitehall. The French chose one unidentified body, found buried with seven of his comrades, also unknown, which was taken from the site of some of the most violent fighting. The Unknown Soldier was buried at the Arc de Triomphe in

▲ The names of 54,896 British soldiers who were lost at Ypres but whose bodies were never found are engraved on the Menin Gate.

Paris in 1920, and three years later a flame of remembrance above the tomb was lit for the first time; it is renewed each evening. The tomb represents the 1,400,000 French soldiers who died for their country.

Such a terrible event demanded that some form of expiation be made. Mausoleums and memorials to the dead started to appear along the length of what had been the Western Front. In each village a monument to the dead was built to recall the days of the men's suffering. On the stones are engraved the names of the dead who had sacrificed themselves for the living.

Those who had escaped death, who had, as John Dos Passos put it, survived 'by accident', wondered how they would endure 'the life that they would one day live again, if they lived that long'. They were like ghosts in a world in which they could no longer share the ordinary lives of those who had not lived as they had done; among civilians they were like strangers, with their changed viewpoints and the weight of the experiences, which they could not talk about. The old soldiers tried to forget so they could go on living. Some suffered nightmares for years, and their cries allowed their families a glimpse of the bottomless despair they suffered. Sometimes the memory of the deaths came back unexpectedly. 'On my wedding day,' remembered one old man, 'even though I was going to be so happy, just as I was crossing the churchyard with its rows of tombstones, I suddenly started to cry. I wept and wept and couldn't stop. It was because of all the others.'

'Old soldier' is an expression that, over the years, no longer evokes much more than the annual services of remembrance and the men with their rows of ribbons and medals, carrying their regimental flags and standing in the grass at the foot of monuments on which the carved names of the fallen can now hardly be deciphered. Their bodies, a little more bent each year, still stand to attention when they hear the bugle. Their eyes are steady, even if their hands shake a little, as they stand to attention each year without fail, despite their frailty. Their faces are serious and reveal what they cannot describe in words. Who could imagine the scenes that have passed before their misty eyes over the years? It was their young selves who had escaped from the mud and the terrible trenches and who had faced the horror of the war with dignity and courage, just as they now stand until the end of the ceremonies to keep alive the memories of those who did not survive.

'My dead comrades, my poor dead comrades, it is now that you are suffering, without a cross to guard you and without loving arms in which you can curl up. I know I can see you prowling round, looking high and low and searching in the everlasting night for all those ungrateful people who have already forgotten you,' wrote Roland Dorgelès in *Les Croix de bois* (1919).

Time has done its work and, from one generation to the next, the memory has become fainter. What was once the history of individual families has become the impersonal history found on the pages of books. Old habits have reasserted themselves. First the plough and then the tractor have taken their place in the fields, filling in the old trenches, even though, decades afterwards, the land is still not completely free of the marks left by the shells nor, in some places, of bones.

When everyone forgets in the end, the earth will remember. The ground will continue to bear the scars of the tragic history of these men.

▶ Part of the memorial at Vimy, which commemorates more than 66,000 Canadian soldiers who died in the war.

BIBLIOGRAPHY

ALAIN, *Souvenirs de guerre*, Hartmann, 1937.

ALAIN, *Correspondance avec Florence et Élie Haléry*, Gallimard, 1958.

ARAGON, Louis, *Les Yeux d'Elsa*, Seghers, 1942.

AUDOIN-ROUZEAU, Stéphane, *À travers les journaux: 14–18 – Les combattants des tranchées*, Armand Colin, 1986.

BARBUSSE, Henri, *Le Feu*, Flammarion, 1965.

BARTHAS, Louis, *Carnets de guerre de Louis Barthas, tonnelier*, La Découverte, 1997.

BECKER, Jean-Jacques, *Les Français dans la Grande Guerre*, Robert Laffont, 1980.

BELMONT, Ferdinand, *Lettres d'un officier de chasseur alpin*, Plon, 1917.

BERNANOS, Georges, *Les Grands Cimetières sous la lune*, Plon, 1938.

BERNIER, Jean, *La Percée*, Albin Michel, 1920.

BEUMELBURG, Werner, *Combattants allemands à Verdun*, Payot, 1934.

BLOCH, Marc, *Souvenirs de guerre 1914–1915*, Armand Colin, 1969.

BOTTI, Louis, *Avec les zouaves*, Berger-Levrault, 1922.

BRIDOUX, André, *Souvenirs du temps des morts*, Albin Michel, 1930.

CARTIER, Raymond and Jean-Pierre, *La Première Guerre Mondiale*, Presses de la Cité, 1982.

CÉLINE, Louis-Ferdinand, *Voyage au bout de la nuit*, Pléiade, Gallimard, 1981.

CENDRARS, Blaise, *La Main Coupée*, Denoël, 1946.

Centre de recherche de l'Historial de Péronne, *14–18. La très grande guerre*, 1994.

CHAINE, Pierre, *Les Mémoires d'un rat*, Payot, 1921.

CHEVALLIER, Gabriel, *La Peur*, Stock, 1930.

COLETTE, *Les Heures longues*, Pléiade, tome II, Gallimard, 1986.

COULSON, Leslie, extracts from *The Wordsworth Book of First World War Poetry*, Wordsworth Editions Ltd, 1995.

DEAUVILLE, Max, *La Boue des Flandres*, M. Lamertin, Bruxelles, 1922.

DÉSAGNEAUX, Henri, *Journal de guerre*, Denoël 1971.

DORGELÈS, Roland, *Les Croix de bois*, Albin Michel, 1919.

DOS PASSOS, John, *One Man's Initiation*, 1919.

DRIEU LA ROCHELLE, Pierre, *La Comédie de Charleroi*, Gallimard, 1934.

DUCASSE, André, Meyer, Jacques and Perreux, Gabriel, *1914–1918. Vie et mort des Français*, Hachette, 1962.

DUHAMEL, Georges, *Vie des martyrs*, Mercure de France, 1917.

DUHAMEL, Georges, *Civilisation*, Mercure de France, 1918.

DURLEWANGER, A., *Le Drame du Linge*, Éditions SAEP, Colmar, 1970.

DUROSELLE, Jean-Baptiste, *La France et les Français, 1914–1920*, Éditions Richelieu, 1972.

FAULKNER, William, *A Fable*, Vintage, 1977.

FERRO, Marc, *La Grande Guerre (1914–1918)*, Gallimard, 1969.

GALTIER-BOISSIÈRE, Jean, *La Fleur au fusil*, Éditions Baudinière.

GALTIER-BOISSIÈRE, Jean, *Un hiver à Souchez*, Éditions Les Étincelles, 1930.

GAUDY, Georges, *Les Trous d'obus de Verdun*, Plon, 1922.

GENEVOIX, Maurice, *Ceux de quatorze*, Flammarion, 1950.

GIONO, Jean, *Le Grand Troupeau*, Gallimard, 1931.

GRANCHER, Marcel-E., *5 de campagne*, Éditions Lugdunum, 1938.

GRAVES, Robert, *Goodbye to All That*, 1929.

Guide de la Première Guerre mondiale des Flandres à l'Alsace, Casterman, 1996.

HENRIOT, Émile, *Rencontres en Île-de-France*. Unedited pages published in *Le Monde*, 4 April 1958.

JOFFRE, Marshal, *Mémoires*, Plon, 1932.

JOHANNSEN, Ernst, *Quatre de l'infanterie*, Éditions de l'Épi, 1929.

JÜNGER, Ernst, *Orages d'acier*, tran. Henri Plard, Christian Bourgois Éditeur, 1994.

JÜNGER, Ernst, *Das Wäldchen 125*, 1925.

JÜNGER, Ernst, *Sturm*, 1923.

LAURENT, André, *La Bataille de la Somme 1916*, Éditions Martelle, 1996.

LE GOFFIC, Charles, *Un chapitre de l'histoire des fusiliers marins*, Plon.

LOMBARD, Laurent, *Ceux de Liège*, G. Lens, Verviers, 1934.

MACDONALD, Lyn, *They Called it Passchendaele*, Michael Joseph, London, 1978.

MAC ORLAN, Pierre, *Verdun*, Nouvelles Éditions du siècle, 1935.

MAC ORLAN, Pierre, *Les Poissons morts*, Payot, 1917.

MALHERBE, Henry, *La Flamme au poing*, Albin Michel, 1917.

MAUROIS, André, *Les Silences du colonel Bramble*, coll. Les Cahiers rouges, Éditions Bernard Grasset.

MEYER, Jacques, *La Biffe*, Albin Michel, 1928.

MEYER, Jacques, *La Guerre, mon vieux...*, Albin Michel, 1931.

MEYER, Jacques, *La Vie quotidienne des soldats pendant la Grande Guerre*, Hachette, 1966.

MIQUEL, Pierre, *La Grande Guerre*, Fayard, 1983.

NOBÉCOURT, R.G., *Les Fantassins du Chemin des Dames*, Robert Laffont, 1965.

NORTON CRU, Jean, *Témoins*, Éditions Les Étincelles, 1924.

OWEN, Wilfred, extracts from *The Wordsworth Book of First World War Poetry*, Wordsworth Editions Ltd, 1995.

PÉZARD, André, *Nous autres, à Vauquois*, Renaissance du livre, 1918.

POURCHER, Yves, *Les Jours de guerre. La vie des Français au jour le jour. 1914–1918*, Hachette Pluriel, 1995.

Proceedings of the 80th Anniversary Symposium, conducted by Claude Carlier and Guy Pedroncini, *La bataille de Verdun*, Economica.

REMARQUE, Erich Maria, *Im Westen Nichts Neues*, 1929.

RENN, Ludwig, *Krieg*, 1928.

ROMAINS, Jules, *Les Hommes de bonne volonté*, Flammarion, 1958.

SASSOON, Siegfried, extracts from *The Wordsworth Book of First World War Poetry*, Wordsworth Editions Ltd, 1995.

SPEARS, General E.L., *En liaison 1914*, Gallimard, 1932.

TARDIEU, André, *Avec Foch*, Flammarion, 1939.

TUFFRAU, Paul, *Carnet d'un combattant*, Albin Michel.

VACHÉ, Jacques, *Lettres de guerre*, Éditions Jean-Michel Place, 1989.

VAN DER MEERSCH, Maxence, *Invasion 14*, Albin Michel.

VIGNES ROUGES, Jean des, *Bourru, soldat de Vauquois*, Perrin, 1916.

ZWEIG, Arnold, *Erziehung vor Verdun*, 1935.

ZWEIG, Stefan, *Der Welt von Gestern. Erinnerungen Eines Europaers*, Fischer, 1955.

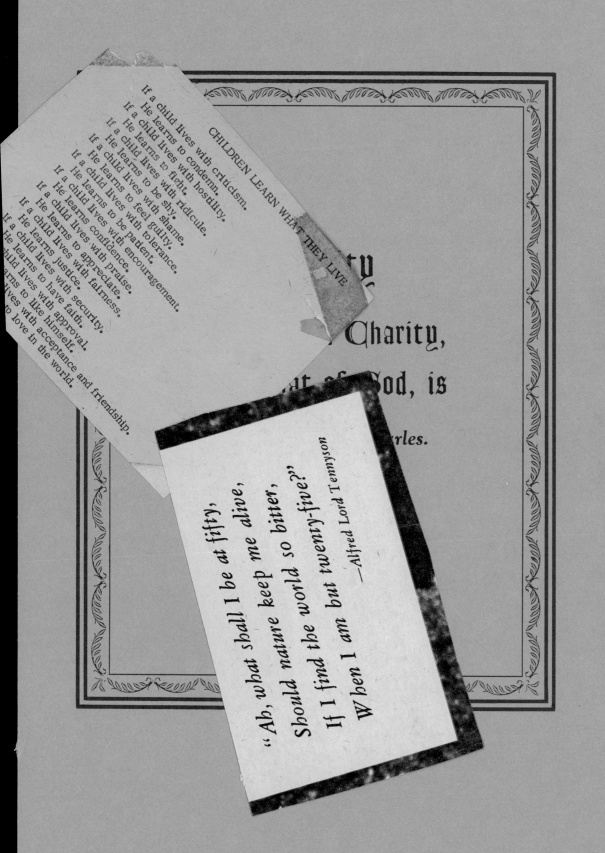

CHILDREN LEARN WHAT THEY LIVE

If a child lives with criticism,
He learns to condemn.
If a child lives with hostility,
He learns to fight.
If a child lives with ridicule,
He learns to be shy.
If a child lives with shame,
He learns to feel guilty.
If a child lives with tolerance,
He learns to be patient.
If a child lives with encouragement,
He learns confidence.
If a child lives with praise,
He learns to appreciate.
If a child lives with fairness,
He learns justice.
If a child lives with security,
He learns to have faith.
If a child lives with approval,
He learns to like himself.
If a child lives with acceptance and friendship,
He learns to love in the world.

Charity,

at of God, is

rles.

"Ah, what shall I be at fifty,
Should nature keep me alive,
If I find the world so bitter,
When I am but twenty-five?"
—Alfred Lord Tennyson

XIII. FAULT FINDING

FUTILE — A wicked man who reproaches a virtuous one is like one who looks up and spits at Heaven; the spittle soils not the Heaven, but comes back and defiles his own face.

—*Sakya-Muni.*

A MIRROR—Search thy own heart; what paineth thee in others in thyself may be.—*Whittier.*

Do you want to know the man against whom you have most reason to guard yourself? Your looking-glass will give a very fair likeness of his face.—*Whateley.*

THE EASIEST WAY — Napoleon said that the man who never makes a mistake never makes war. Those who content themselves with pointing out the mistakes and blunders of those who are in the struggle, are making, themselves, the greatest of all blunders. Nothing is easier than fault-finding. No talent, no self-denial, no brains, no character are required to set up in the grumbling business.—*Robert West.*

CONSIDERATE — There is a good thought in the following incident from a late book: "A dear old friend of mine used to say with the truest Christian charity, when he heard any one being loudly condemned for some fault: 'Ah! well, yes, it seems very bad to me, because that's not my way of sinning'."

—*Williams.*

EVEN IN PARADISE—Some would find fault with the morning-red, if they ever got up early enough. . . The fault-finder will find faults even in Paradise.

—*Thoreau.*

PATIENCE—Endeavor to be always patient of the faults and imperfections of others, for thou hast many faults and imperfections of thy own that require a reciprocation of forbearance. If thou art not able to make thyself that which thou wishest to be, how canst thou expect to mould another in conformity to thy will?

—*Thomas a' Kempis.*

CONFESSION — We confess our little faults only to persuade others that we have no great ones.

—*La Rochefoucauld.*

The Anvil Outlasts the Hammer.—

TRUE RELIGION

I remember that in the time of childhood I was very religious; I rose in the night, was punctual in the performance of my devotions, and abstinent. One night I had been sitting in the presence of my father, not having closed my eyes during the whole time, and with the holy Koran in my embrace, whilst numbers around us were asleep. I said to my father: "Not one of these lifteth up his head to perform his genuflexions, but they are all so fast asleep you would say they are dead." He replied: "Life of your father, it were better if thou also wert asleep than to be searching out the faults of mankind. The boaster sees nothing but himself, having a veil of conceit before his eyes. If he were endowed with an eye capable of discerning God, he would not discern any person weaker than himself."

SAADI—*The Gulistan.*

RID THE WORLD OF A RASCAL
—Make yourself an honest man, and then you may be sure that there is one rascal less in the world.—*Carlyle.*

~

DEAD LEAVES—You will find it less easy to uproot faults, than to choke them by gaining virtues. Do not think of your faults; still less of others' faults; in every person who comes near you look for what is good and strong: honor that; rejoice in it; and, as you can, try to imitate it; and your faults will drop off, like dead leaves, when their time comes.—*Ruskin.*

~

NEVER MIND
Some people think so many things;
So many things that are not so;
Never mind their taunts and stings;
You and I, dear—know.
—Ruth Mason Rice.

~

BLAMELESS — Let him who would move and convince others, be first moved and convinced himself.—*T. L. Cuyler.*

If you would lift me, you must be on higher ground.—*Emerson.*

I can easier teach twenty what were good to be done, than to be one of the twenty to follow mine own teachings.
—Shakespeare.

It is easier to be wise for others than for ourselves.—*La Rochefoucauld.*

~

CRITICISM — Of course, there are some folks who do not seem to be able to cooperate. Their long suit is criticism—destructive and not constructive criticism, at that. To such I would quote the words of Edmund Burke: "Applaud us when we run, console us when we fall, cheer us when we recover, but for God's sake, let us pass on!"

REVENGE—A little girl was making faces at a bulldog. Her mother reprimanded her. "Well, he started it," said the girl. No doubt the girl was right, for it is no trouble for a bulldog to look ugly. The weakness was in the girl's conclusion drawn from the dog's face. The dog was probably innocent, but if not, the girl gained nothing by competing with him in making faces. The person who proceeds on the theory that he must return every ugly face he sees, or every ugly act which is directed toward him, will have a never-ending and profitless job. Hate has injurious effects on the person who resents, so that he is the chief sufferer.—*Telescope.*

~

CRITICS — How humiliating it is to find that I am pained when I learn that N or M does not like my preaching, yet am so calmed when all the alphabet, for years, rejected my Master's message.
—J. W. Alexander.

~

STRIKE AN AVERAGE — I have long been disposed to judge men by their average. If it is reasonably high, I am charitable with faults that look pretty black.—*Ed Howe.*

~

GOSSIP
There is so much good in the worst of us,
And so much bad in the best of us,
That it ill becomes any of us
To find fault with the rest of us.

~

SLANDER—Life would be a perpetual flea hunt if a man were obliged to run down all the innuendoes, inveracities, insinuations and misrepresentations which are uttered against him.
—Henry Ward Beecher.

TEMPTATION is like a winter torrent, difficult to cross. Some, then, being most skilful swimmers, pass over, not being whelmed beneath temptations, nor swept down by them at all, while others who are not such, entering into them, sink in them. As, for example, Judas, entering into the temptation of covetness, swam not through it, but, sinking beneath it, was choked both in body and spirit. Peter entered into the temptation of the denial, but having entered it, he was not overwhelmed by it, but manfully swimming through it he was delivered.—*Cyril.*

Three Gates

If I am tempted to reveal
  A tale someone to me has told
About another, let it pass,
  Before I speak, three gates of gold.

Three narrow gates: First, is it *true?*
  Then, is it *needful?* In my mind
Give truthful answer, and the next
  Is last and narrowest, Is it *kind?*

And if, to reach my lips at last,
  It passes through these gateways, three,
Then I may tell the tale, nor fear
  What the result of speech may be.
            —*Beth Day.*

A FUNDAMENTAL LAW — We are too hasty to believe every evil report. Many an innocent person has been injured by a tale that was without foundation. It is a serious matter to do an injustice to a fellow man by a report that we spread. The first thing, the least thing that one can do before he passes on a story that has come to him, is to stop long enough to ask if it is true. One of the ten fundamental laws of character is, "Thou shalt not bear false witness against thy neighbor."

THE RESPONSIBILITY of tolerance lies with those who have the wider vision.
            —*George Eliot.*

BUSYBODIES — Most of us are fearless critics of other men's conduct and meticulous denouncers of other men's sins. To mind other people's business is a common pastime of our day. There are very few of us who are not deeply concerned over the reform of—somebody else.

Now there is no more lovely experience than to feel the personal interest of a friend in you and your affairs. But there is no more irritating experience than to be aware of unfriendly meddling and prying into your private affairs.

The man who cannot respect personality is hardly qualified to be listened to on any subject.

I FIND the doing of the will of God leaves me no time for disputing about His plans.—*Macdonald.*

DESERVING—To be suspicious is to invite treachery.—*Voltaire.*

TOLERANT SYMPATHY — There are two kinds of tolerance.

The one comes from indifference. It is a supercilious thing. "No matter what you believe," it seems to say, "you will have to take the consequences. That does not affect me, because I have the right creed."

The other kind of tolerance comes through sympathy. "You and I do not profess the same doctrines," it says, "but we seek the same end,—the glory of God and the good of our fellow men. Our points of view, our circumstances, our educations have been different. The road is not easy. Let us help one another."

RECOGNIZING GREATNESS —
There is an old maxim to the effect that
only good should be spoken of the dead.
It is a noble half-truth and ought to be
considered by those who are inclined to
injure the good names of people whose
voices are stilled in death.

But why should generous praise wait
for death? Why can we not introduce
the element of eternity into our judgment
of living men so that greatness may be
recognized and encouraged before it takes
its difficult journey into the valley of the
shadow?

ABSURDITY — What an absurd
thing it is to pass over all the valuable
parts of a man, and fix our attention on
his infirmities.—*Addison.*

SELF-DISCOVERY

"Within my earthly temple there's a
    crowd;
There's one of us that's humble, one that's
    proud;
There's one that's brokenhearted for his
    sins
And one who, unrepentant, sits and grins;
There's one who loves his neighbor as
    himself
And one who cares for naught but fame
    and pelf.
From such corroding care I would be free
If once I could determine which is me."

VAGARY—Worldly fame is but a
breath of wind that blows now this way,
and now that, and changes name as it
changes direction.—*Dante.*

HOW IMMENSE appear to us the
sins that we have not committed.
       —*Madame Necker.*

FERTILIZING—It is not so much the
being exempt from faults, as having
overcome them, that is an advantage to
us; it being with the follies of the mind
as with the weeds of the field, which if
destroyed and consumed upon the place
of their birth, enrich and improve it more
than if none had sprung there before.
       —*Pope.*

FRIEND—I joked about every prominent man in my lifetime, but I never
met one I didn't like.—*Will Rogers.*

DIARY OF A LEGISLATIVE
BODY:

"Monday—Soak the rich.

"Tuesday—Begin hearing from the
rich.

"Tuesday Afternoon — Decide to give
the rich a chance to get richer.

"Wednesday—Tax Wall Street stock
sales.

"Thursday — Get word from Wall
Street: 'Lay off us or you will get no campaign contributions.'

"Thursday Afternoon — Decide: 'We
are wrong about Wall Street.'

"Friday—Soak the little fellow.

"Saturday Morning—Find out there is
no little fellow. He has been soaked until
he is drowned.

"Sunday—Meditate.

"Next Week—Same procedure, only
more talk and less results."—*Will Rogers.*

EVERYONE is eagle-eyed to see
another's faults and deformity.—*Dryden.*

HE CENSURES GOD who quarrels
with the imperfections of men.—*Burke.*

XIV. FRIENDSHIP

TALISMAN—Friendship, in its truest sense, is next to love the most abused of words. One may call many "friend" and be still ignorant of that sentiment, cooler than passion, warmer than respect, more just and generous than either, which recognizes a kindred spirit in another, and, claiming its right, keeps it sacred by the wise reserve that is to friendship what the purple bloom is to the grape, a charm which once destroyed can never be restored.

—*J. Alcott.*

A TRUE FRIEND is somebody who can make us do what we can.—*Emerson.*

A friend hath the skill and observation of the best physician; the diligence and vigilance of the best nurse; and the tenderness and patience of the best mother.

—*Clarendon.*

GOOD MAN—You may depend upon it that he is a good man whose intimate friends are all good, and whose enemies are decidedly bad.—*Lavater.*

SHINING ARMOR—A blessed thing it is for any man or woman to have a friend; one human soul whom we can trust utterly; who knows the best and the worst of us, and who loves us in spite of all our faults; who will speak the honest truth to us, while the world flatters us to our face, and laughs at us behind our back; who will give us counsel and reproof in the day of prosperity and self-conceit; but who, again, will comfort and encourage us in the day of difficulty and sorrow, when the world leaves us alone to fight our own battle as we can.

—*Kingsley.*

THE GREATEST BOON—For true friendship, it is not enough to have emptied a brotherly glass to each other, to have sat on the same form at school, to have met frequently at the same cafe, to have conversed courteously in the street, to have sung the same songs at the same club, to have worn the same colors as politicians, to have extolled one another in the press. Friendship, indeed, is one of the greatest boons God can bestow on man. It is a union of our finest feelings; a disinterested binding of hearts, and a sympathy between two souls. It is an indefinable trust we repose in one another, a constant communication between two minds, and an unremitting anxiety for each other's souls.—*J. Hill.*

Because you love me, I have found
New joys that were not mine before;
New stars have lightened up my sky
With glories growing more and more.
Because you love me I can rise
To the heights of fame and realms
of power;
Because you love me I may learn
The highest use of every hour.

Because you love me I can choose
To look through your dear eyes and
see
Beyond the beauty of the Now
Far onward to Eternity.

Because you love me I can wait
With perfect patience well possessed;
Because you love me all my life
Is circled with unquestioned rest;
Yes, even Life and even Death
Is all unquestioned and all blest.
—*Pall Mall Magazine.*

A FRIEND IS A PERSON—

Who will help you in the hour of sickness;

Who will lend you a dollar without deducting the interest;

Who will help you up hill when you are sliding down;

Who will defend you in the hour when others speak evil of you;

Who will believe in your innocence until you admit your guilt;

Who will say behind your back what he says to your face;

Who will shake hands with you wherever he meets you, even though you wear patches; and

Who will do all these things without expecting any return.

—*Dorothy C. Retsloff.*

OLD FRIENDSHIP

Beautiful and rich is an old friendship,
Grateful to the touch as ancient ivory,
Smooth as aged wine, or sheen of tapestry
Where light has lingered, intimate and
    long.
Full of tears and warm is an old friend-
    ship
That asks no longer deeds of gallantry,
Or any deed at all—save that the friend
    shall be
Alive and breathing somewhere, like a
    song.
            —*Eunice Tietjens.*

Reprinted from LEAVES IN WINDY WEATHER by Eunice Tietjens, by permission of Alfred A. Knopf, Inc. Copyright 1926, by Alfred A. Knopf, Inc.

THE LANGUAGE OF FRIENDSHIP is not words, but meanings. It is an intelligence above language.

WE DO NOT WISH for friends to feed and clothe our bodies—neighbors are kind enough for that—but to do the like office for our spirits.—*Thoreau.*

THESE THREE—Three men are my friends—he that loves me, he that hates me, he that is indifferent to me. Who loves me, teaches me tenderness; who hates me, teaches me caution; who is indifferent to me, teaches me self-reliance.
            —*Dinger.*

SPENDTHRIFTS—Never cast aside your friends if by any possibility you can retain them. We are the weakest of spendthrifts if we let one friend drop off through inattention, or let one push away another, or if we hold aloof from one for petty jealousy or heedless slight or roughness. Would you throw away a diamond because it pricked you? One good friend is not to be weighed against the jewels of all the earth. If there is coolness or unkindness between us, let us come face to face and have it out. Quick, before the love grows cold. Life is too short to quarrel in, or carry black thoughts of friends. It is easy to lose a friend, but a new one will not come for calling, nor make up for the old one when he comes.
            —*Anonymous.*

FLATTERY — The friend who holds up before me the mirror, conceals not my smallest faults, warns me kindly, reproves me affectionately, when I have not performed my duty, he is my friend, however little he may appear so. Again, if a man flattering praises and lauds me, never reproves me, overlooks my faults, and forgives them before I have repented, he is my enemy, however much he may appear my friend.—*Herder.*

INDISPENSABLE — So long as we love, we serve. So long as we are loved by others I would almost say we are indispensable; and no man is useless while he has a friend.—*R. L. Stevenson.*

COMPANIONSHIP — Christ asked His disciples to watch with Him in Gethsemane. Tender touch of nature, to make Him with the whole world kin. Two infants will walk hand in hand "in the dark" where neither would go alone. Invalids, who have counted the strokes of midnight's wakeful hours, conjured by the wall flashes and flickers of dim lamps, and need no other service, cry out, Father! Mother! Some one! We sit by them, long and patiently, perhaps dozing, disciple-like, as we hold their hands, saying and doing nothing, but being near them. Through the streets of Paris, between prison and block, the most desperate were often observed sitting upon the cart's edge, hand in hand. Triumph wants friends also. Jesus wants our sympathy still in His warfare with sin on the earth. He who so wanted the society of men will have His own with Him where He is, at last and forever.—*Evans.*

EACH MAN can interpret another's experience only by his own.—*Thoreau.*

THREE KINDS — There are three kinds of friendships which are advantageous, and three which are injurious. Friendship with the upright, friendship with the sincere, and friendship with the man of much information—these are advantageous. Friendship with a man of specious airs, friendship with the insinuatingly soft, friendship with the glib-tongued—these are injurious.—*Confucius.*

BEAUTY HINT NO. 2—Said Mrs. Browning, the poet, to Charles Kingsley, the novelist, "What is the secret of your life? Tell me, that I may make mine beautiful also." Thinking a moment, the beloved old author replied, "I had a friend."

GOD'S BEST GIFT — Blessed are they who have the gift of making friends, for it is one of God's best gifts. It involves many things, but above all, the power of going out of one's self, and appreciating whatever is noble and loving in another.
—*Thomas Hughes.*

In Tune

I don't remember when I first began
To call you "friend." One day, I only know,
The vague companionship that I'd seen grow
So imperceptibly, turned gold, and ran
In tune with all I'd thought, or dared to plan.
Since then, you've been to me like music, low,
Yet clear; a fire that throws its warm, bright glow
On me as on each woman, child, and man,
And common thing that lies within its rays;
You've been like wholesome food that stays the cry
Of hungry, groping minds; and like a star—
A self-sufficient star—you make me raise
My utmost being to a higher sky,
In tune, like you, with earth, yet wide, and far.
—*Florence Steigerwalt.*

PERFECTION — Friendship is the highest degree of perfection in society.
—*Montaigne.*

A FRIEND is one who incessantly pays us the compliment of expecting from us all the virtues, and who can appreciate them in us.—*Thoreau.*

FRIEND.—A friend is one who needs us and one whom we need. Around us may be many whose companionship we enjoy, but were they suddenly to drop out of their places there would be no soreness, no sense of deprivation, no lack of comfort. We do not need them, neither do they need us. A friend is one to whom we cling, though many leagues of space separate us. Though days pass with no sight of his face or word from his pen, we know our friend loves us and that when we meet again we will be on the same old terms: we shall begin where we left off. A friend is one in whom we can confide. The secret chambers of our soul open to his touch on the latch. Thousands imagine their friends are numbered by scores, but if subjected to these tests every one of them would fall into the great sea of common humanity.—*Dinger.*

IGNORANCE with love is better than wisdom without it.

COMPARISONS

Friendship — Like music heard on the waters,
Like pines when the wind passeth by,
Like pearls in the depths of the ocean,
Like stars that enamel the sky,
Like June and the odor of roses,
Like dew and the freshness of morn,
Like sunshine that kisseth the clover,
Like tassels of silk on the corn,
Like mountains that arch the blue heavens,
Like clouds when the sun dippeth low,
Like songs of birds in the forest,
Like brooks where the sweet waters flow,
Like dreams of Arcadian pleasures,
Like colors that gratefully blend,
Like everything breathing of kindness—
Like these is the love of a friend.
　　　　　　　　　—*A. P. Stanley.*

TRIBUTE — I love you not only for what you are, but for what I am when I am with you. I love you not only for what you have made of yourself, but for what you are making of me. I love you for the part of me that you bring out.

I love you for putting your hand into my heaped-up heart, and passing over all the foolish and frivolous and weak things which you cannot help dimly seeing there, and for drawing out into the light all the beautiful, radiant belongings, that no one else had looked quite far enough to find.

I love you for ignoring the possibilities of the fool and weakling in me, and for laying firm hold on the possibilities of good in me. I love you for closing your eyes to the discords in me, and for adding to the music in me by worshipful listening.

I love you because you are helping me to make of the lumber of my life not a tavern but a Temple, and of the words of my every day not a reproach but a song.

I love you because you have done more than any creed could have done to make me good, and more than any fate could have done to make me happy. You have done it just by being yourself. Perhaps that is what being a friend means after all.

HE THAT DOES a base thing for a friend burns the golden thread which ties their hearts together.—*Jeremy Taylor.*

"Hello" only lasts for a minute,
　It's a short, brisk, queer little word.
But, say! there's a lot of cheer in it;
　It's like the first chirp of a bird
In spring, when the hilltops are greening,
　Right after the cold and the snow.
I think when it comes to real meaning,
　There isn't a word like "Hello!"
　　　　　　　　　—*Ralph Bricker.*

XV. HAPPINESS

ALTERNATIVES—There are two ways of being happy; we may either diminish our wants or augment our means. Either will do, the result is the same. And it is for each man to decide for himself, and do that which happens to be the easiest. If you are idle or sick or poor, however hard it may be for you to diminish your wants, it will be harder to augment your means. If you are active and prosperous or young or in good health, it may be easier for you to augment your means than to diminish your wants. But if you are wise, you will do both at the same time, young or old, rich or poor, sick or well. And if you are very wise, you will do both in such a way as to augment the general happiness of society.—*Benjamin Franklin.*

TASTE—Happiness lies in the taste, and not in things; and it is from having what we desire that we are happy—not from having what others think desirable.
—*La Rochefoucauld.*

HABITS — Gentleness and cheerfulness, these come before all morality; they are the perfect duties . . . If your morals make you dreary, depend upon it they are wrong. I do not say "Give them up," for they may be all you have; but conceal them like vice, lest they should spoil the lives of better and simpler people.
—*Robert Louis Stevenson.*

CHEERFULNESS — The difference between polished iron and iron that is unpolished is the difference between cheerfulness and no cheerfulness. Cheerfulness in a man is that which when people meet him makes them happy.—*Beecher.*

THE SEARCH—If you ever find happiness by hunting for it, you will find it as the old woman did her lost spectacles, safe on her own nose all the time.
—*Josh Billings.*

LOAF AND INVITE YOUR SOUL —There is such a thing as taking ourselves and the world too seriously, or at any rate too anxiously. Half of the secular unrest and dismal, profane sadness of modern society comes from the vain idea that every man is bound to be a critic of life, and to let no day pass without finding some fault with the general order of things, or projecting some plan for its general improvement. And the other half comes from the greedy notion that a man's life does consist, after all, in the abundance of things that he possesseth, and that it is somehow or other more respectable and pious to be always at work trying to make a larger living, than it is to lie on your back in the green pastures and beside the still waters, and thank God that you are alive.—*Henry Van Dyke.*

*Who drives the horses of the sun
    Shall lord it but a day;
Better the lowly deed were done,
    And kept the humble way.*

*The rust will find the sword of fame,
    The dust will hide the crown;
Ay, none shall nail so high his name
    Time will not tear it down.*

*The happiest heart that ever beat
    Was in some quiet breast
That found the common daylight sweet
    And left to Heaven the rest.*
—JOHN VANCE CHENEY.

LAUGH, PREACHER, LAUGH—Ministers are not martyrs. Most ministers have a saving sense of humor and look on the sunny side of life. When Monday morning rolls along, and it is so-called "Ministers' Blue Monday" they get together like birds of a feather. In those ministers' conferences from time to time the preachers are boys again and swap yarns and experiences. In some of these meetings the cream of humor comes to the top.

One summer while vacationing in New York City my eye fell on the announcement in a prominent paper, offering a prize for the funniest experience on the part of the readers. In due time I sent in mine. A few days later a beautiful check was received for my prize-winning experience. Here it is: I had preached in a certain church on Sunday. On Friday I received the following letter: "Dear Brother: Since I heard you preach I have gotten so that I can not walk. Please get me a wheelchair." If any preacher wishes to go in the wheelchair business I will send him some of my old sermons.

A friend of mine married a couple. The girl weighed probably close to 300 pounds. The man would not weigh more than a hundred, judging from his diminutive size. When the time came for the presentation of the wedding ring the little groom was about to place the band of gold on the ring finger of the colossal bride. It did not fit, whereupon the little fellow exclaimed: "Oh baby, it does not fit." The preacher was asked to furnish a file, and the little groom, who was a mechanic as well as an ardent lover, filed the ring off until it fitted, whereupon the ceremony was completed.

A very pompous preacher, whose bay window was the only sign of his greatness and who had a fairly good opinion of himself, was trying to make a gathering of people laugh at the expense of a preacher who was not quite so corpulent as he. The preacher of small stature had a reputation of being a hearty eater. He had also the reputation of being witty. Listen to the historic dialogue: "A great deal of good food has been wasted on Brother Little; it does not seem to have done him much good." Laughter. Whereupon Brother Little quietly arose saying: "Mr. Chairman, food affects different people in different ways. For instance, in some people it makes tissue, in other blood, in others bone, in others muscle. In my case it makes brain. In the case of Brother Big it all goes to his stomach!" Convulsing laughter.

Although this is only the beginning of a much longer story I will close with an incident that occurred in a community in which I was pastor. One of our members was quite sick. In the yard of her home an immense hog attracted curious people from far and near. Annoyed by the constant stream of visitors, a member of the family put the following notice in the newspaper: "Mrs. Z. is very ill. Please do not come to see the big hog until she is better."—*Marinus James.*

VALUES—A laugh is worth one hundred groans in any market.

—*Charles Lamb.*

A WILD GOOSE CHASE — Happiness in this world, when it comes, comes incidentally. Make it the object of pursuit, and it leads us a wild goose chase, and is never attained. Follow some other object, and very possibly we may find that we have caught happiness without dreaming of it; but likely enough it is gone the moment we say to ourselves, "Here it is!" Like the chest of gold that treasure-seekers find.

—*Nathaniel Hawthorne.*

LAUGHTER—while it lasts, slackens and unbraces the mind, weakens the faculties, and causes a kind of remissness and dissolution in all the powers of the soul; and thus far it may be looked upon as a weakness in the composition of human nature. But if we consider the frequent reliefs we receive from it, and how often it breaks the gloom which is apt to depress the mind and dampen our spirit, with transient, unexpected gleams of joy, one would take care not to grow too wise for so great a pleasure of life.—*Addison.*

PLEASANT—You have not fulfilled every duty, unless you have fulfilled that of being pleasant.—*Charles Buxton.*

MISERABLE—If you want to be miserable think about yourself, about what you want, what you like, what respect people ought to pay you and what people think of you.—*Charles Kingsley.*

Happiness

I asked professors who teach the meaning
    of life to tell me what is happiness.
And I went to famous executives who boss
    the work of thousands of men.
They all shook their heads and gave me
    a smile as though I was trying to fool
    with them.
And then one Sunday afternoon I wan-
    dered out along the Desplaines river
And I saw a crowd of Hungarians under
    the trees with their women and chil-
    dren and a keg of beer and an ac-
    cordion.   —*Carl Sandburg.*

From CHICAGO POEMS by Carl Sandburg, by permission of the publishers, Henry Holt and Company, Inc. Copyright, 1916 by Henry Holt and Company. Copyright, 1943 by Carl Sandburg.

SUNSHINE — Those who bring sunshine to the lives of others cannot keep it from themselves.—*James M. Barrie.*

MOVING MOUNTAINS — If you only laugh, things don't come so hard. If you laugh at it, the trouble will not seem so real. I know, for I laugh away a mountain.

Jesus told of the faith that removes mountains. May not cheerfulness in the face of difficulty and privation be an evidence of that wonder working faith?

—*John T. Faris.*

RADIANT WITNESSES—We do not please God more by eating bitter aloes than by eating honey. A cloudy, foggy rainy day is not more heavenly than a day of sunshine. A funeral march is not so much like the music of angels as the songs of birds on a May morning. There is no more religion in the gaunt, naked forest in winter than in the laughing blossoms of the spring, and the rich ripe fruits of autumn. It was not the pleasant things in the world that came from the devil, and the dreary things from God! It was "sin brought death into the world and all our woe;" as the sin vanishes the woe will vanish too. God Himself is the ever-blessed God. He dwells in the light of joy as well as of purity, and instead of becoming more like Him as we become more miserable, and as all the brightness and glory of life are extinguished, we become more like God as our blessedness becomes more complete. The great Christian graces are radiant with happiness. Faith, hope, charity, there is no sadness in them; and if penitence makes the heart sad, penitence belongs to the sinner; not to the saint; as we become more saintly, we have less sin to sorrow over.

—*R. W. Dale.*

PERFUME—Happiness is a perfume you cannot pour on others without getting a few drops on yourself.

TRUE CONTENT—Be content with your surroundings but not with yourself till you have made the most of them.

GLADNESS—The men whom I have seen succeed best in life have always been cheerful and hopeful men, who went about their business with a smile on their faces, and took the changes and chances of this mortal life like men, facing rough and smooth alike as it came.

—*Charles Kingsley.*

THE POWER BEHIND evolution is the mightiest and surest thing in existence. It is the most dependable thing in the Cosmos. It attends every instant upon man's willingness to cooperate with it, ready to respond richly to his most timid demands. It puts its shoulder to the wheel alongside the weakest and most debased of mortals. . . . The cry of hunger is a manifesto more powerful than the parchment of princes, because it is a voice from Nature. The Law is consistently beneficent. There is such a thing as perfect justice to every man. The greatest good to the greatest number is a sophistical make-shift. Its euphonious persuasiveness has captivated the superficial logic of a science which accepted expedients for principle. But in the light of new truth it is a clear and a most thrilling fact, that good and happiness and justice belong to every single man, and to one as much as another. The new philosophy makes for the universal good without a single creature forgotten; according to himself shall each man share in the universal and appropriable all-good.—*Annie F. Cantwell.*

NOT ENOUGH — Be not simply good, but good for something.—*Thoreau.*

GRIEF—Happiness is to feel that one's soul is good; there is no other, in truth, and this kind of happiness may exist even in sorrow, so that there are griefs preferable to every joy, and such as would be preferred by all those who have felt them.

—*Joseph Joubert.*

CHEER—Among Christians so much prominence has been given to the disciplinary effects of sorrow, affliction, bereavement, that they have been in danger of overlooking the other and more obvious side that by every joy, by every favor, by every sign of prosperity—yea, and by these chiefly—God designs to educate and discipline His children. This one-sided view of the truth has made many morbid, gloomy Christians, who look for God's hand only in the lightning and never think of seeing it in the sunlight. They only enjoy themselves when they are miserable.

—*F. E. Clark.*

CLASSIFICATION — Man is the merriest specie of the creation; all above or below him are serious.—*Addison.*

COMPLETE — The out-and-out Christian is a joyful Christian. The half-and-half Christian is the kind of Christian that a great many of you are—little acquainted with the Lord. Why should we live halfway up the hill and swathed in the mists, when we might have an unclouded sky and a radiant sun over our heads if we would climb higher and walk in the light of His face?

—*Alexander Maclaren.*

THE SECRET—The secret of happiness is not in doing what one likes, but in liking what one has to do.—*Barrie.*

XVI. HOME

NEGLECT—A story is told of a young man who stood at the bar of justice to be sentenced for forgery. The judge had known the young man from childhood, for his father had been a famous legal light and his work on the Law of Trusts was the most exhaustive work on the subject. "Do you remember your father," asked the judge, sternly, "that father whom you have disgraced?" The prisoner answered, "I remember him perfectly. When I went to him for advice or companionship, he would look up from his book on the Law of Trusts and say, 'Run away, boy, I am busy.' My father finished his book, and here I am." The great lawyer had neglected his own trust with awful results.

—*Public Speakers Library.*

Joys of Home

Curling smoke from a chimney low,
And only a few more steps to go.
Faces pressed at a window pane
Watching for someone to come again.
And I am the someone they want to see—
These are the joys life gives to me.

So let me come home at night and rest
With those who know I have done my
   best;
Let the wife rejoice and my children
   smile,
And I'll know by their love that I'm worth
   while.
For this is conquest and world success—
A home where abideth happiness.

—*Edgar A. Guest.*

"Joys of Home" is from the book "When Day is Done" by Edgar A. Guest, copyright 1921 by The Reilly & Lee Co., Chicago.

PEACE AT HOME—He is happiest, be he king or peasant, who finds peace in his home.—*Goethe.*

ADOPTION—When Christ receives a soul into His love, He puts upon him the ring of adoption. Adopted! Why, then, we are brothers and sisters to all the good of earth and Heaven, we have the family name and the family dress; and the Father looks down upon us, robes us, defends and blesses, and the insignia of eternal glory is our coat of arms.

—*Gallaway.*

SELF-RELIANCE — If you would have your son be something in the world, teach him to depend on himself. Let him learn that it is by close and strenuous personal application he must rise—that he must, in short, make himself, and be architect of his own fortune.—*Edwards.*

THE WATCHER

She always leaned to watch for us,
   Anxious if we were late,
In winter by the window,
   In summer by the gate;

And though we mocked her tenderly,
   Who had such foolish care,
The long way home would seem more
      safe
   Because she waited there.

Her thoughts were all so full of us,
   She never could forget!
And so I think that where she is
   She must be watching yet,

Waiting till we come home to her,
   Anxious if we are late—
Watching from Heaven's window,
   Leaning from Heaven's gate.

—MARGARET WIDDEMER.

From CROSS CURRENTS by Margaret Widdemer, copyright, 1921, by Harcourt, Brace and Company, Inc. Reprinted by permission.

LOVE has many ways of expressing itself, but in general the ways are two —the practical and the sentimental. Which is the higher and better way? It is merely a question of appropriateness under the circumstances. Love must express itself very often in coal, and cornmeal, and salt pork, and clothes. But let it not be concluded that love may not express itself in acts of pure sentiment. The soul has needs. Sympathy and tenderness and friendship are just as real and more enduring, than coal and wood. Sometimes a flower is more important than flour; sometimes a word of cheer is better than gold.—*Ferral.*

Measuring Rods

I know what mother's face is like,
  Though it I cannot see:
It's like the music of a bell,
It's like the way the roses smell,
It's like the stories fairies tell—
  It's all of these to me.

I know what father's face is like,
  I am sure I know it all:
It's like his whistle in the air,
It's like his step upon the stair,
It's like his arms that take much care,
  And never let me fall.

And so I know what God is like,
  The God whom no one sees:
He's everything my mother means,
He's like my very sweetest dreams,—
He's everything my father seems,
  But greater than all these.

A BOTANY LESSON — If we had paid no more attention to our plants than we have to our children, we would now be living in a jungle of weeds.
—*Luther Burbank.*

HOME-GROWN—Happiness grows at our own firesides, and is not to be picked in strangers' gardens.
—*Douglas Jerrold.*

Apotheosis

("A mother's kiss made me a painter."—Benjamin West.)

Bent breathless o'er a sleeping baby's bed,
A boy whose fingers twitched with restless zeal,
Thrilled as he watched the fitful light reveal
The smile that cross those tender lips had spread.
It seemed to him to be God's very seal.
Those trembling fingers seized a coal still red
And strove to tell in lines what his heart said;—
A boy's crude sketch of innocence ideal.

A mother paused from tasks dark found undone,
And with her worn hand roughly touched his cheek;
Then made her boy an artist with a kiss.
The source of genius is not hard to seek:
Its falt'ring sparks are fanned to flame each one
By trust like this shown in a mother's kiss.

—*Clyde Francis Lytle.*

A LITTLE CHILD SHALL LEAD THEM — In the old days there were angels who came and took men by the hand, and led them away from the city of destruction. We see no white-winged angels now. But yet men are led away from threatening destruction: a hand is put into theirs, which leads them forth gently toward a calm, bright land, so that they look no more backward; and the hand may be a little child's.
—*George Eliot.*

IS THERE A SANTA CLAUS?—

Dear Editor,—I am eight years old. Some of my little friends say there is no Santa Claus. Papa says "If you see it in *The Sun*, it's so." Please tell me the truth; is there a Santa Claus?

—*Virginia O'Hanlon.*

115 West Ninety-fifth St.

Virginia, your little friends are wrong. They have been affected by the scepticism of a sceptical age. They do not believe except they see. They think that nothing can be which is not comprehensible by their little minds.

All minds, Virginia, whether they be men's or children's, are little. In this great universe of ours man is a mere insect, an ant, in his intellect, as compared with the boundless world about him, as measured by the intelligence capable of grasping the whole of truth and knowledge.

Yes, Virginia, there is a Santa Claus. He exists as certainly as love and generosity and devotion exist, and you know that they abound and give to our life its highest beauty and joy. Alas! how dreary would be the world if there were no Santa Claus. It would be as dreary as if there were no Virginias. There would be no childlike faith then, no poetry, no romance, to make tolerable this existence. We should have no enjoyment, except in sense and sight. The eternal light with which childhood fills the world would be extinguished.

Not believe in Santa Claus! You might as well not believe in fairies! You might get your papa to hire men to watch in all the chimneys on Christmas Eve to catch Santa Claus, but even if they did not see Santa Claus coming down, what would that prove? Nobody sees Santa Claus, but that is no sign there is no Santa Claus.

The most real things in the world are those that neither children nor men can see. Did you ever see fairies dancing on the lawn? Of course not, but that's no proof that they are not there. Nobody can conceive or imagine all the wonders there are unseen and unseeable in the world.

You may tear apart the baby's rattle and see what makes the noise inside, but there is a veil covering the unseen world which not the strongest man, nor even the united strength of all the strongest men that ever lived, could tear apart. Only faith, fancy, poetry, love, romance, can push aside that curtain and view and picture the supernal beauty and glory beyond. Is it all real? Ah, Virginia, in all this world there is nothing else real and abiding.

No Santa Claus! Thank God! he lives, and he lives forever. A thousand years from now, Virginia, nay, ten times ten thousand years from now, he will continue to make glad the heart of childhood.—*Casual Essays of the Sun.*

PATIENCE

If we knew the baby fingers,
    Pressed against the window pane,
Would be cold and stiff tomorrow—
    Never trouble us again—
Would the bright eyes of our darling
    Catch the frown upon our brow?
Would the prints of rosy fingers
    Vex us then as they do now?

Ah, those little ice-cold fingers,
    How they point our memories back
To the hasty words and actions
    Strewn along our backward track!
How those little hands remind us,
    As in snowy grace they lie,
Not to scatter thorns—but roses
    For our reaping by-and-by.

—*Selected.*

HEART'S EASE — Every house where love abides and friendship is a guest, is surely home, and home, sweet home, for there the heart can rest.
—*Henry Van Dyke.*

To My Father

It matters not that Time has shed
His thawless snow upon your head,
For he maintains, with wondrous art,
Perpetual summer in your heart.
—*William Hamilton Hayne.*

ALL THE WORLD—There is an enduring tenderness in the love of a mother to a son that transcends all other affections of the heart! It is neither to be chilled by selfishness, nor daunted by danger, nor weakened by worthlessness, nor stifled by ingratitude. She will sacrifice every comfort to his convenience; she will surrender every pleasure to his enjoyment; she will glory in his fame, and exult in his prosperity—and if misfortune overtake him he will be the dearer to her from misfortune; and if disgrace settle upon his name she will still love and cherish him in spite of his disgrace; and if all the world beside cast him off she will be all the world to him.—*Washington Irving.*

Road Maps

Would ye learn the road to Laughtertown,
O ye who have lost the way?
Would ye have young heart though your hair be gray?
Go learn from a little child each day.
Go serve his wants and play his play,
And catch the lilt of his laughter gay,
And follow his dancing feet as they stray;
For he knows the road to Laughtertown,
O ye who have lost the way!
—*Katherine D. Blake.*

A Boy to Train

The man who has a boy to train,
Has work to keep him night and day.
There's much to him he must explain,
And many a doubt to clear away;
His task is one which calls for tact
And friendship of the finest kind,
Because, with every word and act,
He molds the little fellow's mind.
He must be careful of his speech,
For careless words are quickly learned;
He must be wise enough to teach
What corners may be safely turned.

"*A Boy to Train*" *is copyrighted by Edgar A. Guest. Used by permission of the publishers, The Reilly & Lee Co., Chicago.*

What Would You Take?

What would you take for that soft little head
Pressed close to your face at time for bed;
For that white, dimpled hand in your own held tight,
And the dear little eyelids kissed down for the night?
What would you take?

What would you take for that smile in the morn,
Those bright, dancing eyes and the face they adorn;
For the sweet little voice that you hear all day
Laughing and cooing—yet nothing to say?
What would you take?

What would you take for those pink little feet,
Those chubby round cheeks, and that mouth so sweet;
For the wee tiny fingers and little soft toes,
The wrinkly little neck and that funny little nose?
Now, what would you take?
—*Good Housekeeping.*

NEIGHBOR—What is meant by our neighbor we cannot doubt; it is every one with whom we are brought into contact. First of all, he is literally our neighbor who is next to us in our own family and household; husband to wife, wife to husband, parent to child, brother to sister, master to servant, servant to master. Then it is he who is close to us in our own neighborhood, in our own town, in our own parish, in our own street. With these all true charity begins. To love and be kind to these is the very beginning of all true religion. But, beside these, as our Lord teaches, it is every one who is thrown across our path by the changes and chances of life; he or she, whosoever it be, whom we have any means of helping —the unfortunate stranger whom we may meet in traveling, the deserted friend whom no one else cares to look after.

—*A. P. Stanley.*

Motto for Every Home

Whoe'er thou art that entereth here,
Forget the struggling world
And every trembling fear.

Take from thy heart each evil thought,
And all that selfishness
Within thy life has wrought.

For once inside this place thou'lt find
No barter, servant's fear,
Nor master's voice unkind.

Here all are kin of God above—
Thou, too, dear heart: and here
The rule of life is love.

IMMEDIACY — He who helps a child helps humanity with an immediateness which no other help given to human creature in any other stage of human life can possibly give again.—*Phillips Brooks.*

Restoration

Could every time-worn heart but see Thee
once again,
A happy, human child, among the homes
of men,
The age of doubt would pass—the vision
of Thy face
Would silently restore the childhood of
the race.

—*Henry Van Dyke.*

The Bravest Battle

The bravest battle that ever was fought!
Shall I tell you where and when?
On the maps of the world you will find
it not;
'Twas fought by the mothers of men.

Nay, not with cannon or battle-shot,
With a sword or noble pen;
Nay, not with eloquent words or thought
From mouths of wonderful men!

But deep in a walled-up woman's heart—
Of a woman that would not yield,
But bravely, silently bore her part—
Lo, there is that battlefield!

No marshaling troops, no bivouac song,
No banner to gleam and wave;
But oh! these battles, they last so long—
From babyhood to the grave.

Yet, faithful still as a bridge of stars,
She fights in her walled-up town—
Fights on and on in the endless wars,
Then, silent, unseen, goes down.

Oh, ye with banners and battle-shot,
And soldiers to shout and praise!
I tell you the kingliest victories fought
Were fought in those silent ways.

O spotless woman in a world of shame,
With splendid and silent scorn,
Go back to God as white as you came—
The kingliest warrior born!

—*Joaquin Miller.*

89

BUT ONLY ONE MOTHER—Most of all the other beautiful things in life come by twos and threes, by dozens and hundreds. Plenty of roses, stars, sunsets, rainbows, brothers and sisters, aunts and cousins, but only one *mother* in the whole world.—*Kate Douglas Wiggin.*

Boy

For the time when a boy is in danger
Of going a little bit wild
Is when he's too young to be married
Too old to be known as child.
A bird of the wild grass thicket
Just out of the parent tree flown.

Too large to keep in the old nest,
Too small to have one of its own.
When desolate, 'mid his companions,
His soul is a stake to be won,
'Tis then that the devil stands ready
To get a good place to catch on.

—Selected.

THE WATCHMAN — Nothing is sweeter than love, nothing more courageous, nothing higher, nothing wider, nothing more pleasant, nothing fuller nor better in Heaven and earth, because love is born of God, and cannot rest but in God, above all created things. Love feels no burden, thinks nothing of trouble, attempts what is above its strength, pleads no excuse of impossibility . . . It is therefore able to undertake all things, and it completes many things, and warrants them to take effect, where he who does not love would faint and lie down. Love is watchful and sleeping, slumbereth not. Though weary, it is not tired; though pressed, it is not straitened; though alarmed, it is not confounded; but, as a lively flame and burning torch, it forces its way upwards and securely passes all.

—Thomas a' Kempis.

Son

When I look out upon the florid years
  Ensnared in dreams, and castles vainly built
Encumbered with uncertainty and fears
  Of doing — comes propinquity with guilt:
That my own duty, Son, be not well done;
  That should you fail your boyish hands, full grown,
Will mark me cause; that fortunes never won,
  And favors lost, or wisdom scantly known
Shall stand between us: this your credo make:
  To live the truth in speech and deed; to spend
Long efforts toward good courtesy, and take
  Great pains with kindness; all your days commend
To glad God-fearing work, and rightly none
  Shall put a contemny upon you, Son.

—Lillian Arline Walbert.

THE MODEL—Did you ever watch a little child take a lesson in model drawing? Never two strokes of the pencil without a glance at the model. And the first law and the last law of the imitation of Christ is just this—"looking unto Jesus."

—George Jackson.

My Boy

"So let him live,
Love work, love play,
Love all that life can give;
And when he grows too weary to feel joy,
Leave life, with laughter, to some other boy."

—Charles C. Wakefield.

MUTUAL HELP—The family is a school of mutual help. Each member depends on every other. Today the robust father holds the "wee laddie" on his knee, or leads him up the stairway of that schoolroom in which he is to be taught his alphabet. But there is a tomorrow coming by and by when the lisper of the A B C will be the master of a home of his own—with an infirm, gray-haired parent dozing away his sunset years in an armchair. Each helps the other when and where the help is most needed. And every word and deed of unselfish love, comes back in blessings on its author. God puts helpless babes, and infirm parents into our families for this purpose (among others) that the strong may bear the burden of the weak, and in bearing them may grow stronger themselves in Bible graces.—*Cuyler.*

My Mother

She was as good as goodness is,
    Her acts and all her words were kind,
And high above all memories
    I hold the beauty of her mind.
            —*Frederic Hentz Adams.*

A STANDARD—There is nothing by which men display their character so much as in what they consider ridiculous.
            —*Goethe.*

Boundless

They talk about a woman's sphere
As though it had a limit;
There's not a place in earth or Heaven,
There's not a task to mankind given,
There's not a blessing or a woe,
There's not a whispered yes or no,
There's not a life, or death, or birth,
That has a feather's weight of worth—
    Without a woman in it.

FORGIVE—We may, if we choose, make the worst of one another. Every one has his weak points; every one has his faults; we may make the worst of these; we may fix our attention constantly upon these. But we may also make the best of one another. We may forgive, even as we hope to be forgiven. We may put ourselves in the place of others, and ask what we should wish to be done to us, and thought of us, were we in their place. By loving whatever is lovable in those around us, love will flow back from them to us, and life will become a pleasure instead of a pain; and earth will become like Heaven; and we shall become not unworthy followers of Him whose name is Love.

Memories

Like a richly colored flame whose bright
    tip
Draws upward, but is brushed by erring
    storm,
Then relentingly seeks the earth's dark
    form
And buries its deep desires bit by bit;
Thus your life ebbed—though trembling,
    pleading lips
Cried proffering words to a Triune God.
In vain I watched for one familiar nod,
Then pressed my mouth to thin black
    hairy wisps.

Memories? Mother! How can I forget?
Your smiling eyes with sad mystery
    tinged;
Your helping hands, though labor
    wrought with tasks;
Mother! Your clear high laughter had a
    depth
That thrilled my heart, and lifted silence
    winged
With boundless joy. Thank God! Memories last!
            —*Hilda A. Dammtrch.*

XVII. IMMORTALITY

RELEASE—Man is like a bird in a cage until he lives for eternity. He is like a prisoner in a cell until he gives the eternal within him expression. Just as the ripples of the meadow-brook reproduce the swell of the ocean tides towards which the brook flows; and just as the music of the rivulet in its eddies echoes the lap of the mighty sea on the beach where some day the rivulet will measure its waters; so the voices within us are the voices of the larger life for which we are destined and towards which we are going.—*Vance.*

Death, be not proud, though some have
    called thee
Mighty and dreadful, for thou art not
    so;
For those, whom thou think'st thou
    dost overthrow,
Die not, poor Death, nor yet canst
    thou kill me.
From rest and sleep, which but thy
    pictures be,
Much pleasure, then from thee much
    more, must flow,
And soonest our best men with thee
    do go,
Rest of their bones, and soul's delivery.
Thou art slave to fate, chance, kings,
    and desperate men,
And dost with poison, war, and sick-
    ness dwell,
And poppy, or charms, can make us
    sleep as well,
And better than thy stroke. Why
    swell'st thou then?
One short sleep past, we wake eter-
    nally,
And Death shall be no more; Death,
    thou shalt die.

—JOHN DONNE.

WHISPERS OF HOPE—Immortality is a word that Hope through all the ages has been whispering to Love. The miracle of thought we can not understand. The mystery of life and death we can not comprehend. This chaos called world has never been explained. The golden bridge of life from gloom emerges, and on shadow rests. Beyond this we do not know. Fate is speechless, destiny is dumb, and the secret of the future has never yet been told. We love; we wait; we hope. The more we love, the more we fear. Upon the tenderest heart the deepest shadows fall. All paths, whether filled with thorns or flowers, end here. Here success and failure are the same. The ray of wretchedness and the purple robe of power all differences and distinction lose in this democracy of death. Character survives; Goodness lives; Love is immortal.—*Robert G. Ingersoll.*

THE GOOD—Our hope for eternal life in the hereafter does not spring from a longing for a spiritual existence, but grows out of our love for life upon this earth, which we have tried and found good.—*Robert J. Shores.*

LIFE ETERNAL!—How shall I express my thought of it? It is not mere existence, however prolonged and free from annoyance. It is not the pleasures of the senses, however vivid. It is not peace. It is not happiness. It is not joy. But it is all these combined into one condition of spiritual perfection—one emotion of indescribable rapture—the peace after the storm has gone by, the soft repose after the grief is over, the joy of victory when the conflict is ended.—*Hill.*

THE MUDDY VESTURE OF DE-CAY—Death means just this; no more and no less. As Maclaren has vigorously said: "Strip the man of the disturbances that come from a fevered body, and he will have a calmer soul. Strip him of the hindrances which come from a body that is like an opaque tower around his spirit, with only a narrow crevice here and a narrow door there—five poor senses with which he is connected with the outer universe—and, surely, the spirit will have wider avenues out to God. It will have larger powers of reception, because it has become rid of the closer confinements of the fleshly tabernacle. They who die in Jesus live a larger, fuller, nobler life, by the very cessation of care, change, strife, and struggle. Above all, they live a fuller, grander life, because they sleep in Jesus' and are gathered into His embrace, and awake with Him, clothed with white robes, awaiting the adoption—to wit, the redemption of the body."

SYMPATHY—If a friend of mine . . . gave a feast, and did not invite me to it, I should not mind a bit . . . But if . . . a friend of mine had a sorrow and refused to allow me to share it, I should feel it most bitterly. If he shut the doors of the house of mourning against me, I would move back again and again and beg to be admitted, so that I might share in what I was entitled to share. If he thought me unworthy, unfit to weep with him, I should feel it as the most poignant humiliation, as the most terrible mode by which disgrace could be inflicted on me . . . he who can look on the loveliness of the world and share its sorrow, and realize something of the wonder of both, is in immediate contact with divine things, and has got as near to God's secret as any one can get.—*Oscar Wilde.*

WHY WE BELIEVE—If there be an argument which stirs me to indignation at its futility, and to wonder that any mortal ever regarded it as of the slightest force: it is that which is set out in the famous soliloquy in Cato, as to the immortality of the soul. Will any sane man say, that if in this world you wish for a thing very much, and anticipate it very clearly and confidently, you are therefore sure to get it? If that were so, many a little schoolboy would end by driving his carriage and four who ends by driving no carriage at all. No: we cling to the doctrine of a future life: we could not live without it: but we believe it, not because of undefined longings within ourselves, not because of reviving plants and flowers, not because of the chrysalis and the butterfly: but because our Savior Jesus Christ hath abolished death, and brought light and immortality to light through the gospel.—*A. K. H. Boyd.*

Hope Sees a Star

Life is a narrow vale between the cold and barren peaks of two eternities.

We strive in vain to look beyond the heights.

We cry aloud—and the only answer is the echo of our wailing cry.

From the voiceless lips of the unreplying dead there comes no word.

But in the night of death Hope sees a star, and listening Love can hear the rustling of a wing.

He who sleeps here, when dying, mistaking the approach of death for the return of health, whispered with his latest breath, "I am better now."

Let us believe, in spite of doubts and fears, that these dear words are true of all the countless dead.

—*Robert G. Ingersoll, at his brother's grave, June 2, 1879.*

FROM A FULL HEART—Never let the seeming worthlessness of sympathy make you keep back that sympathy of which, when men are suffering around you, your heart is full. Go and give it without asking yourself whether it is worth while to give it. It is too sacred a thing for you to tell what it is worth. God, from whom it comes, sends it through you to His needy child.—*Phillips Brooks.*

REVISED EDITION
The Body
of
Benjamin Franklin, Printer
(Like the cover of an old book,
Its contents torn out,
And stripped of its lettering and gilding,)
Lies here food for worms.
Yet the work itself shall not be lost,
For it will (as he believes) appear once
more
In a new
And beautiful Edition
Corrected and Amended
By
The Author
(*Franklin's self-written epitaph*)

CHARTED—It is not darkness you are going to, for God is Light. It is not lonely, for Christ is with you. It is not an unknown country, for Christ is there.
—*Charles Kingsley.*

EVOLUTION
Out of the dusk a shadow,
  Then a spark;
Out of the cloud a silence,
  Then, a lark;
Out of the heart a rapture,
  Then, a pain;
Out of the dead, cold ashes,
  Life again.
—*John Banister Tabb.*

HEAVEN—When I was a boy I used to think of Heaven as a glorious golden city, with jewelled walls, and gates of pearl, with nobody in it, but the angels, and they were all strangers to me. But after a while my little brother died; then I thought of Heaven as that great city, full of angels, with just one little fellow in it that I was acquainted with. He was the only one I knew there, at that time. Then another brother died, and there were two in Heaven that I knew. Then my acquaintance began to die, and the number of my friends in Heaven grew larger all the time. But, it was not till one of my own little ones was taken that I began to feel that I had a personal interest in Heaven. Then a second went, and a third, and a fourth; and so many of my friends and loved ones have gone there, that it seems as if I know more in Heaven than I know on earth. And now, when my thoughts turn to Heaven, it is not the gold and the jewels, and the pearls that I think of—but the loved ones there. It is not the place so much as the company that makes Heaven seem beautiful.—*Selected.*

ONLY THE BODY — Plato in his Phaedon represents Socrates as saying in the last hour of his life to his inconsolable followers, "You may bury me if you can catch me." He then added with a smile, and an intonation of unfathomable thought and tenderness, "Do not call this poor body Socrates. When I have drunk the poison, I shall leave you, and go to the joys of the blessed. I would not have you sorrow at my hard lot, or say at the interment, 'Thus we lay out Socrates;' or, 'Thus we follow him to the grave, and bury him.' Be of good cheer: say that you are burying my body only."
—*R. J. Cooke.*

FIGURES OF DEATH—You cannot find in the New Testament any of those hateful representations of dying which men have invented, by which death is portrayed as a ghastly skeleton with a scythe, or something equally revolting. The figures by which death is represented in the New Testament are very different. There are two of them which I think to be exquisitely beautiful. One is that of falling asleep in Jesus. When a little child has played all day long, and becomes tired out, and the twilight has sent it in weariness to its mother's knee, where it thinks it has come for more excitement, then, almost in the midst of its frolicking, and not knowing what influence is creeping over it, it falls back in the mother's arms, and nestles close to the sweetest and softest couch that ever cheek pressed, and, with lengthening breath, sleeps; and she smiles and is glad, and sits humming unheard joy over its head. So we fall asleep in Jesus. We have played long enough at the games of life, and at last we feel the approach of death. We are tired out, and we lay our head back on the bosom of Christ and quietly fall asleep.—*H. W. Beecher.*

DISSOLVED — In the laboratory of Faraday a workman one day knocked into a jar of acid a silver cup. It disappeared, was eaten by the acid, and could not be found. The question came up as to whether it could ever be found. The great chemist came in and put certain chemicals into the jar and every particle of the silver was precipitated to the bottom. The mass was then sent to a silversmith and the cup was restored. So a precious soul who has fallen into the sink of iniquity, lost, dissolved in sin can only be restored by the Great Chemist—"Jesus only."
—*S. S. Times.*

RESURRECTION — We see in the Risen Christ the end for which man was made and the assurance that the end is within reach. Christ rose from the grave changed and yet the same; and in Him we have the pledge and type of our rising.

Away

I cannot say, and I will not say
That he is dead. He is just away!

With a cheery smile and a wave of the
hand,
He has wandered into an unknown land.

And left us dreaming how very fair
It needs must be, since he lingers there.

And you—oh you, who the wildest yearn
For the old time step and the glad return—

Think of him faring on, as dear
In the love of There as the love of Here;

And loyal still, as he gave the blows
Of his warrior strength to his country's
foes—

Mild and gentle, as he was brave,
When the sweetest love of his life he gave

To simple things; where the violets grew
Pure as the eyes they were likened to,

The touches of his hands have strayed
As reverently as his lips have prayed;

When the little brown thrush that harshly
chirred
Was dear to him as the mocking-bird;

And he pitied as much as a man in pain
A writhing honey-bee wet with rain.

Think of him still as the same, I say:
He is not dead—he is just—away!
—*James Whitcomb Riley.*

From AFTERWHILES, by permission of the publishers,
The Bobbs Merrill Company.

THE SOUL SURVIVES—The arguments from reason by which the immortality of the soul is maintained are well known. But there is another argument, the scope of which has been so immensely enlarged in modern times that the disregard of it by the ancients does not count against its inherent validity. This is the general consent of the race. The future existence of the soul has been held as a matter of popular belief by the people of every age and country. It is found among the Chinese, the Egyptians, the Hindus, the Persians, the Greeks and Romans, the Druids, the Celts, the Germans, the Slavs, and a great variety of uncivilized tribes in North America and South, in the centre of Africa, and in the islands of the sea. There are exceptions, but these are just enough to confirm the rule. The great body of the human family in every age have held, as they hold now, that the soul survives the body; and there is no way of accounting for this unanimity but by admitting the truth of the doctrine. Either it was derived by tradition from our original ancestors, who obtained it from their Creator, or its evidences lie so deeply impressed upon the constitution of man that they compel assent. A judgment held so long, so widely, and by such different races, must be deemed to be correct.—G. F. Wright.

VESPERS

I know the night is near at hand:
The mists lie low on hill and bay,
The Autumn sheaves are dewless, dry;
But I have had the day.

Yes, I have had, dear Lord, the day;
When at Thy call I have the night,
Brief be the twilight as I pass
From light to dark, from dark to light.
—Silas Weir Mitchell.

CONQUERORS — In this world, he that is today conqueror may tomorrow himself be defeated. Pompey is eclipsed by Caesar, and then Caesar falls by the hands of conspirators; Napoleon conquered nearly all Europe, and was then himself conquered. But the Christian's conquest of death is absolute. The result is final. He has vanquished the last enemy, and has no more battles to fight.—Foster.

Death to a good man is but passing through a dark entry, out of one little dusky room of his Father's house into another that is fair and large, lightsome and glorious, and divinely entertaining.
—A. Clarke.

You have felt the exhilarating change from a convalescent chamber to a bright spring day, with its balmy air, its flowers and fragrance and songs. How fresh the burst of devout feeling in a pious mind amid such a scene! What, then, must be the transition from the gloom of a sick-chamber, and the last of life's struggles, into the tranquillity and joy of the presence of the Lord?—J. Graham.

HEAVEN SATISFIES — If a child were to ask me if there would be harps and pianos—yes, and hobby-horses, in Heaven, I would tell him "yes;" that is, if he was fond of those things; because that would be the truest answer I could make him. What I should mean by it would be, that there would be that there which would just as nicely fit into his Heavenly desires as the hobby-horse does into his earthly desires. Heaven means satisfaction. And if it takes a hobby-horse to satisfy him now, and I tell him there will be nothing of that kind there, then to him I make Heaven unsatisfactory and so falsify the fact. There is an untruthful way of telling the truth and a truthful way of telling an untruth.—Parkhurst.

MORTALITY — I was walking one day in Westminster Abbey. As I paused to survey the monuments of the illustrious departed that are gathered there, my attention was arrested by the appearance of the pavement near to where I stood. A beautiful many-colored light rested upon it, and gave it an aspect that I could not but linger to behold. The cause was apparent. A painted window above me explained the reason. And the pavement, beautiful as it appeared, had no color in itself; it was the window above that gave it the beauteous hue. How many are like that pavement! They appear beautiful, and we are apt to mistake it for "the beauty of holiness;" but it is in a borrowed light—contact with the wise and good it may be; remove that, and their true color appears.—*Selected.*

GETTING READY — There is only one way to get ready for immortality, and that is to love this life and live it as bravely and faithfully, and cheerfully as we can.—*Henry Van Dyke.*

MORTALITY—It is the custom of the Chinese to keep their coffins in their houses where they can be often seen. The ancient Egyptians, at all their feasts, served their guests with some part of a skeleton to put them in mind of their mortality. And, on the day of his coronation, one of the emperors of Constantinople, among other gifts of great value, received the present of a gravestone, to remind him of the coming day when the crown would be taken from his head. And, in the midst of life and health, it would be good for us if we would often think of that hour that will finish our discipline and fix our destiny.

—*Public Speakers Library.*

INTIMATION OF IMMORTALITY—It has always seemed to me a major tragedy that so many people go through life haunted by the fear of death—only to find when it comes that it's as natural as life itself. For very few are afraid to die when they get to the very end. In all my experience only one seemed to feel any terror—a woman who had done her sister a wrong which it was too late to right.

Something strange and beautiful happens to men and women when they come to the end of the road. All fear, all horror disappears. I have often watched a look of happy wonder dawn in their eyes when they realized this was true. It is all part of the goodness of nature and, I believe, of the illimitable goodness of God.

—*A Veteran Nurse.*

Disguise

Out of the pain of night-watching removed
Into the sleep that God gives His beloved,
Into the dawn of a glad resurrection,
Into the house of unbroken affection,
Into the joy of her Lord—thence confessing
Death in disguise is His angel in blessing.

—*Selected.*

THE CROSSING — They that love beyond the world can not be separated by it. Death can not kill what never dies.

Nor can spirits ever be divided, that love and live in the same divine principle, the root and record, of their friendship . . . Death is but crossing the world, as friends do the seas; they live in one another still . . .

This is the comfort of friends, that though they may be said to die, yet their friendship and society are, in the best sense, ever present because immortal.

—*William Penn.*

TRANSITION — We are all of us going to die sometime. . . . Some—and this, I assume, means the majority — in times of health put from them all contemplation of death as a concrete fact; even so, though, there must be hours when they speculate upon it as applying to themselves. So to all such, I, who have skirted the Valley of the Shadow, say that if my own experience is typical — and it surely must have been — then those among us whose lot it will be to face the finish while still in reasonable possession of our faculties will face it without fear and without bitterness, without reluctance and without repinings, without sufferings, whether physical or mental; we shall find it, at the last, but a peaceful transition, an eternal change mercifully accomplished.

—*Irvin S. Cobb.*

The Junk Man

I am glad God saw Death
And gave Death a job taking care of all
    who are tired of living:
When all the wheels in a clock are worn
    and slow and the connections loose
And the clock goes on ticking and telling
    the wrong time from hour to hour
And people around the house joke about
    what a bum clock it is,
How glad the clock is when the big Junk
    Man drives his wagon
Up to the house and puts his big arms
    around the clock and says:
        "You don't belong here,
        You gotta come
        Along with me,"
How glad the clock is then, when it feels
    the arms of the Junk Man close
    around it and carry it away.

—*Carl Sandburg.*

From CHICAGO POEMS by Carl Sandburg, by permission of the publishers, Henry Holt and Company, Inc. Copyright, 1916 by Henry Holt and Company. Copyright, 1943 by Carl Sandburg.

CHARACTER (*Alone Remains*)—In the U. S. Mint there was recently a curiously-engraved medal of elaborate design and the minutest detail. Even the lace on the figure was wrought out with marvelous painstaking. The expense of the medal was $6,500, yet its value there was only the bare metal, about one-twentieth. So men pass with the world at high valuation. Culture, refinement, wealth, social standing, official influence, titular distinctions, give them a temporary importance, but death soon will bring them to the crucible of a final judgment, at which all these extrinsic and adventitious characteristics pass for nothing.

Anticipations

I love preliminary things:
The tuning-up of flutes and strings;
The little scales musicians play
In varying keys to feel their way;
The hum—the hush in which it dies;
But most to see the curtain rise.

I love preliminary things:
The little box the postman brings;
To cut the twine, to break the seals,
And wonder what the lid reveals;
To lift the folds in which it lies
And watch the gift materialize.

The snowdrop and the daffodil,
The catkins hanging straight and still,
The blossom on the orchard trees—
Do you know greater joys than these?
Each represents the hope that springs
In all preliminary things.

—*J. R. J.*

Death

Fearest the shadow? Keep thy trust;
    Still the star-worlds roll.
Fearest death? Sayest, "Dust to dust"?
    No; say "Soul to soul!"

—*John Vance Cheney.*

RENOVATION — If a man has a statue decayed by rust and age, and mutilated in many of its parts, he breaks it up and casts it into a furnace, and after the melting he receives it again in more beautiful form. As thus the dissolving in the furnace was not a destruction, but a renewing of the statue, so the death of our bodies is not a destruction, but a renovation. When, therefore, you see as in a furnace our flesh flowing away to corruption, dwell not on that sight, but wait for the recasting. And advance in your thoughts to a still higher point, for the statuary casting into the furnace a brazen image but makes a brazen one again. God does not thus; but casting in a mortal body formed of clay, He returns you an immortal statue of gold.—*Chrysostom.*

MANSIONS — I understand that the Lord meant by His "Father's house" the whole vast universe; and if so, the point of His comfort to the disciples becomes clear. "In my Father's house," He said, "are many mansions." Do not suppose that this world is all, or that beyond the veil, even the blessedness and joy of this world will not be surpassed. You have found a home here. You have found God here. You have here learned that it is possible to dwell with God. But this is only one mansion and there are many more. You have entered only the first. There are myriads that you have not seen. Do not, therefore, tremble if I leave you. This world is not the whole of the stage on which redemption is to be wrought out. Do not think that death is dissolution to the soul, or that its personal and spiritual relationship to God will be affected by death. If such had been the case I would certainly have told you, and my course of instruction would have been very different. This world is but one place of abode with God. There are innumerably more, and only with these in thought can you realize the worth and promise of a Christian life.—*Purves.*

MEASURED BY THE SOUL—The size of one's Heaven is the exact dimensions of his soul. Happiness is a matter of appetite and capacity. As well prepare dinner for a corpse as Heaven for a soul whose spiritual functions are dead. The problem of the hereafter is not the matter of a celestial climate and a city beautiful. It is the problem of the eternal in man. The kingdom is within him. The greatest concern of a human being therefore should be to feel God's presence, to be stirred by His message, to have faith in the invisible, and to follow aspirations which leap over the boundaries of time and seek satisfaction in the infinite. For to be devoid of all this is to fall a victim to the disease that destroys character, paralyses progress, and forbids happiness.—*Vance.*

Song

When I am dead, my dearest,
  Sing no sad songs for me;
Plant thou no roses at my head,
  Nor shady cypress-tree;
Be the green grass above me
  With showers and dewdrops wet;
And if thou wilt, remember,
  And if thou wilt, forget.

I shall not see the shadows,
  I shall not feel the rain;
I shall not hear the nightingale
  Sing on, as if in pain;
And dreaming through the twilight
  That doth not rise nor set,
Haply I may remember,
  And haply may forget.
      —*Christina G. Rossetti.*

99

XVIII. MEMORY

WHAT TO FORGET — If you would increase your happiness and prolong your life, forget your neighbor's faults. Forget all the slander you have ever heard. Forget the temptations. Forget the fault finding, and give a little thought to the cause which provoked it. Forget the peculiarities of your friends, and only remember the good points which make you fond of them. Forget all personal quarrels or histories you may have heard by accident, and which, if repeated, would seem a thousand times worse than they are. Blot out as far as possible all the disagreeables of life; they will come, but will only grow larger when you remember them, and the constant thought of the acts of meanness, or, worse still, malice, will only tend to make you more familiar with them. Obliterate everything disagreeable from yesterday; write upon today's clean sheet those things lovely and loveable.

THE SCENT OF THE ROSES

*Let Fate do her worst; there are relics
    of joy,
Bright dreams of the past, which she
    cannot destroy;
Which come in the night-time of sor-
    row and care,
And bring back the features that joy
    used to wear.
Long, long be my heart with such
    memories filled,
Like the vase in which roses have once
    been distilled—
You may break, you may shatter the
    vase if you will,
But the scent of the roses will hang
    round it still.*

    —THOMAS MOORE.

REJOICE

Grave on thy heart each past "red-letter
    day"!
Forget not all the sunshine of the way
By which the Lord hath led thee; answer-
    ed prayers,
And joys unasked, strange blessings, lifted
    cares,
Grand promise-echoes! Thus thy life shall
    be
One record of His love and faithfulness
    to thee.

    —*F. R. Havergal.*

THEY SAY—Die when I may, I want it said of me by those who knew me best, that I always plucked a thistle and planted a flower where I thought a flower would grow.—*Abraham Lincoln.*

REMEMBER

Remember me when I am gone away,
    Gone far away into the silent land;
    When you can no more hold me by
        the hand,
Nor I half turn to go yet turning stay.
Remember me when no more, day by day,
    You tell me of our future that you
        planned:
    Only remember me; you understand
It will be late to counsel then or pray.
Yet if you should forget me for a while
    And afterwards remember, do not
        grieve;
    For if the darkness and corruption
        leave
    A vestige of the thoughts that once I
        had,
Better by far you should forget and smile
    Than that you should remember and
        be sad.

    —*Christina G. Rossetti.*

FORGET

It is better to forget the things that hurt us,
And to live each day and take whatever
    comes,
With the hope that by tomorrow
There will come a balm for sorrow
And help to master life's important sums!
There's a strength comes to us every time
    we suffer,
And our will grows stronger every time
    we fight,
Let us then be doubly grateful
For the things that disappoint us;
They only come to lead us to the light!
        —*Helen Mocksett Stork.*

MEMORABILIA

My mind lets go a thousand things
Like dates of wars and deaths of kings,
And yet recalls the very hour—
'Twas noon by yonder village tower,
And on the last blue noon in May—
The wind came briskly up this way,
Crisping the brook beside the road;
Then, pausing here, set down its load
Of pine-scents, and shook listlessly
Two petals from that wild-rose tree.
        —*Thomas Bailey Aldrich.*

SAINTED

He loved the House of God;
His dearest wish to be
A minister within her walls
In service full and free.

Beautifully he lived,
We who well loved him know,
Blessing with kindly hands our dead,
Softening death's cruel blow.

Beautifully he died—
The temple floors he trod,
To pass to his reward within
The altar of his God!
        —*Estella Shields Fahringer.*

REMEMBER—The value of time.
The success of perseverance.
The pleasure of working.
The dignity of simplicity.
The worth of character.
The power of kindness.
The influence of example.
The obligation of duty.
The wisdom of economy.
The virtue of patience.
The improvement of talent.
The joy of originating.
        —*Bulletin.*

THE COIN

Into my heart's treasury
    I slipped a coin,
That time cannot rust
    Nor a thief purloin;
Oh, better than the minting
    Of a gold-crowned king
Is the safe-kept memory
    Of a lovely thing.
        —*Sara Teasdale.*

From THE COLLECTED POEMS of Sara Teasdale.
By permission of The Macmillan Company, publishers.

FORGET IT

Forget the slander you have heard,
Forget the hasty, unkind word;
Forget the quarrel and the cause,
Forget the whole affair, because
Forgetting is the only way.
Forget the storm of yesterday,
Forget the chap whose sour face
Forgets to smile in any place.
Forget you're not a millionaire,
Forget the gray streaks in your hair.
Forget the coffee when it's cold,
Forget to kick, forget to scold,
Forget the plumber's awful charge,
Forget the iceman's bill is large;
Forget the coalman and his ways,
Forget the winter's blustery days.
        —*Anonymous.*

THINK ON THESE THINGS — Psychologists tell us that the vividness of our memory depends on the stress of attention. Therefore, says St. Paul, "if there be any virtue, if there be any praise, *think on these things.*"

You

Deep in the heart of me,
Nothing but You!
See through the art of me—
Deep in the heart of me
Find the best part of me,
Changeless and true.
Deep in the heart of me
Nothing but You!

—*Ruth Guthrie Harding.*

THINK ON THESE THINGS —

What to remember,—what to forget,— that is the question.

It seems to me that the good things, the heavenly guidance, the help that other men have given us to keep the right path, are the things to remember.

The mistakes, the false leads, the devilish influences, are the things to forget.

Love Can Never Lose Its Own

Yet Love will dream and Faith will trust
(Since He who knows our need is just)
That somehow, somewhere, meet we must.
Alas for him who never sees
The stars shine through his cypress trees!
Who, hopeless, lays his dead away,
Nor looks to see the breaking day
Across the mournful marbles play!
Who hath not learned, in hours of faith,
The truth to flesh and sense unknown
That Life is ever lord of Death,
And Love can never lose its own!

—*John Greenleaf Whittier.*

HIM—Dr. S. D. Gordon tells of an old Christian woman whose age began to tell on her memory. She had once known much of the Bible by heart. Eventually only one precious bit stayed with her, "I know whom I have believed, and am persuaded that He is able to keep that which I have committed unto Him against that day." By and by part of that slipped its hold, and she would quietly repeat, "That which I have committed unto Him." At last as she hovered on the borderland between this and the spirit world, her loved ones noticed her lips moving. They bent down to see if she needed anything. She was repeating over and over again to herself the one word of the text, "Him —Him—Him." She had lost the whole Bible but one word. But she had the whole Bible in that one word.

Because

Because of your strong faith I kept the track
  Whose sharp-set stones my strength had well-nigh spent.
I could not meet your eyes if I turned back;
  So on I went.

Because you would not yield belief in me,
  The threatening crags that rose my way to bar,
I conquered inch by crumbling inch—to see
  The goal afar.

And though I struggle toward it through hard years,
  Or flinch, or falter blindly, yet within,
"You can!" unwavering my spirit hears
  And I shall win.

KEEP ON—Before you give up hope, turn back and read the attacks that were made upon Lincoln.—*Bruce Barton.*

THERE IS A REMEMBRANCE of the dead, to which we turn even from the charms of the living. This we would not exchange for the song of pleasure or the bursts of revelry.—*Washington Irving.*

SAFETY ZONES—In great crisis, the memory of the word of some wise and gracious teacher often comes to our rescue, and the new and bewildering experience in which we stand assumes a familiar and orderly aspect. We are set free from fear and panic and enabled to act with sanity and wisdom. For those whose memory is full of the words of Christ, there is strength in all life's emergencies.

JOY'S RECOLLECTION is no longer joy, while sorrow's memory is sorrow still.—*Byron.*

ROADSIDE MEETINGS

A little more tired at close of day,
A little less anxious to have our way;
A little less ready to scold and blame;
A little more care for a brother's name—
And so we are nearing the journey's end,
Where time and eternity meet and blend.
The book is closed and the prayers are said,
And we are a part of the countless dead.
Thrice happy then if some soul can say
"I live because he has passed this way."
　　　　　　　—*Stephen Crane.*

MEMORY IS NOT WISDOM; idiots can by rote repeat volumes.—Yet what is wisdom without memory?
　　　　　　　—*Tupper.*

THE TRUE ART of memory is the art of attention.—*Johnson.*

DEFINED—Memory is the cabinet of imagination, the treasury of reason, the registry of conscience, and the council chamber of thought.—*Basil.*

COMPENSATION — If the memory is more flexible in childhood, it is more tenacious in mature age; if childhood has sometimes the memory of words, old age has that of things, which impress themselves according to the clearness of the conception of the thought which we wish to retain.—*Bonstetten.*

BOOK OF JUDGMENT — That memory is the book of judgment, I can well believe. I have, indeed, seen the same thing asserted in modern books, and accompanied by a remark which I am convinced is true, namely: that the dread book of account, which the Scriptures speak of is, in fact, the mind itself of each individual. Of this, at least, I feel assured —that there is no such thing as forgetting, possible to the mind; a thousand accidents may and will interpose a veil between our present consciousness and the secret inscriptions on the mind; accidents of the same sort will also rend away this veil; but whether veiled or unveiled, the inscription remains forever; just as the stars seem to withdraw before the common light of day; whereas, in fact, we know that it is the light which is drawn over them as a veil, and that they are waiting to be revealed, when the obscuring daylight shall have withdrawn.
　　　　　　　—*De Quincey.*

A JOY FOREVER—A memory without blot or contamination must be an exquisite treasure, an inexhaustible source of pure refreshment.—*Charlotte Bronte.*

XIX. MYSTICISM

SPIRITUAL VALUES—And now comes the new day in which we live—a day of social reconstruction and spiritual awakening. The typical Christian of this new day will be the practical mystic. He will be a mystic—sensitive to the spiritual values of life and its deepest music; but he will also be a man of practical power, facing the social problems of the age and contributing to their solution.—*Albert W. Parker.*

GUIDANCE—In the daily events of our life we mistake the Divine for the human. You may cross a street, and not know the reason why, and in that very crossing you may unconsciously be obeying a Divine suggestion. You may hold over the letter box a letter, and suddenly you may say, "I'll not send it by this post," and your not sending it may occasion you a blessing that you never thought of. You cannot account for these things. You say, "I thought just at the last moment I would not do so;" but that is a fool's explanation of life. I rather believe that God's angels are just overhead, or just by our side, and that we do things by Divine impulse without always knowing what we are in reality doing. You say, "Yes, but don't let us be superstitious." I answer, I am more afraid of people losing veneration than I am afraid of their becoming superstitious; and it is a poor life that does not begin in veneration, and continue in worship to the end.—*J. Parker.*

THE MYSTERY

He came and took me by the hand
　Up to a red rose tree,
He kept His meaning to Himself,
　But gave a rose to me.

I did not pray Him to lay bare
　The mystery to me;
Enough the rose was heaven to smell,
　And His own face to see.
　　　　　—Ralph Hodgson.

From POEMS. By permission of The Macmillan Company, publishers.

A PRAYER

Soul of Christ, sanctify me!
Body of Christ, save me!
Blood of Christ, inebriate me.
Water from the side of Christ, cleanse me.
Passion of Christ, strengthen me!
O good Jesus, hear me!
Within Thy wounds, hear me!
Suffer me never to be separated from
　Thee!
From the malicious enemy defend me!
At the hour of my death call me!
And bid me come to Thee!
That with Thy saints I may praise Thee!
For ever and ever!
Amen.
　　　　　—St. Ignatius.

SEARCH FOR GOD

I sought His love in lore of books,
　In charts of science's skill;
They left me orphaned as before—
　His love eluded still;
Then in despair I breathed a prayer;
The Lord of Love was standing there!

I sought His love in sun and stars,
　And where the wild seas roll,
And found it not. As mute I stood,
　Fear overwhelmed my soul;
But when I gave to one in need,
I found the Lord of Love indeed.
　　　　　—THOMAS CURTIS CLARK.

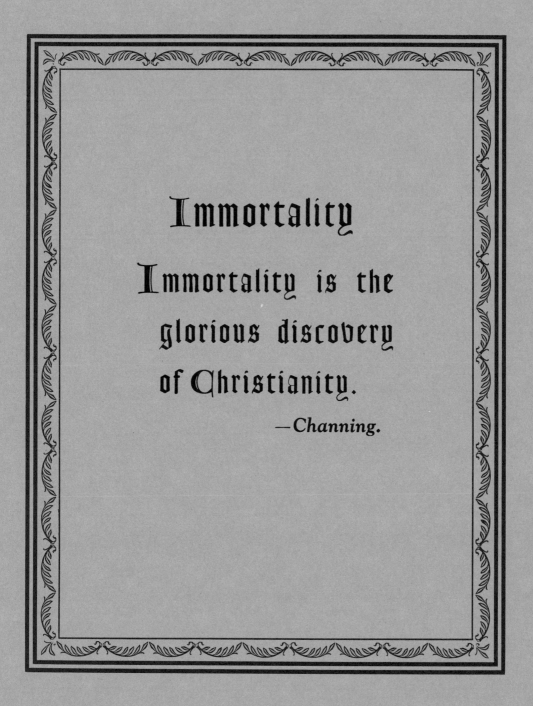

Immortality

Immortality is the glorious discovery of Christianity.

—Channing.

SONG OF THE MYSTIC

I walk down the Valley of Silence
Down the dim, voiceless valley—alone!
And I hear not the fall of a footstep
Around me, save God's and my own;
And the hush of my heart is as holy
As havens where angels have flown.

Long ago was I weary of voices
Whose music my heart could not win,
Long ago was I weary of noises
That fretted my soul with their din,
Long ago was I weary of places
Where I met but the human—and sin.

And I toiled on, heart-tired of the Human,
And I moaned midst the mazes of men
Till I knelt, long ago, at an altar
And I heard a voice call me. Since then
I walk down the Valley of Silence
That lies far beyond human ken.

Do you ask what I found in the Valley?
'Tis my trysting place with the Divine,
And I fell at the feet of the Holy
And above me, a voice said: "Be mine."
And there rose from the depths of my
    spirit
An echo: "My heart shall be thine."

Do you ask me the place of the Valley,
Ye hearts that are harrowed by Care?
It lieth afar between mountains,
And God and His angels are there:
And one is the dark mount of Sorrow,
And one the bright mountain of Prayer.
                    —Abram J. Ryan.

REFLECTIONS — The world is a
looking-glass, and gives back to every man
the reflection of his own face. Frown at it,
and it in turn will look sourly upon you;
laugh at it and with it, and it is a jolly,
kind companion.
            —William Makepeace Thackeray.

THE MYSTIC'S PRAYER

Lay me to sleep in sheltering flame
    O Master of the Hidden Fire!
Wash pure my heart, and cleanse for me
    My soul's desire.

In flame of sunrise bathe my mind,
    O Master of the Hidden Fire,
That, when I wake, clear-eyed may be
    My soul's desire.
                    —William Sharp.

THE ESSENCE OF RELIGION—
The efficacy of religion lies precisely in
that which is not rational, philosophic,
nor external; its efficacy lies in the unforeseen, the miraculous, the extraordinary.
Thus religion attracts more devotion in
proportion as it demands more faith—
that is to say, as it becomes more incredible to the profane mind. The philosopher
aspires to explain away all mysteries, to
dissolve them into light. It is mystery, on
the other hand, which religious instinct
demands and pursues; it is mystery which
constitutes the essence of worship . . .
No positive religion can survive the supernatural element, which is the reason for
its existence.
                —Henri-Frederic Amiel.

THE UNKNOWN GOD

Far up the dim twilight fluttered
    Moth wings of vapour and flame:
The lights danced over the mountains,
    Star after star they came.

The lights grew thicker unheeded,
    For silent and still were we;
Our hearts were drunk with a beauty
    Our eyes could never see.
        —A.E. (George William Russell)

From SELECTED POEMS of AE. By permission of
The Macmillan Company, publishers.

105

The Old Kent Road

The weary tavern yawns, so to confess
The dissipation of the night before
And lack of interest in the crowds that
    pour
Along the street; and therefore none
    would guess
That, deep beneath its morning conscious-
    ness,
Lie buried holy memories a score
Of how, where recent ale-slops foul its
    floor,
The soil received a martyr's selfishness!
Small room for thoughts like this amidst
    the din
Of traffic: few seem able to afford
The time to gather heavenly treasures in
When hunger drives, or Mammon is
    abroad.
But lo! through haunts of care and ways
    of sin
Moves some one with the Body of the
    Lord!

—Leo Rowlands.

THE GLORY OF COMMUNION
—Father Dalgairns declared, "The human heart is incurably mystical. . ."
Cardinal Manning, in his blessed little classic, *The Eternal Priesthood*, says, "The priest stands every morning upon the shores of the eternal world." We catch glimpses of the Supernal. As we speak the mystic words of the Mass, the thin, ethereal curtain between the two worlds is blown aside for a moment and we see at least briefly and dimly what the Mass really means. When we come away from the altar, returning so to speak from the other world to this, it is our duty and our privilege to convey, or at least to try to convey to the people what we have seen and heard. We shall do it with the help of the sacred words in which the mystery of the Mass is en-shrined, by means of the ritual and the liturgy, the combination of word and action that makes the Mass. In whatever proportion we succeed in imparting to the people a realization of the Mass, not as a poem, a form of beautiful words expressing profound thought; not as a drama, impressive, fascinating like the Passion Play, but as at once Poem, Drama, Fact, Reality, a Reality from the other world strangely taking place in this world; in proportion as we make the people see that the Mass is the Only Genuine Reality we shall teach them to love the Mass and cling to the Mass, even though like so many martyrs in Rome, in England, in Ireland, in Russia, in China, in Japan, they shall have to die for the Mass.—*James M. Gillis.*

The Virgin

Mother, whose virgin bosom was uncrost
With the least shade of thought to sin
    allied;
Woman, above all women glorified,
Our tainted nature's solitary boast;
Purer than foam on central ocean tost,
Brighter than eastern skies at daybreak
    strewn
With fancied roses, than the unblem-
    ished moon
Before her wane begins on heaven's blue
    coast,
Thy image falls to earth. Yet some, I ween,
Not unforgiven the suppliant knee might
    bend
As to a visible form in which did blend
All that was mixed and reconciled in
    thee
Of mother's love with maiden purity,
Of high with low, celestial with terrene.

—William Wordsworth.

WHEN men cease to wonder, God's secrets remain unrevealed.

ENOUGH FOR THE PRESENT.—
"Religion is full of questions that we cannot answer," declared Dr. James McCosh in an address to his students at Princeton University, "because we only know in part,"—a long pause, then with thrilling emphasis,—"but we know!"

There are things of which we may be positively certain though we cannot comprehend all their connections and relations. We know that our souls exist as truly as our bodies. We know that there is a God, who is not blind force, but a spirit who answers the souls who seek peace and joy. Evil brings discord and death to the soul. We know that Jesus Christ is absolutely good, the perfect union of the Divine and the human spirits. We know through Him that love is the source of power, and that life continues after death.

Beyond our ken lie the mysteries unexplored. But we have light enough to steer by, if we will. We know as much as we need. If we live by it we shall know more, some day.

Symbol

My faith is all a doubtful thing,
  Wove on a doubtful loom,—
Until there comes, each showery spring,
  A cheery tree in bloom.

And Christ who died upon the tree
  That death had stricken bare,
Comes beautifully back to me,
  In blossoms, everywhere.
                    —David Morton.

DISCOVERY — It is not when I am going to meet Him, but when I am just turning away and leaving Him, that I discover that God is.—Thoreau.

IMMANENT.—The most real fact in this universe is God. The whole creation bears witness to His presence. The sunlight that floods the earth, the glories of the firmament, night and day, winter and spring, all declare that the Creator is everywhere in His world. The rose that was blooming one morning in my garden, with colors more delicate than the brush of a Turner could paint, told me that the great Artist was there. The laughter of little children, the love of friends, the upward march of the races of men proclaim that God is about us and within us richly imparting His grace. The unsatisfied aspiration of the heart, its pain, its joy, its penitence, its thoughts too deep for words tell us how near God is.

WHAT SHADOWS we are, and what shadows we pursue!—Burke.

Acceptance

I cannot think or reason,
I only know he came
With hands and feet of healing
And wild heart all aflame.

With eyes that dimmed and softened
At all the things he saw,
And in his pillared singing
I read the marching Law.

I only know he loves me,
Enfolds and understands—
And oh, his heart that holds me,
And oh, his certain hands!
                    —Willard Wattles.

I WOULD FAIN KNOW ALL that I need, and all that I may.—I leave God's secrets to Himself.—It is happy for me that God makes me of His court, and not of His council.—Joseph Hall.

WHERE THE SEARCH ENDS.—"I searched the world over for God and found Him in my heart," said Augustine. In the heart of the believer a still small voice speaks in clearest accents, bearing "witness with our spirits that we are the children of God." Nothing on earth is so heavenly as that—so like "the voice of angels singing in the silence." It is as clear as bells at eventime. It is assuring like the familiar voice of a friend beloved. The Holy Spirit speaking in the secret chambers of the heart is the climax of God's revelation to us!

EACH PARTICLE of matter is an immensity; each leaf a world; each insect an inexplicable compendium.—*Lavater.*

MYSTERY is but another name for our ignorance; if we were omniscient, all would be perfectly plain.
—*Tryon Edwards.*

MORTAL.—When Anaxagoras was told of the death of his son, he only said, "I knew he was mortal." So we in all casualties of life should say, "I knew my riches were uncertain, that my friend was just a man." Such considerations would soon pacify us, because all our troubles proceed from their being unexpected.
—*Plutarch.*

USE IT.—While reason is puzzling itself about mystery, faith is turning it to daily bread, and feeding on it thankfully in her heart of hearts.—*F. D. Huntington.*

EVANESCENT.—Man must be prepared for every event of life, for there is nothing that is durable.—*Menander.*

I DO NOT KNOW HOW the great loving Father will bring out light at last, but He knows, and He will do it.
—*David Livingstone.*

STAY ON YOUR LEVEL.—Happy is the man who is content to traverse this ocean to the haven of rest, without going into the wretched diving-bells of his own fancies.—There are depths; but depths are for God.—*Evans.*

A RELIGION without mystery must be a religion without God.

BEYOND REASON — It has been well said that a thing is not necessarily against reason, because it happens to be above it.—*Colton.*

SPECULATE NOT TOO MUCH on the mysteries of truth or providence.— The effort to explain everything, sometimes may endanger faith.—Many things God reserves to Himself, and many are reserved for the unfolding of the future life.—*Tryon Edwards.*

WHICH?—The idea of philosophy is truth; the idea of religion is life.
—*Peter Bayne.*

OUR LORD has written the promise of the resurrection, not in books alone, but in every leaf in springtime.
—*Martin Luther.*

NONE BUT GOD can satisfy the longing of the immortal soul; as the heart was made for Him, He only can fill it.
—*Trench.*

XX. NATURE

GOD'S THOUGHTS—The mountains are God's thoughts piled up. The ocean is God's thoughts spread out. The flowers are God's thoughts in bloom. The dew drops are God's thoughts in pearls.—*Sam Jones.*

ON EVERY ROSE

I see His blood upon the rose
   And in the stars the glory of His eyes,
His body gleams amid eternal snows
   His tears fall from the skies.

I see His face in every flower;
   The thunder and the surging of the birds
Are but His voice—and carven by His power
Rocks are His written words.

All pathways by His feet are worn,
   His strong heart stirs the ever-beating sea,
His crown of thorns is twined with every thorn
   His cross is every tree.
        —*Joseph Mary Plunkett.*

FLOWERS—I do not believe a child, brought up under my ministry in this Church, will ever see flowers till he dies without having some thought of religion, of the sanctuary, and of the inspiration of flowers. So, flowers at our service have a meaning. They are not in any special way a symbolization; they simply bring things common into higher relations on a principle of association; and having them on the platform, besides affording pleasure, to a certain extent interprets a part of my idea of the Christian ministry.
        —*Beecher.*

COMMONPLACE

"A commonplace life," we say, and we sigh,
But why should we sigh as we say?
The commonplace sun in the commonplace sky
Makes up the commonplace day;
The moon and the stars are commonplace things,
And the flower that blooms, and the bird that sings;
But dark were the world, and sad our lot,
If the flowers failed, and the sun shone not;
And God, who studies each separate soul,
Out of commonplace lives makes His beautiful whole.
        —*"Susan Coolidge."*

From *A FEW MORE VERSES*, by Susan Coolidge. By permission of Little, Brown & Company, Publishers.

A BALLAD OF TREES AND THE MASTER

Into the woods my Master went,
Clean forspent, forspent.
Into the woods my Master came,
Forspent with love and shame.
But the olives they were not blind to Him;
The little gray leaves were kind to Him;
The thorn-tree had a mind to Him
When into the woods He came.

Out of the woods my Master went,
And He was well content.
Out of the woods my Master came,
Content with death and shame.
When death and shame would woo Him last,
From under the trees they drew Him last:
'Twas on a tree they slew Him—last
When out of the woods He came.
        —SIDNEY LANIER.
By permission of Charles Scribner's Sons, Publishers.

TEACHERS

"The eye—it cannot choose but see;
We cannot bid the ear be still;
Our bodies feel, where'er they be,
Against and with our will.

"Nor less I deem that there are Powers
Which of themselves our minds impress;
That we can feed this mind of ours
In a wise passiveness."

One impulse from a vernal wood
May teach you more of man,
Of moral evil and of good,
Than all the sages can.
—*William Wordsworth.*

TRANSCENDENT

Dear heart, perhaps you can not find
        God's hand
Or see His face through some hour of
        despair.
Do not be grieved, go seek the good,
        clean land,
And you will find Him there.

He is a part of every wind that sweeps
Across the furrows, down their upturned
        length.
Breathe deeply of it—here is where God
        keeps
Stored healing and stored strength.

Wander awhile down some still wooded
        way;
Stoop to the lichen, dig through the
        mossy sod.
Stir in the leafmold—and the feathery
        spray
Of a fern can show you God.

You can touch Him as you touch the bark
        of a tree;
You can hear His voice in the voice of the
        singing birds.
Dear God, may we listen—God, may we
        look and see
Thy face, and hear Thy words.

MAN was made last because he was worthiest. The soul was inspired last, because yet more noble. No air, no earth, no water was here used to give help to this work; Thou, that breathest upon man and gavest him the Holy Spirit, didst also breathe upon the body and gavest it a living spirit; we are beholden to nothing but Thee for our soul. Our flesh is from flesh, our spirit is from the God of spirits.
—*Joseph Hall.*

THE BIRTH OF THE FLOWERS

God spoke! and from the arid scene
Sprang rich and verdant bowers,
Till all the earth was soft with green,—
He smiled; and there were flowers.
—*Mary McNeil Fenollosa.*

OUT IN THE FIELDS WITH GOD

The little cares that fretted me
    I lost them yesterday,
Among the fields above the sea,
    Among the winds at play,
Among the lowing of the herds,
    The rustling of the trees,
Among the singing of the birds,
    The humming of the bees.

The foolish fears of what might happen,
    I cast them all away
Among the clover-scented grass,
    Among the new-mown hay,
Among the husking of the corn,
    Where drowsy poppies nod
Where ill thoughts die and good are
        born—
    Out in the fields with God.
—*Louise Imogen Guiney.*

REALITY—Nature forever puts a premium on reality. What is done for effect, is seen to be done for effect; what is done for love, is felt to be done for love.

BE STILL WITH GOD.—To be idle sometimes is the part of wisdom. It is the needful rest and relaxation which Christ invited His disciples to share with Him when they were overstrained and worn out with labour. The best way to enjoy it is to get away from the crowd into some quiet place where the heart can be still with God in the open air. It is most sweet when it is shared by true friends.

Such idleness may be very fruitful. It reaps

"The harvest of a quiet eye
That broods and sleeps on His own heart."

OVERTONES

I heard a bird at break of day
Sing from the autumn trees
A song so mystical and calm,
So full of certainties,
No man, I think, could listen long
Except upon his knees.
Yet this was but a simple bird,
Alone, among dead trees.
—William Alexander Percy.

TOGETHER.—Lyman Abbott says: I pluck an acorn and hold it to my ear, and this is what it says to me: "By and by the birds will come and nest in me. By and by I will furnish shade for the cattle. By and by I will provide warmth for the home. By and by I will be shelter from the storm to those who have gone under the roof. By and by I will be the strong ribs of a great vessel, and the tempest will beat against me in vain, while I carry men across the Atlantic." "O foolish little acorn, wilt thou be all this?" I ask. And the acorn answers, "Yes, God and I."

THE GATES.—The man who can really, in living union of the mind and heart, converse with God through nature, finds in the material forms around him a source of power and happiness inexhaustible and like the life of angels.— The highest life and glory of man is to be alive unto God; and when this grandeur of sensibility to Him, and this power of communion with Him is carried, as the habit of the soul, into the forms of nature, then the walls of our world are as the gates of Heaven.—G. B. Cheever.

MARVEL.—The ignorant man marvels at the exceptional; the wise man marvels at the common; the greatest wonder of all is the regularity of nature.
—G. D. Boardman.

STOREHOUSE.—A man finds in the productions of nature an inexhaustible stock of material on which he can employ himself, without any temptation to envy or malevolence, and has always a certain prospect of discovering new reasons for adoring the sovereign author of the universe.—Johnson.

PANACEA.—It were happy if we studied nature more in natural things; and acted according to nature, whose rules are few, plain, and most reasonable.
—Penn.

WELLSPRING.—Nature is the armoury of genius. Cities serve it poorly, books and colleges at second hand; the eye craves the spectacle of the horizon; of mountain, ocean, river and plain, the clouds and stars; actual contact with the elements, sympathy with the seasons as they rise and roll.—A. B. Alcott.

THE LAWS OF NATURE are just, but terrible. There is no weak mercy in them. Cause and consequence are inseparable and inevitable. The elements have no forbearance. The fire burns, the water drowns, the air consumes, the earth buries. And perhaps it would be well for our race if the punishment of crimes against the law of man were as inevitable as the punishment of crimes against the laws of nature,—were man as unerring in his judgment as nature.—*Longfellow.*

SYMPATHY WITH NATURE is a part of the good man's religion.
—*F. H. Hedge.*

NATURE
The day before April
Alone, alone,
I walked to the woods
And I sat on a stone.

I sat on a broad stone
And sang to the birds.
The tune was God's making
But I made the words.
—*Mary Carolyn Davies.*

NATURE AND WISDOM always say the same.—*Juvenal.*

THE BEST PEDAGOGUE—Nature is man's teacher. She unfolds her treasures to his search, unseals his eye, illumes his mind, and purifies his heart; an influence breathes from all the sights and sounds of her existence.—*Street.*

EVEN THE LEAST — Nature hath nothing made so base, but can read some instruction to the wisest man.—*C. Aleyn.*

NATURE is commanded by obeying her.—*Bacon.*

CLOAK — Nature is the time-vesture of God that reveals Him to the wise, and hides Him from the foolish.—*Carlyle.*

ALL SUNSHINE makes the desert.
—*Arabian Proverb.*

PROSECUTOR—There is no witness so terrible—no accuser so powerful as conscience which dwells within us.
—*Sophocles.*

IGNORANCE AND FAITH — In dwelling on divine mysteries, keep thy heart humble, thy thoughts reverent, thy soul holy. Let not philosophy be ashamed to be confuted, nor logic to be confounded, nor reason to be surpassed. What thou canst not prove, approve; what thou canst not comprehend, believe; what thou canst believe, admire and love and obey. So shall thine ignorance be satisfied in thy faith, and thy doubt be swallowed up in thy reverence, and thy faith be as influential as sight. Put out thine own candle, and then shalt thou see clearly the sun of righteousness.—*Jeremy Taylor.*

STUDY NATURE as the countenance of God.—*Kingsley.*

NATURE is but a name for an effect whose cause is God.

LOOK THROUGH nature up to nature's God—*Pope.*

112

XXI. OPPORTUNITY

OPTIMISM—I have told you of the Spaniard who always put on his spectacles when about to eat cherries, that they might look bigger and more tempting. In like manner, I make the most of my enjoyments, and pack away my troubles in as small a compass as I can.—*Robert Southey.*

CIVILIZATION itself is simply a granary into which society has swept all the rich harvests of the mind. Now ten-talent men are few. Thus far philosophers have found five men whose genius is of the first order, and whose work has been epic-making and revolutionary. But the dizzy space that separates these men from the rudest savage is not so great as the space that separates earth's five greatest intellects from this divine carpenter, whose achievements for home and friendship, for law and liberty, for learning and religion, make His forehead to strike against the stars.—*Hillis.*

LUCK—Luck is an ignis fatuus. You may follow it to ruin, but not to success.
—*James A. Garfield.*

IT is not the position but the disposition that makes men and women happy.

Circumstances may make a man, but circumstances never made a man out of unprepared material.

About the only exercise some folks take is jumping at conclusions.

Make a man believe he is worthless, and he will act worthlessly.

Good clothes on some folks remind you of pretty labels on empty bottles.

Character stands for all that this moral demanding century wants.—*Dinger-isms.*

THE GREAT CONQUEROR—Jesus of Nazareth, without money and arms, conquered more millions than Alexander, Caesar, Mahomet, and Napoleon; without science and learning, He shed more light on things human and Divine than all philosophers and scholars combined; without the eloquence of schools, He spoke words of life as never were spoken before or since, and produced effects which lie beyond the reach of orator or poet; without writing a single line, He has set more pens in motion, and furnished themes for more sermons, orations, discussions, learned volumes, works of art, and sweet songs of praise, than the whole army of great men of ancient and modern times. Born in a manger, and crucified as a malefactor, He now controls the destinies of the civilized world, and rules a spiritual empire which embraces one-third of the inhabitants of the globe. There never was in this world a life so unpretending, modest, and lowly in its outward form and condition, and yet producing such extraordinary effects upon all ages, nations, and classes of men. The annals of history produce no other example of such complete and astonishing success in spite of the absence of those material, social, literary, and artistic powers and influences which are indispensable to success for a mere man.
—*Schaff.*

THE SAYING OF OMAR IBN, AL HALIF, THE SECOND CALIPH

Four things come not back:
The spoken word;
The sped arrow;
Time past;
The neglected opportunity.

OBSCURING TRUTH — I cannot think but that the world would be better and brighter if our teachers would dwell on the Duty of Happiness as well as the Happiness of Duty.—*John Lubbock.*

Every duty we omit obscures some truth we should have known.—*Ruskin.*

RENEWAL—There is one illustration of the value of the constant renewal of society from the bottom that has always interested me profoundly. The only reason why government did not suffer dry rot in the Middle Ages under the aristocratic system which then prevailed was that so many of the men who were efficient instruments of government were drawn from the church,—from that great religious body which was then the only church, that body which we now distinguish from other religious bodies as the Roman Catholic Church. The Roman Catholic Church was then, as it is now, a great democracy. There was no peasant so humble that he might not become a priest, and no priest so obscure that he might not become Pope of Christendom; and every chancellery in Europe, every court in Europe, was ruled by these learned, trained and accomplished men, —the priesthood of that great and dominant body. What kept government alive in the Middle Ages was this constant rise of the sap from the bottom, from the rank and file of the great body of the people through the open channels of the priesthood.—*Woodrow Wilson.*

SPECIAL PROVIDENCES—People talk about special providences. I believe in the providences, but not in the specialty. I do not believe that God lets the thread of my affairs go for six days, and on the seventh evening takes it up for a moment.—*George Macdonald.*

RESOURCES—No man is blamed for being a fourteen-foot catboat instead of a steam yacht or an Atlantic liner. It is only required of him that he heave up whatever sail he carries and be headed right. This simplifies the whole matter and makes the path of duty plain. How much energy and wisdom, how much goodness and spiritual efficiency have you? "Not much," you say. No matter, bring it along! As you live in the spirit of Christian devotion your life will unfold in faith, in hope, and in love until men will say of your Master, "This of a truth is that prophet that should come into the world."

There is a false self-distrust which denies the worth of its own talent. It is not humility—it is petty pride, withholding its simple gifts from the hands of Christ because they are not more pretentious. There are men who would endow colleges, they say, if they were millionaires. They would help in the work of Bible study if they were as gifted as Henry Drummond. They would strive to lead their associates into the Christian life if they had the gifts of Dwight L. Moody. But they are not ready to give what they have and do what they can and be as it has pleased God to make them, in His service—and that is their condemnation.
—*Charles Reynolds Brown.*

TALENT—It is your duty to use your talents. Remember if you do not use you will lose. It is reported of Charles Darwin that when he had finished his scientific work, he settled down to enjoy life. He thought that he would now enjoy poetry, music and art. Sad to say he soon discovered that these things did not strike a response in his being. Later he said, "It is too late now because I have allowed these parts of my being to atrophy."
—*Zollars.*

USE WHAT YOU HAVE—A ship lost at sea for many days suddenly sighted a friendly vessel. From the mast of the unfortunate vessel was seen the signal: "Water, water; we die of thirst!" The answer from the friendly vessel at once came back: "Cast down your bucket where you are." A second and a third time the signal, "Water, water, send us water!" ran up from the distressed vessel, and was answered: "Cast down your bucket where you are." . . . The captain of the distressed vessel at last heeding the injunction, cast down his bucket, and it came up full of fresh, sparkling water from the mouth of the Amazon River. To those of my race who depend on bettering their condition I would say: "Cast down your bucket where you are—cast it down in making friends in every manly way of the people of all the race by whom we are surrounded."

We shall prosper in proportion as we learn to dignify and glorify common labor and put brains and skill into the common occupations of life; shall prosper in proportion as we learn to draw the line between the superficial and the substantial, the ornamental gewgaws of life and the useful. No race can prosper till it learns that there is as much dignity in tilling a field as in writing a poem. It is at the bottom of life we must begin, and not at the top.—*Booker T. Washington.*

HITCH HIKERS—If you want to succeed in the world, you must make your own opportunities as you go on. The man who waits for some seventh wave to toss him on dry land will find that the seventh wave is a long time a-coming. You can commit no greater folly than to sit by the roadside until some one comes along and invites you to ride with him to wealth and influence.—*John B. Gough.*

WHAT LUCK MEANS — Luck means the hardships and privations which you have not hesitated to endure; the long nights you have devoted to work. Luck means the appointments you have never failed to keep; the trains you have never failed to catch.—*Max O'Rell.*

CLOSED DOORS — When God shuts a door He opens a window.

EXTRAORDINARY—The true calling of a Christian is not to do extraordinary things, but to do ordinary things in an extraordinary way.—*Dean Stanley.*

INDIVIDUALITY — Whoso would be a man must be a nonconformist. He who would gather immortal palms must not be hindered by the name of goodness, but must explore if it be goodness. Nothing is at last sacred but the integrity of your own mind. . .

What I must do is all that concerns me, not what the people think . . . It is easy to live after our own; but the great man is he who in the midst of the crowd keeps with perfect sweetness the independence of solitude . . .

A foolish consistency is the hobgoblin of little minds, adored by little statesmen and philosophers and divines. With consistency a great soul has simply nothing to do.—*Ralph Waldo Emerson.*

SELF-MADE MEN — I am tired of hearing about self-made men. There is not a self-made man in the world. The so-called self-made man is the man who has seized his opportunities, and those given him by circumstances, and has made use of them.—*Lucius Tuttle.*

SUI GENERIS — All truly wise thoughts have been thought already thousands of times; but to make them really ours we must think them over again honestly, till they take firm root in our personal experience.—*Goethe.*

GREAT QUALITIES—It is not sufficient to have great qualities; we must be able to make proper use of them.
—*La Rochefoucauld.*

FUTILE—One does not gain much by mere cleverness.—*Vauvenargues.*

PERSONALITY—As the world was plastic and fluid in the hands of God, so it is ever to so much of His attributes as we bring to it. To ignorance and sin, it is flint . . . The great man makes the great thing. Wherever Macdonald sits, there is the head of the table . . . The day is always his who works in it the serenity and great aims.
—*Ralph Waldo Emerson.*

MAKING THE BEST—My business is not to remake myself, but to make the absolute best of what God made.
—*Robert Browning.*

DUTY — All higher motives, ideals, conceptions, sentiments in a man are of no account if they do not come forward to strengthen him for the better discharge of the duties which devolve upon him in the ordinary affairs of life.
—*Henry Ward Beecher.*

ORIGINALITY — To do easily what is difficult for others is the mark of talent. To do what is impossible for talent is the mark of genius.—*Henri-Frederic Amiel.*

DISCOURAGEMENT — Never let us be discouraged with ourselves; it is not when we are conscious of our faults that we are the most wicked; on the contrary, we are less so. We see by a brighter light; and let us remember, for our consolation, that we never perceive our sins till we begin to cure them.
—*Francois de la Mothe Fenelon.*

COMPLAINING—You are never to complain of your birth, your training, your employments, your hardships; never to fancy that you could be something if only you had a different lot and sphere assigned you. God understands His own plan, and He knows what you want a great deal better than you do. The very things that you most deprecate, as fatal limitations or obstructions, are probably what you most want. What you call hindrances, obstacles, discouragements, are probably God's opportunities. Bring down your soul, or rather, bring it up to receive God's will and do His work, in your lot, in your sphere, under your cloud of obscurity, against your temptations, and then you shall find that your condition is never opposed to your good, but really consistent with it.—*H. Bushnell.*

EVEN THE POOREST—There has been no man of pure genius; as there has been none wholly destitute of genius.
—*Thoreau.*

FAIRY GOLD — Of all good gifts which ever came out of the wallet of the Fairy Godmother, the gift of natural gladness is the greatest and best. It is to the soul what health is to the body, what sanity is to the mind, the test of normality.
—*Bliss Carman.*

XXII. OTHERS

INFLUENCE — Alice Freeman Palmer, the second president of Wellesley College, was happiest when she was doing most for others. When she left the college she gave herself so unweariedly to her self-imposed task of lightening the burdens of the unfortunate, that her husband, a Harvard professor, expostulated. He thought she should give her time and strength to writing books that would make her still more famous. "You are building no monument," he said. "When you are gone people will ask who you are, and no one will be able to say." "Well, why should they?" was the answer. "I am trying to make girls happier and wiser. Books don't help much toward that. It is people that count. You want to put yourself into people; they touch other people; these, others still, and so you go on working forever."

—John T. Faris.

THE TORCH BEARER—The hero is one who kindles a great light in the world, who sets up blazing torches in the dark streets of life for men to see by. The saint is the man who walks through the dark paths of the world, himself a light.

—Felix Adler.

THE SPEECH OF ANGELS—Music is well said to be the speech of angels; in fact, nothing among the utterances allowed to man, is felt to be so Divine. It brings us near to the Infinite; we look for moments across the cloudy elements into the eternal light, when song leads and inspires us. Serious nations, all nations that can listen to the mandate of nature, have prized song and music as a vehicle for worship, for prophecy, and for whatsoever in them was Divine.—Carlyle.

UNSELFISHNESS—There is nothing like putting the shine on another's face to put the shine on our own. Nine-tenths of all loneliness, sensitiveness, despondency, moroseness, are connected with personal interests. Turn more of these selfish interests into unselfish ones, and by so much we change opportunities for disheartenment into their opposite.

—W. C. Gannett.

NEIGHBOR—Love your neighbor for God's sake, and God for your own sake, who created all things for your sake, and redeemed you for His mercy's sake. If your love hath any other motive, it is false love; if your motive hath any other end, it is self-love. If you neglect your love to your neighbor, in vain you profess your love of God; for by your love of God, your love to your neighbor is acquired; and by your love to your neighbor, your love of God is nourished.

—The Beauties of Thought.

WHO WALKS THE WORLD WITH SOUL AWAKE

Who walks the world with soul awake
  Finds beauty everywhere;
Though labor be his portion,
  Though sorrow be his share,
He looks beyond obscuring clouds,
  Sure that the light is there!

And if, the ills of mortal life
  Grown heavier to bear,
Doubt come with its perplexities
  And whisper of despair,
He turns with love to suffering men—
  And, lo! God, too, is there.

—FLORENCE EARLE COATES.

INFLUENCE—The least may influence the greatest. It was St. Andrew that influenced St. Peter to "come and see" Jesus. One least spoken of among the apostles influenced the one who took the foremost place among them as if to show that such power is independent of personal superiority. It is not the great and gifted alone who exercise this mysterious power of influence. It is a universal law of life. These personal influences, first of Jesus on Andrew, then of Andrew on Peter, were the beginning of the conversion of the world.—*T. T. Carter.*

HELPFULNESS — "Did you know Dr. Osler?" someone asked another. "Yes," was the answer, "intimately, but I only saw him once. It was late twilight; the city square was almost deserted when a woman carrying a heavy child came slowly up the square and sat down to rest on the coping bordering the pavement. The child's heavy head was pressed against her bosom and she seemed all in. I started to speak to her when up the square came jauntily a man in full evening dress, top coat, silk hat, flower in his buttonhole, light gloves in one hand and his can swinging in the other, evidently singing. In an instant he saw the woman and her burden. He stopped, made a playful dive with his cane at the child, then throwing cane and gloves on the grass, he gently lifted the child into his arms, holding its head against his own breast as he talked to the mother. Then whistling to a little boy who chanced in sight he said: 'Get a cab as quick as you can and if you are back in five minutes, riches! for you!' and he patted his breast pocket. The boy flew off and was back quickly with the cab. Dr. Osler put the woman in the cab, carefully placed the child on her lap —then he wrote on a card, 'This is Mrs. Osler's youngest. See that he is well taken care of until I come tomorrow night.' He read what he had written aloud to the woman, winked his eye at me, gave the driver his fare, told him to drive at once to the Hopkins Hospital, see that the woman and boy were safely attended to—then pressed a five dollar bill in the woman's hand, said: 'Your laddie will be well looked after at the hospital. I will see him tomorrow.' Then he slammed the door of the cab and was off. All done while I was trying to say, 'Can I help you?' "

—*Edith G. Reid.*

OBEDIENCE—The man who would lift others must be uplifted himself, and he who would command others must learn to obey.—*Charles K. Ober.*

MARCHING TOGETHER—In the Roman army of old the soldier carried a large oblong shield on his left arm. When a city was beseiged the men in close rank locked their shields together over their heads and then marched in safety to the gate. So is it, in an organization where brotherhood prevails. We lock our shields over our heads as we march against the vicissitudes, the trials and temptations of life, and not over our own heads alone, but others are sheltered beneath them. A comrade falls, but our locked shields ward off hardship and penury from his widow and her little ones. A companion is prostrated with sickness, but he is cared for and the wants of both him and his are supplied.

SELF-POISON — Bad temper is its own scourge. Few things are bitterer than to feel bitter. A man's venom poisons himself more than his victim.

—*Charles Buxton.*

A SOLDIER OF THE COMMON GOOD—A life without love in it is like a heap of ashes upon a deserted hearth—with the fire dead, the laughter stilled, and the light extinguished. It is like a winter landscape—with the sun hidden, the flowers frozen, and the wind whispering through the withered leaves. God knows we need all the unselfish love that can come to us. For love is seldom unselfish. There is usually the motive and the price. Do you remember William Morris, and how his life was lived, his fortune spent, his hands busied—in the service of others? He was the father of the settlement movement, of cooperative homes for working people, and of the arts and crafts revival, in our day. He was a "soldier of the common good." After he was gone—his life began to grow in radiance and power, like a beacon set high upon a dangerous shore. In the twilight of his days he wrote what I like to think was his creed—and mine: "I am going your way, so let us go hand in hand. You help me and I'll help you. We shall not be here very long, for soon death, the kind old nurse, will come back and rock us all to sleep. Let us help one another while we may."

—*Frank P. Tebbetts.*

FOLLY — Consider how few things are worthy of anger, and thou wilt wonder that any fools should be wroth.

—*Robert Dodsley.*

KINGDOM—The kingdom of God is a society of the best men, working for the best ends, according to the best methods. Its law is one word—loyalty; its gospel one message—love. If you know anything better, live for it; if not, in the name of God and of humanity, carry out Christ's plan.

—*Henry Drummond.*

TRAVELING HOMEWARD — To be strong and true; to be generous in praise and appreciation of others; to impute worthy motives even to enemies; to give without expectation of return; to practise humility, tolerance, and self-restraint; to make the best use of time and opportunity; to keep the mind pure and the judgment charitable; to extend intelligent sympathy to those in distress; to cultivate quietness and non-resistance; to seek truth and righteousness; to work, love, pray, and serve daily, to aspire greatly, labor cheerfully, and take God at His word—this is to travel heavenward.

—*Grenville Kleiser.*

SOULS

My soul goes clad in gorgeous things,
　　Scarlet and gold and blue;
And at her shoulder sudden wings
　　Like long flames flicker through.

And she is wallow-fleet, and free
　　From mortal bonds and bars.
She laughs, because Eternity
　　Blossoms for her with stars!

O folk who scorn my stiff gray gown,
　　My dull and foolish face,—
Can ye not see my Soul flash down,
　　A singing flame through space?

And folk, whose earth-stained looks I
　　hate,
Why may I not divine
Your Souls, that must be passionate,
　　Shining and swift, as mine!

—*Fannie Stearns Davis.*

BREAKING BARRIERS — This, then, is Christianity: to smash the barriers and get next to your fellowman.

—*John T. Faris.*

THE MOST POWERFUL MOTIVE—The sense of somebody's need is, I believe, the most powerful motive in the world, one that appeals to the largest number of people of every age, race, and kind. It wakes up the whole nature, the powers that learn as well as those that perform; it generates the vigor of interest that submerges selfishness and cowardice; it rouses the inventiveness and ingenuity that slumber so soundly in students' classrooms. For many of us . . . work that is service taps a great reservoir of power, sets free some of our caged and leashed energy.—*Richard C. Cabot.*

KEEP THEM TO YOURSELF — What right have I to make every one in the house miserable because I am miserable? Troubles must come to all, but troubles need not be wicked, and it is wicked to be a destroyer of happiness.
—*Amelia E. Barr.*

SECOND CHANGES—We all have to learn, in one way or another, that neither men nor boys get *second* chances in this world. We all get *new* chances till the end of our lives, but not second chances in the same set of circumstances; and the great difference between one person and another is, how he takes hold of and uses his first chance, and how he takes his fall if it is scored against him.—*Thomas Hughes.*

Church

A reading church is an informed church;
An informed church is an interested church;
An interested church is an acting church;
An acting church is a serving church;
A serving church is a Christian church.
—*Selected.*

SINS OF SOCIETY—Some one has said that the seven deadly sins of society are these: Policies without principles; wealth without work; pleasure without conscience; knowledge without character; commerce and industry without morality; science without humanity; worship without sacrifice.—*Observer.*

WHEN A MAN COMES TO HIMSELF—Surely a man has come to himself only when he has found the best that is in him, and has satisfied his heart with the highest achievement he is fit for. It is only then that he knows of what he is capable and what his heart demands. And, assuredly, no thoughtful man ever came to the end of his life, and had time and a little space of calm from which to look back upon it, who did not know and acknowledge that it was what he had done unselfishly and for others, and nothing else, that satisfied him in the retrospect, and made him feel that he had played the man. And so men grow by having responsibility laid upon them, the burden of other people's business. Their powers are put out at interest, and they get usury in kind. They are like men multiplied. Each counts manifold. Men who live with an eye only upon what is their own are dwarfed beside them—seem fractions while they are integers. The trustworthiness of men trusted seems often to grow with the trust.—*Woodrow Wilson.*

SACRIFICE—There can be no real and abiding happiness without sacrifice. Our greatest joys do not result from our efforts toward self-gratification, but from a loving and spontaneous service to other lives. Joy comes not to him who seeks it for himself, but to him who seeks it for other people.—*H. W. Sylvester.*

TUNING-UP — Every morning compose your soul for a tranquil day, and all through it be careful often to recall your resolution, and bring yourself back to it, so to say. If something discomposes you, do not be upset, or troubled; but having discovered the fact, humble yourself gently before God, and try to bring your mind into a quiet attitude. Say to yourself, "Well, I have made a false step; now I must go more carefully and watchfully." Do this each time, however frequently you fall. When you are at peace use it profitably, making constant acts of meekness, and seeking to be calm even in the most trifling things. Above all, do not be discouraged; be patient; wait; strive to attain a calm, gentle spirit.

—St. Francois de Sales.

GOODNESS — You can only make others better by being good yourself.

—Hugh R. Hawies.

ICH DIEN — The crest of the Prince of Wales bears the simple watchword, "I serve," and no more princely motto can be found.

We cannot determine whether our faces shall be beautiful or ugly, our bodies graceful or deformed. But the shaping of our life is in our own hands. We make that great or small, noble or mean, as we will.

The motto, "I serve," always betokens real power and lasting authority. More, it is a truly Christian motto and proclaims eternal kinship with the highest.

—George Henry Hubbard.

COOPERATION — Never one thing and seldom one person can make for a success. It takes a number of them merging into one perfect whole.—*Marie Dressler.*

DEPENDENCE — We can't play alone in the game of life. We're dependent, my friend, on others; we cannot "get by" in the struggle and strife, except for the help of our brothers! Whatever we plan, or whatever we do, whatever we give of our best, is meant to include all our fellow men too, and add to the joy of the rest.

REWARD — Service to a just cause rewards the worker with more real happiness and satisfaction than any other venture of life.—*Carrie Chapman Catt.*

FOR THOSE WHO LOVE ME

I live for those who love me,
For those who know me true,
For the Heaven that smiles above me,
   And awaits my coming too;
For the cause that lacks assistance,
For the wrong that needs resistance,
For the future in the distance,
   And the good that I can do.

—G. Linnaeus Banks.

BURNING BRIDGES—He who can not forgive others breaks the bridge over which he must pass himself.

—George Herbert.

ROBBING ONESELF — Of all the passions that are incident to a man, there is none so impetuous, or that produceth so terrible effect as anger; for besides that intrinsical mischief which it works in a man's own heart, in regard whereof Hugo said well, "Pride robs me of God, envy of my neighbor, anger of myself." What bloody tragedies doth this passion act every day in the world, making the whole earth nothing but either an amphitheatre for fight or a shambles for slaughter.

—Joseph Hall.

TEAMWORK — We may call it by this name, or call it by that—"teamwork" or "cooperation;" together we stand, by ourselves we fall flat; together, my friend, we're the Nation! Whatever we do, or whatever we plan—we can't stand alone, e'en the best of us; but must share of our gifts with our good fellowman—for we're only a part of the rest of us!

FELLOWSHIP — We are told that William Penn, clad in simple garb, stood in the center of a company of Indian chieftains and said, "My friends, we have met on the broad pathway of good faith. We are all one flesh and blood. Being brethren, no advantage shall be taken on either side. Between us there shall be nothing but openness and love." Jumping to their feet these Indian chiefs replied, "While the rivers run and the sun shines, we shall live in peace with the children of William Penn." Although no record of this treaty was made on parchment, yet the war whoop of the Indian was not heard again in Pennsylvania for more than seventy years.—*Selected.*

GIFTS

He gives nothing but worthless gold
  Who gives from a sense of duty;
But he who gives but a slender mite,
And gives to that which is out of sight,
  That thread of the all-sustaining
    Beauty
Which runs through all and doth all
    unite,—
The hand cannot grasp the whole of his
  alms,
The heart outstretches its eager palms,
For a god goes with it and makes it store
To the soul that was starving in darkness
  before.
          —*James Russell Lowell.*

PURGE—Out of every heart the lurking grudge. Give us the grace and strength to forebear and to persevere. Offenders, give us the grace to accept and to forgive offenders. Forgetful ourselves, help us to bear cheerfully the forgetfulness of others. Give us courage and gaiety and the quiet mind. Spare to us our friends, soften to us our enemies. Bless us, if it may be, in all our innocent endeavors. If it may not, give us the strength to encounter that which is to come, that we be brave in peril, constant in tribulation, temperate in wrath, and in all changes of fortune, and down to the gates of death, loyal and loving one to another.
          —*Robert Louis Stevenson.*

A TEST — A cobbler at Leyden, who used to attend the public disputations held at the academy, was once asked if he understood Latin. "No," replied the mechanic; "but I know who is in the wrong in the argument by seeing who is angry first.

TOGETHER—These seven "togethers" are seven links of a chain which bind us indissolubly to Christ: Crucified together; quickened together; raised together; seated together in Heavenly places; sufferers together; heirs together; and glorified together with Christ. They indicate the everlasting purpose of God in our redemption, and His plan in effecting that purpose.

COURTESY is not the creation of effort, it is the product of grace; it is born, not made. Paul was born of grace, and therefore he was gracious, and instinctively his courtesy fitted itself to all the changing requirements of the day . . . Grace is the bountiful mother of all the graces.—*J. H. Jowett.*

SELF-PRESERVATION — The use of anger is to stir us up to self preservation, and to put us upon our guard against injuries. When it has done this, it has performed all that belongs to it; for what measures we may take to effect this, how we may secure ourselves, and how we should behave towards those who offend us—these are the points concerning which we must not consult our passions, but our reason, which was given us to moderate our passions, and to prescribe laws for our actions.—*Jortin.*

TEMPER—If religion has done nothing for your temper, it has done nothing for your soul.—*Clayton.*

Vain Regret

My mind was ruffled with small cares
   today,
And I said pettish words, and did not keep
Long-suffering patience well, and now
   how deep
My trouble for this sin! in vain I weep
For foolish words I never can unsay.
                    —*H. S. Sutton.*

TASTE—If I had my life to live over again, I would have made a rule to read some poetry and listen to some music at least once a week; for perhaps the parts of my brain now atrophied would thus have been kept active through use.

The loss of these tastes is a loss of happiness, and may possibly be injurious to the intellect, and more probably to the moral character, by enfeebling the emotional part of our nature.—*Darwin.*

IT TAKES TWO—Labor and trouble one can always get through alone, but it takes two to be glad.—*Ibsen.*

UNCONSCIOUS GROWTH—Art creates an atmosphere in which the proprieties, the amenities, and the virtues unconsciously grow.—*Robert G. Ingersoll.*

CALMNESS — We often forget this, most of us; but it is true. Noise, anger, explosive tones, superlatives, exaggerations of passion, add nothing to the force of what we say, but rather rob our words of the power that belongs to them. But the utterance that shows a spirit subdued by truth and mastered by wisdom is the utterance that sweeps away opposition, that persuades and overcomes. Go into a heated political convention, and you will find that it is not the men who get angry and storm and swear who carry the day. But the men who never lose their tempers and never raise their voices; who keep talking quietly and placidly as if they were discussing the weather. This is a truth that all of us who seek to influence our fellow beings, in the family, in the church, in the school, in society, in politics, anywhere, must lay to heart. We are prone to forget it; but we make a great mistake when we do forget it. The soft tongue breaketh the bone. The tamed tongue subdues the adversary.—*Gladden.*

DISSATISFACTION with our condition is often due to the false idea we have of the happiness of others.—*Churchman.*

THIS is the final test of a gentleman: His respect for those who can be of no possible service to him.
                    —*William Lyon Phelps.*

MANY HANDS — By many hands the work of God is done.
                    —*Richard Le Gallienne.*

CHRISTMAS SPIRIT — I am the Christmas spirit!

I enter the home of poverty, causing palefaced children to open their eyes wide, in pleased wonder.

I cause the miser's clutched hand to relax, and thus paint a bright spot on his soul.

I cause the aged to renew their youth and to laugh in the old, glad way.

I keep romance alive in the heart of childhood, and brighten sleep with dreams woven of magic.

I cause eager feet to climb dark stairways with filled baskets, leaving behind hearts amazed at the goodness of the world.

I cause the prodigal to pause a moment on his wild, wasteful way, and send to anxious love some little token that releases glad tears—tears which wash away the hard lines of sorrow.

I enter dark prison cells, reminding scarred manhood of what might have been, and pointing forward to good days yet to be.

I come softly into the still, white home of pain, and lips that are too weak to speak just tremble in silent, eloquent gratitude.

In a thousand ways I cause the weary world to look up into the face of God, and for a little moment forget the things that are small and wretched.

I am the Christmas spirit!

—*E. C. Baird.*

ARRANGEMENT — A child, desirous of presenting his father with a bouquet, goes into the garden and gathers a lapful of flowers and weeds, all mixed together. His mother selects, arranges, and binds the flowers, and makes the gift acceptable. So Christ makes ever our poor services acceptable to God as a sweet-smelling savor.—*Ambrose.*

MUSIC is nature's high-water mark. It is when the brook is full and goes with strong pulsing current toward the sea that it sings sweet music. When the writer of the book of Job would give us the noblest idea of beauty and harmony in the universe, he declares that in creation's dawn "The morning stars sang together." When God would give the most glorious prelude to the birth of Jesus, angels sang together on the plains of Bethlehem.

—*Gordon.*

Who Is Brother?

He who understands your silence.

He who will be a balance in the seasaw of life.

He who considers your needs before your deservings.

He who to himself is true and therefore must be so to you.

He who, when he reaches the top of the ladder, does not forget you if you are at the bottom.

He who is the same today when prosperity smiles upon you, and tomorrow when adversity and sorrows come.

He who cheerfully comes in when all the world has gone out; who weeps with you when the laughing is away.

He who guards your interests as his own, neither flatters nor deceives, gives just praise to your good deeds, and equally condemns your bad acts.

He who is the same to you in the society of the wealthy and proud, as in the solitude of poverty; whose cheerful smile sheds sunshine in every company.

—*Lodge Record.*

HAVING AND GETTING—There is no happiness in having and getting, but only in giving. Half the world is on the wrong scent in the pursuit of happiness.—*F. W. Gunsaulus.*

COURTESY—Some friends of mine, motoring in winter over the Spanish Guadarramas, stuck in a deep snowdrift and asked a passing muleteer if he would be kind enough to drag their car to the top of the pass. He agreed, and at the top they offered him a tip which must have seemed to him a small fortune. But he waved it aside with an apologetic smile, as if unwilling to hurt their feelings, saying: "All that the poor can offer is favors."

—Howard of Penrith.

OUTWITTED

He drew a circle that shut me out—
Heretic, rebel, a thing to flout.
But love and I had the wit to win:
We drew a circle that took him in.

—Edwin Markham.

Reprinted by permission.

LOVE is the medicine of all moral evil. By it the world is to be cured of sin. Love is the wine of existence. When you have taken that, you have taken the most precious drop that there is in the cluster. Love is the seraph, and faith and hope are but the wings by which it flies. The nature of the highest love is to be exquisitely sensitive to the act of forcing itself unbidden and unwelcomed upon another. The finer, the stronger, the higher love is, the more it is conditioned upon reciprocation. No man can afford to invest his being in anything lower than faith, hope, love—these three, the greatest of which is love.

—Henry Ward Beecher.

I WILL NOT FOLLOW where the path may lead, but I will go where there is no path, and I will leave a trail.

—Muriel Strode.

RICH men have built our hospitals, endowed our colleges, founded our orphan homes, assisted the scientists in combating disease, and they have in a thousand ways blessed this old world. Let us be fair. We have no right to pick out a few who have worshipped the dollar and lived for self at the expense of human life and judge all by them. The world is full of good men and women who have accumulated wealth and who are blessing the world in which they live. Every man and woman to their task: Ability, Labor and Capital must each make its contribution to civilization and prosperity. Prosperity is a granary that can be filled to overflowing only when all workers unite in bringing in their contributions, large and small.

—Public Speakers Library.

BACKWARD — By putting his best foot forward, many a man pulls his worst foot back. *—Ralph W. Sockman.*

HOLD OUT A LIGHT

Hold out a light,
  The way is dark,
No ray to guide
  Yon struggling bark.
Rough rocks are near,
  And wild waves roar;
Hold out a light
  To show the shore.

Hold out a light;
  Your brother may
Win back to land
  With your small ray;
New courage find
  Life's storms to face
With strengthened faith
  To win the race.

—Addison Howard Gibson.

GOOD NATURE—A cheerful temper, joined with innocence, will make beauty attractive, knowledge delightful, and wit good-natured. It will lighten sickness, poverty, and affliction; convert ignorance into an amiable simplicity, and render deformity itself agreeable.

—*Addison.*

Via Crucis

If thou wouldst follow Me upon the way,
Take up My cross where I have laid it
    down.
Cast off thy life of luxury and ease,
Take to thy heart My hyssop and My
    crown.

Tread where I trod, each step a thing of
    pain,
Meeting nor help nor succor on the road.
Strengthen thine ears to listen to the gibes
Flung at thee as thou fallest 'neath thy
    load.

Thy friends will be the sad at heart and
    poor,
Those who are burdened with a life of
    shame,
Those sufferers who are the halt andd
    blind,
Those to whom Beauty is a distant name.

Take up My cross where I have laid it
    down,
My mantle wrap about thee and My pain,
Give of My love to all thy fellow-men—
This being done, I'll not have died in vain!

—*Hesper Le Gallienne.*

SELF-DENIAL — Our superfluities should be given up for the convenience of others. Our conveniences should give place to the necessities of others. And even our necessities give way to the extremities of the poor.—*John Howard.*

PATIENCE — We have need of patience with ourselves and with others; with those below, and those above us, and with our own equals; with those who love us and those who love us not; for the greatest things and for the least; against sudden inroads of trouble, and under daily burdens; disappointments as to the weather, or the breaking of the heart; in the weariness of the body, or the wearing of the soul; in our own failure of duty; or others' failure toward us; in every-day wants, or in the aching of sickness or the decay of old age; in disappointment, bereavement, losses, injuries, reproaches; in heaviness of the heart; or its sickness amid delayed hopes. In all these things, from childhood's little troubles to the martyr's sufferings, patience is the grace of God, whereby we endure evil for the love of God—*E. B. Pusey.*

Liberality

He is dead whose hand is not open wide
    To help the need of a human brother;
He doubles the length of his lifelong ride
    Who gives his hand to another.
And a thousand million lives are his
Who carries the world in his sympathies.
To give is to live. To deny is to die.

—*Selected.*

LAYMEN—Preachers and laymen are each rowing different oars, but they are both in the same boat. When only one oar is being pulled, there is a lot of splash but no progress. Let us see that both oars are being pulled. We are facing great problems and must work them out together, each with confidence in the other, each with love for the other, and each unselfishly thinking of the generations to come, with less thought for ourselves.

—*Roger Babson.*

BROTHERHOOD—There is an old legend of a general who found his troops disheartened. He believed it was owing to the fact that they did not realize how close they were to the other divisions of the same army on account of a dense growth of small trees and shrubbery. Orders therefore were given to "Burn the underbrush." It was done and they saw they were not isolated, as they had supposed, but were part of one great army. The result was that their courage revived, and they went forward in triumph. So let us burn the brushwood between the workingman and the church—the brushwood of prejudice, mistrust and separation. We all have far more in common than we think. We are all under the same great Captain. Let the brushwood be burned away in the glow of united song, and in the enthusiasm of common worship.—*Messenger.*

YOU WANT to double your wealth without gambling or stock-jobbing. Share it. Whether it be material or intellectual, its rapid increase will amaze you. What would the sun have been had he folded himself up in darkness? Surely he would have gone out. So would Socrates.

—*J. C. Hare.*

Right

The world is a difficult world indeed,
 And the people are hard to suit,
And the man who plays on the violin
 Is a bore to the man with a flute.
And I myself have often thought,
 How very much better 'twould be
If every one of the folks that I know
 Would only agree with me.
But since they will not, the very best way
 To make the world look bright,
Is never to mind what others say,
 But do what you think is right.

—*Light and Life Evangel.*

SUNSHINY — Have you ever had your day suddenly turn sunshiny because of a cheerful word? Have you ever wondered if this could be the same world, because someone had been unexpectedly kind to you? You can make today the same for somebody. It is only a question of a little imagination, a little time and trouble. Think now, "What can I do today to make someone happy?"—old persons, children, servants—even a bone for the dog, or sugar for the bird! Why not?—*Babcock.*

ENEMIES—Ye have enemies; for who can live on this earth without them? Take heed to yourselves; love them. In no way can thy enemy so hurt thee by his violence as thou dost hurt thyself if thou love him not. And let it not seem to you impossible to love him. Believe first that it can be done, and pray that the will of God may be done in you. For what good can thy neighbor's ill do to thee? If he had no ill, he would not even be thine enemy. Wish him well, then, that he may end his ill, and he will be thine enemy no longer. For it is not the human nature in him that is at enmity with thee, but his sin. . . . Let thy prayer be against the malice of thine enemy, that it may die, and he may live. For if thine enemy were dead, thou hast lost, it might seem, an enemy, yet has thou not found a friend. But if his malice die, thou hast at once lost an enemy and found a friend.

—*St. Augustine.*

Twins

Devotion borrows Music's tone,
And Music took Devotion's wing;
And like the bird that hails the sun.
They soar to heaven, and soaring, sing.

—*The Hermit of St. Clement's Wall.*

SELF-CONTROL.—Self-Control implies command of temper, command of feeling, coolness of judgment, and the power to restrain the imagination and curb the will. It means such thorough mastery over self as Robert Ainsworth, the lexicographer, possessed, who, when his wife, in a fit of passion, committed his voluminous manuscript to the flames, calmly turned to his desk, and recommenced his labors.

—*W. H. Davenport Adams.*

Measure of Success

When sunset falls upon your day
And fades from out the west,
When business cares are put away
And you lie down to rest,
The measure of the day's success
Or failure may be told
In terms of human happiness
And not in terms of gold.

Is there beside some hearth tonight
More joy because you wrought?
Does some one face the bitter fight
With courage you have taught?
Is something added to the store
Of human happiness?
If so, the day that now is o'er
Has been a real success.

—*Selected*

CHIVALRY.—Some say that the age of chivalry is past. The age of chivalry is never past, so long as there is a wrong left unredressed on earth, or a man or woman left to say, "I will redress that wrong, or spend my life in the attempt." The age of chivalry is never past, so long as we have faith enough to say, "God will help me to redress that wrong; or, if not me, He will help those that come after me, for His eternal Will is to overcome evil with good."—*Kingsley.*

HARMONIUM — Besides Theology, music is the only art capable of affording peace and joy of the heart like that induced by the study of the science of Divinity. The proof of this is that the Devil, the originator of sorrowful anxieties and restless troubles, flees before the sound of music almost as much as he does before the Word of God. This is why the prophets preferred music before all the other arts, proclaiming the Word in psalms and hymns.

My heart, which is full of overflowing, has often been solaced and refreshed by music when sick and weary.

—*Martin Luther.*

A CHALLENGING FACT.—Brotherhood is no longer simply a religious ideal, but a challenging material fact; for there is no peace but universal peace, no enduring prosperity that does not comprehend all mankind. It was Dante who said seven centuries ago that no soul could ever be quite happy in Heaven while it was conscious of a single suffering soul in Hell.—*Edgar White Burrill.*

ENEMIES.—If we would read the secret history of our enemies, we would find in each man's life sorrow and suffering enough to disarm all hostility.

—*Longfellow.*

True

He's true to God who's true to man; wherever wrong is done
To the humblest and the weakest, neath the all-beholding sun.
That wrong is also done to us; and they are slaves most base
Whose love of right is for themselves and not for all their race.

—*James Russell Lowell.*

PREACHING — Every problem that the preacher faces leads back to one basic question: how well does he understand the thoughts and lives of his people? That he should know his gospel goes without saying, but he may know it ever so well and yet fail to get it within reaching distance of anybody unless he intimately understands people and cares more than he cares for anything else what is happening inside of them. Preaching is wrestling with individuals over questions of life and death, and until that idea of it commands a preacher's mind and method, eloquence will avail him little and theology not at all.
—*Harry Emerson Fosdick.*

BENEVOLENCE — God is positive. Evil is merely primitive, not absolute. It is like cold, which is the privation of heat. All evil is so much death to nonentity. Benevolence is absolute and real. So much benevolence as a man hath, so much life hath he; for all things proceed out of this same spirit, which is differently named love, justice, temperance, in its different applications, just as the ocean receives different names on the several shores which it washes.—*Emerson.*

RECOMMENDATION — The memorial tablet to Dr. Geddie, at Aneitum, New Hebrides, bears the words: "When he landed in 1840, there were no Christians here; when he left in 1872, there were no heathen." These words are more suggestive than hundreds of pages of history. They are the best that can be said about any Christian worker. It is the nullification of self and the exaltation of the Master that are more eloquent than words or deeds. As John said, "He must increase but I must decrease." It is "Christ in us, the hope of glory." It is not what we say, but what we are.

MEASURING RODS—At the close of life the question will be not, how much have you got, but how much have you given; not how much have you won, but how much have you done; not how much have you saved, but how much have you sacrificed; how much have you loved and served, not how much were you honored.—*Nathan C. Schaeffer.*

JUSTICE is the paying universally what we owe. St. Paul explains this, and at the same time shows the profound connection between love and justice when he says, "Owe no man anything, but to love one another;" for "he that loveth another hath fulfilled the law." Here love is the eternal debt of righteousness, which justice must be forever paying. Now charity does not suppress righteousness either in God or in man; in us, it is the strength by which the debt is paid, as well as the watchful requital of the debt itself. The Christian ethics of justice are deeply affected by the supremacy of love.
—*W. B. Pope.*

INVISIBILITY—No man can wrap his cloak about him and say that he will stand alone, that his life shall not influence nor be influenced by other lives. Even the mountain that lifts its snow-capped summit to the clouds is enclosed around with influences that constantly change its characteristics, the sun, the mighty king of day, melts its ice-bound top, and the rain plows furrows in its gigantic sides. So these different organizations throw around human lives, sunshine of friendship and rain drops of charity and love, protecting the living, soothing the dying, holding in fond remembrance the dead, assisting with tender care the loved ones who remain.—*Brotherhood.*

THE REAL TEST—Society affects to estimate men by their talents, but really feels and knows them by their character. —*Thoreau.*

SELF-SACRIFICE—Shortly after the death of Phillips Brooks, his oldest brother said to Dr. McVicker, "Phillips might have saved himself, and so prolonged his life. Others do; but he was always giving himself to any who wanted him." Dr. McVickers answered: "Yes, indeed, he might have saved himself, but in so doing he would not have been Phillips Brooks. The glory of his life was that he did not save himself." Ah! the glory of any life is that it does not save itself. Like Mary, Bishop Brooks gave the best he had to God and humanity, and that is why the fragrance of his life has filled two continents with its sweetness.—*Tidings.*

GIVING—Never be afraid of giving up your best, and God will give you His better.—*Hinton.*

PEACEABLE—A peaceable disposition is a distinguishing mark of Christian character, and the want of it is a serious defect in the character of any one "that nameth the name of Christ." Upon all who claim to be His followers it is enjoined, in the words of an inspired apostle: "If it be possible, as much as lieth in you, live peaceably with all men." —*The Watchman.*

I HAVE SOMEWHERE MET with the epitaph on a charitable man which has pleased me very much. I cannot recollect the words, but here is the sense of it: "What I spent I lost; what I possessed is left to others; what I gave away remains with me."—*Addison.*

ENVY is called a passion; and means suffering. Envy is a mysterious and terrible disease. The nerves of sensation within the man are attached by some unseen hand to his neighborhood all around him, so that every step of advancement which they make tears the fibres that lie next his heart. The wretch enjoys a moment's relief when the mystic chord is temporarily slackened by a neighbor's fall; but his agony immediately begins again, for he anticipates another twitch as soon as the fallen is restored to prosperity.—*W. Arnot.*

REPRESENTATIVES—We are here to represent Christ—to present Him again, to re-present Him.—*Babcock.*

EXAMPLE—We reprove each other unconsciously by our own behavior. Our very carriage and demeanor in the streets should be a reprimand that will go to the conscience of every beholder. An infusion of love from a great soul gives a color to our faults which will discover them as lunar caustic detects impurities in water. —*Thoreau.*

DEPORTMENT — Godliness is that outward deportment which characterizes a heavenly temper.—*G. Crabb.*

BENEVOLENCE—He that lays out for God, God lays up for him. But, alas! God's credit runs low in the world; few care to trust Him. Give and spend, and be sure that God will send; for only in giving and spending do you fullfill the object of His sending.—*J. G. Holland.*

TAPERS—If you have knowledge, let others light their candles at it.

CONSIDERATENESS — One imbued with this high quality never sees deformity or blemish. A lame man could easily classify his friends, as to their breeding, by drawing a line between those who ask how it happened, and those who refrain from all questions. The gentleman will not talk to the beggar of his rags, nor boast of his health before the sick, nor speak of his wealth among the poor; he will not seem to be fortunate among the hapless, nor make any show of his virtue before the vicious. He will avoid all painful contrast, always looking at the thing in question from the standpoint of the other person.—*T. T. Munger.*

UPRIGHTNESS

Who serves his country best?
  Not he who guides her senates in debate,
And makes the laws which are her prop and stay;
  Not he who wears the poet's purple vest,
  And sings her songs of love and grief and fate;
    There is a better way.

He serves his country best
  Who lives pure life, and doeth righteous deed,
And walks straight paths, however others stray,
And leaves his sons as uttermost bequest
  A stainless record which all may read;
    This is a better way.
        —*Selected.*

PUNCTUALITY — Punctuality preserves peace and good temper in a family or a business; it gives calmness of mind; it gives weight to character; it is contagious, and thus leads to a general saving of time and temper and money.
        —*Adams.*

INFLUENCE — Every human being has influence. It is inseparable from existence. Its effects are as penetrating as ointment. Its presence is as manifest in every life as the leaven that swells the meal.

Each moral action and utterance is linked to a chain of sequences no mortal can foretell. Each is a vast whispering gallery, where words and actions live on and ring on forever.

Scientists tell us that the words spoken by Abraham and Elijah are still influencing the air; that the atmosphere is a mighty library, on whose pages human actions and utterances have all been impressed. Influence is born with us like fire in the flint. It walks with us, flashes from the eyes and radiates from us like light from the sun. Influence is posthumous; and of an evil man, like the fallen Abel, it may be said, "He being dead, yet speaketh!"—*Morgan.*

CHARITY

Knowledge shall fail, and prophecy shall cease:
Yea, constant faith and holy hope shall die,
One lost in certainty, and one in joy;
While thou, more happy power, fair Charity,
Triumphant sister, greatest of the three,
Thy office and thy nature still the same,
Lasting thy lamp, and unconsumed thy flame,
Still shalt survive;
Shalt stand before the host of heaven confest,
For ever blessing, and for ever blest!
        —*Prior.*

CHARACTER—Keep clear of a man who does not value his own character.

LIMITLESS—The Church must grope her way into the alleys, and courts, and purlieus of the city, and up the broken staircase, and into the bare room, and beside the loathsome sufferer; she must go down into the pit with the miner, into the forecastle with the sailor, into the tent with the soldier, into the shop with the mechanic, into the factory with the operative, into the field with the farmer, into the countingroom with the merchant. Like the air, the Church must press equally on all the surfaces of society; like the sea, flow into every nook of the shore line of humanity; and like the sun, shine on things foul and low as well as fair and high, for she was organized, commissioned, and equipped for the moral renovation of the whole world.—*Simpson.*

HATE — I will tell you what to hate. Hate hypocrisy, hate cant, hate intolerance, oppression, injustice; hate pharisaism; hate them as Christ hated them— with a deep, living, godlike hatred.
—*F. W. Robertson.*

Parable of the Rhone
Erstwhile, beside the placid river Rhone,
Paused I and pondered as I stood alone,
And marveled at the beauty of the scene.
The massive stream flows on its great
    course,
So wide and deep, yet noiseless in its glee,
Still rushes mad-like with tremendous
    force,
As on it wends its way towards the sea.
From this majestic memory, oft I scan
The field of effort shown in human skill.
See how true merit in the life of man
Runs broad and deep, to execute his will,
How, like a river, man in varied poise,
The greater be the life, the less the noise.
—*Octave F. Ursenbach.*

EMPTINESS — Do, and it shall be done. Do with another, that it may be done with thee; for thou aboundest and thou lackest. Thou aboundest in things temporal, thou lackest things eternal. A beggar is at thy gate, thou art thyself a beggar at God's gate. Thou art sought, and thou seekest. As thou dealest with thy seeker, even so God will deal with His. Thou art both empty and full. Fill thou the empty out of thy fulness, that out of the fulness of God thine emptiness may be filled.—*St. Augustine.*

The Bridge Builder
An old man traveling a lone highway,
Came at the evening cold and gray,
To a chasm vast and deep and wide,
Through which was flowing a sullen tide.
The old man crossed in the twilight dim,
The sullen stream held no fears for him;
But he turned when safe on the other side,
And builded a bridge to span the tide.

"Old man," cried a fellow pilgrim near,
"You're wasting your time in building
    here.
Your journey will end with the closing
    day;
You never again will pass this way.
You have crossed the chasm deep and
    wide,
Why build you this bridge at even-tide?"

The builder lifted his old gray head:
"Good friend, in the path I have come,"
    he said,
"There followeth after me today
A youth whose feet must pass this way.
This stream which has been as naught
    to me,
To that fair-haired youth may pitfall be;
He, too, must cross in the twilight dim—
Good friend, I am building this bridge
    for him." —*Will Allen Dromgoole.*

132

AMIABLE — How shall a man cultivate an amiable temper, and exhibit a becoming example? Why, by adopting the following rules:

Reflect upon and deliberately weigh the peculiar advantages resulting from such a temper and conduct. To an individual this will bring serenity, peace, and joy; to a family, comfort, harmony, and help.

Carefully guard against such things as have the least tendency to disturb the mind and awaken uneasy tempers.

Assiduously avoid being ruffled or moved by little events. Neglect of this maxim has been the source of most little animosities.—*Evangelical Magazine.*

HELPFULNESS — Mark how the hand comes to the defense of the eye in its weakness; and how the eye with its sight, and from its elevated position, keeps watch for the welfare of the lowly, blind, but laborious and useful foot. The mutual helpfulness of these members is absolutely perfect. Such should be the charity between brother and brother of God's family on earth.—*W. Arnot.*

GOODNESS conditions usefulness. A grimy hand may do a gracious deed, but a bad heart cannot. What a man says and what a man is must stand together, —must consist. His life can ruin his lips or fill them with power. It is what men see that gives value to what we say. Being comes before saying or doing. Well may we pray, "Search me, O God! Reveal me to myself. Cleanse me from secret faults, that those who are acquainted with me, who know my downsittings and my uprisings, may not see in me the evil way that gives the lie to my words."
—*Babcock.*

FORGIVENESS — How great is the contrast between that forgiveness to which we lay claim from God towards us, and our temper towards others! God, we expect, will forgive us great offences—offences many times repeated; and will forgive them freely, liberally, and from the heart. But we are offended at our neighbor, perhaps, for the merest trifles, and for an injury only once offered; and we are but half reconciled when we seem to forgive. Even an uncertain humor, an ambiguous word, or a suspected look, will inflame our anger; and hardly any persuasion will induce us for a long time to relent.—*H. Thornton.*

SO IT HAS ALWAYS BEEN—they come to Christ, the brainiest come to the manger. Who was the greatest metaphysician this country ever has produced? Jonathan Edward, the Christian. Who was the greatest poet ever produced? John Milton, the Christian. Why is it that every college and university in the land has a chapel? They must have a place for the wise men to worship.—*Scoville.*

MIRACLES — Some skeptics say, "Oh, the miracles, I can't accept miracles." One may drop a brown seed in the black soil and up comes a green shoot. You let it grow and by and by you pull up its root and you find it red. You cut the red root and find it has a white heart. Can any one tell how this comes about—how brown cast into black results in green and then in red and white? Yet you eat your radish without troubling your mind over miracles. Men are not distressed by miracles in the dining room; they reserve them all for religion!
—*Bryan.*

XXIII. PERSEVERANCE

FAILURES—Scarcely a great man can be named who has not failed the first time. In such defeat no shame lies; the shame consists in one's not retrieving it. Lord Beaconsfield made, as everybody knows, a signal failure in his maiden speech in the House of Commons. But he was not cowed by the derisive laughter which greeted him. With astonishing self-control, and no less astonishing self-knowledge, he exclaimed, "I have begun several times many things, and have succeeded in them at last. I shall sit down now; but the time will come when you will hear me." The command of temper, the mastery over self, which these words displayed, is almost sublime. The late Lord Lytton made many failures. His first novel was a failure; so was his first play; so was his first poem. But he would not yield to disappointment. He subdued his mortification, and resumed his pen, to earn the eventual distinction of a foremost place among our foremost novelists, and to contribute to the modern stage two of its most popular dramas. We should be disposed to define genius as the capacity of surviving failure; in self-control, at all events, it finds a powerful auxiliary and agent.—*Lucas.*

SAILING — To reach the port of Heaven we must sail sometimes with the wind and sometimes against it. But we must sail, and not drift nor lie at anchor.
—*Oliver Wendell Holmes.*

HABIT — We are spinning our own fates, good or evil, never to be undone. Every smallest stroke of virtue or vice leaves its ever-so-little scar. The drunken Rip Van Winkle, in Jefferson's play, excuses himself for every fresh dereliction by saying, "I won't count this time!" Well, he may not count it, and a kind Heaven may not count it; but it is being counted none the less. Down among his nerve-cells and fibers the molecules are counting it, registering and storing it up to be used against him when the next temptation comes. Nothing we ever do is, in strict scientific literalness, wiped out.
—*William James.*

HAND IN HAND — The greatest work has always gone hand in hand with the most fervent moral purpose.
—*Sidney Lanier.*

HOW DID YOU DIE?

*Did you tackle that trouble that came
    your way,
With a resolute heart and cheerful?
Or hide your face from the light of day
    With a craven soul and fearful?
Oh, a trouble's a ton, or a trouble's an
    ounce,
    Or a trouble is what you make it,
And it isn't the fact that you're hurt
    that counts,
    But only how did you take it?*

*And though you be done to the death,
    what then?
    If you battled the best you could,
If you played your part in the world
    of men,
    Why, the critic will call you good.
Death comes with a crawl or comes
    with a pounce,
    And whether he's slow or spry,
It isn't the fact that you're dead that
    counts,
    But only how did you die?*

—EDMUND VANCE COOKE.

LIFE'S HARD TASKS — Among some skaters was a boy so small and so evidently a beginner that his frequent mishaps awakened the pity of a tender-hearted, if not wise, spectator. "Why, sonny, you are getting all bumped up," she said. "I wouldn't stay on the ice and keep falling down so; I'd just come off and watch the others." The tears of the last down fall were still rolling over the rosy cheeks, but the child looked from his adviser to the shining steel on his feet, and answered, half-indignantly, "I didn't get some new skates to give up with; I got them to learn how with." The whole philosophy of earthly discipline was in the reply. Life's hard tasks are never sent for us "to give up with;" they are always intended to awaken strength, skill, and courage in learning how to master them.
—*Forward.*

GROWTH—To have failed is to have striven, to have striven is to have grown.
—*Maltbie D. Babcock.*

STRUGGLE—There is no royal road to the temple of melody, where St. Cecilia dwells. There is no short cut to the temple of the beautiful, where Apollo reigns as lord of the arts of color, form, and music. The eager aspirant for eloquence, or wealth, or wisdom, begins a long, long way from the excellence that crowns one's life-work. Every morning Mother Nature whispers to the youth, "Strive, struggle." Every night her last message is, "Sleep to waken again to new struggles, wrestlings, and achievements." In the realms of conscience and character man must work out his own salvation through ceaseless struggling, toiling long, hard, and patiently. And just in proportion as he goes toward excellence does the work become difficult.—*Newell Dwight Hillis.*

DISCONTENT—There are two kinds of discontent in this world; the discontent that works, and the discontent that wrings its hands. The first gets what it wants, and the second loses what it has. There's no cure for the first but success; and there's no cure at all for the second.
—*Gordon Graham.*

DO IT BETTER—When the first volume of Thomas Carlyle's *French Revolution* had been completed with tremendous travail, Carlyle entrusted the manuscript to John Stuart Mill for critical reading. It was a black night in Mill's life when, white-faced and trembling, he was obliged to return with the news that except for a few stray sheets, the manuscript had gone up in smoke. The chambermaid had found it handy to start a fire!

When the door finally closed behind their distraught visitor, leaving them to the privacy of their despair, Carlyle said to his wife: "Well, Mill, poor fellow, is terribly cut up. We must endeavor to hide from him how very serious this business is to us." Serious, because they were penniless. Above all, serious because he had written at white heat and, when each chapter was finished, had triumphantly torn up his notes as plaguy and toilsome things which he would never need or wish to see again.

Next day all the Scotch Presbyterian blood in his veins bade him order a fresh supply of paper and make in his diary this entry: "It is as if my invisible school master had torn my copybook when I showed it and said, 'No, boy, thou must write it better'."—*Alexander Woollcott.*

POWER — People do not lack strength; they lack will.—*Victor Hugo.*

DETERMINATION — The longer I live, the more I am certain that the great difference between men — between the feeble and the powerful, the great and the insignificant—is energy, invincible determination—a purpose once fixed, and then death or victory. That quality will do anything that can be done in this world, and no talents, no circumstances, no opportunities, will make a two-legged creature a man without it. There are hindrances without and within, but the outer hindrances could effect nothing if there were no inner surrender to them. Fear of opinion, timidity, dread of change, love of ease, indolence, unfaithfulness, are the great hindrances. Optimism is believing that you can eat the rooster that scratches over your grave.—*Sam Jones.*

Man-Making

We all are blind until we see
That in the human plan
Nothing is worth the making if
It does not make the man.

Why build these cities glorious
If man unbuilded goes?
In vain we build the world, unless
The builder also grows.
—*Edwin Markham.*
Reprinted by permission.

BEGIN GREATLY—A life without a purpose is a languid, drifting thing.— Every day we ought to renew our purpose, saying to ourselves: This day let us make a sound beginning, for what we have hitherto done is nought.—Our improvement is in proportion to our purpose.—We hardly ever manage to get completely rid even of one fault, and do not set our hearts on daily improvement. —Always place a definite purpose before thee.—*Thomas a' Kempis.*

A MASTER INFLUENCE — Perseverance is the master impulse of the firmest souls; the discipline of the noblest virtues; and the guarantee of acquisitions the most invigorating in their use and inestimable in their worth.—*E. L. Magoon.*

Perpetual pushing and assurance put a difficulty out of countenance, and make a seeming impossibility give away.
—*Jeremy Collier.*

CAFETERIA — Life is a cafeteria. There are no waiters to bring success to you. Help yourself. Paul evidently felt that there was no standstill to human life. He was a part of a great procession and must keep step with alert and eager tread. It will be well if we can catch his spirit. Of all the Apostles, Paul attained the sublimest heights. He had greater capacities to begin with, perhaps, and he bent all the energies of his great soul to the end to which he had consecrated himself completely. Great men have purposes; others have wishes.
—*Public Speakers Library.*

LITTLE BY LITTLE—No great work is ever done in a hurry. To develop a great scientific discovery, to paint a great picture, to write an immortal poem, to become a minister, or a famous general—to do anything great requires time, patience, and perseverance. These things are done by degrees, "Little by Little." Milton did not write "Paradise Lost" at a sitting, nor did Shakespeare compose "Hamlet" in a day. The greatest writers must begin with the alphabet, the most famous musicians once picked out their notes laboriously; a child must learn to draw a straight line before he can develop into a Titian or a Michael Angelo.
—*W. J. Wilmont Buxton.*

Prayer

A prayer in its simplest definition is merely a wish turned God-ward. —Phillips Brooks.

WILL—Our bodies are our gardens, to the which our wills are gardeners; so that if we will plant nettles or sow lettuce, set hyssop and weed up thyme, supply it with one gender of herbs or distract it with many, either to have it sterile with idleness or manured with industry—why, the power and incorrigible authority of this, lies in our wills.—*Shakespeare.*

In the moral world there is nothing impossible if we can bring a thorough will to it. Man can do everything with himself, but he must not attempt to do too much with others.
—*Wilhelm von Humboldt.*

A character is a perfectly formed will.
—*Novalis.*

PERSEVERANCE gives power to weakness, and opens to poverty the world's wealth. It spreads fertility over the barren landscape, and bids the choicest flowers and fruits spring up and flourish in the desert abode of thorns and briars.
—*S. G. Goodrich.*

PATIENCE — Let it be remembered that "steadfast application to a fixed aim" is the law of a well-spent life. When Giardini was asked how long it would take to learn the violin, he replied, "Twelve hours a day for twenty years together." Alas, too many of us think to play our fiddles by a species of inspiration! The Leotards and Blondins whose gymnastic achievements attract such admiring crowds—what labor must they have undergone; what "painful diligence" must they have exhibited! The same energy, the same adherence to a settled purpose, might assuredly have made them benefactors of mankind, had they been animated by a nobler impulse.

WILLING SERVICE—A musician is not recommended for playing long, but for playing well; it is obeying God willingly, that is accepted; the Lord hates that which is forced, it is rather a tax than an offering. Cain served God grudgingly; he brought his sacrifice, not his heart. To obey God's commandments unwillingly is like the devils who came out of the man possessed, at Christ's command, but with reluctancy and against their will. Good duties must not be pressed and beaten out of us, as the waters came out of the rock when Moses smote it with his rod; but must freely drop from us, as myrrh from the tree, or honey from the comb. If a willing mind be wanting, there wants that flower which should perfume our obedience, and make it a sweet-smelling savor unto God.—*T. Watson.*

Will

One ship drives east, and another west
With the self-same winds that blow;
'Tis the set of the sails
And not the gales,
Which decides the way to go.

Like the winds of the sea are the ways
    of fate;
As the voyage along through life;
'Tis the will of the soul
That decides its goal,
And not the calm or the strife.
—*Ella Wheeler Wilcox.*

MAXIMS VERIFIED—For the conduct of life, habits are more important than maxims, because a habit is a maxim verified. To take a new set of maxims for one's guide is no more than to change the title of a book; but to change one's habits is to change one's life. Life is only a tissue of habits.—*Amiel.*

A TASK—To be honest, to be kind, to earn a little, and to spend a little less, to make upon the whole a family happier for his presence, to renounce when that shall be necessary and not to be embittered, to keep a few friends, but these without capitulation; above all, on the same condition, to keep friends with himself; here is a task for all a man has of fortitude and delicacy.—*Robert Louis Stevenson.*

LITTLE STROKES — Jacob Riis, in his drive against slums, never allowed a chance to pass of telling the people of New York what they were harboring. But it took a lot of telling, and he sometimes grew discouraged. "But," he said, "when nothing seems to help I go and look at a stonecutter hammering away at his rock perhaps 100 times without as much as a crack showing in it. Yet at the 101st blow it will split in two, and I know it was not that blow that did it, but all that had gone before."

"THIS ONE THING I DO."—The power of a man increases steadily by continuance in one direction. He becomes acquainted with the resistance and with his own tools; increases his skill and strength and learns the favorable moments and favorable accidents. He is his own apprentice, and more time gives a a great addition of power, just as a falling body acquires momentum with every foot of the fall.—*Emerson.*

Perseverance, dear my lord, keeps honor bright. To have none, is to hang quite out of fashion, like a rusty nail in monumental mockery.—*Shakespeare.*

Great works are performed not by strength, but by perseverance.
—*Book of Reflections.*

FORTITUDE — In November, 1915, the papers told of the death, at Saranac Lake, New York, of Dr. Edward L. Trudeau, who was not different from many another young man until after his physician told him he must die of tuberculosis. But he did not lose courage. He went to the Adirondack wilderness, not because he thought the air would help him, but because he longed for the joy of the out-of-doors life. The air and the exposure were what he needed. As he began to recover his strength he thought of other sufferers whom he might help. During the next forty years he became one of the world leaders in investigations as to the cause and cure of tuberculosis, and he succeeded in building up a great sanitarium for sufferers from the disease, from which thousands have gone with new hope—the first of hundreds of similar institutions, whose builders took their inspiration from him. The secret of his success was optimism, which with him was another name for faith in God. Because of his faith he was able to work with joy, in spite of the slow but steady progress of his disease.—*John T. Faris.*

The Way Back

To keep my health . . . To do my work . . .
    To live!
To see to it I grow, and gain, and give.
Never to look behind me for an hour.
To wait in meekness and to walk in
    power.
But always fronting onward toward the
    right;
Always and always facing toward the
    light.
Robbed, starved, defeated, fallen, wide
    astray,—
On with what strength I have, back to the
    Way!
    —*Charlotte Perkins Gilman.*

XXIV. PERSPECTIVE

VIEW POINTS—There is a story of two Greek sculptors who competed for the placing of a statue on a pillar in the public square. And one worked skilfully and well, until the features of his figure were smoothed and polished to look as if living. But the other left his block of marble crude and jagged and uncouth, so that one could hardly tell if indeed it were a human being at all. And they put the statue of the first up on the pillar, where all might see; but high up on the pillar it was blurred by distance, and it could not be seen clearly from any angle. So they took it down, and put up the other's, and, behold, that which had not seemed true to life was now in its right perspective, and became life-like and beautiful, true to the imagination.
—*Edgar White Burrill.*

FAIRY TALES—Every man's life is a fairy tale written by God's fingers.
—*Hans Christian Andersen.*

NOBILITY—King Philip with a large company of soldiers in splendid array, went to visit Socrates. When the grand procession reached the city where Socrates lived a part of the time, they learned that Socrates was out in the country. The king was astonished! He exclaimed, "Socrates, come with me, I will let you reign over a part of my kingdom." Socrates said, "Then I would be like King Philip?" "Yes." "Well," replied Socrates, "I can see how Socrates could be made like King Philip, but I do not see how King Philip could be made like Socrates." King Philip is buried in the tomb of forgetfulness. Socrates lives on, linked with the harbingers of Christ.

FAITHFULNESS — When Pompeii was destroyed, there were very many buried in the ruins of it, who were afterwards found in very different situations. There were some found who were in the streets, as if they had been attempting to make their escape. There were some found in deep vaults, as if they had gone thither for security. There were some found in lofty chambers; but where did they find the Roman sentinel? They found him standing at the city gate, with his hand still grasping the war weapon, where he had been placed by his captain; and there, while the Heaven threatened him; there, while the earth shook beneath him; there, while the lava stream rolled, he had stood at his post; and there, after a thousand years had passed away, was he found. So let Christians stand to their duty, in the post at which their Captain has placed them.—*Evangelist.*

PESSIMISM—If it wasn't for the optimist, the pessimist would never know how happy he wasn't.

> It is not growing like a tree
> In bulk, doth make Man better be;
> Or standing long an oak, three hundred year,
> To fall a log at last, dry, bald, and sere:
> A lily of a day
> Is fairer far in May,
> Although it fall and die that night—
> It was the plant and flower of light.
> In small proportions we just beauties see;
> And in short measures life may perfect be.
>
> —BEN JONSON.

ADAPTATIONS — In "The Natural Law in the Spiritual World," Prof. Henry Drummond has a striking passage, in which he describes "the wonderful adaptation of each organism to its surroundings—of the fish to the water, of the eagle to the air, of the insect to the forest bed; and of each part of every organism—the fish's swim-bladder, the eagle's eye, the insect's breathing tubes." All these, he says, inspire us with a sense of the boundless resources and skill of nature in perfecting her arrangements for the individual life. "Down in the last details the world is made for what is in it; and by whatever process things are as they are, all organisms find in surrounding nature the ample complements of themselves."

All this holds as one ascends the scale of being. Man finds every want met and need answered. It is as true of his mental as of his physical make-up. When we reach the apex of the pyramid of being we must hold that the same law obtains. Faith must have realities adjusted to its varying needs. For faith, the supernatural is the natural. It is faith's medium, its native air. Therefore, the incomprehensible, instead of destroying or preventing faith, permits it. It creates faith. It demands faith. It is faith's glory.—*Brooks.*

ARRIVING — We picture death as coming to destroy; let us rather picture Christ as coming to save. We think of death as sending; let us rather think of life as beginning, and that more abundantly. We think of losing; let us think of gaining. We think of parting; let us think of meeting. We think of going away; let us think of arriving. And as the voice of death whispers, "You must go from earth," let us hear the voice of Christ saying, "You are but coming to Me!"
—*Norman Macleod.*

IMITATION—To be in Christ, is to live in His ideas, character, spirit, as the atmosphere of being. Men everywhere are living in the ideas and characters of others. He who lives in the spirit of Raphael, becomes a painter; he who lives in the spirit of Milton, becomes a poet; he who lives in the spirit of Bacon, becomes a philosopher; he who lives in the spirit of Caesar, becomes a warrior; he who lives in the spirit of Christ, becomes a man.—*Anonymous.*

STEWARDSHIP

I bought gasoline; I went to the show;
I bought some new tubes for my radio;
I bought candy and peanuts, nut bars and
ice cream;
While my salary lasted, life sure was a
scream.

It takes careful spending to make money
go round;
One's methods of finance must always be
sound.
With habits quite costly, it's real hard to
save;
My wife spent ten "bucks" on a permanent wave.

The church came round begging. It sure
made me sore!
If they'd let me alone, I'd give a lot more.
They have plenty of nerve! They forgot all
the past!
I gave them a quarter the year before last.
—*Lookout.*

VIRTUE— Chinamen wear five buttons only on their coats, that they may keep in sight something to remind them of the five principal moral virtues which Confucius recommended. These are: Humility, Justice, Order, Prudence, and Rectitude.

GOOD.—Live for something. Do good and leave behind you a monument of virtue that the storm of time can never destroy. Write your name in kindness, love, and mercy on the hearts of thousands you come in contact with year by year; you will never be forgotten. No, your name, your deeds will be as legible on the hearts you leave behind as the stars on the brow of evening. Good deeds will shine as the stars of heaven. —*Chalmers.*

WORTH LIVING

Is life worth living? Yes, so long
  As there is wrong to right,
Wail of the weak against the strong,
  Or tyranny to fight;
Long as there lingers gloom to chase,
  Or streaming tear to dry,
One kindred woe, one sorrowing face
  That smiles as we draw nigh;
Long as a tale of anguish swells
  The heart, and lids grow wet
And at the sound of Christmas bells
  We pardon and forget;
So long as faith with Freedom reigns,
  And loyal hope survives;
And gracious charity remains
  To leaven lowly lives;
While there is one untrodden tract
  For intellect or will,
And men are free to think and act
  Life is worth living still.
              —*Alfred Austin.*

PEBBLES ON THE SHORE.—I do not know what I may appear to the world, but to myself I seem to have been only like a boy playing on the seashore, and diverting myself in now and then finding a prettier shell or a smoother pebble than ordinary, whilst the great ocean of truth lay all undiscovered before me.
              —*Isaac Newton.*

FIRST.—When Leonardo da Vinci resolved to paint the Last Supper, he threw all his energies into the work. He labored early and late. No pains were spared by him. He pondered devoutly those pages of the New Testament which record the first sacramental feast, in order that he might do his best to realize and reproduce the memorable scene. At length his task was done. Having given the finishing stroke, he invited a few confidential friends to a private inspection. They gazed attentively, and various remarks were made. An observation from one of them, however, led, as will be seen, to unexpected results. He spoke with great admiration of a golden chalice represented as being on the table at which our Lord and His disciples sat. Its shape, color, size, were all that could be desired. "That," exclaimed the critic, "is the most beautiful object in the picture." Hearing what was said, the artist took up a brush, and dipping it in black paint, deliberately smeared it over the whole canvas. He soon explained it—"If," said he, "what you tell me is true, then my picture is a failure, for I meant my Master's face to be the chief and most beautiful object."

All are artists; a good or bad picture each of us is painting—the picture of life. Too often, alas! men make inferior things the most conspicuous objects on the canvas of their daily history, bestowing rich colors and careful handicraft upon trifles. But the Saviour should be the grand center of our souls, and should have our chief and first attention.—*T. Stevenson.*

TEMPERANCE.— There is no difference between knowledge and temperance; for he who knows what is good and embraces it, who knows what is bad and avoids it, is learned and temperate.
              —*Socrates.*

MISTAKES — There are six mistakes of life that many of us make, said a famous writer, and then he gave the following list:

The delusion that individual advancement is made by crushing others down.

The tendency to worry about things that can not be changed or corrected.

Insisting that a thing is impossible because we ourselves can not accomplish it.

Refusing to set aside trivial preferences in order that important things may be accomplished.

Neglecting development and refinement.

The failure to establish the habit of saving money.—*Southern Bulletin.*

MANY-SIDEDNESS—I tell you that Jesus challenges the attention of this world by His many-sidedness. He meets the needs of all classes and conditions of men. As deep answereth unto deep, so does He respond to the movings of each soul of men. Call the roll of the world's workers and ask, "What think ye of Christ?" Their answers amaze us! To the artist, He is the One altogether lovely. To the architect, He is the Chief Corner Stone. To the astronomer, He is the Sun of Righteousness. To the baker, He is the living Bread. To the biologist, He is Life. To the builder, He is the Sure Foundation. To the carpenter, He is the Door. To the doctor, He is the Great Physician. To the educator, He is the Great Teacher. To the farmer, He is the Sower. To the florist, He is the Rose of Sharon. To the geologist, He is the Rock of Ages. To the philanthropist, He is the Unspeakable Gift. To the servant, He is the Good Master. What is He to you?
—*Selected.*

THE FOOTPATH TO PEACE—
A Thought for the Opening Year

To be glad of life, because it gives you the chance to love and to work and to play and to look up at the stars; to be satisfied with your possessions, but not contented with yourself until you have made the best of them; to despise nothing in the world except falsehood and meanness, and to fear nothing except cowardice; to be governed by your admirations rather than by your disgusts; to covet nothing that is your neighbor's except his kindness of heart and gentleness of manners; to think seldom of your enemies, often of your friends and every day of Christ; and to spend as much time as you can with body and with spirit, in God's out-of-doors—these are little guideposts on the footpath of peace.
—*Henry Van Dyke.*

LIFE IS EARNEST—Live as though life was earnest, and life will be so.
—*Owen Meredith.*

Voiceless

Vain is the chiming of forgotten bells
That the wind sways above a ruined
   shrine.
Vainer his voice in whom no longer
   dwells
Hunger that craves immortal Bread and
   Wine.

Light songs we breathe that perish with
   our breath
Out of our lips that have not kissed the
   rod.
They shall not live who have not tasted
   death.
They only sing who are struck dumb by
   God.

—*Joyce Kilmer.*

GUIDE—A man's conscience may be mistaken; but still, after all, it is the only light that he has got which will enlighten him in each separate case where he has a choice of conduct. A man's conscience may be mistaken; but if so, obedience to it is a mistake and not a sin, and we know that mistakes are very different from sins. If our conscience be mistaken because we have not taken due trouble to enlighten it, then for that neglect of cultivating our conscience we are responsible. But even then the conscience claims our obedience, and if to obey it is a mistake, to disobey is a sin. All other authorities speak to men in general; this voice speaks to the very soul that hears it, and to none other. All other authorities speak of the general rules by which we must live; this voice speaks of what is to be done now, here, in these circumstances. Now, no one can help feeling that a command given to him personally to do, or not to do, a given act at the moment, must have more weight than a general command given to all men, given for all times. It is as if God Himself had interfered for our guidance, and had thereby superseded all other guidance. And though the messenger who thus comes direct from God may after all be mistaken, yet surely we can do nothing but obey him, and pray God to guard him against mistakes.
—*John Foster.*

COMRADES

I walked with poets in my youth,
 Because the world they drew
Was beautiful and glorious
 Beyond the world I knew.

The poets are my comrades still,
 But dearer than in youth,
For now I know that they alone
 Picture the world of truth.
—*William Roscoe Thayer.*

LIFE'S LESSONS—We've all got to go to school, I expect, and we don't all get the same lesson to learn, but the one we do get is our'n, 'taint nobody else's, and if it's real hard, why, it shows the teacher thinks we're capable.
—*Rose Terry Cooke.*

FORGETTING GOD—No man can be without his god. If he have not the true God to bless and sustain him, he will have some false god to delude and to betray him. The Psalmist knew this, and therefore he joined so closely forgetting the name of our God and holding up our hands to some strange god. For every man has something in which he hopes, on which he leans, to which he retreats and retires, with which he fills up his thoughts in empty spaces of time; when he is alone, when he lies sleepless on his bed, when he is not pressed with other thoughts; to which he betakes himself in sorrow or trouble, as that from which he shall draw comfort and strength—his fortress, his citadel, his defence; and has not this good right to be called his god? Man was made to lean on the Creator; but if not on Him, then he leans on the creature in one shape or another. The ivy cannot grow alone; it must twine round some support or other; if not the goodly oak, then the ragged thorn; round any dead stick whatever, rather than have no stay nor support at all. It is even so with the heart and affections of man; if they do not twine around God, they must twine around some meaner thing.
—*Trench.*

CREATING SYMPHONIES — We can read poetry, and recite poetry, but to *live* poetry—is the symphony of life.
—*S. Frances Foote.*

SELF RELIANCE—Napoleon, when he was only a boy in years, spread out his future before his uncle. His uncle shook his head and said, "Dreams!" Napoleon stepped quickly to the window, and pointing up into the noonday sky, said, "Do you see that star?" "No," was the reply. "I do," he answered, and that star led him to the summit of human renown. Faith is one condition of greatness, and no man ever yet held the confidence of his fellows who did not believe in himself. The story goes that Colonel Roosevelt went to Heaven. Going up to Saint Peter, he asked if he could have ten thousand soprano singers. The reply was in the affirmative. He then asked for ten thousand alto singers and was told he could have those. Next he asked for ten thousand tenor singers and Saint Peter replied that he could have those. Roosevelt thanked him and started to turn away. Saint Peter stopped him with: "What about bass singers?" "Oh, I am going to sing bass myself."—*Fowler.*

Per Aspera

Thank God, a man can grow!
He is not bound
With earthward gaze to creep along the
  ground:
Though his beginnings be but poor and
  low,
Thank God, a man can grow!
The fire upon his altars may burn dim,
  The torch he lighted may in darkness
  fail,
  And nothing to rekindle it avail,—
Yet high beyond his dull horizon's rim,
Arcturus and the Pleiades beckon him.
              —*Florence Earle Coates.*

HE WHO IS FIRM in will, moulds the world to himself.—*Goethe.*

BETTER—We have read of the young artist, wearied and discouraged, who slept by the picture which he had done his best to complete. The master quietly entered the room and bending over the sleeping pupil, placed on the canvas with his own skilful hand the beauty which the worn artist had striven in vain to portray. And when we, tired and spent, lay down earth's toil, our own great Master will make perfect our picture for the Father's many mansioned house. From our service He will remove every stain, every blemish, and every failure. To our service He will give the brightest luster and highest honor. Shall we not bring ourselves to the One who can make us better?—*Public Speakers Library.*

PROGRESS, in the sense of acquisition, is something; but progress in the sense of being is a great deal more. To grow higher, deeper, wider, as the years go on; to conquer difficulties, and acquire more and more power; to feel all one's faculties unfolding, and truth descending into the soul—this makes life worth living.
              —*J. F. Clarke.*

TEMPTATION—No man was ever lost in a straight road. This famous saying which is attributed to the Emperor Akbar, is worthy of a place among the proverbs of Solomon. It is worthy, too, of a place in the memory of every Christian who would walk worthily of his holy profession, and would keep off forbidden ground. Going on pilgrimage to Heaven in the days of John Bunyan, was not always an easy business, nor is it in our days. Then the chief hindrance arose in the form of violent opposition and persecution; now the danger comes from alluring temptations.—*Cuyler.*

INVICTUS—The soul of perseverance cannot be beaten; imprison it and you get Pilgrim's Progress; blind it, and you get Paradise Lost; deafen it, and you get a wizard in electricity; put it into a log cabin, and it will work its way to the White House; commit to the frozen seas of the Arctic regions, and it finds the north pole; return its poems three score and ten times, and you get a poet for the nation's homes.

THE PROSPECT

Methinks we do as fretful children do,
Leaning their faces on the windowpane
To sigh the glass dim with their own
    breath's stain,
And shut the sky and landscape from their
    view;
And thus, alas! since God the maker
    drew
A mystic separation 'twixt those twain,—
The life beyond us and our souls in
    pain,—
We miss the prospect which we are call-
    ed unto
By grief we are fools to use. Be still and
    strong,
O man, my brother! hold thy sobbing
    breath,
And keep thy soul's large window free
    from wrong
That so, as life's appointment issueth,
Thy vision may be clear to watch along
The sunset consummation-lights of death.
    —Elizabeth Barrett Browning.

NEW YEAR—1. Face the New Year with the Old Book.

2. Face the New Needs with the Old Promises.

3. Face the New Problems with the Old Gospel.

4. Face the New Life with the Old Remedies.—Selected.

CHRISTIANITY — The Christian life is an enlistment for the whole man and for life. The call of Christ is a call to detach ourselves from many things that we may attach ourselves to one thing.—Tyler.

VERBS — No one really knows what it is to live until he can truly say these eleven great verbs of life: I am, I think, I know, I feel, I wonder, I see, I believe, I can, I ought, I will, I serve. Life is but the process of learning through daily experience the meaning of these eleven wonderful little verbs of life and acquiring the personal power of each:

I AM: the power of self-knowledge.

I THINK: the power to investigate.

I KNOW: the power to master facts.

I FEEL: the power to appreciate, to value and to love.

I WONDER: the power of reverence, curiosity, worship.

I SEE: the power of insight, imagination, vision.

I BELIEVE: the power of adventurous faith.

I CAN: power to act and skill to accomplish.

I OUGHT: the power of conscience, the moral imperative.

I WILL: will power, loyalty to duty, consecration.

I SERVE: power to be useful, devotion to a cause.
    —George Walter Fiske.

LIFE'S LOYALTIES — I am not bound to win, but I am bound to be true. I am not bound to succeed, but I am bound to live by the light that I have. I must stand with anybody that stands right, stand with him while he is right, and part with him when he goes wrong.
    —Abraham Lincoln.

RECIPE FOR A HAPPY NEW YEAR — Take twelve, fine, full-grown months, see that these are thoroughly free from all old memories of bitterness, rancor, hate and jealousy; cleanse them completely from every clinging spite; pick off all specks of pettiness and littleness; in short, see that these months are freed from all the past—have them as fresh and clean as when they first came from the great storehouse of Time.

Cut these months into thirty or thirty-one equal parts. This batch will keep for just one year. Do not attempt to make up the whole batch at one time (so many persons spoil the entire lot in this way), but prepare one day at a time, as follows:

Into each day put twelve parts of faith, eleven of patience, ten of courage, nine of work (some people omit this ingredient and so spoil the flavor of the rest), eight of hope, seven of fidelity, six of liberality, five of kindness, four of rest (leaving this out is like leaving the oil out of the salad —don't do it), three of prayer, two of meditation, and one well selected resolution. If you have no conscientious scruples, put in about a teaspoonful of good spirits, a dash of fun, a pinch of folly, a sprinkling of play, and a heaping cupful of good humor.

Pour into the whole love *ad libitum* and mix with a vim. Cook thoroughly in a fervent heat; garnish with a few smiles and a sprig of joy; then serve with quietness, unselfishness, and cheerfulness, and a Happy New Year is a certainty.

—*H. M. S.*

IMAGINATION — There are two worlds: the world that we can measure with line and rule, and the world that we feel with our hearts and imagination.
—*Leigh Hunt.*

PROGRESS—Our business in life is not to get ahead of other people, but to get ahead of ourselves. To break our own record, to outstrip our yesterdays by to-days, to bear our trials more beautifully than we ever dreamed we could, to whip the tempter inside and out as we never whipped him before, to give as we never have given, to do our work with more force and a finer finish than ever,—this is the true ideal—to get ahead of ourselves. To beat some one else in a game, or to be beaten, may mean much or little. To beat our own game means a great deal. Whether we win or not, we are playing better than we ever did before, and that's the point after all—to play a better game of life.—*Evangelist.*

I have a rendezvous with Life,
In days I hope will come,
Ere youth has sped and strength of mind,
Ere voices sweet grow dumb.
I have a rendezvous with Life,
When Spring's first heralds hum.

Sure some would cry it better far
To crown their days with sleep,
Than face the wind, the road, the rain,
To heed the falling deep.
Though wet, nor blow, nor space I fear,
Yet fear I deeply too,
Lest Death should greet and claim me ere
I keep Life's rendezvous.

—*Countee Cullen.*

"*I Have a Rendezvous With Life*" *is from COLOR, by Countee Cullen. Copyright, 1925, by Harper & Brothers.*

GREATNESS—It is great—and there is no other greatness—to make one nook of God's creation more fruitful, better, more worthy of God; to make some human heart a little wiser, manlier, happier, more blessed, less accursed.—*Carlyle.*

XXV. POSSESSIONS

VAIN GLORY—A little while ago, I stood by the grave of the old Napoleon—a magnificent tomb of gilt and gold, fit almost for a dead deity—and gazed upon the sarcophagus of rare and nameless marble, where rest at last the ashes of that restless man. I leaned over the balustrade and thought about the career of the greatest soldier of the modern world.

I saw him walking upon the banks of the Seine, contemplating suicide. I saw him at Toulon—I saw him putting down the mob in the streets of Paris—I saw him at the head of the army of Italy—I saw him crossing the bridge of Lodi with the tricolor in his hand—I saw him in Egypt in the shadows of the pyramids—I saw him conquer the Alps and mingle the eagle of France with the eagles of the crags. I saw him at Marengo—at Ulm and Austerlitz.

I saw him in Russia, where the infantry of the snow and the cavalry of the wild blast scattered his legions like winter's withered leaves. I saw him at Leipsic in defeat and disaster—driven by a million bayonets back upon Paris—clutched like a wild beast—banished to Elba. I saw him escape and retake an empire by the force of his genius. I saw him upon the frightful field of Waterloo, where Chance and Fate combined to wreck the fortunes of their former king. And I saw him at St. Helena, with his hands crossed behind him, gazing out upon the sad and solemn sea.

I thought of the orphans and widows he had made—of the tears that had been shed for his glory, and of the only woman who ever loved him, pushed from his heart by the cold hand of ambition. And I said I would rather have been a French peasant and worn wooden shoes. I would rather have lived in a hut with a vine growing over the door, and the grapes growing purple in the kisses of the autumn sun. I would rather have been that poor peasant with my loving wife by my side, knitting as the day died out of the sky—with my children upon my knees and their arms about me—I would rather have been that man and gone down to the tongue-less silence of the dreamless dust, than to have been that imperial impersonation of force and murder, known as "Napoleon the Great."—*Robert G. Ingersoll.*

MONEY — Luther used to say that each one needed a three-fold conversion, that of his heart, his head and his pocketbook. Some one has said that the book with the seven seals that no one could open was the pocketbook. We need to feel that every dollar in our keeping belongs to God and must be used so as to best promote the interests of His kingdom. The greatest thing you can do for God and yourself today, is to consecrate everything to the Lord.

TREASURE

I am rich today, a baby ran to meet me,
And put her tiny hand within my own
And smiled, her rosy lips a flower,
The light within her eyes, from heaven
  shone.
And when I crossed the fields the
  birds were singing,
A golden blossom in my pathway lay,
It wasn't much; but, oh, the joy there's
  in it,
To have a baby smile at you
  In just that way.
  —MARGUERITE A. GUTSCHOW.

SANDALPHON

Have you read in the Talmud of old,
In the Legends the Rabbins have told
 Of the limitless realms of the air,
Have you read it,—the marvelous story
Of Sandalphon, the Angel of Glory,
 Sandalphon, the Angel of Prayer?

How, erect, at the outermost gates
Of the City Celestial he waits,
With his feet on the ladder of light,
That, crowded with angels unnumbered,
By Jacob was seen as he slumbered
 Alone in the desert at night?

But serene in the rapturous throng,
Unmoved by the rush of the song,
 With eyes unimpassioned and slow,
Among the dead angels, the deathless
Sandalphon stands listening breathless
 To sounds that ascend from below:—

And he gathers the prayers as he stands,
And they change into flowers in his
 hands,
 Into garlands of purple and red;
And beneath the great arch of the portal,
Through the streets of the City Immortal
 Is wafted the fragrance they shed.

When I look from my window at night,
And the welkin above is all white,
 All throbbing and panting with stars,
Among them majestic is standing
Sandalphon the angel, expanding
 His pinions in nebulous bars.

And the legend, I feel, is a part
Of the hunger and thirst of the heart,
 The frenzy and fire of the brain,
That grasps at the fruitage forbidden,
The golden pomegranates of Eden,
 To quiet its fever and pain.
 —*Henry Wadsworth Longfellow.*

THRIFT—"My other piece of advice," said Mr. Micawber, "you know. Annual income twenty pounds, annual expenditure nineteen six, result happiness. Annual income twenty pounds, annual expenditure twenty pounds ought and six, result misery. The blossom is blighted, the leaf is withered, the god of day goes down upon the dreary scene, and—and in short, you are forever floored. As I am."
 —*Dickens*—"*David Copperfield.*"

UTILITARIANISM — Whatever strengthens and purifies the affections, enlarges the imagination, and adds spirit to sense, is useful.—*Shelley.*

WHAT MONEY CAN'T BUY—It's good to have money and the things that money can buy, but it's good, too, to check up once in a while and make sure you haven't lost the things that money can't buy.—*George Horace Lorimer.*

VIEWPOINT — One day a rich but miserly Chassid came to a Rabbi. The Rabbi led him to the window. "Look out there," he said, "and tell me what you see."
 "People," answered the rich man.
 Then the Rabbi led him to a mirror. "What do you see now?" he asked.
 "I see myself," answered the Chassid.
 Then the Rabbi said, "Behold—in the window there is glass and in the mirror there is glass. But the glass of the mirror is covered with a little silver, and no sooner is a little silver added than you cease to see others and see only yourself."—*S. Ansky.*

WITHIN—Joy is not in things; it is in us.—*Wagner.*

TREASURE—A happy man or woman is a better thing to find than a five-pound note. He or she is a radiating focus of good-will; and their entrance into a room is as though another candle had been lighted. We need not care whether they could prove the forty-seventh proposition; they do a better thing than that—they practically demonstrate the great Theorem of the Livableness of Life.

—*Robert Louis Stevenson.*

REWARD—I made courtiers; I never pretended to make friends, said Napoleon . . . On a rocky little island he fretted away the last years of his life—alone.

—*Bruce Barton.*

HONEY — My Dear Robert, — One passage in your letter a little displeased me * * * You say that "this world to you seems drained of all its sweets!" At first I had hoped you only meant to insinuate the high price of Sugar! but I am afraid you meant more. O Robert, I don't know what you call sweet. Honey and the honeycomb, roses and violets, are yet in the earth. The sun and moon yet reign in Heaven, and the lesser lights keep up their pretty twinklings. Meats and drinks, sweet sights and sweet smells, a country walk, spring and autumn, follies and repentance, quarrels and reconcilements, have all a sweetness by turns. So good humor and good nature, friends at home that love you, and friends abroad that miss you—you possess all these things, and more innumerable; and these are all sweet things. You may extract honey from everything; do not go a-gathering after gall * * * I assure you I find this world a very pretty place.

—*Charles Lamb to Robert Lloyd.*

PRIDE—The man who has not anything to boast of but his illustrious ancestors is like a potato—the only good belonging to him is underground.

—*Thomas Overbury.*

GAIN — What is gain? The worldly man says money: the Word of God says godliness. What can money do? Can it cure an aching head? Can it ease an aching heart? Can it scare away disease? Can it restore health to the sickly frame, or hope to the hopeless heart? Ah, no! It may purchase a softer pillow to nurse the pain; it may secure a more experienced physician to battle with the disease; it may find a sunnier clime, in which the wasted frame may pine and languish till it be laid to rest in its long home: but there the power of money ends. How is it with godliness? It cannot purchase the softer pillow. Yes, it can. It can place the aching head, the aching heart, on the pillow—the soft, the downy pillow of contentment. "Father, not my will, but Thine be done." It can secure the services of the Great Physician and the balm of Gilead —the hand that heals both soul and body. It can waft the wearied heart, that feels the pangs of suffering, the inroads of disease, or the approach of death—that heart it can waft into the sunnier regions of eternal day; and, while the wasted body pines, the brightening spirit, hovering on the outskirts of Heaven, tastes a peace that passeth all understanding, a joy unspeakable and full of glory.

—*R. B. Nichol.*

Superfluous wealth can buy superfluities only. Money is not required to buy one necessary of the soul.—*Thoreau.*

Goodness is the only investment that never fails.—*Thoreau.*

OVER-EQUIPPED—David was not the first, nor is he the last man to find himself handicapped by too much equipment. Many a man's native skill is restrained by the heavy armour laid on him by foolish friends or by his silly self.

Preachers keep themselves from preaching the Gospel because they desire to make a great display of their learning.

Churches fail to win the allegiance of men because they devote too much time to material equipment. Colleges and schools provide the latest things in dormitories and class-rooms and laboratories, but take too much for granted the teaching and studying that is supposed to justify them.

Parents spend huge sums of money on the clothing of their children, their external manners and appearance and in preparing the positions in life which they are to occupy. But like as not the poor youths will rattle around in it all like dry peas in a pod.

The finest equipment is sometimes only a handicap.

CHRIST

He is a path, if any be misled;
　He is a robe, if any naked be;
If any chance to hunger, He is bread;
　If any be a bondman He is free;
If any be but weak, how strong is He!
To dead men life He is, to sick men health;
To blind men sight, and to the needy
　　wealth;
A pleasure without loss, a treasure without stealth.
　　　　　　　　—Giles Fletcher.

COMPENSATION — Fortune, to show us her power, and abate our presumption, seeing she could not make fools wise, has made them fortunate.
　　　　　　　　—Montaigne.

THE GOLDEN AGE—Over a doorway in an old Dutch banking house is this inscription in French:

"The Golden Age is the age in which gold does not rule."

The value of money lies in its control by spiritual purpose. To desire it for its own sake is to destroy all human values.

CHOKING WEEDS—I knew a boy whose education was stifled because his father gave him two automobiles and a motorboat.

I knew a man who could never accomplish anything seriously worthwhile because he was always tinkering with trifles. I knew another man whose house was so full of rare and costly bric-a-brac that he was a slave to the care of his collections.

Unless we know the difference between flowers and weeds we are not fit to take care of a garden.

It is not enough to have truth planted in our minds. We must learn and labor to keep the ground clear of thorns and briars, follies and perversities, which have a wicked propensity to choke the word of life.

THREE WAYS — There are three things a man can do with himself and his possessions. He may selfishly hoard them; he may lavishly waste them; he may intelligently spend them.

The temporary nature of earthly strength and riches is plain to all men who think.

Only he who spends it freely and gladly for the purposes of his soul may experience the full meaning of life and say at the end:

"Glad did I live and gladly die,
　And I laid me down with a will."

GET RID OF THE WEEDS — An old Vermont farmer was talking with a young neighbor. The young man was complaining because the devil's paint-brush (that bright but destructive weed) was ruining his hay crop. "Fertilize your land, my boy, fertilize your land," said the old man, "I've noticed that the devil's paintbrush is like lots of folks. It can't stand prosperity."

BOOKS—I would rather be a poor man in a garret with plenty of books than a king who did not love reading.
—*Macauley*.

CHECKMATE — In life, as in chess, one's own pawns block one's way. A man's very wealth, ease, leisure, children, books, which should help him to win, more often checkmate him.
—*Charles Buxton*.

TRUE OWNERSHIP—One's own— what a charm there is in the words! how long it takes boy and man to find out their worth! how fast most of us hold on to them! faster and more jealously, the nearer we are to the general home into which we can take nothing, but must go naked as we came into the world. When shall we learn that he who multi-plieth possessions multiplieth troubles, and that the one single use of things which we call our own, is that they may be his who hath need of them?—*Hughes*.

FALSE GOD—Worldly wealth is the devil's bait; and those whose minds feed upon riches, recede in general from real happiness, in proportion as their stores increase; as the moon, when she is fullest of light, is farthest from the sun.—*Burton*.

THE GREATEST HUMBUG in the world is the idea that money can make a man happy. I never had any satisfaction with mine until I began to do good with it.—*C. Pratt*.

WHY DEPRESSIONS — Everything in the world can be endured, except continual prosperity.—*Goethe*.

A SMOOTH SEA never made a skilful mariner; neither do uninterrupted prosperity and success qualify men for usefulness and happiness.

COUNT THE COSTS—No man is prosperous whose immortality is forfeited. —No man is rich to whom the grave brings eternal bankruptcy.—No man is happy upon whose path there rests but a momentary glimmer of light, shining out between clouds that are closing over him in darkness forever.—*H. W. Beecher*.

VIEWPOINT — He is not poor that has little, but he that deserves much.
—*Daniel*.

POVERTY is no disgrace to a man but it is confoundedly inconvenient.
—*Sydney Smith*.

OF ALL THE ADVANTAGES which come to any young man, I believe it to be demonstrably true that poverty is the greatest.—*J. G. Holland*.

HELPLESS—In a terrible crisis there is only one element more helpless than the poor, and that is the rich.
—*Clarence Darrow*.

XXVI. PRAYER

AS THOU WILT—O Lord, Thou knowest what is best for us; let this or that be done, as Thou shalt please. Give what Thou wilt, and how much Thou wilt, and when Thou wilt. Deal with me as Thou thinkest good. Set me where Thou wilt, and deal with me in all things just as Thou wilt. Behold, I am Thy servant, prepared for all things: for I desire not to live unto myself, but unto Thee! and oh, that I could do it worthily and perfectly!—*Thomas a' Kempis.*

Lord, what a change within us one short hour
Spent in Thy presence will avail to make!
What heavy burdens from our bosoms take!
What parched grounds refresh as with a shower!
We kneel, and all around us seem to lower;
We rise, and all, the distant and the near,
Stands forth in sunny outline, brave and clear;
We kneel, how weak; we rise, how full of power!
Why, therefore, should we do ourselves this wrong,
Or others—that we are not always strong—
That we are sometimes overborne with care—
That we should ever weak or heartless be,
Anxious or troubled—when with us is prayer,
And joy and strength and courage are with Thee?

—RICHARD C. TRENCH.

HEART—Pray Him to give you what Scripture calls "an honest and good heart," or "a perfect heart;" and, without waiting, begin at once to obey Him with the best heart you have. Any obedience is better than none. You have to seek His face; obedience is the only way of seeing Him. All your duties are obediences. To do what He bids is to obey Him, and to obey Him is to approach Him. Every act of obedience is an approach —an approach to Him who is not far off, though He seems so, but close behind this visible screen of things which hides Him from us.—*J. H. Newman.*

FACULTIES — If we stand in the openings of the present moment, with all the length and breadth of our faculties unselfishly adjusted to what it reveals, we are in the best condition to receive what God is always ready to communicate.—*T. C. Upham.*

CONFIDING — Lord, I know not what I ought to ask of Thee; Thou only knowest what I need; Thou lovest me better than I know how to love myself. O Father! give to Thy child that which he himself knows not how to ask. I dare not ask either for crosses or consolations; I simply present myself before Thee; I open my heart to Thee. Behold my needs which I know not myself; see, and do according to Thy tender mercy. Smite, or heal; depress me, or raise me up; I adore all Thy purposes without knowing them; I am silent; I offer myself in sacrifice; I yield myself to Thee! I would have no other desire than to accomplish Thy will. Teach me to pray; pray Thyself in me.

—*Selected.*

THREE DEGREES — Poor, broken-winded things our prayers are, like a wounded bird fluttering along the ground, rising like an arrow shot from a child's hand, going a little way to the sky, and then dropping down again. I am afraid most of us have three degrees of temperature in regard to our prayers or our desires. The highest is for temporal wants for ourselves; medium, spiritual good for ourselves; the most tepid of them all for the progress of Christ's kingdom. It takes a man with a spirit to pray, "Thy will be done in earth as it is in Heaven," as it ought to be prayed.—*Maclaren.*

PRAYER AT EARLY MASS

Deep in the east the dawn is white,
Pale like Thy Face beneath the thorn.
High in the east the dawn is red,
Red like the Heart a lance had torn.
Deep in the east the dawn is white,
Pale like the Bread You bid us break.
High in the east the dawn is red,
Red like the Wine You bid us take.
Uplifted Host! Uplifted Cup of Wine
Cry within this morning! And the sweet
Sweet pleading comes again that once
    was Thine
Upon a hill whereon no sun would shine!
O Lord, I know not if Thy Paradise
Shall keep such moment for the wakened
    dead,
Nor any dawn to flame it in their skies,
But if the beauty that the east has worn
Be gathered still and still be white and
    red,
Then in my heart a single prayer is born:
Lord, let me be, wherever it is morn.
                        —*John W. Lynch.*

UNANSWERED — I have lived to thank God that all my prayers have not been answered.—*Jean Ingelow.*

HELP—God brings no man into the conflicts of life to desert him. Every man has a Friend in Heaven whose resources are unlimited; and on Him he may call at any hour and find sympathy and assistance.—*Morris.*

ASKING

1. "Ask ye of the Lord." (Zec. 10:1). "My God shall supply all your need."
2. "Ask and it shall be given you." (Matt. 7:7). "The testimony of the Lord is sure."
3. "Ask in a prayer." (Matt. 21:22). There must be prayerful dependence.
4. "Ask in faith." (James 1:6). "He that cometh to God must believe."
5. "Ask what I shall give thee." (1 Kings 3:5). "His ears are open unto our prayers." (2 Chron. 1:7).
6. "Ask diligently." (Deut. 13:14). "Abound in faith and all diligence."

PRIVATE PRAYER is our refuge from troubles. High above the beating waves, and near Heaven, it is our fortress. What sometimes would become of us, if we might not shut the door upon mankind, and find repose in our Father's bosom? The afflicted Christian, entering his citadel, says, like persecuted David, "I give myself unto prayer." Thou, who knowest all, and changest never, art on my side. If I grieve any, I would not grieve Thee. I would not make Thee my enemy, I would retain Thy favor. Oh my Almighty Friend, "say unto my soul, I am thy salvation." Heavenly Father, Thy smile invigorates me. I am glad and safe when I hear Thy voice.—*Robinson.*

REPOSE — Thou hast made us for Thyself, O Lord; and our heart is restless until it rests in Thee.—*St. Augustine.*

LOVE—We sometimes fear to bring our troubles to God, because they must seem so small to Him who sitteth on the circle of the earth. But if they are large enough to vex and endanger our welfare, they are large enough to touch His heart of love. For love does not measure by a merchant's scales, nor with a surveyor's chain. It hath a delicacy which is unknown in any handling of material substances.—*Torrey.*

FAITH—During the Civil War fourteen inmates of Andersonville Prison, on August 20, 1864, bowed in prayer to the Almighty that he would send them water; and a spring broke out on the outside of the wall and ran through the prison. The people there were unanimous in their belief that it was of divine origin, the water in the nearby stream being fearfully unwholesome. The spring is reported to be still flowing.—*Christian Endeavor World.*

SORROWS — Learn to entwine with your prayers the small cares, the trifling sorrows, the little wants of daily life. Whatever affects you be it a changed look, an altered tone, an unkind word, a wrong, a wound, a demand you cannot meet, a change you cannot notice, a sorrow you cannot disclose—turn it into prayer, and send it up to God. Disclosures you may not make to man you can make to the Lord. Man may be too little for your great matters: God is not too great for your small ones. Only give yourself to prayer, whatever be the occasion that calls for it.—*Winslow.*

PROVISION — Good prayers never come creeping home. I am sure I shall receive either what I ask or what I should ask.—*Joseph Hall.*

THE EXPRESSION OF THE SOUL—Prayer is not necessarily in fluency of speech; it is not in painted imagery; it is not in deep thoughts; it is not in burning words; it is not in the length and breadth and fulness of petition. Prayer is something more: it is the wish of the heart—the expression of the soul.—*Dear.*

PRAYER has been defined to be a wish referred to God; and if we could keep this thought before us, it would help us to acquire the habit of prayer by making us refer each wish, as it comes into our minds, to God, for His assistance in furtherance or frustration.—*J. R. Illingworth.*

The Kneeling Camel

The camel, at the close of day
   Kneels down upon the sandy plain
To have his burden lifted off
   And rest to gain.

My soul, thou too shouldst to thy knees
   When the daylight draweth to a close,
And let thy Master lift thy load
   And grant repose:

Else how canst thou tomorrow meet,
   With all tomorrow's work to do,
If thou thy burden all the night
   Dost carry through?

The camel kneels at break of day
   To have his guide replace his load,
Then rises up again to take
   The desert road.

So thou shouldst kneel at morning's dawn
   That God may give thee daily care,
Assured that He no load too great
   Will make thee bear.
      —*Anna Temple.*

APPEAL TO AUTHORITY—Prayer is the application of want to Him who alone can relieve it, the voice of sin to Him who alone can pardon it. It is the urgency of poverty, the prostration of humility, the fervency of penitence, the confidence of trust. It is not eloquence, but earnestness; not figures of speech, but compunction of soul. It is the "Lord, save, I perish" of drowning Peter. . . . It is not a mere conception of the mind nor an effort of the intellect, nor an act of the memory, but an elevation of the soul towards its Maker. It is the devout breathing of a creature struck with a sense of its own misery and of the infinite holiness of Him whom it is addressing, experimentally convinced of its own emptiness and of the abundant fulness of God, of His readiness to hear, of His power to help, of His willingness to save . . . Prayer is right in itself as the most powerful means of resisting sin and advancing in holiness. It is above all might, as everything is, which has the authority of Scripture, the command of God, and the example of Christ.—*Hannah More.*

Surrender

O Father, grant Thy love divine,
To make these mystic temples Thine
When wasting age and weary strife
Have sapped the leaning walls of life.
When darkness gathers over all
And the last tottering pillars fall,
Take the poor dust Thy mercy warms,
And mould it into heavenly forms.
—*Selected.*

SUBMISSION — May our Lord's sweet hand square us and hammer us, and strike off all kinds of pride, self-love, world-worship, and infidelity, so that He can make us stones and pillars in His Father's house.—*Samuel Rutherford.*

ABOVE — A Jewish legend tells us that during the famine in Canaan, Joseph ordered his officers to throw wheat and chaff upon the waters of the Nile that the people below might see that there was plenty above. God puts upon the River of Life wheat from the heavenly fields in order that we may seek things that are above.—*Torrey.*

THE SUM OF ALL—All subjects for thought are represented in this prayer which begins with God, comprehends Heaven and earth, and terminates in eternity.—*W. N. Percival.*

If you run over and through all the words of all holy prayers, you will find nothing which this prayer of the Lord doth not comprehend and contain.
—*St. Augustine.*

For like as the law of love is the sum and abridgment of the other laws, so this prayer is the sum and abridgment of all other prayers; all the other prayers are contained in this prayer; yea, whatsoever mankind hath need of to soul and body, that same is contained in this prayer.

Any clause of it might suffice a whole day as a fountain of pious thought, a base of manifold petition, a medium of rich communication with the Father.
—*Robinson.*

REMEMBERING — We talk about God's remembering us, as if it were a special effort. But if we could only know how truly we belong to God, it would be different. God's remembrance of us is the natural claiming of our life by Him as true part of His own.—*Phillips Brooks.*

THE ABLEST MEN in all walks of modern life are men of faith. Most of them have much more faith than they themselves realize.—*Bruce Barton.*

THE MODEL — In one of Carlyle's letters to an old-time Scottish friend, a few years ago, he said:—"Our Father which art in Heaven, hallowed be Thy name, Thy will be done." What else can we say? The other night, in my sleepless tossings about, which were growing more and more miserable, these words, that brief and grand prayer, came strangely into my mind, with an altogether new emphasis; as if written and shining for me in mild, pure splendor, on the black bosom of the night there; when I, as it were, read them word by word—with a sudden check to my imperfect wanderings, with a sudden softness of composure which was much unexpected. Not for perhaps thirty or forty years had I once formally repeated that prayer. Nay, I never felt before how intensely the voice of man's soul it is; the inmost aspiration of all that is high and pious in poor human nature; right worthy to be recommended with an "After this manner pray ye."

BRIEF LET ME BE — The fewer words the better prayer.—*Luther.*

HE WHO RUNS from God in the morning will scarcely find him the rest of the day.—*Bunyan.*

PREFATORY—Prayer is the preface to the book of Christian living; the text of the new life sermon; the girding on of the armor for battle; the pilgrim's preparation for his journey. It must be supplemented by action or it amounts to nothing.—*A. Phelps.*

PRAYER BOOK—Open thy heart to God; if He be there, the outspread world will be thy book of prayer.—*Tholuck.*

THE LORD'S PRAYER contains the sum total of religion and morals.
—*Wellington.*

Thy Will

To know Thy will, Lord of the seeking mind,
To learn Thy way for me, Thy purpose kind,
Thy path to follow and Thy guide find—
    For this I pray.
To do Thy will, Lord of the eager soul,
To bring my restlessness 'neath Thy control,
To give Thee, not a part, but all—the whole—
    For this I pray.
To love Thy will, Lord of the ardent heart,
To bid all selfishness, all sloth depart,
To share with gladness all Thou dost and art—
    For this I pray.
—*Alice M. Kyle.*

ANY HEART turned God-ward, feels more joy in one short hour of prayer, than e'er was raised by all the feasts on earth since its foundation.—*Bailey.*

WHEN TO PRAY — Prayer, as the first, second, and third element of the Christian life, should open, prolong, and conclude each day. The first act of the soul in early morning should be a draught at the heavenly fountain. It will sweeten the taste for the day. A few moments with God at that calm and tranquil season, are of more value than much fine gold. And if you tarry long so sweetly at the throne, you will come out of the closet as the high priest of Israel came from the awful ministry at the altar of incense, suffused all over with the heavenly fragrance of that communion.—*H. W. Beecher.*

XXVII. SPEECH

KIND WORDS — Cold words freeze people, and hot words scorch them, and bitter words make them bitter, and wrathful words make them wrathful. Kind words also produce their own image on men's souls; and a beautiful image it is. They smooth, and quiet, and comfort the hearer.

—Pascal.

POWER OF THE PULPIT — The power of preaching is not gone, says C. J. Brown, D.D., of Edinburgh. But, he adds, "I will tell you, though, what is gone. The power of a neat little manuscript, carried to the pulpit and prettily read, that is gone. If such a practice is to continue, the pulpit cannot indeed compete with the press. We shall be miserably beaten in the competition. But carry to the pulpit a different thing altogether; carry to it well-digested thoughts with suitable words to express them, written in your inmost soul; thoughts and words wherewith to stir the souls of your hearers to their inmost depths, wherewith to hold living intercourse with them; tell them, indeed, what God has been telling you, and both you and they shall find that the pulpit still wields a power altogether its own."

PREPARATION — A celebrated preacher being asked, "How long does it take you to prepare an address?" replied, "If I am only to speak for fifteen or twenty minutes, it requires at least a week's preparation and prayerful thought beforehand; if I may occupy thirty or forty minutes, two or three days' preparation will do; but if I may speak for an hour, a few minutes forethought will be sufficient."

ORATORY — "And the common people heard Him gladly," for "He taught them as one having authority." These sentences reveal the very heart of effective speaking. Considered from the human viewpoint alone, the Son of Mary was the prince of speakers. He alone has delivered a perfect address—the Sermon on the Mount. The two other speeches that approach it are Paul's appeal to the Athenians on Mars Hill and the speech of Abraham Lincoln at Gettysburg. These have no tricks, no devices, no tinsel gilt. They do not attempt to "split the ears of the groundlings," and yet they are addressed to the commonest of the world's common people.—*Beveridge.*

THE VOICELESS

We count the broken lyres that rest
  Where the sweet wailing singers
    slumber,
But o'er their silent sister's breast
  The wild flowers who will stoop to
    number?
A few can touch the magic string,
  And noisy Fame is proud to win
    them:—
Alas for those that never sing,
  But die with all their music in them!

O hearts that break and give no sign
  Save whitening lip and fading
    tresses,
Till Death pours out his longed-for
    wine
  Slow-dropped from Misery's crush-
    ing presses,—
If singing breath or echoing chord
  To every hidden pang were given,
What endless melodies were poured,
  As sad as earth, as sweet as heaven!
    OLIVER WENDELL HOLMES.

ILLUSTRATIONS — The subject matter of Christian teaching pre-eminently requires illustration. The barrister has, in a new case, that which stimulates attention, while the preacher has an oft-told tale to set before his people.

—*Andrew Fuller.*

The aim of the teacher, who would find his way to the hearts and understandings of his hearers, will never be to keep down the parabolical element in his teaching, but rather to make as much and as frequent use of it as he can.

—*Trench.*

To have one's page alive the author must be alive himself, constantly acquiring fresh thought.

—*Matthews.*

Genius lights its own fire, but it is constantly collecting materials to keep alive the flame.—*Wilmott.*

A Narrow Window

A narrow window may let in the light,
A tiny star dispel the gloom of night,
A little deed a mighty wrong set right.

A rose, abloom, may make a desert fair,
A single cloud may darken all the air,
A spark may kindle ruin and despair.

A smile, and there may be an end to strife;
A look of love, and Hate may sheathe the
    knife;
A word—ah, it may be a word of life!
—*Florence Earle Coates.*

ELOQUENCE — There is no power like that of oratory. Caesar controlled men by exciting their fears, Cicero by captivating their affections and swaying their passions. The influence of the one perished with its author, that of the other continues to this day.—*H. Clay.*

SELF-EXAMINATION — If any speak ill of thee, flee home to thy own conscience, and examine thy heart; if thou be guilty, it is a just correction; if not guilty, it is a fair instruction; make use of both, so shalt thou distill honey out of gall, and out of an open enemy create a secret friend.—*Quarles.*

EXCEPT a living man there is nothing more wonderful than a book! a message to us from the dead—from human souls we never saw, who lived, perhaps, thousands of miles away. And yet these, in those little sheets of paper, speak to us, arouse us, terrify us, teach us, comfort us, open their hearts to us as brothers.

—*Charles Kingsley.*

KIND WORDS are the bright flowers of earthly existence; use them, and especially around the fireside circle. They are jewels beyond price, and powerful to heal the wounded heart and make the weighed-down spirit glad.

Let us use our speech as we should wish we had done when one of us is silent in death. Let us give all the communications, make all the explanations, speak all the loving words ere it is too late.

A genuine word of kindness is often the best lever to raise a depressed spirit to its natural level.

The art of saying appropriate words in a kindly way is one that never goes out of fashion, never ceases to please, and is within the reach of the humblest.

Always say a kind word if you can, if only that it may come in, perhaps, with singular opportuneness, entering some mournful man's darkened room, like a beautiful firefly, whose happy circumvolutions he cannot but watch, forgetting his many troubles.—*Arthur Helps.*

THOUGHT — The three foundations of thought: perspicuity, amplitude, and justness.

The three ornaments of thought: clearness, correctness, and novelty.

The three properties of just thinking: What is possible, what is commendable, and what ought to be—*Catherall.*

DIRECTNESS — The ability to state our convictions with clearness and completeness yields two benefits. It makes our convictions respected. There is persuasion in the forceful putting of a thought, and in sentences sharply drawn and well considered. Considerable of what passes as the weightiness of an opinion is no more than the gravity and dignity of its presentation. The effect of words, as of soldiers, can be trebled by their manner of marshaling. A word aptly chosen is an argument, and a phrase judiciously contrived a syllogism. "A word fitly spoken is like apples of gold in pictures of silver." It was the transparent terseness of the man born blind which so inconvenienced the Pharisees. "I was blind, now I see." There was all there that was said, and more beside—a conclusion without its being stated. Here lies the power of proverbs, in their lucid brevity.—*Parkhurst.*

GOODNESS—His words had power because they accorded with his thoughts; and his thoughts had reality and depth because they harmonized with the life he had always lived. It was not mere breath that this preacher uttered; they were the words of life, because a life of good deeds and holy love was melted into them. Pearls, pure and rich, had been dissolved into the precious draught.

—*Nathaniel Hawthorne.*

PLAINNESS (*not puerility*)—A style may be lofty yet clear. As a medieval preacher has said, "The stars, clear and distinct as they are, are most lofty; so is a sermon like stars that all can see, yet few measure." True loftiness is shown not in rhetoric so much as in nobility of thought and wealth of experience. Here is the power of some early Puritan sermons that were "studied in a jail, preached under a hedge, printed in a garret, sold at a peddler's stall, bought by a priest's footman, applauded by a bishop and ordered to the press by a procession of gentry."

The Poet

Ever I must sing
As poets have;
The old tradition keep,
To laugh or weep
In some forgotten attic
As they have done
Rousing the world from sleep
To laugh or weep.

Ever must I bring
As poets have
The passions of life and truth
From the bosom of youth
That never rouses itself in me
But leaves in its wake
A verse; an ache.
  —*Lillian Arline Walbert.*

WAKE UP—Sydney Smith, the prince of clerical wit, speaking of a preacher noted for his dull sermons made this remark: "He evidently thought sin was to be taken from man, as Eve was from Adam, by casting him into a deep sleep." A Scotch minister advised a lady who was given to sleeping in church to take some snuff. She replied: "Put more snuff into your sermons."—*Boen.*

The Parson's Prayer

I do not ask
That crowds may throng the temple,
That standing room be priced,
I only ask that as I voice the message,
They may see Christ!

I do not ask
For churchly pomp or pageant,
Or music such as wealth alone can buy,
I only ask that as I voice the message,
He may be nigh!

I do not ask
That men may sound my praises
Or headlines spread my name abroad,
I only pray that as I voice the message,
Hearts may find God!

I do not ask
For earthly place or laurel,
Or of this world's distinctions any part,
I only ask when I have voiced the message,
My Savior's heart!—*Ralph S. Cushman.*

From PRACTISING THE PRESENCE by Ralph S. Cushman. Copyright, 1936. Used by permission of the publisher, Abingdon-Cokesbury Press.

AUTHORS — When Addison had completed the Guardian, he was asked to publish another work, but said, "I must take time to relax and lay in fuel for it." Samuel Johnson declined to be introduced to a popular author, saying that he did not wish to talk with a man who wrote more than he read.

Fuller said that he "guessed good housekeeping, not by the number of chimneys, but by the smoke." Many capacious mental fireplaces lack fuel, and many large libraries lack readers. Only as we get can we give.

"I have two poems, one on the 'Bible' and the other on the 'Ocean,' but cannot find a publisher to take them." "Throw one into the other!" was the wise advice of a sarcastic friend.

LEARNING — The preacher should keep his learning subordinate to his love and respect for men. There are times when it must be crucified, and the preacher must literally "die daily." It may be for him the right eye to be plucked out. Dr. Duff, on his way to India, was shipwrecked near Cape Town. He had purchased a large library to gratify his love for classical literature. All this was lost. Strangely enough, his Bagster's Bible and hymn-book were washed ashore. He accepted this as an intimation that henceforth "human learnings must be to him a means, and not an end."—*E. P. Abbott.*

SERMON—As the preacher goes on (giving living bread, and not "critical" stones), yonder tired mother opens her heart, and is inspired with new hope to go on in her pressed home-life; the business man hears God's voice, and he, too, is encouraged; some word reaches that young man, and he is kept from doing the evil thing he had planned that very night. But no demonstration is made; in some way the burning words of the preacher have lifted the whole congregation Heavenward. Measure that sermon? Yes, if you can measure a sunbeam; yes, if you can measure a mother's love; yes, if you can measure a spiritual uplift by the miserable yardsticks of human measurement! No, no, my friend, the effect of that word given in that service, can only be measured by Him in that day when the final judgment of every man's work is made.—*Parkhurst.*

"LET ME SEE YOUR TONGUE" —One of the first things which a physician says to his patient is, "Let me see your tongue." A spiritual adviser might often do the same.—*N. Adams.*

PROFANITY—It is no mark of a gentleman to swear. The most worthless and vile, the refuse of mankind, the drunkard and the prostitute, swear as well as the best dressed and educated gentleman. No particular endowments are requisite to give a finish to the art of cursing. The basest and meanest of mankind swear with as much tact and skill as the most refined; and he that wishes to degrade himself to the very lowest level of pollution and shame should learn to be a common swearer. Any man has talents enough to learn to curse God, and imprecate perdition on himself and his fellow men. Profane swearing never did any man any good. No man is the richer or wiser or happier for it. It helps no one's education or manners. It commends no one to any society. It is disgusting to the refined, abominable to the good, insulting to those with whom we associate, degrading to the mind, unprofitable, needless, and injurious to society; and wantonly to profane His name, to call His vengeance down, to curse Him, and to invoke His vengeance, is perhaps of all offenses the most awful in the sight of God.—*Luther.*

BREVITY — That which Guthrie would have spread over an entire page, elaborating every particular with pre-Raphael-like minuteness, Arnot would have given in a sentence; and while the hearer of the former would have said, "What a beautiful illustration!" that of the latter would have exclaimed, "How clear he made it all by that simple figure!"
—*W. M. Taylor.*

ELOQUENCE — He is an eloquent man who can treat humble subjects with delicacy, lofty things impressively, and moderate things temperately.—*Cicero.*

BREVITY — The American audience appreciates most of all the story that is brief. Nothing in my experience so well serves to illustrate a point and to make a slight break in the tension, as the story that can be put in half a dozen words.

As an example, perhaps the following will serve: in discussing the low average intelligence of the common people I throw in this thought: "You would be amazed if you knew how many people don't even know that the epistles were not the wives of the apostles." I find that humorous relief does not check the flow of thought, but does serve to revive and reconcentrate upon a technical discourse the flagging attention of an audience.
—*Charles Henry Mackintosh.*

READING is to the mind what exercise is to the body. As by the one, health is preserved, strengthened and invigorated: by the other, virtue (which is the health of the mind) is kept alive, cherished and confirmed.—*Addison.*

ORATORY is the greatest art known to man and embraces a number of great arts. In music tradition furnishes the ideas. The poet clothes them in words. The composer sets these to music, and the singer renders them into song. The orator must be able to do all these things. He must furnish the ideas, he must clothe them in words, he must give these a rhythmic arrangement, and he must deliver them with all the care with which a singer sings a song. Each of these elements is of supreme importance. The ideas must be bright and seem alive. The language must be chaste and expressive. The arrangement must be logical, natural and effective. There must be a natural unfolding of the subject matter.—*King.*

A LOST ANGEL'S SONG — Kind words are the music of the world. They have a power which seems to be beyond natural causes, as if they were some angel's song which had lost its way and come on earth. It seems as if they could almost do what in reality God alone can do—soften the hard and angry hearts of men. No one was ever corrected by a sarcasm—crushed, perhaps, if the sarcasm was clever enough—but drawn nearer to God, never.—*F. W. Faber.*

Speak Gently

Speak gently: It is better far
  To rule by love than fear;
Speak gently: Let no harsh words mar
  The good we might do here.

Speak gently to the little child
  Its love be sure to gain,
Teach it in accents soft and mild
  It may not long remain.

Speak gently to the aged one,
  Grieve not the careworn heart;
The sands of life are nearly run,
  Let such in peace depart.

Speak gently, kindly to the poor;
  Let no harsh tone be heard.
They have enough they must endure
  Without an unkind word.

Speak gently to the erring; know
  They must have toiled in vain;
Perchance unkindness made them so,
  Oh, win them back again.
                    —*David Bates.*

THREE TESTS — When I want to speak let me think first. Is it true? Is it kind? Is it necessary? If not, let it be left unsaid.—*Babcock.*

PLEASANT — God has given us tongues that we may say something pleasant to our fellow-men.—*Heinrich Heine.*

SERMONS — A sermon is too often like Hodge's horse. It is overdone with brasses and bells, harness and harmony, but there is no real strength in it, no life and vigor. It is fine, but not forcible. Now, it strikes everybody that the trappings of a poor old half-starved horse look like mockery. You cannot plough fields with ribbons and bells; you want muscle and sinew; and so there is no moving men's hearts with pretty phrases and musical nothings. What is needed is thought, truth, and sound doctrine, and the Spirit of God. Young men are apt to think less of what to say than of how to say it; but our advice is, think of both in due proportion. Set the matter before the manner; get the horse first, and get a good one, and then harness him. Give the people the grand old Gospel, and plenty of it, and they will not much mind the way in which you bring it forth. A good horse should be decently harnessed, and Divine truth should be fitly spoken; the mischief is that some appear to think that the harness makes the horse, and that a fine style is the main thing in a sermon. Churches and chapels would not so often be empty if ministers would take heed what they preach as well as how they preach.
                    —*Spurgeon.*

DRAMA—To me it seems as if when God conceived the world, that was poetry; He formed it, and that was sculpture; He varied and colored it, and that was painting; and then, crowning all, He peopled it with living beings, and that was the grand divine, eternal drama.
                    —*Charlotte Cushman.*

SPEAKING — Daniel Webster said: "If all my talents and powers were to be taken from me by some inscrutable Providence, and I had my choice of keeping but one, I would unhesitatingly ask to be allowed to keep the Power of Speaking, for through it, I would quickly recover all the rest."

TALES — As a basket of silver filled with apples of gold,
So is the preached word with tales well told.

Always carry with you into the rostrum a sense of the immense consequences which may depend on your full and faithful presentation of the truth.—*R. S. Storrs.*

The orator is thereby an orator that he keeps his feet ever on a fact.
—*Emerson.*

HOW SWEET the words of truth breathed from the lips of love.
—*James Beattie.*

SYCOPHANT — Only experience can show how salt is the savor of another's bread, and how sad a path it is to climb and descend another's stairs.
—*Dante.*

ONE GREAT USE of words is to hide our thoughts.—*Voltaire.*

KIND WORDS cost no more than unkind ones. Kind words produce kind actions, not only on the part of those to whom they are addressed, but on the part of those by whom they are employed; and this not incidentally only, but habitually in virtue of the principle of association.
—*Jeremy Bentham.*

ORNAMENT — It is not to be used for its own sake. Dr. Taylor once suggested to a workman a certain embellishment in making a library case. The man replied, "I could not do that, sir, for it would be contrary to one great rule in art." "What rule?" "That we must never construct ornament, but only ornament construction." "It was quaintly spoken, but it was to me a word in season. I saw in a moment that this principle held as truly in the architecture of a sermon as in that of a cathedral—in the construction of a discourse as in that of a bookcase; and often since, when I have caught myself making ornament for its own sake, I have destroyed what I had written; and I have done so simply from the recollection of that artisan's reproof."

Proud Words

'Tis sweet to hear "I love you"
Beneath a giggling moon;
'Tis fun to hear "You dance well"
To a lilting, swinging tune;
'Tis great to be proposed to
And whisper low, "I do;"
But the sweetest words in all the world,
"I've got a job for you."
—*Margaret Deeney.*

REMINDING—The object of preaching is, constantly to remind mankind of what mankind are constantly forgetting; not to supply the defects of human intelligence, but to fortify the feebleness of human resolutions; to recall mankind from the by-paths where they turn, into that broad path of salvation which all know, but few tread.—*Sydney Smith.*

INDEX — Speech is the index of the mind.—*Seneca.*

BRIEF—Be brief; for it is with words as with sunbeams—the more they are condensed the deeper they burn.—*Southey.*

PULPIT TEMPTATIONS — The Christian pulpit needs to be on guard against the snare of words. One of the greatest curses that can come to a young preacher is that of a glib tongue. It means almost certain ruin. How futile, no matter how pleasing, are the efforts of a mere ministerial rhetorician! Language was meant to reveal thought, to open up to human minds the vast riches of reality; often, however, words constitute simply a dust storm to conceal every vestige of truth. When a minister ceases to think and study he takes refuge in shibboleths, he shuffles the symbols, and "rings the changes" on old words and phrases, with many an appeal to the "faith of our fathers" and the "good old-time religion." Then straightway he becomes a problem for the bishop and the cabinet, for such a preacher's sole stock in trade is an outfit of moth-eaten verbalisms. He may be saved, of course, if he is willing to begin to buy books, to read, and to study; for in this way, and in this way only, can a speaker put new life into his words and give them meaning and content. After all, the most important thing is to have something to say. If a mind be filled with the abundant resources of thought, the soul of the man will come bursting through into eloquent speech, sometimes crowding even into a commonplace word marvels of beauty and power.

Zion's Herald.

LOVE — What are our lame praises in comparison with His love? Nothing, and less than nothing; but love will stammer rather than be dumb.

—Robert Leighton.

RULES FOR SPEAKERS—Be prepared.

Speak distinctly.
Look your audience in the eyes.
Favor your deep tones.
Speak deliberately.
Cultivate earnestness.
Be logical.

Don'ts for Speakers—

Don't be afraid of your voice.
Don't forget your audience can think.
Don't be ashamed of your own opinion.
Don't cover too much ground.
Don't forget to practice.

First Aid to Speakers—

Be prepared and don't rely on inspiration.
Originality comes from meditation.
Have a definite purpose.
Avoid irrelevancy.
Be sincere, earnest and enthusiastic
Don't hurry into your subject.
Wait for attention.
Begin in a conversational tone but loud enough to be heard.
Don't force gestures.
Cultivate the straight-forward open eye.
Don't walk about while speaking.
Don't be didactic.
Good diction is a passport recognized by everyone.
Let your grammar, vocabulary and pronunciation be the best.
Cultivate a genial manner.
Pauses are of great oratorical value.
Write much and often.
Read aloud and regularly.
The best way to learn to speak is to speak.

—Walter Robinson.

POWER—To have what we want is riches; but to be able to do without is power.—*George Macdonald.*

SAYINGS—The best preaching is uncomfortable preaching.

No church ever saved a community by quarreling among themselves.

I know a lot of people who desecrate Sunday on Saturday night.

Most church quarrels arise over some one's rights, not over some one's prayers.

God loveth a cheerful giver who does not talk too much about it nor expect too much credit for it.

Blessed is the man who does not insist upon talking about his children when I want to talk about mine.

Blessed is the man who appreciates his own time too highly to waste the time of some one else.—*Roy L. Smith.*

FORCE — From the lawyer, the minister may learn to establish his case. The minister usually starts out with a proposition stated in the form of a text, the truth of which he is presumably going to prove. To do this he must present his evidence, marshal his facts, and set them forth in a logical and convincing manner. This the minister often fails to do. It is not required that every sermon shall be an exercise in logic, a sample of argument, but that it will seek to inform, to instruct, and to convince. Our sermons frequently lack facts, convincing facts, moving facts. We are inclined to forget that, "in all our preaching we must preach for verdicts. We must present our case, we must seek a verdict, and we must ask for an immediate execution of the verdict."—*Smith.*

MISOGYNIST — Any time Europe wants us to fall for somepin they got, they tell us they want our moral leadership. We should sympathize with Europe and all that, but we don't have to marry her.
—*Will Rogers.*

MULTUM IN PARVO—The people that throw mud always have dirty hands.

The road to Somewhere is not paved. The paved road passes through Anywhere and stops at Nowhere.

You can't whitewash yourself by blackening others.

Face the sunshine and the shadows will fall behind you.

For every bad habit you give up you automatically contract a good one.

Swear off on talking and see what a good listener you become.

Use the Golden Rule.

Oil your brain occasionally with a good brand of constructive thoughts.

It's a hard job to work with rusty tools.

Every time you frown you vaccinate yourself against happiness.

Keep it up and it is bound to take.

Be patient with the faults of others— they have to be patient with you.

The man who keeps himself and machine under control at all times never becomes angry—or kills anybody.

The pathway of Life is just about like any other congested street. If you don't keep going you get crowded to one side.
—*Charles H. Cowgill.*

BEHAVIOR—Christianity is pre-eminently the religion of the heart. It does not always ask words, but it always wants work. The motives and not the means are the things on which it passes judgment. And the man who shows by his life that he is not ashamed of the Gospel will assuredly one day find that the Gospel is not ashamed of him. There is much more which might be said, but I refrain. Ere I close, you will let me add my emphasis to the fact that it is in our life and conduct that we must show our devotion to Christ. The silent Gospel reaches further than the grandest rhetoric.—*Wilson.*

XXVIII SUCCESS

A RECIPE — I leave these words with you. It is only a young man's message to young men. The message is simple enough. There's nothing impossible about it to any young man, so long as he bears in mind the salient points: First—What success means; the successful doing, the doing well of whatever he does in whatever position he is. Second—The price of success; hard work, patience, and a few sacrifices.

Then for his keys—In his religious life: A firm, unwavering belief in God and in prayer, and a life consistent with that belief for himself and for others. In his social life: Moderation. In his marriage: Love. And in business: Thoroughness. Not thoroughness alone in large things or what is apparent to the eye; but thoroughness in all things; not slighting small things.—*Edward Bok.*

IMPOSSIBLE — The engineer, when he cannot carry his tunnel across or around a mountain, tunnels through it. "Impossibilities!" cried Lord Chatham, " I trample upon impossibilities! "Impossible!" exclaimed Mirabeau, "Talk not to me of that blockhead of a word." If a man's faith in himself and his mission be real and earnest, he cannot fail to gain a certain measure of success. If he does not satisfy the world, he will at least satisfy the voice of conscience. When we look back upon the history of humanity, we see nothing else but a record of what has been achieved by men of strong will. Their will it is that has opened up the way to their fellows. Their enthusiasm of purpose, their fixity of aim, their heroic perseverance—we are all inheritors of what these high qualities have won. "The world is no longer clay," says Emerson, "but rather iron in the hands of its workers, and men have got to hammer out a place for themselves by steady and rugged blows."

HOW TO WIN—Keep up the fires of thought, and all will go well . . . You fail in your thoughts or you prevail in your thoughts alone.—*Thoreau.*

VICTORY—There is a serene Providence which rules the fate of nations, which makes little account of time, little of one generation or race, makes no account of disasters, conquers alike by what is called defeat or by what is called victory, thrusts aside enemy or obstruction, crushes everything immortal as inhuman, and obtains the ultimate triumph of the best race by everything which resists the moral laws of the world.
—*Ralph Waldo Emerson.*

TRIUMPH—There never shall be one lost good. *All* we have willed or hoped or dreamed of good shall exist.
—*Robert Browning.*

HOME AT LAST

To an open house in the evening,
Home shall men come,
To an older place than Eden,
And a taller town than Rome.
To the end of the way of the wandering star,
To the things that cannot be and that are,
To the place where God was homeless,
And all men are at home.

GILBERT K. CHESTERTON.

Copyright, 1932, by Dodd, Mead & Company, Inc. From THE COLLECTED POEMS of G. K. Chesterton. Reprinted by permission of Dodd, Mead & Company.

An Inspiration

However the battle is ended,
   Though proudly the victor comes
With fluttering flags and prancing nags
   And echoing roll of drums,
Still truth proclaims this motto,
   In letters of living light,—
No question is ever settled,
   Until it is settled right.

Though the heel of the strong oppressor
   May grind the weak to dust,
And the voices of fame with one acclaim
   May call him great and just,
Let those who applaud take warning,
   And keep this motto in sight,—
No question is ever settled
   Until it is settled right.

Let those who have failed take courage;
   Tho' the enemy seems to have won,
Tho' his ranks are strong, if he be in the
      wrong
   The battle is not yet done;
For, as sure as the morning follows
   The darkest hour of the night,
No question is ever settled
   Until it is settled right.

O man bowed down with labor!
   O woman, young, yet old!
O heart oppressed in the toiler's breast
   And crushed by the power of gold!
Keep on with your weary battle
   Against triumphant might;
No question is ever settled
   Until it is settled right.
               —*Ella Wheeler Wilcox.*

RECOLLECTION is the only paradise here on earth from which we cannot be turned out.—*Richter.*

WHATEVER DISUNITES man from God disunites man from man.
               —*Burke.*

SUCCESS.—He has achieved success who has lived well, laughed often and loved much; who has gained the respect of intelligent men and the love of little children; who has filled his niche and accomplished his task; who has left the world better than he found it, whether by an improved poppy, a perfect poem or a rescued soul; who has never lacked appreciation of earth's beauty or failed to express it; who has looked for the best in others and given the best he had; whose life was an inspiration; whose memory is a benediction.—*Mrs. A. J. Stanley.*

Together

Ho, brother, it's the hand clasp and the
   good word and the smile
That does the most and helps the most
   to make the world worth while!
It's all of us together, or it's only you
   and I—
A ringing song of friendship, and a word
   or two of cheer,
Then all the world is gladder, and the
   bending sky is clear.
It's you and I together—and we're brothers
   one and all
Whenever through good fellowship we
   hear the subtle call,
Whenever in the ruck of things we feel
   the helping hand
Or see the deeper glow that none but we
   may understand—
Then all the world is good to us and all is
   worth the while;
Ho, brother, it's the hand clasp and the
   good word and the smile!

POWER — Responsibility gravitates toward him who gets ready for it, and power flows to him and through him who can use it.—*George Walter Fiske.*

WATCH AND PRAY—Jesus commands both vigilance and supplication, readiness and dependence.

"Pray to God and row to shore," says the proverb of the Russian fishermen. "Pray to God and keep your powder dry," runs the saying of our pioneer forefathers.

There are two sides to man's religious life: his own honest efforts and God's guidance and support. Either without the other is inadequate.

Hidden Treasure

" 'Twas long ago I read the story sweet—
Of how the German mothers, o'er the sea,
Wind in, throughout the yarn their girlies knit,
Some trinkets small, and tiny shining coins,
That when the little fingers weary grow,
And fain would lay aside the tiresome task,
From out the ball will drop the hidden gift,
To please and urge them on in search for more.
And so, I think, the Father kind above
Winds in and out the skein of life we weave,
Through all the years, bright tokens of His love,
That when we weary grow and long for rest
They help to cheer and urge us on for more;
And far adown within the ball we find,
When all the threads of life at last are spun,
The grandest gift of all—eternal life."

—*Anonymous.*

THINK BACK — Often a retrospect delights the mind.—*Dante.*

STAND YOUR GROUND — The following story is told about Henry Ward Beecher as a boy:

The teacher in the school he attended asked a boy a question which the boy answered. Apparently the teacher was much incensed at the answer and cried testily: Sit down! The abashed boy sat abruptly down. Several boys were asked the same question and gave the same answer and promptly became confused when the teacher voiced his unexplained disapproval.

Finally Beecher was called and gave the same answer as the other boys. Sit down! roared the teacher. But Beecher held his ground and insisted that the answer was correct. For a few moments the teacher stormed at him, but seeing Beecher obdurate and convinced, he smiled and said: Well, boys, you were all correct, but Beecher was the only one sure enough to stand up for it.

It is important not only to give the right answer but to stick to it through thick and thin.

My Wage

I bargained with Life for a penny,
  And Life would pay no more,
However I begged at evening
  When I counted my scanty score.

For Life is a just employer,
  He gives you what you ask,
But once you have set the wages,
  Why, you must bear the task.

I worked for a menial's hire,
  Only to learn, dismayed,
That any wage I had asked of Life,
  Life would have paid.

—*Jessie B. Rittenhouse.*

From THE DOOR OF DREAMS, by Jessie Belle Rittenhouse. Used by permission of the publishers, Houghton Mifflin Company.

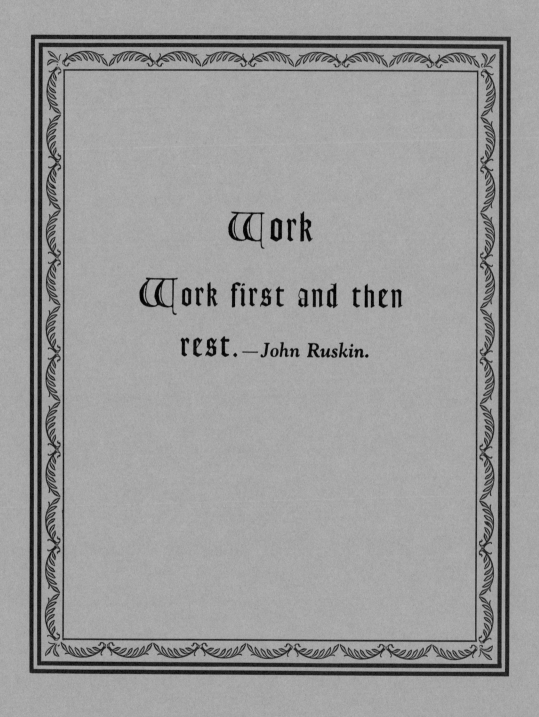

Work

Work first and then

rest.—John Ruskin.

THE FOLLY OF IMPATIENCE — Action taken under the impulse of haste and impatience is usually foolish. A superficial glance often seems to justify a course which a little patience reveals as the utterest folly.

Impatience accounts for many wild schemes in days of emergency and creates many a frightful panic. Action is the result toward which thought tends, but impatient action is always the result of folly.

Can you hope to hit the mark if you go off at half-cock?

WHOEVER sincerely endeavors to do all the good he can will probably do much more than he imagines or will ever know to the day of judgment when the secrets of all hearts shall be made manifest.—*Anonymous.*

PREPAREDNESS

For all your days prepare,
And meet them ever alike:
When you are the anvil, bear;
When you are the hammer, strike.
—*Edwin Markham.*
Reprinted by permission.

I HAVE come to see life, not as a chase of forever impossible personal happiness, but as a field for endeavor toward the happiness of the whole human family. There is no other success. I know indeed of nothing more subtly satisfying and cheering than a knowledge of the real good will and appreciation of others. Such happiness does not come with money; nor does it flow from a fine physical state. It cannot be bought. But it is the keenest joy, after all, and the toiler's truest and best reward.
—*William Dean Howells.*

OVER-CONFIDENCE — Sir James M. Barrie said: "We are all of us failures —at least all the best of us are."

The man who is in real danger is the man who thinks he is perfectly safe.

EFFICIENCY — "Nothing," said Carlyle, "is more terrible than activity without insight."

The tragedy of life is not hardship, labour, suffering; but meaninglessness, emptiness, effort without objective. The fever-racked man who aimlessly passes through the motions of his accustomed daily conduct is a pitiable object. How much more so those whose daily conduct is merely the expression of the fever of life.

Only the man whose activity is directed by a great purpose can be fundamentally happy. Life easily degenerates into the mere dance of death unless it be intelligently directed. Behind the expenditure of the precious energy of life there must be the highest degree of wisdom. Otherwise that energy which can never be recaptured is wasted.

THE HUMAN RACE is in the best condition when it has the greatest degree of liberty.—*Dante.*

MAKE YOUR OWN LUCK—If a man exercises foresight and develops the strength and courage to include various contingencies in the scope of his plans, he puts luck in its proper place as the minor uncertainty that lends savour to life. Luck is too much dependent on men to be a god.

Nansen once said of Amundsen's discovery of the South Pole: "Let no one come and prate about luck and chance, Amundsen's luck is that of the strong man who looks ahead."

169

XXIX. TODAY

BANISH THE FUTURE—Banish the future; live only for the hour and its allotted work. Think not of the amount to be accomplished, the difficulties to be overcome, but set earnestly at the little task at your elbow, letting that be sufficient for the day; for surely our plain duty is "not to see what lies dimly at a distance, but to do what lies clearly at hand."—*Osler.*

THE MAN-I-YET-MAY-BE — Yesterday I dragged wearily along, passively resigned—the Man-I-Am—between the Man-I-Might-Have-Been and the Man-I-Yet-May-Be. But now, today, I feel that with Christ's help all things are possible to the aspirations, the energy, and courage that are thrilling in me in this beautiful new-born life of today, and the Man-I-Yet-May-Be draws closer to my side.
—*O. F.*

DAYS

Daughters of Time, the hypocritic Days,
Muffled and dumb like barefoot dervishes,
And marching single in an endless file,
Bring diadems and fagots in their hands.
To each they offer gifts after his will,
Bread, kingdoms, stars, and sky that holds them all.
I, in my pleached garden, watched the pomp,
Forgot my morning wishes, hastily
Took a few herbs and apples, and the Day
Turned and departed silent. I, too late,
Under her solemn fillet saw the scorn.
EMERSON.

ONLY ONCE — We live but once. The years of childhood, when once past, are past for ever. It matters not how ardently we may wish to live them over; it avails us nothing. So it is with the other stages of life. The past is no longer ours. It has gone beyond our reach. What we have made it, it shall remain. There is no power in Heaven or on earth that can change it. The record of our past stands forth in bold and ineffaceable characters, open to the all-seeing eye of God. There it stands, and one day we shall give an account of it. The present moment alone is ours. "Now is thy treasure possessed unawares." Today is a day which we never had before, which we shall never have again. It rose from the great ocean of eternity, and again sinks into its unfathomable depths.—*Talmage.*

FEELINGS—For a few brief days the orchards are white with blossoms. They soon turn to fruit, or else float away, useless and wasted, upon the idle breeze. So will it be with present feelings. They must be deepened into decision, or be entirely dissipated by delay.
—*Theodore Cuyler.*

GONE—Lost wealth may be replaced by industry, lost knowledge by study, lost health by temperance, but lost time is gone for ever.—*Smiles.*

THRIFT—Believe me when I tell you that thrift of time will repay you in afterlife, with a usury of profit beyond your most sanguine dreams; and that waste of it will make you dwindle alike in intellectual and moral stature, beyond your darkest reckoning.—*W. E. Gladstone.*

FILL THE SPACES—Select a large box, and place in it as many cannon balls as it will hold, and it is, after a fashion, full; but it will hold more if smaller matters be found. Bring a quantity of marbles; very many of these may be packed in the spaces between the larger globes; the box is now full, but still only in a sense; it will contain more yet. There are interstices in abundance, into which you may shake a considerable quantity of small shot, and now the chest is filled beyond all question; but yet there is room. You cannot put in another shot or marble, much less another ball; but you will find that several pounds of sand will slide down between the larger materials, and, even then between the granules of sand, if you empty yonder jug, there will be space for all the water, and for the same quantity several times repeated. Where there is no space for the great, there may be room for the little; where the little cannot enter, the less can make its way; and where the less is shut out, the least of all may find ample room. So, where time is, as we say, fully occupied, there must be stray moments, occasional intervals, and snatches, which might hold a vast amount of little usefulness in the course of months and years. What a wealth of minor good, as we think it to be, might be shaken down into the interstices of ten years' work, which might prove to be as precious in result by the grace of God, as the greater works of the same period.
—*C. H. Spurgeon.*

Building

For Yesterday is but a Dream,
And To-Morrow is only a Vision;
But To-Day, well lived,
Makes every Yesterday
A dream of Happiness,
And every To-Morrow a Vision of Hope.

TOMORROW — Today is the wise man's day; tomorrow is the fool's day. The wise man is the man who, when he sees what ought to be done, does it today. The foolish man is the man who, when he sees what ought to be done, says, "I will do it tomorrow." The men who always do today the thing they see ought to be done today are the men who make a success for time and for eternity. The men and women who put off until tomorrow what ought to be done today are the men and women who make a shipwreck of time and of eternity.—*Banks.*

WELL-EARNED SLEEP — Make a rule, and pray God to help you to keep it, never, if possible, to lie down at night without being able to say, "I have made one human being, at least, a little wiser, a little happier, or a little better this day."
—*Charles Kingsley.*

DO IT NOW—There is no moment like the present. The man who will not execute his resolutions when they are fresh upon him can have no hope from them afterwards: they will be dissipated, lost, and perish in the hurry and scurry of the world, or sunk in the slough of indolence.—*Maria Edgeworth.*

MOMENTS—The small stones which fill up the crevices have almost as much to do with making the fair and firm wall as the great rocks; so the wise use of spare moments contributes not a little to the building up in good proportions a man's mind.—*E. Paxton Hood.*

PROMPTNESS — I owe all my success in life to having been always a quarter of an hour beforehand.—*Lord Nelson.*

171

WATCH your way then, as a cautious traveler; and don't be gazing at that mountain or river in the distance, and saying, "How shall I ever get over them?" but keep to the present little inch that is before you, and accomplish that in the little moment that belongs to it. The mountain and the river can only be passed in the same way; and when you come to them, you will come to the light and strength that belong to them.

—M. A. Kelty.

PUPIL—Today is yesterday's pupil.

—Franklin.

WAYFARERS — I expect to pass through this world but once. Any good thing, therefore, that I can do or any kindness I can show to any fellow human being let me do it now. Let me not defer nor neglect it, for I shall not pass this way again.—Stephen Grellet.

INDECISION—The sun rose; it rose upon no sadder sight than the man of good abilities, and good emotions, incapable of their directed exercise, incapable of his own help and his own happiness, sensible of the blight upon him, and resigning himself to let it eat him away.

—Dickens—"Tale of Two Cities."

HELPFULNESS—Today is your day and mine, the only day we have, the day in which we play our part. What our part may signify in the great whole we may not understand; but we are here to play it, and now is our time. This we know: it is a part of action, not of whining. It is a part of love, not cynicism. It is for us to express love in terms of human helpfulness.—David Starr Jordan.

DAY-BREAK — The morning, which is the most memorable season of the day, is the awakening hour . . . Little is to be expected of that day, if it can be called a day, to which we are not awakened by our Genius. . . All memorable events, I should say, transpire in morning time and in a morning atmosphere . . . To him whose elastic and vigorous thought keeps pace with the sun, the day is a perpetual morning . . . Morning is when I am awake and there is a dawn in me. . .

—Thoreau—"Walden."

The Time Is Brief

Because the longest life is brief
I must be swift in keeping
The little trysts with kindliness,
Before the time of sleeping!

I must be swift in reaching out,
To those whose hearts are yearning;
O, swift indeed to love them much
Before the long road's turning!

Before a sudden summons comes,
I surely must be saying
The words that I have failed to say—
The prayers I should be praying.

—Grace Noll Crowell.

THE ANSWER—We will never get anywhere with our finances till we pass a law saying that every time we appropriate something we got to pass another bill along with it stating where the money is coming from.—Will Rogers.

ALL OTHER KNOWLEDGE is hurtful to him who has not honesty and good nature.—Montaigne.

STUDY THE PAST if you would divine the future.—Confucius.

"IMPROVE YOUR OPPORTUNITIES," said Bonaparte to a school of young men, "every hour lost now is a chance of future misfortune."

~

TOO LATE— The foolish virgins of Christ's parable faced the fact that there is a point in life at which no excuses will avail.

The door was shut. There is absolutely nothing to be done about it. All action should have been taken beforehand. Now it is too late.

But the important thing to remember is that the arrival at the inexorable point of hopelessness is always the culmination of what has gone before; and that this desperate plight is avoidable if we are continually ready.

Many of us are going to do great things —tomorrow. But tomorrow never comes. For the only day we have is today. And this corrupting habit of running behind schedule—even in small things—has for its inevitable result the bringing of us face to face with a shut door.

The demand that life makes on all of us is to be ready at all times, to live neither in the past nor in the future but in the present.

Until we learn that lesson we cannot escape the certain consequence that we shall one day stand, sorrowful but too late, before the one door through which we desire to enter but cannot—because it is shut.

~

ESSENTIAL — There can be no persevering industry without a deep sense of the value of time.—*Mrs. Sigourney.*

~

DOST THOU LOVE LIFE? then do not squander time, for that is the stuff life is made of.—*Franklin.*

POSTPONED DUTIES—Tomorrow is never what we think it will be. In that sense tomorrow never comes. Today we think we will be happy and please ourselves. Tomorrow we will do our duty. But we only make ourselves wretched pleasure-seekers.

For human nature is fundamentally such that it can only find enduring gladness in the incidental accompaniments of duty performed today.

~

THE KEEN SPIRIT seizes the prompt occasion; makes the thought start into instant action, and at once plans and performs, resolves and executes.
—*Hannah More.*

~

A SECRET OF GREATNESS —
"The flighty purpose never is o'ertook
Unless the deed go with it."

Is this not one of the secrets of greatness? Certainly it is not a common characteristic of men.

We have an impulse to send a note to a friend. But postpone it and perhaps forget it.

We encounter a noble idea in conversation or a book. But let it slide through our leaky minds.

We hear or read a strange word or idea. Instead of turning to the dictionary or other book of reference or making a note for later investigation, we let it go.

Is it any wonder that our minds grow dull or that we are oppressed with the sense of unfulfilled purposes? Greatness may not be within our reach, but mental growth is. And no one need be oppressed by the haunting memory of unaccepted opportunities.

~

PROGRESS is the activity of today and the assurance of tomorrow.—*Emerson.*

PARADISE—If the state of the dead until the resurrection morning be one of entire unconsciousness, our Lord's parable of the rich man and Lazarus is worse than unmeaning. It is untrue in a sense which we forbear here to characterize. Nor is this the only decisive statement of His. The promise to the dying thief, "This day shalt thou be with Me in paradise," would be worse than unmeaning if the dying man were to lapse that instant into unconsciousness and continue in that state till the moment of the general awakening.—*J. B. Heard.*

TIME IS PAINTED with a lock before, and bald behind, signifying thereby that we must take time by the forelock, for when it is once passed there is no recalling it.—*Swift.*

PUNCTUALITY is the stern virtue of men of business, and the graceful courtesy of princes.—*Bulwer.*

TIME! the corrector where our judgments err; the test of truth, and love; the sole philosopher, for all beside are sophists.—*Byron.*

INDEPENDENCE—It is a miserable thing to live a life of suspense; it is the life of a spider.—*Swift.*

SPEND YOUR TIME in nothing which you know must be repented of; in nothing on which you might not pray the blessing of God; in nothing which you could not review with a quiet conscience on your dying bed; in nothing which you might not safely and properly be found doing if death should surprise you in the act.—*Baxter.*

IT IS BETTER to be doing the most insignificant thing than to reckon even a half hour insignificant.—*Goethe.*

NOW — There is a time to be born, and a time to die, says Solomon, and it is the memento of a truly wise man; but there is an interval between these two times of infinite importance.—*Richmond.*

TO CHOOSE TIME is to save time.
—*Bacon.*

USE THE DAY — Keep forever in view the momentous value of life; aim at its worthiest use—its sublimest end; spurn, with disdain, those foolish trifles and frivolous vanities, which so often consume life, as the locusts did Egypt; and devote yourself, with the ardor of a passion, to attain the most divine improvements of the human soul. In short, hold yourself in preparation to make the transition to another life, whenever you shall be claimed by the Lord of the world.
—*J. Foster.*

TO KILL TIME is, by definition, to murder it.

SPENDTHRIFTS — If time be of all things the most precious, wasting time must be the greatest prodigality, since lost time is never found again; and what we call time enough is always little enough. Let us then be up and doing, and doing to the purpose; so by diligence shall we do more with less perplexity.
—*Franklin.*

AFTER ALL—It's a great country but you can't live in it for nothing.
—*Will Rogers.*

XXX. TRIFLES

FRAGMENTS—Macaulay tells the story of a man who had the contract for putting in the stained windows for a great cathedral. He was much annoyed by the persistent request of his apprentice for the privilege of designing and arranging the glass, for just one window. He did not wish to discourage the young man's ambition, nor did he wish an experiment to be made with costly material. So he said to him, "If you will furnish your own material, you may try your hand on that window," pointing to one not very prominent. But what was his surprise to find him gathering up the little bits of glass that he himself had cut off and thrown away. He set to work with these, and suceeded in working out a design of rare beauty. When the doors were thrown open, and the people came to view the work, they stood in great groups before that window, admiring its charming excellence, until the master artist became exceedingly jealous of the rising reputation of his apprentice. So we may gather up the little bits of time, and influence, and money, and opportunity, which we generally throw away, and weave them into a life so pure and beautiful, that the angels will stand before it in admiration and praise.—*Moffitt.*

THE KEY—Study the big problems all the time, but never to skip a small task, for one of the simple duties may hold the key to the biggest problem.
—*John T. Faris.*

IMPOTENCY — Those who bestow too much application on trifling things become generally incapable of great ones.
—*La Rochefoucauld.*

LITTLE SINS — It is Satan's custom by small sins to draw us to greater, as the little sticks set the great ones on fire, and a wisp of straw enkindles a block of wood.—*T. Manton.*

A spark is the beginning of a flame; and a small disease may bring a greater.
—*Baxter.*

Small twigs will prove thorny bushes if not timely stubbed up.—*Swinnock.*

What great difference is there whether your eternal burning be kindled by many sparks, or by one fire brand? Whether you die by smaller wounds, or by one great one? Many little items make a debt desperate, and the payment impossible.
—*Hopkins.*

WASTE —"Do not waste five-dollar time on a five-cent job."—*John T. Faris.*

LITTLE THINGS

"Little words are the sweetest to hear; little charities fly farthest, and stay longest on the wing; little lakes are the stillest; little hearts are the fullest, and little farms are the best tilled. Little books are read the most, and little songs the dearest loved. And when Nature would make anything especially rare .and beautiful, she makes it little; little pearls, little diamonds, little dews. Agar's is a model prayer; but then it is a little one; and the burden of the petition is for but little. The Sermon on the Mount is little, but the last dedication discourse was an hour long. Life is made up of littles; death is what remains of them all. Day is made up of little beams, and night is glorious with little stars."

LITTLE THINGS — "A cup of cold water"—a little thing! But life is made up of little things, and he who would rise to higher usefulness is wise if he cherishes the loving yet seeming trifles of daily living.—*Floyd W. Tomkins.*

BEGINNINGS—Little sins, so called, are the beginning of great ones. The explosion is in the spark, the upas in its seed, the fiery serpent in its smooth egg, the fierce tiger in the playful cub. By a little wound death may be caused as surely as by a great one. Through one small vein the heart's blood may flow not less fatally than through the main artery. A few drops oozing through an embankment may make a passage for the whole lake of waters. A green log is safe in the company of a candle; but if a few shavings are just lighted, and then some dry sticks, the green log will not long resist the flames. How often has a character which seemed steadfast been destroyed by little sins. Satan seldom assails in the first instance with great temptations. Skilful general! he makes his approach gradually, and by zigzag trenches creeps towards the fortress he intends at length to storm. Therefore watch against little sins.—*Newman Hall.*

A MEASURING ROD
That best portion of a good man's life,
His little nameless unremembered acts
Of kindness and of love.
—*William Wordsworth.*

THE OBLIGATION — The million little things that drop into our hands, the small opportunities each day brings He leaves us free to use or abuse and goes unchanging along His silent way.
—*Helen Keller.*

GOD SEES—Perhaps at the Last Day all that will remain worth recording of a life full of activity and zeal, will be those little deeds that were done solely beneath the eye of God.—*Gold Dust.*

MANY FACETS—If falsehood had, like the truth, but one face only, we should be upon better terms; for we should then take the contrary to what the liar says for certain truth; but the reverse of truth hath a hundred figures, and is a field indefinite without bound or limit.—*Montaigne.*

THE HOURS—The bell strikes one. We take no note of time, but from its loss. To give it then a tongue is wise in man. As if an angel spoke. I feel the solemn sound. If heard aright, it is the knell of my departed hours. Where are they? With the years beyond the flood. It is the signal that demands dispatch; how much is to be done!—*Young.*

MUCH MAY BE DONE in those little shreds and patches of time, which every day produces, and which most men throw away, but which nevertheless will make at the end of it no small deduction from the life of man.—*Colton.*

TRIFLES? — Sometimes when I consider what tremendous consequences come from little things—a chance word, a tap on the shoulder, or a penny dropped on a newstand—I am tempted to think . . . there are no little things.
—*Bruce Barton.*

OBSTINACY AND CONTRADICTION are like a paper kite: they are only kept up so long as you pull against them.

KINDNESS AND LOVE — If you will study the history of Christ's ministry from Baptism to Ascension, you will discover that it is mostly made up of little words, little deeds, little prayers, little sympathies, adding themselves together in unwearied succession. The Gospel is full of divine attempts to help and heal, in body, mind, and heart, individual men. The completed beauty of Christ's life is only the added beauty of little inconspicuous acts of beauty — talking with the woman at the well; going far up into the North country to talk with the Syrophenician woman; showing the young ruler the stealthy ambition laid away in his heart that kept him out of the kingdom of Heaven; shedding a tear at the grave of Lazarus; teaching a little knot of followers how to pray; preaching the Gospel one Sunday afternoon to two disciples going out to Emmaus; kindling a fire and broiling fish that His disciples might have a breakfast waiting for them when they came ashore from a night of fishing, cold, tired, and discouraged. All of these things, you see, let us in so easily into the real quality and tone of God's interests, so specific, so narrowed down, so enlisted in what is small, so engrossed with what is minute.
—*Parkhurst.*

BE CAUTIOUS — Springs are little things, but they are sources of large streams; a helm is a little thing, but we know its use and power; nails and pegs are little things, but they hold the parts of a large building together; a word, a look, a smile, a frown, are all little things, but powerful for good or evil. Think of this, and mind the little things.—*Hillis.*

DISCRETION—We may outrun by violent swiftness that which we run out, and lose by overrunning.—*Shakespeare*

LITTLE BUT MIGHTY—Size is not always an indication of importance. We all stop to look at a big man walking in a crowd. But he is not always superior to his less noticeable companions. The giant Goliath was no doubt a splendid figure on the field of battle; but he was no match for the ruddy stripling David.

There are small things which wield a mighty influence.

A rudder is a small thing compared to to the ship which it steers. But who wants to be on a rudderless ship?

Your home may be very small and humble, but would you exchange it and all that it means for a residence in the biggest hotel in the world?

A man may be a very small creature, but would you rather be an elephant or the man who controls him?

Words are little things, but what tremendous power for good or evil they may exert!

DREAM PEDLARY

If there were dreams to sell,
  What would you buy?
Some cost a passing bell;
  Some a light sigh,
That shakes from Life's fresh crown
Only a rose-leaf down.
If there were dreams to sell,
Merry and sad to tell,
And the crier rang the bell,
  What would you buy?

A cottage lone and still,
  With bowers nigh,
Shadowy, my woes to still,
  Until I die.
Such pearl from Life's fresh crown
Fain would I shake me down.
Were dreams to have at will,
This would best heal my ill,
  This would I buy.
—*Thomas Lovell Beddoes.*

ANGER — When some of those cutting, sharp, blighting words have been spoken which send the hot, indignant blood to the face and head, if those to whom they are addressed keep silence, look on with awe, for a mighty work is going on within them, and the spirit of evil, or their guardian angel, is very near to them in that hour. During that pause they have made a step towards Heaven or towards hell, and an item has been scored in the book which the day of judgment shall see opened.—*Emerson.*

PRIME MOVER — Whosoever shall review his life will find that the whole tenor of his conduct has been determined by some accident of no apparent moment.
—*Johnson.*

TRUE GREATNESS—Johnson well says, "He who waits to do a great deal of good at once will never do anything." Life is made up of little things. It is very rarely that an occasion is offered for doing a great deal at once. True greatness consists in being great in little things.
—*C. Simmons.*

GIVE-AWAYS — Trifles discover a character more than actions of importance. In regard to the former, a person is off his guard, and thinks it not material to use disguise. It is no imperfect hint toward the discovery of a man's character to say he looks as though you might be certain of finding a pin upon his sleeve.
—*Shenstone.*

A STRAY HAIR, by its continued irritation, may give more annoyance than a sharp blow.—*Lowell.*

MEN are led by trifles.—*Napoleon.*

CONTRAST — There is a care for trifles which proceeds from love of conscience, and is most holy; and a care for trifles which comes of idleness and frivolity, and is most base.—*Ruskin.*

BUZZ BUZZ—The mind of the greatest man on earth is not so independent of circumstances as not to feel inconvenienced by the merest buzzing noise about him; it does not need the noise of a cannon to disturb his thoughts. The creaking of a vane or pulley is quite enough. Do not wonder that he reasons ill just now; a fly is buzzing in his ear; it is quite enough to unfit him for giving good counsel.—*Pascal.*

A LITTLE and a little, collected together, become a great deal; the heap in the barn consists of single grains, and drop and drop make the inundation.
—*Saadi.*

LOST—It is in those acts which we call trivialities that the seeds of joy are forever wasted.—*George Eliot.*

IN EVERYTHING—There is a kind of latent omniscience not only in every man, but in every particle.—*Emerson.*

GREAT MERIT, or great failings, will make you respected or despised; but trifles, little attentions, mere nothings, either done or neglected, will make you either liked or disliked in the general run of the world.—*Chesterfield.*

THE SUM — Trifles make perfection, but perfection itself is no trifle.
—*Michael Angelo.*

XXXI. WORK

CHOICES — All through life we must keep choosing. Destiny hangs on "yes" and "no." As we look back, it is to wonder what would have happened if we had gone the other way when the road forked.

On life's bargain-counter are wares piled up for the pleasing of all tastes. We marvel that some eagerly select what we contemptuously reject. * * * Our tastes are as various as our natures.

How can Nature originate so great a variety of patterns? We speak of the mass of mankind as if it was all one. But it presents a bewildering variation. Human beings are as different from one another as their parental influences and their environments and their personal natures are different. Flesh and blood can never be run in a mould of monotonous uniformity. The fascination of travel is in the endless variety of mankind that one encounters, more than in silent buildings or inarticulate scenery.

The choice of personal associates is the all-influencing choice. To go wrong here is the likeliest way to cripple one's chances of eminence or of plain, everyday success. A man goes into business with partners guilty of malfeasance, and they pull him down. A woman marries the wrong husband, and though her courage may keep her at the sticking point and may enable her to preserve the appearance of domestic felicity, all that makes for the ideal relationship is absent. The basis of happiness is not in things, but in people. Those of us who are thoroughly normal cannot get along without congenial society. The kind of persons we choose to be with is the first and surest indication of character. The worthiest must be uneasy and unhappy in the company of the worst; and the best will naturally seek the best. What a man chooses, he is.

— *Philadelphia Public Ledger.*

DOING — Whatever your hands find to do, that do with all the might that is in you. That is the lesson of all experience. Face every task with a determination to conquer its difficulties and never to let them conquer you. No task is too small to be done well. For the man who is worthy, who is fit to perform the deeds of the world, even the greatest, sooner or later the opportunity to do them will come. He can abide his time, can rest— "safe in himself as in a fate."— *G. W. Goethals.*

MY TASK

To love some one more dearly every
    day,
To help a wandering child to find his
    way,
To ponder o'er a noble thought and
    pray,
And smile when evening falls—
    This is my task.
To follow truth as blind men seek for
    light,
To do my best from dawn of day till
    night,
To keep my heart fit for His holy sight,
And answer when He calls—
    This is my task.
And then my Savior by and by to meet,
When faith hath made her task on
    earth complete,
And lay my homage at the Master's
    feet,
Within the jasper walls—
    This crowns my task.

MAUDE LOUISE RAY.

WEEDS come of themselves; flowers require cultivation. There is depravity in the soil, a tendency to thorns and thistles. It is under the curse. Good things are brought out of the soil, like good things out of the human heart, only as the result of much labor. It takes no pains to produce a harvest of weeds, nor to produce the harvest that the thief or the drunkard reaps—no more effort than is required to float down stream. This is depravity.—*Gleanings for Sermons.*

FINDING ONE'S WORK—The desire to begin over again is one of those longings so common and universal that we may say it is a native instinct. . . that we have failed, and failed again and again, need not intimidate us for a new trial. Aspirations, imperfections, and failures are intimations of future achievements. Defeats foretell future successes. The sin to be dreaded is the unlit lamp and ungirt loin. Our light must be burning, however dimly, and we must keep on the right road, however often we stumble on the way. Under no circumstances can it be true that there is not something to be *done*, as well as something to be suffered. Let us sit down before the Lord and count our resources, and see what we are *not* fit for, and give up wishing for it. Let us decide honestly what we *can do*, and then do it with all our might.

—*Amelia E. Barr.*

Faith and Works

If faith produce no works, I see
That faith is not a living tree:
Thus faith and works together grow;
No separate life they e'er can know;
They're soul and body, hand and heart—
What God hath joined, let no man part.

—*Hannah More.*

THE COMMON TASK—It is not the straining for great things that is most effective; it is the doing the little things, the common duties, a little better and better—the constant improving—that tells.

We often see young people who seem very ambitious to get on by leaps and bounds, and are impatient of what they call the drudgery of their situation, but who are doing this drudgery in a very ordinary, slipshod way. Yet it is only by doing the common things uncommonly well, doing them with pride and enthusiasm, and just as well, as neatly, as quickly, and as efficiently as possible, that you take the drudgery out of them. This is what counts in the final issue. How can you expect to do a great thing well when you half do the little things? These are the stepping-stones to the great things.

The best way to begin to do great things is to improve the doing of the little things just as much as possible,—to put the uncommon effort into the common task, to make it large by doing it in a great way. Many a man has dignified a very lowly and humble calling by bringing to it a master spirit. Many a great man has sat upon a cobbler's bench, and has forged at an anvil in a blacksmith's shop. It is the man that dignifies the calling. Nothing that is necessary to be done is small when a great soul does it.

—*Orison Swett Marden.*

HIT IT HARD—The temper of life is to be made good by big, honest blows; stop striking and you will accomplish nothing; strike feebly, and you will do almost as little. Success rides on every hour—grapple it, and you may win; but without a grapple it will never go with you. Work is the weapon of honor, and who lacks the weapon will never triumph.—*Ik Marvel.*

DURABLE SATISFACTIONS — A great deal of the joy of life consists in doing perfectly, or at least to the best of one's ability, everything which he attempts to do. There is a sense of satisfaction, a pride in surveying such a work—a work which is rounded, full, exact, complete in all its parts—which the superficial man, who leaves his work in a slovenly, slipshod, half-finished condition, can never know. It is this conscientious completeness which turns work into art. The smallest thing, well done, becomes artistic.

—William Mathews.

RESOLVE—The "bull's-eye" may not be hit by the rifleman whose hand is uncertain, and his footing infirm. The goal will never be reached by the runner who swerves from a straight course, and wanders into a pathless wilderness. The student will accomplish nothing who flies from study to study with the restlessness of disease; and no man, whatever his condition or mental powers, will win or deserve success, unless he fixes upon some special object to be carried out, and through cloud and sunshine steadily perseveres in his settled purpose.

Purpose, indeed, is the very essence—the main element—of an heroic character. It was purpose which animated Ignatius Loyola in his ascetic labors; in persecution, and captivity, and physical suffering, still toiling at the fulfillment of his cherished design, the establishment of that "Society of Jesus," whose influence on the world's history has been so signal and remarkable. Martin Luther's "purpose" achieved the Reformation. Oliver Cromwell's "purpose" turned the tide of battle at Naseby, and placed him in the seat of the English kings. Mahomet's "purpose" built up a mighty empire, and fixed the firm foundations of a new creed.

The man who concentrates his energies upon the fulfilment of an unalterable design will assuredly wring success from the hands of a reluctant fortune. Such a man will take no heed of "impossibilities." "Impossible?" exclaimed Napoleon, "there is nothing impossible; it is a word only found in the dictionary of fools." The difference between genius and mediocrity lies chiefly in this matter of "purpose;" for true genius has, what mediocrity usually wants, the capacity of labor. "Work and purpose" is the moral of every heroic life.

—Public Speakers Library.

WANTED—Men,
Not systems fit and wise,
Not faiths with rigid eyes,
Not wealth in mountain piles,
Not power with gracious smiles,
Not even the potent pen—
Wanted: Men.

—Anonymous.

CARPENTER—"Is not this the carpenter?" As though no words of wisdom or works of power could come from a carpenter! If Jesus had been a rabbi, in a scholar's robe, it would have been another thing. Yes: and what another thing for us, and for all the world's workers! Celsus sneered at the carpenter, and said that word proved he was an impostor. How could God so demean Himself? But the world has left Celsus behind, along with the critics of Nazareth, and blessed God for the gentleness and comfort, the sympathy and hope, which were given to us by the hands of the Carpenter.

—Vance.

LABOR—Labor, the symbol of man's punishment; Labor, the secret of man's happiness.—*James Montgomery.*

ZEAL—If there was ever a man who seemed to spend his life for nothing, it was Henry Martyn—a man of an exquisite nature, great power, and a sweet and loving disposition. Taking the highest honors at the university, and having the best prospects in the Church, he was led by the Spirit of God to consecrate himself to the cause of foreign missions. For that object he sacrificed that which was dearer to him than life—for she to whom he was affianced declined to go with him. He forsook father, and mother, and native land, and love itself, and went an elegant accomplished scholar, among the Persians, the Orientals, and spent a few years almost without an apparent conversion. Still he labored on, patient and faithful, until, seized with a fever, he staggered. And the last record that he made in his journal was, that he sat under the orchard trees and sighed for that land where there should be sickness and suffering no more. The record closed—he died, and a stranger marked his grave. A worldly man would say, "Here was an instance of mistaken zeal and enthusiasm. Here was a man who might have produced a powerful effect on the Church in his own country, and built up a happy home, and been respected and honored; but, under the influence of a strange fanaticism, he went abroad, and sickened and died, and that was the last of him."
The last of him! Henry Martyn's life was the seed-life of more noble souls, perhaps, than the life of any other man that ever lived. Scores and scores of ministers in England and America, who have brought into the Church hundreds and thousands of souls, and multitudes of men in heathen lands, all over the world, have derived inspiration and courage from the eminently fruitful, but apparently wasted and utterly thrown away, life of Henry Martyn.—*H. W. Beecher.*

NOT KNOWLEDGE, BUT APTITUDE—It isn't what a man knows that matters, but how near to a straight line he can drive the processes of his mind; how near to a lean and useful muscle he can make that mind; how near he can come to lassoing a truth or method. No man should be judged by what he doesn't know; he should be judged only by how quickly and sensibly he assumes new duties.—*Struthers Burt.*

BUILDING CATHEDRALS—Three men, all engaged at the same employment, were asked what they were doing. One said he was making five dollars a day. Another replied that he was cutting stone. The third said he was building a cathedral. The difference was not in what they were actually doing, although the spirit of the third might quite possibly have made him the more expert at his task. They were all earning the same wage; they were all cutting stone; but only one held it in his mind that he was helping build a great edifice. Life meant more to him than to his mates, because he saw further and more clearly.

The farmer may be only planting seed, but if he opens his eyes he is feeding the world. The railroad man, the factory hand, the clerk in the store, likewise are building their cathedrals. The investors in stocks and bonds, the executives of great corporations — they are building cathedrals likewise, if only they can catch the vision. The housewife does not count the dollars she receives for her exertions. If she did, her life would be unhappy indeed. The rest of us, the great figures of the industrial world more than the humble ones, are thinking too much about such things as cutting stone and making profits, fully to be realizing the beauty of life.
—*Omaha Bee.*

DEEDS REMAIN—Life passes; work is permanent. It is all going—fleeting and withering. Youth goes. Mind decays. That which is done remains. Through ages, through eternity, what you have done for God, that, and only that, you are. Deeds never die.—*F. W. Robertson.*

FAITH and works are as necessary to our spiritual life as Christians, as soul and body are to our natural life as men; for faith is the soul of religion, and works the body.—*Colton.*

Faith without works is like a bird without wings; though she may hop with her companions on earth, yet she will never fly with them to Heaven; but when both are joined together, then doth the soul mount up to her eternal rest.
—*J. Beaumont.*

Christian works are no more than animate faith, as flowers are the animate springtide.—*Longfellow.*

Faith and works are related as principle and practice. Faith—the repose in things unseen, the recognition of eternal principles of truth and right, the sense of obligation to an eternal Being who vindicates these principles—must come first. Faith is not an intellectual assent, nor a sympathetic sentiment. It is the absolute surrender of self to the will of a being who has a right to command this surrender. It is this which places men in personal relation to God, which (in St. Paul's language) justifies them before God.—*Lightfoot.*

It is an unhappy division that has been made between faith and works, though in my intellect I may divide them, just as in a candle I know there is both light and heat; but yet, put out the candle and they are both gone; one remains not without the other. So it is betwixt faith and works.—*Seldon.*

No good thing is ever lost. Nothing dies, not even life which gives up one form only to resume another. No good action, no good example dies. It lives forever in our race. While the frame moulders and disappears, the deed leaves an indelible stamp, and moulds the very thought and will of future generations.
—*Samuel Smiles.*

Work

Let me do my work from day to day,
  In field or forest, at the desk or loom,
  In roaring market-place or tranquil
    room;
Let me but find it in my heart to say
When vagrant wishes beckon me astray:
  "This is my work; my blessing, not my
    doom;
  Of all who live, I am the one by whom
This work can best be done in the right
    way."

Then shall I see it not too great, no small,
  To suit my spirit and to prove my
    powers;
  Then shall I cheerful greet the laboring
    hours,
And cheerful turn when the long shadows
    fall
At eventide, to play and love and rest,
Because I know for me my work is best.
—*Henry Van Dyke.*

SLIPSHOD METHODS — Do your best, not because your work is worth it, but because you are. Whatever you are doing, you are making manhood. Half-hearted work makes only half a man. Slipshod methods mean loose principles. The only way to keep character up to the standard is by continually living up to the highest standard in all that you do.
—*Young People's Weekly.*

MAKE A DUST—My son, remember you have to work. Whether you handle pick or wheelbarrow or a set of books, digging ditches or editing a newspaper, ringing an auction bell or writing funny things, you must work. Don't be afraid of killing yourself by overworking on the sunny side of thirty. Men die sometimes, but it is because they quit at nine p. m. and don't go home until two a. m. It's the intervals that kill, my son. The work gives you appetite for your meals; it lends solidity to your slumber; it gives you a perfect appreciation of a holiday. There are young men who do not work, but the country is not proud of them. It does not even know their names; it only speaks of them as old So-and-So's boys. Nobody likes them; the great, busy world doesn't know they are here. So find out what you want to be and do. Take off your coat and make dust in the world. The busier you are, the less harm you are apt to get into, the sweeter will be your sleep, the brighter your holidays, and the better satisfied the whole world will be with you.—*Bob Burdette.*

INSPIRE—Men cannot be made wise or strong or moral by exterior laws or agencies. There are two ways to help a thriftless man. One is to build him a house and place him therein. The other is to inspire in him the sense of industry, economy, and ambition, and then he will build his own house. All tools, books, pictures, laws, on the outside, begin with ideas on the inside. Inspire the reason, and man will fill the library with books. Wake up the taste and imagination in young men, and they will fill the galleries with pictures. Stir the springs of justice, and men will go forth to cleanse iniquities and right wrongs.—*Parkhurst.*

UPWARD—Infinite toil would not enable you to sweep away a mist; but by ascending a little you may often look over it altogether. So it is with our moral improvement; we wrestle fiercely with a vicious habit, which could have no hold upon us, if we ascended into a higher moral atmosphere.—*Helps.*

HEROES—"No man has earned the right to intellectual ambition until he has learned to lay his course by a star which he has never seen—to dig by the divining rod for springs which he may never reach . . . To think great thoughts you must be heroes as well as idealists. Only when you have worked alone—when you have felt around you a black gulf of solitude more isolating than that which surrounds the dying man, and in hope and in despair have trusted to your own unshaken will — then only will you have achieved. Thus only can you gain the secret isolated joy of the thinker, who knows that, a hundred years after he is dead and forgotten, men who never heard of him will be moving to the measure of his thought—the subtle rapture of a postponed power, which the world knows not because it has no external trappings, but which to his prophetic vision is more real than that which commands an army."
—*Oliver Wendell Holmes.*

LIVING — A life spent in brushing clothes, and washing crockery, and sweeping floors—a life which the proud of the earth would have treated as the dust under their feet; a life spent at the clerk's desk; a life spent in the narrow shop; a life spent in the laborer's hut, may yet be a life so ennobled by God's loving mercy that for the sake of it a king might gladly yield his crown.—*Farrar.*

PICTURES IN THE FIRE—You can always see a face in the fire. The laborer, looking into it at evening, purifies his thoughts of the dross and earthiness which they have accumulated during the day.

—*Thoreau.*

ATTITUDES AND APTITUDES— Have an apitude for the thing you do, and have an attitude of respect or reverence toward it.

Some people learn the motions of their work without ever bothering to study the meaning of those motions; such are doubtless working without an aptitude for their jobs. On the other hand, perhaps the great failures are the persons who, having an aptitude for their work, have the wrong attitude. They do a poor job, knowing it to be poor, but they lack respect for their own handiwork, and have so little thought for their fellow beings, that they are willing to waste their time doing something worthless.

In medieval times people approached their work with prayer. Whether it was ultimately viewed by the many or the few, it was all, no matter how it might be hidden, seen by God; and it was done primarily for God.

When we were knee-high to grasshoppers we were taught: "What is worth doing at all is worth doing well." All else is waste.—*Boston Herald.*

WORKINGMAN—Jesus Christ was a workingman. His hands were fitted to labor as His voice was fitted to music. He entered into the condition of the great majority of mankind and became one of them in the fellowship of toil and from that time it has been hard for a man to get into better company than that of working people.—*George Hall.*

ENTHUSIASM makes men strong. It wakes them up, brings out their latent powers, keeps up incessant action, impels to tasks requiring strength; and these develop it. Many are born to be giants, yet few grow above common men, from lack of enthusiasm. They need waking up; if set on fire by some eager impulse, inspired by some grand resolve, they would soon rise head and shoulders above their fellows. But they sleep, doze, wait for public sentiment, cling to the beaten paths, dread sacrifices, shun hardships, and die weaklings.

—*Theological Framework.*

THE CURE — The most unhappy of all men is the man who cannot tell what he is going to do, that has got no work cut out for him in the world, and does not go into any. For work is the grand cure of all the maladies and miseries that ever beset mankind—honest work which you intend getting done.—*Carlyle.*

CONSCIENCE—It is a great source of encouragement to man to feel that he has conscience on his side. He does not feel it necessary to stop at every stage that he may build up a labored argument as to the truth of the positions which he has laid down or announced; he is not compelled to be forever busy with the process of demonstration, as though what he uttered had no self-evidencing power, but must be fenced about with an array of credentials, or he could not otherwise look to gain assent to its truthfulness. He knows that the work which he does carries with it its own proof. It goes straightway into the recesses of the mind, and there enforces truth, however unwillingly recognized, and however speedily forgotten, of its being precisely such as the Almighty might be expected to send.—*Melvill.*

LASTING SATISFACTION—There is no truer and more abiding happiness than the knowledge that one is free to go on doing, day after day, the best work one can do, in the kind one likes best, and that this work is absorbed by a steady market and thus supports one's own life. Perfect freedom is reserved for the man who lives by his own work and in that work does what he wants to do.

—*R. G. Collingswood.*

A MAN is a worker. If he is not that he is nothing.—*Joseph Conrad.*

PAY ENVELOPE—Folks who never do any more than they get paid for, never get paid for any more than they do.

—*Elbert Hubbard.*

AS A CURE for worrying, work is better than whiskey.—*Thomas A. Edison.*

I BELIEVE in work, hard work and long hours of work. Men do not break down from overwork, but from worry and dissipation.—*Charles Evans Hughes.*

FOR ACTION—Not alone to know, but to act according to thy knowledge, is thy destination, proclaims the voice of thy inmost soul. Not for indolent contemplation and study of thyself, nor for brooding over emotions of piety—no, for action was existence given thee; thy actions, and thy actions alone, determine thy worth.

—*Fichte.*

GREASING THE SKIDS — They that do nothing are in the readiest way to do that which is worse than nothing.

—*Zimmermann.*

I LIKE WORK; it fascinates me. I can sit and look at it for hours.

—*Jerome K. Jerome.*

NO HOPE—In idleness there is perpetual despair.—*Carlyle.*

VITAL FUNCTION — Work is as much a necessity to man as eating and sleeping.—Even those who do nothing that can be called work still imagine that they are doing something.—The world has not a man who is an idler in his own eyes.

—*Humboldt.*

THE PLAN IS DIVINE — The moment a man can really do his work, he becomes speechless about it; all words are idle to him; all theories. Does a bird need to theorize about building its nest, or boast of it when built? All good work is essentially done that way; without hesitation; without difficulty; without boasting.—*Ruskin.*

BUDGETING—The more business a man has to do the more he is able to accomplish, for he learns to economize his time.—*M. Hale.*

THE ONE CAUSE—It is to labor and to labor only, that man owes everything of exchangeable value. Labor is the talisman that has raised him from the condition of the savage; that has changed the desert and the forest into cultivated fields; that has covered the earth with cities, and the ocean with ships; that has given us plenty, comfort and elegance, instead of want, misery, and barbarism.

—*McCulloch.*

XXXII. WORTHY THOUGHTS

PATIENCE — A certain lady met with a serious accident, which necessitated a painful surgical operation, and many months of confinement in bed. When the physician had finished his work and was taking his leave, the patient asked: "Doctor, how long shall I have to lie here helpless?" "Oh, only one day at a time," was the cheery answer. And the poor sufferer was not only comforted for the moment, but many times during the succeeding weary weeks did the thought, "Only one day at a time," come back with its quieting influence.—*The Free Churchman.*

CHARACTER — Build character for God. Make it four-square, with a spiritual side, a moral side, a mental side, and a physical side. On the spiritual side square it with Jesus Christ; let it be your ambition to be as spiritual as your Master; on the moral side be satisfied with nothing less than the standard set by Christ, Himself; on the mental side let the thoughts of God rule, and on the physical side strive to make the body as clean as you believe was the body of the Lord Jesus Christ. Build the whole life for God.—*Speer.*

CHRIST'S STANDARD — Our nation has had heated political discussions as to what is the proper standard of value in the financial world. But in the spiritual realm the followers of Jesus Christ have no room for "difference of opinion" as to what is the standard of value. When His disciples were debating the question as to who should be the greatest in the kingdom of Heaven, Christ put before them a little child.—*Moore.*

KINDNESS — In a remote district of Wales a baby boy lay dangerously ill. The widowed mother walked five miles through the night in the drenching rain to get the doctor. He hesitated about making the unpleasant trip. He questioned "Would it pay?" He knew that he would receive little money for his services, and besides, if the child were saved, he would only become a poor laborer. But love for humanity and a sense of professional responsibility conquered, and the little child's life was saved. Years after when this same child became first Chancellor of the Exchequer, and later Prime Minister of England, the old doctor said, "I never dreamed that in saving that child on the farm hearth, I was saving the life of a national leader." God is constantly justified in the responsibilities He has placed upon us for preserving both material and spiritual life.—*Selected.*

WORSHIP

God made my cathedral
  Under the stars;
He gave my cathedral
  Trees for its spires;
He hewed me an altar
  In the depth of a hill
He gave for a hymnal
  A rock-bedded rill;
He voiced me a sermon
  Of heavenly light
In the beauty around me—
  The calmness of night;
And I felt as I knelt
  On the velvet-like sod
I had supped of the Spirit
  In the Temple of God.

—RUTH FURBEE.

WHISPERS—There is hardly ever a complete silence in our soul. God is whispering to us wellnigh incessantly. Whenever the sounds of the world die out in the soul, or sink low, then we hear these whisperings of God. He is always whispering to us, only we do not always hear, because of the noise, hurry, and distraction which life causes as it rushes on.
—*Faber.*

Love's Garden

Love planted a rose,
    And the world turned sweet,
Where the wheatfield blows
    Love planted a rose.
Up the mill-wheel's prose
    Ran a music beat.
Love planted a rose,
    And the world turned sweet.
—*Katharine Lee Bates.*

Taken from THE RETINUE AND OTHER POEMS, by Katharine Lee Bates, published and copyright by E. P. Dutton & Co., Inc., 1918.

AMBITION — While visiting in a nearby city I was shown an unfinished mansion. A retired capitalist had planned to spend the remainder of his days in this luxurious home. But death ended his dream and deprived him of achieving his ambition. For eight years no workman had scaled the scaffolds; no sound of hammers heard. There was no sight of life save one black crow perched on the summit of an unfinished spire. What a tragedy, but one frequently enacted in human life.

And so that unfinished house stood amidst those stately pines as the symbol to me of unfilled ambition; a monument to the uncertainty of life and the certainty of death; a silent message urging us to strive not for the things which are seen, but for the things which are not seen; for the things which are seen are temporal; but the things which are not seen are eternal.—*Laws.*

AN ACRE of performance is worth the whole world of promise.—*Howell.*

UNIVERSAL—It has been said that Julius Caesar was the greatest man who ever lived. Ridpath says that he was head and shoulders above the age in which he lived. Did angels announce the birth of Julius Caesar? Did the sun refuse to witness his assassination in the senate chamber? Did Julius Caesar have the power to lay down his life, then take it up again? Was it at the name of Julius Caesar that apostles proclaimed and martyrs died? Caesar and his kingdom are things of the past, and were it not for history they would have been forgotten long ago. The name of Jesus is lauded today more than ever before. You may go to the remote isles of the sea and His name is there. You may sail the boundless ocean and His name is there. You may visit every land and clime and His name is there. His name spans eternity past and eternity to come. There have been great spirits in every race, but only one Great Spirit of the race.—*Lookout.*

THERE ARE THREE great principles in life which weave its warp and woof, apparently incompatible with each other, yet they harmonize and in their blending create this strange life of ours. The first is, our fate is in our own hands, and our blessedness and misery the exact result of our own acts. The second is, "There is a divinity that shapes our ends, rough-hew them how we will." The third is, "The race is not to the swift, nor the battle to the strong; but time and chance happeneth to them all." Accident, human will, the shaping will of Diety,—these things make up life.
—*Frederick W. Robertson.*

SAFEGUARDS OF YOUTH — I was standing in Tiffany's great store in New York, and I heard the salesman say to a lady who had asked him about some pearls, "Madam, this pearl is worth $17,000." I was interested at once. I said, "Let me see the pearl that is worth $17,-000." The salesman put it on a piece of black cloth, and I studied it carefully. I said, "I suppose Tiffany's stock is very valuable?" and as I looked around that beautiful store, I imagined them bringing all their stock up to my house, and saying, "We want you to take care of this to-night." What do you think I would do? I would go as quickly as I could to the telephone and call up the chief of police, and say, "I have all Tiffany's stock in my house, and it is too great a responsibility. Will you send some of your most trusted officers to help me?" You would do the same, wouldn't you? But I have a little boy in my home, and for him I am responsible. I have had him for nine years, and some of you may have just such another little boy. I turn to this old Book and I read this word: "What shall it profit a man if he gain the whole world, and lose his own soul?" or "What shall he give in exchange for his soul?" It is as if he had all the diamonds and rubies and pearls in the world, and held them in one hand, and just put a little boy in the other, and the boy would be worth more than all the jewels. If you would tremble because you had seventeen thousand dollars' worth of jewels in your house one night, how shall you go up to your Father and the lad be not with you?

—*J. Wilbur Chapman.*

IMPOSSIBILITIES—Law never does anything constructive. We have had enough of legislators promising to do that which laws can not do.—*Henry Ford.*

STRENGTH — I wonder if you remember the story that Carlyle tells about the dying of Oliver Cromwell. If ever there was a big man and a strong man in the place of ruler in Britain, it was Oliver. His chaplain had been reading to him, and amongst other sentences he had read this: "I can do all things through Christ which strengtheneth me," — all things, even die triumphantly. It was a great word, and the Protector for a time stumbled at it. And in a moment he was heard saying to himself: "Paul's Christ is my Christ. What Christ would help Paul to do, He would help me to do." And he faced that last fight and won it by the grace of Jesus Christ.—*J. D. Jones.*

From Gray's ELEGY

The boast of heraldry, the pomp of power,
  And all that beauty, all that wealth
  e'er gave,
Awaits alike the inevitable hour:—
  The paths of glory lead but to the grave.
Can storied urn or animated bust
  Back to its mansion call the fleeting
  breath?
Can Honor's voice provoke the silent dust,
  Or Flattery soothe the dull cold ear of
  death?

Full many a gem of purest ray serene
  The dark unfathomed caves of ocean
  bear;
Full many a flower is born to blush
  unseen,
  And waste its sweetness on the desert
  air.

GENERAL OBSERVATIONS drawn from particulars are the jewels of knowledge, comprehending great store in a little room.—*Locke.*

USE THE FRAGMENTS — Regret for time wasted can become a power for good in the time that remains. And the time that remains is time enough, if we will only stop the waste and the idle, useless regretting.—*Arthur Brisbane.*

CONFESSION

Last night my little boy confessed to me:
Some childish wrong;
And kneeling at my knee
He prayed with tears—
"Dear God, make me a man
Like Daddy—wise and strong,
I know you can."
Then while he slept
I knelt beside his bed,
Confessed my sins,
And prayed with low-bowed head,
"Oh God, make me a child
Like my child here—
Pure, guileless,
Trusting Thee with faith sincere."
　　　　　　—*Andrew Gillies.*

UNPREPARED — There is a legend of an oriental king, whose servant was also his personal friend and favorite. The king, one day, impatiently presented him with a golden bell, saying, "If ever you find a greater fool than you are, give this to him." Years passed and the king lay on his dying bed. To his servant the king said, "I am going on a long journey, and alas, am ill prepared." "Is it an unexpected journey?" "No, on the contrary, I have been forewarned these many years; but so engrossing have been the cares of government and the pleasures of court that I have given this matter little attention." Whereupon the servant silently handed him the golden bell. He had found a greater fool than himself at last.
　　　　　　—*Selected.*

ONWARD — We are never present with, but always beyond ourselves.—Fear, desire, and hope are still pushing us on toward the future.—*Montaigne.*

THE ABIDING PRESENCE — The Lord Jesus Christ was here long enough to remove all doubt as to His personal identity, yet He withdrew Himself immediately. He had secured for His personality an unquestioned place in human history. Nothing more was to be gained by His visible continuance on earth; His bodily mission had been wholly fulfilled, and therefore He vanished out of the sight of men. But what of the future of His work? Then, according to Christian teaching, was to come manifestation without visibility; instead of bodily presence, there was to be a new experience of life, spirituality, insight, sensibility, and sympathy almost infallible in holy instinct. In one word, the Holy Man was to be followed by the Holy Ghost. As the disciples were to be sent abroad into all coasts, to be scattered all over the earth to preach the gospel, and not to stay together still, in one place, Christ's corporeal presence would have stood them in small stead. He could have been resident but in one place, to have comforted some one of them. . . The Spirit, that was to succeed, was much more fit for men dispersed. He could be, and was, present with them all, and with every one by himself, as filling the compass of the whole world.—*Andrews.*

FIRST — The greatest prayer is patience.—*Buddha.*

TO HIM who harkens to the gods, the gods give ear.—*Homer.*

SEVEN WONDROUS WORDS—
Last words are precious words; how we cling to them, and let them gently stir through the memory and persist through the years. Men build about them great paeans and songs.

The last words of Jesus, matchless for pathos and forgiveness and trust, form a garland of seven flowers that shall never fade while the world lasts. There are three before the darkness; one during the darkness, and three after the darkness. The first is the word of intercession: "Father, forgive them, they know not what they do." These hired soldiers, who are driving the nails and raising the cross, He would forgive them.

The second word is the world of hope beyond death, spoken to the young thief: "This day shalt thou be with Me in paradise." The third word is one of loving provision, "Woman, behold thy son." One of the tenderest acts in all history. Jesus did not forget His mother; He was a son as well as a Saviour; a Son to the last. The fourth: "Why hast thou forsaken Me?" spoken in the awful darkness, we shall never understand. It is the word of loneliness. The first three were spoken for others: He cared for others before He thought of Himself. The great heart broke and He cried, "My God." He lost His sense of God for a moment but not His trust. As the darkness passes He speaks three more words—"I thirst!" "It is finished," the word of victory. The seventh word is the word of trust—"Father, into Thy hands." Father! a precious word for God. The word of supreme confidence, of assurance, of victory.—*A. E. Gregory.*

HABIT — The diminutive chains of habit are generally too small to be felt, till they are too strong to be broken.

READY—Robert Hardy had a dream, and in that dream he thought he was to live only seven days. If you had only seven days to live, how would you live them? How did Robert Hardy begin? He began to study. He began to get ready. Did all in his power each day. He came to the seventh day; and he came near the end of the day. But all at once it was made known to him that he wasn't to die. He looked around and was glad, but he said, "Some seven days will be my last seven," and he lived every day as though he were in his last. You will be in your last seven days soon, and may be even there now.
—*Scoville.*

WHO IS EDUCATED?—There are five tests of the evidence of education— correctness and precision in the use of the mother tongue; refined and gentle manners, the result of fixed habits of thought and action; sound standards of appreciation of beauty and of worth, and a character based on those standards; power and habit of reflection; efficiency or the power to do.

PROTECTION—Dr. Forsyth has told how a friend of his was on a sheep farm in Australia and saw the owner take a little lamb and place it in a huge enclosure where there were several thousand sheep whose bleating, together with the shouting of the sheep-shearers, was deafening. Then the lamb uttered its feeble cry, and the mother sheep at the other end of the enclosure heard it and started to find her lamb. "Do not imagine that you are beyond the reach of the Good Shepherd," said the preacher. "He sees you, He hears you, every good desire of yours is known to Him, and every secret longing for better things. He sees you as if there were no other child in the whole world."

TWO GREAT WANTS — Man's two great wants, viewed as an immortal spirit—are a want of infinite truth, and a want of the infinite good; a want of light and a want of love. These wants are for ever making themselves felt in the human consciousness in various forms. Man is like a noble tree planted in the earth, which can live only by drinking in the air and sunlight of Heaven. The fall has walled him up in a dark enclosure of selfishness and sensuality; but as he cannot live without light and warmth he tries to expand his branches towards certain wretched tapers which are burning in the interior. But they are never enough for him. Without the sun he cannot thrive. "His soul is athirst for God."

—*Goulburn.*

HOME AT LAST — Who seeks for heaven alone to save his soul may keep the path, but will not reach the goal; while he who walks in love may wander far, yet God will bring him where the blessed are.—*Henry Van Dyke.*

HUMILITY—The tree falls with any gust of wind when the root is near the surface; the house which has a shallow foundation is soon shaken. High and wide as the noblest trees spread, so deep and wide their roots are sunk below; the more majestic and noble a pile of building, the deeper its foundation; their height is but an earnest of their lowliness; you see their height, their lowliness is hidden; the use of sinking thus deep is not plain to sight, yet were they not thus lowly, they could not be thus lofty. Dig deep, then, the foundation of humility; so only mayest thou hope to reach the height of charity; for by humility alone canst thou reach that Rock which shall not be shaken, that is, Christ.—*Pusey.*

WHAT MEN HAVE SAID ABOUT THE WORD — The Bible is a book in comparison with which all others are of minor importance, and which in all my perplexities and distresses has never failed to give me light and strength.
—*Robert E. Lee.*

The Bible is the book of all others to be read at all ages and in all conditions of human life. . . . I speak as a man of the world to men of the world, and I say to you, "Search the Scriptures."
—*John Quincy Adams.*

The foundations of our society and our government rest so much on the teachings of the Bible that it would be difficult to support them if faith in these teachings should cease to be practically universal in our country.—*Calvin Coolidge.*

Every soldier and sailor of the United States should have a Testament . . . We plead for a closer, wider and deeper study of the Bible, so that our people may be in fact, as well as in theory, "doers of the Word and not hearers only."
—*Theodore Roosevelt.*

ABYSMAL IGNORANCE — Few things could be culturally more deplorable than that today the average college graduate, who fancies himself educated, should never have read the Book of Job, should be unfamiliar with Isaiah, and should be hardly able to identify those mighty men of valor, Joshua, Gideon, Jephthah, or those most famous of scarlet women, Rahab, Delilah, Bath-sheba, — and should be not only thus abysmally ignorant but should feel no incentive to be otherwise. For this is nothing less than a loss of racial memory, a forgetfulness of our cultural heritage that is as serious in the life of nations as is for the individual the loss of personality attendant upon neurotic disease,

THE VALUE OF MORAL COURAGE—How much self-torture would Jean Jacques Rousseau have saved himself had he known the virtue of moral courage! How different would have been the fate of poor Goldsmith, that bright intellect and tender heart, if he could have resolved to put aside his little vanities and extravagances! Moral courage would have saved Haydon, the artist, from a suicide's death. It would have saved Pope from a thousand petty follies. It would have rescued many a man from a premature grave, a prison, or a workhouse; for, be assured, our sufferings and failures in life are nearly always the result of our own errors. If we but look steadfastly to what is true and right, resisting every effort to divert us from the one straight path— ah, we should not find ourselves lost in quagmires and quicksands! The road before us is different; but it is so plain, and it leads to such a glorious goal!—*Adams.*

TIME TO RE-WIND—One morning Donald observed that the big clock was striking the hour very slowly, and heard his Uncle John remark: "Sounds as if the striking part of it is nearly run down." Donald then not only saw him wind it, but did not forget. The following Sunday morning, while his uncle was reading the paper, his wife came in and inquired if he were going to church. He replied very slowly: "Oh, I—I suppose so." Donald eyed him wonderingly as he remarked: "Why, Uncle John, that sounds as if the meeting side of you was nearly run down! Is it?" Aunt Hannah laughed, and Uncle John flushed as he threw the paper aside, saying: "Maybe it is, Donald. But we'll wind it up again and get a little stronger movement. Neither clocks nor people are of much use when the springs that ought to keep them going are neglected."

RESURRECTION—There are many historical facts in the world that were not attended by one-tenth as many witnesses as was the resurrection of Jesus Christ. As examples I might speak of the birth of princess, the signing of treaties, the remarks of cabinet officers and the deeds of assassins. I say these great events that men receive upon testimony and accept as facts, these have not had one-tenth the number of witnesses as had the resurrection of Jesus Christ. Therefore I need not beg anybody's pardon for what I believe. I believe with all my heart that Jesus, the Christ, is risen indeed. I believe that He was seen after His ressurection, by 641 eye witnesses. During those forty days, Jesus appeared to different men under different circumstances at various places. He ate with them, walked with them, and talked with them. They positively could not have been deceived. Such deception would be without parallel in history and without an analogy in the annals of men. Christ's enemies became the charter members of His church, in Jerusalem on the day of Pentecost. Account for that fact if you deny the resurrection.—*Scoville.*

POINT-OF-VIEW — If anything seems to be wrong with you, first examine the point-of-view. If you do this conscientiously, you will probably find the fault therein and seek a remedy by changing the point-of-view.—*Horace Fletcher.*

When a man's duty looks like an enemy, dragging him into the dark mountains, he has no less to go with it than when like a friend with loving face, it offers to lead him along green pastures by the river side.—*George Macdonald.*

GENERAL INDEX